Small Customers, Big Market:
Commercial Banks in Microfinance

MALCOLM HARPER
and
SUKHWINDER SINGH ARORA

Published by ITDG Publishing
Schumacher Centre for Technology and Development
Bourton Hall, Bourton-on-Dunsmore, Warwickshire CV23 9QZ, UK
www.itdgpublishing.org.uk

ISBN 1-85339-608-7

© ITDG Publishing 2005

First published in 2005

Published in India by TERI Press
The Energy and Resources Institute
Darbari Seth Block, IHC Complex, Lodhi Road, New Delhi – 110 003, India
www.teriin.org

ISBN 81-7993-066-1

All rights reserved. No part of this publication may be reprinted
or reproduced or utilized in any form or by any electronic, mechanical,
or other means, now known or hereafter invented, including photocopying
and recording, or in any information storage or retrieval system,
without the written permission of the publishers.

A catalogue record for this book is available from the British Library.

ITDG Publishing is the publishing arm of the Intermediate Technology
Development Group. Our mission is to build the skills and capacity of people
in developing countries through the dissemination of information in all
forms, enabling them to improve the quality of their lives and that of
future generations

Front cover photograph by Vijay Kulkarni
Designed and typeset by Christian Humphries
Printed in India

Contents

About the authors	v
Preface	ix
Acknowledgements	xi
List of acronyms	xii

Introduction
Why should commercial banks be interested in microfinance? — 1

1 The Microbanking Division of Bank Rakyat Indonesia: a flagship of rural microfinance in Asia — 7
   HANS DIETER SEIBEL

2 Mainstreaming Grameen banking in Philippines — 21
   FABRIZIO FELLONI, HANS DIETER SEIBEL and ANDRES CORNEJO

3 The Bank of Khyber, Pakistan — 37
   AMJAD ALI ARBAB

4 Wholesale microfinance: Sonali Bank, Bangladesh — 55
   M. ABDUL AWAL and ABUL KALAM AZAD

5 Microfinance through self-help groups – case study of Bank of India — 69
   VIJAY KULKARNI

6 Canara Bank, Alanganallur branch, Madurai district, Tamil Nadu, India — 77
   R. SRINIVASAN

7 Oriental Bank of Commerce's microfinance project, India — 93
   RAVINDER YADAV

8 ICICI Bank, India — 103
   TARA NAIR, M.S. SRIRAM and VISWANATH PRASAD

9 Microfinance at Banque du Caire, Egypt — 115
   CATHRYN CARLSON

10 Strategic partnerships in microfinance: the case of the Commercial Bank of Zimbabwe 131
KENNETH RUFASHA

11 Equity Building Society's market-led approach to microfinance in Kenya 147
GRAHAM A.N. WRIGHT and JAMES MWANGI

12 FINADEV SA: the first commercial bank for microfinance in Benin 165
LATÉ LAWSON and HERMAN MESSAN

13 Banco Solidario, Ecuador 179
MELITA SAWYER and MARÍA SOLEDAD JARRÍN

14 Bancafé, Guatemala 195
JOB BLIJDENSTEIN

15 The service company model: Sogesol in Haiti 209
ELISABETH RHYNE

16 The American Bank of Kosovo 223
VERONICA GILBERT and ROSHIKA SINGH

17 Commercial banks in microfinance in Georgia 239
TEONA MIKADZE and GUILLEMETTE JAFFRIN

18 Agricultural Bank of Mongolia (Khan Bank) 257
J. PETER MORROW, JAY DYER and ROBIN YOUNG

Conclusions 275

Endnotes 293
References 299
Index 302

About the authors

Amjad Ali Arbab is Executive Vice-President of the Bank of Khyber. He has spent 22 years in leading positions at financial and non-financial institutions, including 12 years with the Bank of Khyber. He has worked to strengthen the microfinance and SME sector in the North West Frontier Province of Pakistan, and has collaborated closely with ADB, SDC and IFAD.

M. Abdul Awal was a senior executive in Sonali Bank as a microfinance specialist. He now works for the Credit and Development Forum (CDF) as director (Network and Advocacy). He has also worked with PKSF.

Abul Kalam Azad is a microfinance practitioner and a former senior executive of Grameen Bank. He has worked in the micro-credit sector for the last 20 years, and is now working with CDF.

Job Blijdenstein has worked in micro and small business development since 1976, employed by ILO, RVB (now MSM) and others. Since 1992, he has been Director and co-owner with FACET B.V., of FACETA Central, doing consultancy and project management in Central America for organizations such as IADB, SDC, DGIS and World Bank.

Cathryn Carlson worked for 15 years in project finance and capital markets in commercial banks in Asia, Europe and the USA. She has recently set up as an independent consultant in microfinance, based in Singapore where she has lived for the past nine years.

Andres Cornejo is the President of Producers Rural Banking Corporation in Nueva Ecija (Philippines), which he established in 1995.

Jay Dyer has worked for the DAI Group of Companies since 1995. He has 16 years of experience in commercial banking, product development, financial institution development and project management. Before joining DAI, he spent eight years working in commercial banks in the United States as vice president of commercial lending.

Fabrizio Felloni, an agricultural economist, works in the Office of Evaluation at IFAD. He has worked in project, thematic and country programme evaluations in Asia, North and sub-Saharan Africa.

Veronica Gilbert is the Director of the Public Sector Services unit of Deloitte Touche Tohmatsu Emerging Markets Group, which focuses on building the capacity of public sector institutions via international development programmes. She set up and co-ordinated the Kosovo Business Finance Fund (KBFF), followed by the American Bank of Kosovo.

Guillemette Jaffrin worked in Georgia in 2001–2002 for Bannock Consulting as a Banking Adviser on an EBRD-funded programme to support commercial banks to enter microfinance. Since 2003, Guillemette has worked for the International Labour Organization in Vietnam on microfinance issues.

ABOUT THE AUTHORS

María Soledad Jarrín is Technical Sub-Director of Fundación Alternativa, Grupo Solidario in Ecuador. She has 20 years' experience in NGOs and private development organizations. She is also a faculty member of the Catholic University of Ecuador.

Vijay Kulkarni is a consultant in microfinance. He has worked for SIDBI, NABARD, GTZ and other national and international agencies. He is also the Director of the Development Resource Centre (DRC), based at Dharwad in Karnataka, western India. He worked earlier with Basix Finance, Canara Bank and Malaprabha Grameen Bank.

Laté M. Lawson-Lartégo is responsible for policy, strategy, backstopping technical support and capacity building for microfinance in CARE Gulf of Guinea (Ghana, Togo and Benin). Before this, he worked in other senior positions in microfinance for CARE in Benin, and has also worked for PlaNet Finance in France as project manager.

Teona Mikadze worked as a Marketing Associate for Bannock Consulting in Georgia during 2001–2002 on an EBRD-funded programme to support commercial banks to enter microfinance. She is now managing the media research division of the Institute for Polling and Marketing in Georgia.

J. Peter Morrow is an international banker and consultant with 34 years' experience in the USA and developing countries. He has been CEO of the AgBank of Mongolia since its turnaround began in June 2000. He has also served as CEO of two banks and executive officer of two others in Western economies.

Tara Nair is an Associate Professor at the Mudra Institute of Communications, Ahmedabad, India. She has also worked for EDA Rural Systems and other institutions.

Elisabeth Rhyne is Senior Vice President, International Operations/ Africa and Policy and Financial Analysis Department, for ACCION of Washington, D.C. She was earlier the Director of the Office of Microenterprise Development at the US Agency for International Development (USAID) from 1994 to 1998, and before that she designed and co-ordinated USAID's GEMINI project.

Kenneth Rufasha is a Doctoral Researcher at Nottingham Business School, Nottingham Trent University. He also lectures at the university. He has previous experience as a bank manager, an entrepreneur and a business development consultant.

Melita Sawyer is Project Assistant in the Grupo Solidario Project to strengthen savings and credit co-operatives in Ecuador. She has also worked in microfinance in Chiang Mai, northern Thailand; Boston, Massachusetts as well as in Quito, Ecuador.

Hans Dieter Seibel is Professor of Sociology at Cologne University, Germany. From 1999-2001 he was a Rural Finance Adviser at the International Fund for Agricultural Development (IFAD) in Rome. From 1998-2001, he was GTZ team leader of the project 'Linking Banks and Self-Help Groups in Indonesia'.

Roshika Singh is currently a member of the Financial Services Practice unit at Deloitte Touche Tohmatsu Emerging Markets Group. She has worked in many countries on the design of tax, state registry, collateral registry and real-time gross settlement systems, as well as banking supervision programmes.

R. Srinivasan is an Assistant General Manager with the National Bank for Agriculture and Rural Development (NABARD) of India. He is presently District Development Manager for Madurai District in Tamil Nadu. He has worked for NABARD for 20 years, and before that was employed at a national-level commercial bank in India.

M.S. Sriram is a Professor at the Indian Institute of Management, Ahmedabad. He was previously employed by Basix Finance and by the Indian Institute of Management in Bangalore.

S. Viswanatha Prasad works for the Basix group of companies, based in Hyderabad, India, where he was earlier Managing Director of Bhartiya Samruddhi Finance, Ltd., the main non-bank operating unit of the group.

Graham Wright is a reformed accountant. Graham has worked in development for 15 years, and is currently Programme Director for the MicroSave programme, which promotes the development and implementation of market-led financial services for the poor.

Ravinder Yadav started his career as a university teacher and researcher. He then joined a leading commercial bank, where he worked as an agricultural officer, an instructor and then as manager of a large branch. He has managed the microfinance department in the corporate office of the Oriental Bank of Commerce since 1996.

Robin Young has worked for Development Alternatives for 12 years, in research and programme implementation related to microenterprise finance. Before joining DAI, she worked as a consultant to the Microenterprise Unit of the Inter-American Development Bank, conducting research on guarantee funds for microfinance institutions, and as an Associate of Resource Development for ACCION International.

Preface

In the past ten to 15 years, microfinance has moved from a virtually unknown development tool to one of the key topics in economic development work. The success of a number of institutions, particularly the well-publicized achievements of the Grameen Bank of Bangladesh, Bank Rakyat Indonesia (BRI) and BancoSol in Bolivia, have shown that there are different, more commercially-minded ways to help the poor. These approaches, which treat the poor as clients, not as beneficiaries, are reaching more people and are proving more sustainable than earlier efforts based on directly subsidizing financial transactions. In this way, microfinance has become a key factor in transforming fundamental attitudes towards development and alleviating poverty. The focus shifts to how we can best serve the vast 'bottom of the pyramid' markets with win-win models – models which become more sustainable the better they perform.

However, the microfinance field and its achievements remain only partially understood. Most attention has been focused on the work of specialized institutions, many initially set up as non-governmental organizations (NGOs). Several of these rightly have earned the world's praise. But the vast majority of the world's poor cannot rely on such institutions for their critical financial services and they still have few options. If they look past the local moneylenders for credit, savings, money transfer or insurance services, the poor look to the formal sector financial institutions in their countries, institutions that until recently overlooked them and their informal businesses. These formal sector banks and other institutions have the greatest physical presence, the strongest capital base, and the largest management and systems infrastructure to support large-scale financial services delivery.

In all too many countries this potential of the formal financial sector is not realized. When it has been tapped, the results can be amazing as can be witnessed by the tens of millions of poor clients served profitably by BRI in Indonesia. In fact, the world is just awakening to the importance of commercial banks, and other financial service providers such as Western Union, in delivering the huge quantities of 'aid' that arrives in the form of remittances from expatriate family members. Where banks and other formal financial institutions have taken their local markets seriously, have invested in developing products that fit these markets, and have re-engineered operations to make these products accessible to the masses, they are reaping great rewards.

To date there has been too little praise for or notice of these achievements. This has in part to do with the reality that good bankers are successfully promoting themselves and their services to clients so as to stay in business, instead of promoting their activities to donors and the development field. Unfortunately, this misses an opportunity to convince other bankers of the vast potential in serving the bottom of the pyramid. Bankers are by nature conservative. It is not enough that an NGO can do microfinance as a serious business; bankers also need to see that 'real financial institutions' like themselves can profitably serve the poor.

This is why DAI is so pleased to sponsor this book. We believe it will draw attention to the less heralded but no less laudable work that commerical banks are doing to bring better, more diverse financial services to the poor. We believe it will illuminate new practices and insights on how we can bring more formal sector financial institutions into these 'bottom of the pyramid' markets, to provide healthy competition for informal sector providers and NGOs. At a minimum, we believe it will broaden thinking about who can do microfinance, and to whom we should reach out as we strive to broaden access to basic financial services.

Matthew Gamser and Colleen Green
Development Alternatives, Inc

Acknowledgements

This book carries our names on the title page, but it has been very much a collaborative effort. Our own role has mainly been to identify, assemble and present the various case studies, which form the bulk of its content.

The writers of the individual case studies, whose contribution is much more than ours, are recognized in the text, and we have also included a brief note on each writer's career. The study of microfinance has tended to be excessively dominated by external donors, academics and other so-called 'experts'. It is gratifying that so many of our colleagues in this venture are staff of the local institutions that they have described. They may or may not have believed at the outset that the modest honorarium we were able to offer would adequately compensate them for their efforts, but in the event they all put in much more time and effort than might have been expected; we are duly grateful.

We thank Development Alternatives for their generous assistance, which made the book possible, and we are also grateful to the Financial Sector Team of the Department for International Development's (DFID) Policy Division for encouraging Sukhwinder to participate. We both also owe a great debt to the various institutions with which we have been associated over the past many years.

The Technical Advisory Division of the International Fund for Agricultural Development (IFAD) showed an early interest in the work, and this has encouraged us to accelerate its completion. ITDG Publishing has responded enthusiastically to the challenge of publishing a somewhat disparate collection to a tight deadline, and we thank them for their co-operation.

Finally, through our collaborating case study writers, we should like to thank the management and staff of the banks that are described. They are busy people, and their priority is, quite rightly, to do things, not to write about them, or even to help others to write about them. The case studies give some flavour of the quality and originality of some of the things that they are doing. We admire their work, and we are very grateful to them for their help. We hope that their efforts will be rewarded by a wider recognition of the potential of the microfinance market for commercial banks, and in the availability of affordable and sustainable financial services to more of the enormous numbers of people for whom such services are presently inaccessible.

Malcolm Harper and Sukhwinder Singh Arora

Acronyms

ABA	Alexandria Business Association
ABK	American Bank of Kosovo
ACPC	Agricultural Credit Policy Council (Philippines)
ADAB	Association of Development Agencies in Bangladesh
ADB	Asian Development Bank
AgBank	Agricultural Bank of Mongolia
ATM	automatic teller machine
Bancafé	Banco del Café, Guatemala
BANDESA	Agricultural Development Bank, Guatemala
BANRURAL	Rural Development Bank, Guatemala
BAST	Bajram Abdullahu & Sylejman Topanica (ABK customer)
BCC	*Bancafé Communitario* (Community Bancafé)
BCCI	Bank of Credit and Commerce International
BdC	Banque du Caire
BLF	block level federation (of CLAs) (Tamil Nadu, India)
BOK	Bank of Khyber
BPK	Banking and Payments Authority of Kosovo
BRBD	Bangladesh Rural Development Board
BRI	Bank Rakyat Indonesia
BSP	*Bangko Sentral ng Pilipinas*
CBA	Commercial Bank of Zimbabwe
CBK	Central Bank of Kenya
CDF	Credit and Development Forum (Bangladesh)
CGC	Credit Guarantee Corporation (Egypt)
CIS	Commonwealth of Independent States
CLA	cluster level association (of SHGs) (Tamil Nadu, India)
CO	community organization (Pakistan)
CREDIREF	Credit Reference Corporation
DAI	Development Alternatives, Inc.
DFID	Department for International Development (UK)
EBRD	European Bank for Reconstruction and Development
EQI	Environmental Quality International (Egypt)
FBB	Financial Bank Benin
FECECAM	*Fédération des Caisses d'Epargne et de Crédit Mutuel* (Benin)
FLDG	first loss default guarantee
FMFBL	First Microfinance Bank Limited (Pakistan)
FSAC	Financial Sector Adjustment Credit (World Bank programme)
GTZ	*Deutsche Gesellschaft für Technische Zusammenarbeit* GmbH
IADB	Inter-American Development Bank
IFAD	International Fund for Agricultural Development
IFC	International Finance Corporation (World Bank affiliate)
IMI	Internationale Micro Investments (network of microfinance banks)

IPC	International Project Consult (German microfinance company operating in Haiti)
KBF	Kosovo Business Finance
KBFF	Kosovo Business Finance Fund
KCB	Kenya Commercial Bank
KPOSB	Kenya Post Office Savings Bank
KUPEDES	*kredit umum pedesaan* or general rural credit (Indonesia)
MEB	Micro Enterprise Bank (Kosovo)
MFI	microfinance institution
MFU	Microfinance Unit (of Bank of Khyber)
MSME	micro-, small and medium businesses
NABARD	National Bank for Agriculture and Rural Development (India)
NCBA	National Cooperative Business Association (USA)
NGO	non-governmental organization
NWFP	North West Frontier Province (Pakistan)
OBC	Oriental Bank of Commerce (India)
OBGP	Oriental Bank Grameen Project
PADME	*Programme d'Appui au Développement des Micro Entreprises* (Benin)
PAPME	*Programme d'appui aux Petites et Moyennes Entreprises* (Benin)
PAR	portfolio at risk
PCFC	People's Credit and Finance Corporation (Philippines)
PDBR	Palli Daridro Bimochon Foundation (Bangladesh)
PMN	Pakistan Microfinance Network
PPAF	Pakistan Poverty Alleviation Fund
RBI	Reserve Bank of India
RBKO	Raiffeisen Bank Kosovo (formerly ABK)
RMBG	Rural and Micro Banking Group (ICICI Bank)
ROC	revolving online credit
ROSCA	rotating savings and credit association
RSP	rural support programme (Pakistan)
SACCO	Savings and Credit Co-operative (Kenya)
SBI	State Bank of India
SDC	Swiss Agency for Development and Co-operation
SEB	Small Emerging Businesses (USAID programme in Egypt)
SELP	Small Enterprise Lending Programme (EBRD programme in Georgia)
SHG	self-help group (India)
SIMPEDES	*simpanan pedesaan* or rural savings (Indonesia)
SKDRDP	*Shree Kshetra Dharmshthala* Rural Development Project
TUB	Tbiluniversalbank (Georgia)
UGB	United Georgian Bank
UNMIK	UN Interim Administration Mission in Kosovo
USAID	United States Agency for International Development
WAEMU	West Africa Economic and Monetary Union

Introduction
Why should commercial banks be interested in microfinance?

What is this book about?

This volume might have been called 'Microfinance institutions are redundant', or, still more aggressively, 'Who needs MFIs?' We decided against such contentious titles, in order to avoid giving offence to our potential readers, and especially to the institutions with which we are ourselves closely connected, but these discarded titles do reflect the challenge inherent in what the book is about. We assume that our readers accept that efficient and profitable financial services are necessary for sustainable economic development, and that such services should be available not only to the elite but to the mass of the population. But why should donors, governments and other institutions or individuals who want to extend financial services to poorer people, to 'reach the unreached', spend so much money, time and effort on building entirely new institutions, when there are hundreds of thousands of banking outlets already in place? What is microfinance, other than the extension of profitable banking to a new market which has not been properly served before? Who could be better qualified to provide banking services to this new market than institutions which are already offering such services to large numbers of customers in the same towns and even the same villages?

Our readers will have their own answers to these questions, and there are of course many good explanations for all the effort that has been and indeed is still being put into the establishment and development of microfinance instutions (MFIs). Microfinance as we know it might not exist at all if Professor Muhammad Yunus and other pioneers had not demonstrated that the poor are bankable. Moreover, there may be no bank branches in some of the places where poor people need financial services, and even if there are banks their staff may be reluctant to address this new market. Government regulations may also make it very difficult for banks to offer the sorts of financial products which poorer people need.

These arguments are less persuasive than they were 30 years ago or so, when 'new paradigm' microfinance first made its appearance, but they are still valid in some places, for some groups of potential clients and for some institutions. We suggest, however, that times have changed. Donors and policy makers should look beyond MFIs, and should try to encourage and assist banks and other formal financial institutions to replace them, to collaborate or compete with them, to take them over, or to initiate microfinance themselves in places where there are no existing MFIs. More directly, bankers themselves should look more closely at what MFIs and a few other banks have achieved, and should seriously consider entering this market themselves, with or without subsidy or other external support. We hope that this collection of examples from around the world will encourage and help them to do this.

Most commercial banks have large numbers of branches. These are rapidly being supplemented and often replaced by automatic teller machines (ATMs) in many countries, and some MFIs, and banks, deliver micro-financial services even to very poor and illiterate people in this way. Personal contact is, however, still fundamental, particularly to people who have no previous experience of formal institutions, and the scale and outreach of their existing branch networks is one of the most important reasons why banks are beginning to look at the microfinance market.

The physical area covered by each branch is also important, since convenient access is vital, particularly for poorer people without their own vehicle. Table 0.1 shows how many people and how many square kilometres were covered by each bank branch in some of the countries represented in our case studies, and for comparison purposes, similar figures for the UK and the USA.

Table 0.1 Bank coverage in population and area

Country	Approximate number of bank branches	Approximate population per bank branch	Approximate square kilometres per bank branch
Bangladesh	6 230	21 800	23
Egypt	2 600	26 000	388
Georgia	225	22 400	70
Guatemala	1 280	9 340	85
India	66 000	16 000	50
Kenya	490	63 000	1 174
Pakistan	6 920	21 000	115
Philippines	6 400	13 000	47
United Kingdom	12 000	4 900	20
United States	61 000	4 200	158

Source: Web-based data, *World Development Indicators 2004* and *International Comparison of bank branches; an update*, Reserve Bank of Australia, Canberra 1999.

We could not trace more up-to-date data, and the figures do not reveal how many branches are in rural and in urban areas, or in wealthier or poorer neighbourhoods. They also omit many non-bank financial service outlets, such as the 93 000 rural primary co-operative societies in India, most of which can offer both savings and loan facilities.

Nevertheless, the figures show that, with the possible exception of Kenya, the numbers of financial service delivery points far exceeds anything that MFIs are likely ever to achieve. When the numbers of ATMs and electronic point-of-sale facilities are included, the statistics are even more impressive.

The case studies

In the following chapters, we provide 18 case studies, from 15 countries, which show how commercial banks have successfully engaged in microfinance. When we identified the case studies, we loosely defined microfinance as 'the provision of financial services to poorer people who have previously not had access to them'. We deliberately included both public and private sector institutions in our definition of commercial banks, which we stipulated must be 'for-profit full-service regulated financial institutions'. A great deal has been written about the achievements of specialist MFIs, and all the banks described in this book have learned from them. We felt, however, that bankers would be more likely to identify with the experiences of other bankers than with NGOs or MFIs; hence this book.

kthe microfinance initiative within the financial institution itself, but they all include information about the national context and the competitive position of the microfinance market. Some cases have a rather different focus. The Georgia case (Chapter 18) compares the performance of one new microfinance bank with two other existing banks which have gone 'down market' into microfinance, and the Canara Bank case study from India (Chapter 7) focuses on one branch which has been particularly successful.

Each case demonstrates a number of different factors, and it would be unhelpful to suggest that any of them is only included because it represents one single aspect of the topic. Table 0.2 (on the next page) summarizes some of the main features of each of the institutions which are described.

As Table 0.2 reveals, the cases cover a wide variety of ages and types of institutions, which also have a diversity of strategies for entry into microfinance.

All but one of the institutions is a full-service commercial banks; Equity Building Society of Kenya is the exception, but its different legal form makes no effective difference to its operations.

State Bank of India, which is by some measures the world's largest commercial bank, has been in existence since the early years of the nineteenth century, while the American Bank of Kosovo only started in 2001, as an important part of the process of building a new nation. Several of the banks were active in microfinance from their inception, either as one part of or often as the main thrust of their business. In

Table 0.2 *Features of the financial institutions in the case studies*

Chapter	Institution	Country	Date established	Microfinance initiative started	Ownership - Majority govt. ownership	Ownership - Majority private ownership	Going down-market	New institution/ subsidiary
1	Bank Rakyat Indonesia	Indonesia	1904	1984	✓		✓	
2	Producers Bank	Philippines	1995	1995		✓		
3	The Bank of Khyber	Pakistan	1991	1995	✓		✓	
4	Sonali Bank	Bangladesh	1972	1972	✓			
5	State Bank of India	India	1806	1992	✓		✓	
6	Canara Bank	India	1910	1993	✓		✓	
7	Oriental Bank of Commerce	India	1943	1995	✓		✓	
8	ICICI Bank	India	1994	2001		✓		
9	Banque du Caire	Egypt	1952	2001	✓		✓	
10	Commercial Bank of Zimbabwe	Zimbabwe	1991	1996		✓	✓	
11	Equity Building Society	Kenya	1984	1984		✓		
12	Finadev	Benin	1998	1998		✓		✓
13	Banco Solidario	Ecuador	1995	1995		✓	✓	
14	Bancafé	Guatemala	1978	1999		✓		✓
15	Sogesol	Haiti	2000	2000		✓		✓
16	American Bank of Kosovo	Kosovo	2001	2001	✓			✓
17	ProCredit Bank	Georgia	1999	1999		✓		✓
18	Agricultural Bank	Mongolia	1991	2000	✓			

most cases, however, the banks' microfinance activities started many years after the banks themselves. The case studies show the reasons why their management entered this new field, and they describe the often very difficult process by which the new initiative was 'sold' within the bank. In many of the banks, this struggle is still going on.

Their ownership is diverse, and covers the full range from 100 per cent government ownership to 100 per cent private. It might have been expected that governments would have pushed their own institutions into microfinance, for social and political reasons, or perhaps that they were incapable of such an innovative step and that only privately owned banks would do it. In fact, both types of institution have entered this new and unfamiliar market, and there is no indication that either public or privately owned banks are more or less likely to succeed.

The table does not show, however, that many of the public banks were, at the time of the case studies, already in the process of being part- or fully privatized. The American Bank of Kosovo and AgBank Mongolia, for instance, had both been fully privatized by the middle of 2004. Others, such as the three nationalized banks from India, are gradually admitting some private shareholders. Microfinance has often played a major part in the privatization process, by dramatically improving portfolio quality or otherwise.

Table 0.2 also shows the wide variety of strategies that the banks are adopting to enter the microfinance market. Eight are 'going down-market'. They have an established traditional client base, and have taken quite dramatic steps to move 'down' toward smaller and usually unbanked customers. The new customer group usually makes up only a small proportion of the total portfolio, but it is growing in importance. Six others were set up from the outset to address the microfinance market. Unlike most institutions which have started with microfinance, however, they were and are banks, not 'MFIs' or NGOs.

The 18 institutions have also taken a wide variety of routes through which to reach the microfinance market. Two, ICICI Bank in India and Sonali Bank in Bangladesh, are wholesaling funds to MFIs, and are not themselves directly engaged in providing 'new paradigm' micro-financial services at the retail level; they have chosen to use MFIs to retail their funds for them. Seven of the remaining institutions are using informal institutions, such as women's self-help groups, as their primary delivery channel, and the balance are dealing direct with their individual micro-clients.

The case studies show what many microfinance practitioners are only recently beginning to appreciate; that poor people need financial services for many different purposes, and not just to finance micro-enterprise. Few readers of this volume would be interested in doing business with a financial institution whose main or only purpose was to lend them money for investing in a small business. The Mongolian herders, the Kenyan pensioners, the Haitian vendors and the Guatemalan coffee farmers – like all the other people described in the book, who are able for the first time to access financial services from formal institutions – are making use of the full range of banking facilities. Banks can provide this range, and their prosperity depends on their doing so. Banks have generally ignored half the population, namely women. MFIs have shown that women are not only socially deserving, they are better customers. The case studies show that commercial banks have learned this lesson; 99 per cent of Producers Bank and some 80 per cent of FINADEV's customers are women.

Each case study is followed by three or four 'discussion questions'.

These do not by any means cover all the critical issues in the case. They are sometimes quite deliberately contentious, and do not necessarily represent our views. We hope, however, that they will encourage readers to question some assumptions and to confirm, or revise, their own opinions. We hope that some readers may use the book as a source of case studies for full-time post-graduate education courses or for in-service training. The questions should be useful as a basis for initiating class discussion.

Finally, we complete the book with an attempt to summarize some of the conclusions and lessons which we believe it to contain. As with any material of this sort, however, we anticipate and indeed hope that every reader will draw his or her own conclusions from the case studies. If, as a result of this, some more commercial banks consider entering the microfinance market, the book will have more than served its purpose.

Chapter One
The Microbanking Division of Bank Rakyat Indonesia: a flagship of rural microfinance in Asia

HANS DIETER SEIBEL

Rural microfinance in Indonesia: a highly differentiated sector[1]

Rural financial infrastructure

Indonesia has one of the most differentiated rural financial sectors of any developing country, comprising 53 500 banking and semi-formal financial units, 800 000 channelling groups, which are used by various government institutions to reach the rural poor, and millions of rotating savings and credit associations (*arisan*) of indigenous origin. After the establishment of the first rural bank in 1895, a three-tiered system of rural finance developed rapidly, comprising national, district and village institutions. At the top is a century-old agricultural bank, now known as Bank Rakyat Indonesia (BRI). At the community level were originally two types of village banks that specialized in banking-in-kind and banking-in-money. In 1910, there were 12 542 rice banks (*Lumbung Desa*) and 585 money banks (*Bank Desa*). Since then, money has gradually replaced kind. By 1940, their numbers had changed to 5451 *Lumbung Desa* and 7443 *Bank Desa*; and by 1989 there were 2056 *Lumbung Desa* and 3297 *Bank Desa*. (The two types of bank were counted together after 1989.) There is much similarity between today's policy concerns in rural finance and those at the start of the twentieth century: an emphasis on demand-oriented financial services, institutional viability, sustainability of the system as a whole, as well as experimentation to expand services to the poor with individual and group technologies (Holloh 1998, 2001; Seibel 1989; Steinwand 2001).

The finance sector now comprises some 6300 formal and 47 200 semi-formal microfinance outlets, serving about 47 million deposit accounts and 32 million loan accounts (see Table 1.1, overleaf), but it should be noted that figures differ widely according to source. These institutions are predominantly rural and peri-urban. A number of institutions with outreach into rural microfinance are not included, among them private national and regional commercial banks and regional government-owned development banks (BPD).

The BRI Units (formerly *unit desa*) account for 80 per cent of micro-savings balances and 54 per cent of micro-loans outstanding. Outside the formal and semi-formal institutional sector are some 800 000 groups

Table 1.1 Number and outreach of formal and semi-formal MFIs

	Outlets	Deposit Account in '000s	%	Deposit volume in '000s	%	Loan accounts in '000s	%	Loans outstanding		
								Rp bn	%	Av. loan Rp.
Banks										
BRI Units	4049	29 859	64	27 420	80	3100	10	14 183	54	4 575 000
Rural banks (BPR)	2213	4698	10	5 066	15	1745	5	5628	21	3 225 000
*Financial co-operatives	40 527	11 043	24	1 659	5	11 093	34	4787	18	431 500
Non-bank financial institutions										
Village MFIs (BKD)	4482	535	1	24	0	414	1	193	1	466 000
Other MFIs (LDKP)	1428	834	2	218	1	419	1	328	1	783 000
Pawnshops	772	0	0	0	0	15 692	48	1355	5	86 000
TOTAL All institutions	53 471	46 969	101	34 387	101	32 463	99	26 474	100	815 500

* Comprising 35 218 *Unit Simpan Pinjam*, 1123 KSP, 1071 credit unions, 2938 BMT and 177 Swamitra. ** Errors in percentage totals due to rounding.

Source data relates to December 2003 for BRI and BKD and to 2000 for others

of the poor and the ubiquitous *arisan*, a grassroots institution of most of the poor as well as the non-poor. Despite the extremely high level of institutional differentiation, some 50 per cent of rural households are reported to remain without access to formal or semi-formal finance.

Policy framework

After the oil price increases of 1973 and 1979, Indonesia invested large amounts in development, using directed credit as one of its tools. The decline in oil prices after 1982 initiated an era of liberalization, shifting the prime mover of development from government to market forces. Inflation fell from 20 per cent in 1973/74 to 5.7 per cent in 1985/86: an important prerequisite for financial market liberalization. In rural finance, the policy environment evolved rapidly during the 1980s and 1990s. This was highlighted by:

- full interest-rate deregulation and elimination of credit ceilings in 1983 – following the oil crisis of 1982 – which led to the market-oriented reform of the BRI unit system

- institutional liberalization and the passing of a rural banking law in 1988 – before the oil crisis of 1986 – which led to the rise of rural banks as part of the formal financial sector
- the phasing out of 32 of 36 subsidized credit programmes in 1990
- a new banking law in 1992, recognizing two types of banks: commercial banks and rural banks
- 1997–2002: financial sector crisis-management geared to prudential regulation and effective supervision.

This was paralleled by annual GDP growth rates averaging 7 per cent during 1979–96 and a reduction of the percentage of poor people from 60 per cent in 1970 to 11.5 per cent (22.5m people) in 1996 (World Bank 1999). Indonesia's process of steady growth was unexpectedly interrupted by the Asian financial crisis, *krismon*, which revealed, first the dangers of financial deregulation without effective supervision, that is, enforcement of prudential regulation, and second, the risks of excessive short-term external borrowings. At the same time, it revealed the fragility of poverty alleviation, and the number of poor doubled. Since 2000, there have been signs of recovery. New efforts have been made to extend the protection of the law to financial institutions of the poor and near-poor by preparing a draft microfinance law in September 2001.

The failure of subsidized targeted credit in a repressive policy environment

Until 1983, interest rates in Indonesia were regulated, the state banks dominated the financial sector, and the establishment of new banks and branches was restricted. BRI was the main provider of agricultural credit. Most prominent among a multitude of priority programmes was BIMAS, an agricultural diversification programme with a micro-credit component. BIMAS loans were channelled at heavily subsidized rates through BRI, which had greatly expanded its sub-branch network to the level of 3300 so-called village units (*unit desa*) which were set up at the sub-district or *kecamatan* level to handle the BIMAS loans. However, in the absence of incentives for small farmers to repay, or for the 14 300 BRI members of staff to enforce credit discipline, repayment rates lingered around 40–50 per cent, resulting in heavy losses. To the borrowers, the benefits of subsidized credit were drastically reduced: transaction costs shifted from lenders to borrowers, including under-the-table charges, onerous procedures, frequent delays beyond the agricultural input times and restriction of loan purposes to production-oriented agricultural targets. When oil prices dropped and GDP fell, the Indonesian government decided it could no longer afford massive support for such a poorly performing micro-credit programme. 'Close it or reform it', was the directive from a number of policy makers in the financial sector.

Transforming BRI units into viable rural MFIs in a deregulated policy environment

After the interest-rate deregulation in June 1983, the new management of BRI decided to commercialize the units (*unit desa*) into self-sustaining profit centres. With technical assistance from the Harvard Institute for International Development supported by USAID, the bank estimated micro-savings and micro-credit transaction costs, and carefully crafted two commercial products. One was a rural savings scheme with a lottery component, SIMPEDES (*simpanan pedesaan*, 'rural savings'), which proved to be immensely attractive and at the same time served as an instrument of resource mobilization at village level. The gross interest rate on this product was 13 per cent; savers received 11.5 per cent, while 1.5 per cent was put into a lottery fund. The other product was a non-targeted credit scheme, KUPEDES (*kredit umum pedesaan*, 'general rural credit') open to all for any purpose. Its features included simple procedures, short maturities, regular monthly instalments mainly from non-agricultural income, flexible collateral requirements (none for very small loans), incentives for timely repayment, repeat loans contingent upon successful repayment of previous loans, and market rates of interest amounting to 2 per cent flat per month, which is equal to an effective rate of 44 per cent per annum. A discount of 11 per cent for timely repayment gave a rate of 33 per cent per annum to cover all costs and risks. For loans of Rp25m–50m (US$25 000–5000), the current flat rate is 1.6 per cent per month, minus a rebate of 25 per cent for timely loan repayment.

In 1998, in response to the financial crisis, BRI was reorganized into three divisions: a Corporate Banking Division for loans above Rp3bn (US$300 000 at the October 1998 exchange rate), a Retail Banking Division with 323 branches which offer savings deposit services, provide loans on commercial terms from Rp25m–3bn (US$2,500-US$300,000) and handle the remaining subsidized targeted credit progammes; and a Microbanking Division, with 4185 outlets (2566 village units, 1220 peri-urban units and 379 village posts) for smaller loans. At the time of writing (March 2004), the loans from the units may range from Rp25 000 (US$2.90) to Rp50m (US$5800); but BRI reports that in the field actual minimum loan sizes are more like Rp300 000 (US$35). BRI's regulations allow loans up to Rp5m (US$580) to be collateral-free, but most unit managers ask for collateral, which may be land or mobile collateral such as bicycles or television sets.

In February 1984, at the start of the new scheme, all BRI's village units were turned into profit centres with substantial profit-sharing incentives for staff, paralleled by penalties for arrears exceeding 5 per cent. Below this level, unit managers lost their credit authority. The incentives were based on the potential business in each unit's area. Programmes carried out on behalf of the government or donors were kept away from the village units and confined to the branch level.

Table 1.2 *Savings and loans outstanding in BRI village units, December 1984–December 2003*

Years	Savings deposits		Loans outstanding		Savings to loan ratio %	Excess liquidity US$m	12-month loss ratio %	Arrears ratio %*	Return on assets	US$ exchange rate**
	No. of accounts	Amount US$m	No. of accounts	Amount US$m						
1984	2 655	39.3	640 746	103.4	38	-64.2	1 0	5.4	n.a.	1 074
1985	36 563	75.5	1 034 532	203.6	37	-128.1	1 8	2.1	n.a.	1 125
1986	418 945	107.1	1 231 723	203.7	53	-96.6	2 7	4.5	n.a.	1 641
1987	4 183 983	174.2	1 314 780	260.4	67	-86.1	3 0	5.8	n.a.	1 650
1988	4 998 038	284.8	1 386 035	313.3	91	-28.5	4 6	7.4	n.a.	1 731
1989	6 261 988	484.6	1 643 980	427.7	113	56.9	2 3	5.4	n.a.	1 979
1990	7 262 509	891.5	1 893 138	726.9	123	164.7	2 0	4.1	3.0	1 901
1991	8 587 872	1 275.4	1 837 549	730.8	174	544.6	4 9	8.6	2.7	1 992
1992	9 953 294	1 648.4	1 831 732	799.5	206	849.0	3 4	9.1	2.6	2 062
1993	11 431 078	2 049.9	1 895 965	927.7	221	1 122.2	2 2	6.5	3.3	2 110
1994	13 066 854	2 381.4	2 053 919	1 118.8	213	1 262.5	0 7	4.5	5.1	2 197
1995	14 482 763	2 633.8	2 263 767	1 397.2	188	1 236.6	1 1	3.5	6.5	2 284
1996	16 147 260	3 002.4	2 488 135	1 725.7	174	1 276.7	1 6	3.7	5.7	2 362
1997	18 143 316	1 622.0	2 615 679	860.0	189	761.9	2 2	4.7	4.7	5 448
1998	21 698 594	2 043.5	2 457 652	594.5	344	1 449.1	1 9	5.7	4.9	7 901
1999	24 235 889	2 420.1	2 473 923	844.9	286	1 575.2	1.7	3.1	6.1	7 050
2000	25 823 228	1 986.0	2 715 609	813.2	244	1 172.7	1.1	2.5	5.7	9 625
2001	27 045 184	2 105.2	2 790 192	945.2	223	1 160.0	0.5	2.2	5.8	10 446
2002	28 262 073	2 627.3	3 056 103	1 343.9	195	1 283.4	1.7	1.6	6.4	8 937
2003	29 869 197	3 527.3	3 100 358	1 678.2	210	1 849.1	1.9	2.5	5.7	8 451

* Total payments overdue one day or more in percentage of total loans outstanding, excluding loans written off.
** End-of-year rates. *Sources*: 1984–92: Bank Indonesia, Badan Pusat Statistik Indonesia; 1993–2003: http://www.oanda.com/convert/classic
Note: exchange rates varied from Rp8000 to Rp10 000 = US$1 during this period

At the time of its twentieth anniversary in December 2003, the Microbanking Division served 3.1m loan accounts, with loans outstanding amounting to US$1.68bn; or US$542 per loan account; the number of savings accounts had grown to 29.9m, amounting to US$3.53bn; or US$118 per account (Table 1.2, above). In recent years, the Microbanking Division has been extremely profitable, and it made US$186m in 2002. Since 1989, savings mobilized have exceeded loans outstanding, with excess liquidity increasing from US$ 1.12bn in 1993 to US$ 1.85bn in 2003.

Savings as a source of funds: making BRI self-reliant and donor funding superfluous

With this model, BRI became what is probably the most successful microfinance bank with a rural mandate in the developing world. Three major sources of funds have been involved:

1. an injection of Rp210bn (US$20m) of seed capital in 1984 by the government as start-up liquidity for loans and initial administrative costs, which were fully used by 1986, when the units were turning a profit;
2. a World Bank loan of US$102 million, US$5 million of which was provided in 1987 for technical assistance and US$97 million in 1989 for on-lending (Table 1.3) – at a time when it was no longer needed as the unit system had broken even with its internally mobilized resources;
3. savings deposits, vigorously mobilized at local village level and remunerated at positive real terms.

Table 1.3 *Sources of funds of the BRI village units, 1984–1989, and as at December 1996 and June 2003*

Source of funds	Year	Amount in US$m
Government initial capital injection	1984	20

World Bank loan:
  Technical assistance
  Liquidity fund for on-lending
	
	1987
	1989
		
		5
		97

Deposits*	1989 1996 6/2003	534 2 976 2 990
Loans outstanding	1989 1996 6/2003	471 1 710 1 600

* Including current accounts, passbook savings and time deposit accounts

SIMPEDES, voluntary savings with a lottery component that could be withdrawn at any time, proved to be BRI's most attractive savings product, out-performing time deposits by a wide margin. By December 1989, BRI had broken even: fully mobilizing its loan funds through village-level savings and generating excess resources thereafter (Table 1.3). Disbursement of the World Bank loan in 1989 thus came at a time when BRI had outgrown the actual need for it; and the funds were used at mostly unprofitable or even loss-making corporate and branch levels. Since then, BRI's *unit desa* network has been completely self-reliant, mobilizing its own resources, and viable, covering its costs and making a profit. The number of savings accounts has continually increased, particularly during the financial crisis of 1997-98. At the end of June 2003, BRI units served close to 30 million savings accounts in probably about 50 per cent of households in Indonesia, at a borrower-to-saver ratio of roughly 1:10. Savings balances on that date amounted to US$2.99bn, averaging US$102 per account. BRI's self-reliance in terms of fund mobilization and profitability has created the material base for its autonomy and freedom from political interference which has so severely afflicted the rest of the banking system.

Outreach, transaction costs and profitability

The BRI units reached their break-even point 18 months after their reform, generating a profit of Rp9.8bn (US$8.7m) in 1985. For the period from February 1984 to December 2003, the long-term loss ratio (total overdue one day or more, including amounts written off, divided by total which has fallen due during that period) was 1.9 per cent. Total payments in arrears one day or more as a percentage of total loans outstanding, excluding write-offs, were 2.2 per cent in December 2001, 1.6 per cent in 2002 and 2.2 per cent in 2003. Since 1994, return on assets (ROA) has been consistently around 5 per cent-6 per cent. ROA was 6.4 per cent in 2002 and 5.7 per cent in 2003 (see Table 1.2, page 11). Consolidated profits at unit level amounted to US$177m in 1996, US$94m in 1998, US$167m in 1999, US$119m in 2000, US$129m in 2001 and US$186m in 2002. Since 1987, the BRI units' subsidy dependency index (SDI) has been negative (Charitonenko et al. 1998). After 20 years, there is still no sign of the often-quoted iron law in microfinance of an increase in defaults and a fall in profits over time.

BRI has demonstrated that in a deregulated policy environment, a public bank is capable of serving vast numbers of micro-savers and micro-borrowers at competitive interest rates: mobilizing its resources internally, covering its costs, and financing its expansion from its profits. BRI has proven that institutional viability, sustainability and outreach to low-income people are compatible.

Today, the BRI units are the biggest provider of rural financial services within Indonesia's highly differentiated rural financial infrastructure (see Table 1.1, page 8). Among the 54 000 outlets listed, 7 per cent are BRI units, 4 per cent formal sector rural banks (BPR), 3 per cent are semi-formal rural banks (LDKP), and 10 per cent are non-formal village banks (BKD) which report to Bank Indonesia but are not regulated; the remaining 76 per cent are co-operatives. The BRI units account for 62 per cent of all savings deposit accounts, 74 per cent of deposits, 8 per cent of all loan accounts and 39 per cent of loans outstanding.

The superior performance of the BRI units in terms of outreach is due to various factors. One is the attractive design of their savings and credit products; another one the lowering of transaction costs through economies of scale. BRI includes among its customers both poor and non-poor borrowers and cross-subsidizes small loans with the profits from larger loans, which have substantially lower transaction costs. On principle, the poorest have access to the units; however, in remote areas, they are more likely to be serviced by special programmes of limited outreach such as P4K, handled at branch level. Reaching out to poorer segments of the rural population and contributing to their overall uplifting remain one of the big challenges to the units.

Transaction costs of two BRI *unit desa* were studied by Feekes (1993) on behalf of Bank Indonesia and compared with four commercial bank branches, five formal rural banks and three semi-formal rural banks (BKK), all in Central Java. It was found that transaction costs vary, as expected, by credit size. In the case of BRI units, they amounted to 26 per cent of loans below US$250, 10 per cent of loans from US$250 to US$2,500, and 3 per cent of loans between US$2,500 and US$12,500, which at that time were the units' main source of profitability, cross-subsidizing the micro-loans. Smaller institutions were found to be relatively more efficient in the delivery of very small loans, with estimated loan size break-even points of US$105 among the BKK sample units, US$225 among the rural banks, somewhat above US$250 among BRI units, and above US$12,500 among the commercial banks. Three major conclusions follow.

1. For an institution like the BRI to maximize its outreach and yet remain profitable, it has to include among its customers both the poor and the non-poor and cater for their respective demands for smaller and larger loan sizes. The latter then cross-subsidize the former. If the BRI exclude the non-poor from its clientele, it would substantially reduce the bank's outreach to the poor.
2. Only small local financial institutions, such as co-operatives and other village-based institutions, can handle very small loans cost-effectively.
3. In order to reach all segments of the rural population with financial services, there must be a differentiated rural financial infrastructure in which various types and sizes of financial institutions compete with each other.

BRI units since the Asian financial crisis: stronger than before

The impact of the crisis on MFIs has not been uniform, bringing out both the strengths and the weaknesses of different sub-sectors. However, one basic observation applies to the sector as a whole. While the commercial banking sector virtually collapsed, microfinance weathered the crisis well. This testifies, on the one hand, to the strength of the legal and institutional foundations of the microfinance sector, its self-reliance, and the public's trust in MFIs; and, on the other hand, to the absence of two fundamental problems of the commercial banks:

political interference in lending decisions; and excessive foreign exchange risk exposure of the banks and their clients. In contrast, MFIs have mobilized their own resources domestically; and most of them have applied sound lending practices.

On a more detailed level, the impact of the crisis has been stunningly positive on the BRI units. During the crisis year September 1997 to August 1998, total savings deposits in BRI almost doubled: in the BRI units from Rp7.98 trillion to Rp15.13 trillion (+89.6 per cent); and in all of BRI from Rp17.86 trillion to Rp35.17 trillion (+96.9 per cent): an increase well above the inflation rate of 56 per cent during the period. During the three-month period June–August 1998, after Indonesia had been hit by both a drought and an economic crisis, 1.29 million new savings deposit accounts were opened in BRI units (bringing the total up to 20.93 million); and an additional Rp2.84 trillion (US$284 million at the October 1998 exchange rate) were deposited. There was only a slight nominal increase in the credit portfolio, which stood at Rp4.61 trillion in August 1998 (up only 4.5 per cent from Rp4.41 trillion in August 1997), amounting to a substantial decrease in real terms.

Table 1.4 Savings, loans and excess liquidity in BRI units during the crisis year, August 1997 to August 1998

Date	Savings deposits Rp.	Loans outstanding Rp.	Excess liquidity Rp.
8/1997	7.98 trillion	4.41 trillion	3.57 trillion
8/1998	15.13 trillion	4.61 trillion	10.52 trillion
Increase in %	+89.6	+4.5	+194.67

Because of uncertainty over future developments, people reportedly were cautious to take up new loans. The number of BRI *KUPEDES* borrowers, which had steadily increased from 640 746 in December 1984 to 2 615 696 in December 1997, stagnated. During 1998 numbers actually declined every month – from a peak of 2 628 559 in January to 2 508 049 in August – a decrease of 4.6 per cent for that eight-month period and a decrease of 1.4 per cent from August 1997. The amount of loans outstanding continued to increase slowly in nominal terms from Rp4.41 trillion in August 1997 to Rp4.69 trillion in December 1997. After a nominal peak of Rp4.75 trillion in January 1998, it declined to Rp4.55 trillion in May and reached Rp4.61 trillion in August 1998. The amount of loans outstanding thus decreased by 3.0 per cent during the first eight months of 1998, although there was an increase of 4.5 per cent from August 1997.

The crisis had no negative effect on repayment, testifying to the resilience of both the BRI village units and their farmer and microenterprise customers. The 12-month loss ratio (2.16 per cent) during the crisis period is virtually identical with the long-term loss ratio since

1984 (2.17 per cent). Up to December 1998 it further improved to 1.94 per cent. In August 1998, right after the peak of the crisis, BRI even experienced an unprecedented negative one-month loss-ratio where more was repaid than was due.

The new challenges of microfinance profits and savings: cross-subsidization in reverse

BRI is generally renowned as the bank which revolutionized rural microfinance. The micro-banking division is indeed highly profitable, and its outreach is vast; but it is only one of three divisions, accounting for 34 per cent of total assets, 31 per cent of loans outstanding and 41 per cent of deposits in 2001 (see Table 1.5, below). However, the bank as a whole is lossmaking, and, without its Microbanking Division, might have been closed down after the financial crisis of 1997–98. The units have cross-subsidized the bank in two ways:

- through the continual transfer of profits from the units to the consolidated bank; and
- through the transfer of savings mobilized at village level to the local branches.

Table 1.5 BRI consolidated and BRI units, selected balance sheet data 2001 (in US$ million)

	BRI consolidated	BRI village units
Total assets	7 326	2 511
Government re-capitalization bonds	2 616	-
Placements with BRI branch system	-	1 361
Net loans outstanding	2 843	885
Liabilities	6 861	2 307
Savings and time deposits	5 125	2 115
Total equity	465	210
Paid-up capital	166	98
Retained earnings/Profit current year	-2 508	112
Additional paid-in capital	2 807	-

Source: Hiemann 2003: 82-83

Transferring profits

Accumulated losses amounted to US$4.0bn in 1999, US$2.8bn in 2000, US$2.5bn in 2001 and US$2.8bn in 2002 (see Table 1.6), despite the continual transfer of profits from the village units since 1986. Without its microfinance division, it would probably have been among the banks closed down after the Asian financial crisis, when huge amounts of corporate loans turned bad. With total equity at –US$3.65bn, the bank was technically bankrupt in 1999. In 2000, new management took over, and the government injected some US$3bn. The corporate market was all but abandoned, and the bank focused fully on the micro, retail and SME markets. This resulted in a turn-around of the bank, which was internationally rated as BBB in 2001 (a better risk than the country at C). This new policy has been so successful that around the turn of 2003–04, the bank is now being partially privatized and traded on the stock market.

Table 1.6 *Paid-up capital, capital injections, and earnings of BRI consolidated and BRI Units, 1999–2002 (in US$ million)*

	BRI consolidated			BRI units		
Year	Paid-up capital	Capital injections & other	Retained earnings	Capital and reserves	Net profit	Retained earnings
1999	244	83	–3,996.8	92	167	
2000	180	3,055	–2,802.3	85	119	Transferred
2001	166	2,807	–2,497.1	98	129	annually to
2002	193	3,252	–2,808.8	262	186	BRI branches

Sources: Hiemann 2003: 82, 89; *Laporan Statistik* BRI Unit, June 2003 and Jan. 2004

Siphoning off savings

While the credit bias in development finance from the 1960s onwards has never given way to a savings bias, despite a widespread demand for savings services among the poor, savings are no longer 'the forgotten half of rural finance'. In a good number of institutions without a bias either way, ratios of borrowers to savers are between 1:4 and 1:10. To those familiar with the early history of microfinance in Europe during the eighteenth and nineteenth century, this comes as no surprise (Seibel 2003a). However, not all donors have learned that lesson: that the poor need both savings and credit services; but more of the poor need savings deposit facilities than credit. The BRI units, with 30 million savings accounts (including various types of savings and fixed deposits) and a balance of US$3.53bn as at December 2003, have responded to that demand.

Yet, the units' success in savings mobilization has created a new problem: recycling the savings within the village economy rather than siphoning them off. Since 1989, the units have produced excess liquidity, for the past 10 years consistently above US$1bn per year. These levels have been highest during the crisis years 1998 and 1999, with US$1.43bn and US$1.56bn, respectively – at a time when donors rushed to Indonesia to provide fresh credit lines, thereby further raising the country's mountain of external debts. The units are required to place their excess liquidity with the BRI branch system; net placements amounted to US$1.60bn in 1999, US$1.24bn in 2000, US$1.23bn in 2001 and US$1.645 in 2002.

Despite the outreach of the various types of rural MFIs in Indonesia, numerous studies (ADB 2003; Holloh 2001; Seibel 2003b) have shown that there still is a vast unsatisfied demand for credit: in villages at a distance from the sub-district centre where the BRI units are located, and in remote and marginal areas, particularly on the outer islands, where large areas are totally unserved. Here is not the place to propose new strategies and products to BRI. However, there are two questions deserving an answer:

1. Should the unit system extend its single credit product strategy, KUPEDES, and develop additional credit products, with village-level and perhaps even doorstep services, at least in the more profitable units?
2. Should the unit system invest part of its profits in remoter areas by establishing agencies of a smaller size than the usual staff of four, perhaps simultaneously reducing transaction costs through linkages with self-help groups in co-operation with Bank Indonesia's revamped linkage banking programme? (Seibel and Parshuip 2003; Steinwand 1997)

Summary

The case of BRI is evidence that, in a deregulated policy environment, the microfinance section of a government-owned bank can be transformed into a highly profitable, self-reliant financial intermediary; and can turn into a major microfinance provider, offering carefully crafted micro-savings and micro-credit products to low-income people at market rates of interest. Making good use of government seed money and the technical assistance portion of a World Bank loan during an initial phase, it has now fully substituted savings deposits for external loans as its source of funds. With a saver outreach to 30 million accounts and a borrower outreach to 3.1 million accounts (December 2003) through a network of 4185 outlets (3786 units operating as profit centres and 379 village posts), BRI covers its costs from the interest rate margin and finances its expansion from its profits; arrears of over one day stood at 2.2 per cent, the long-term loss ratio since 1984 at 1.62 per cent, and return on assets at 5.7 per cent. With non-targeted loans available from US$3 in theory and US$35 in practice, up to US$5800 at rural market rates of interest as well as unrestricted deposit services, the BRI Microbanking Division has weathered the Asian financial crisis well, in stark contrast to the overall government banking sector including BRI as a whole, which is a loss-making bank. As of December 2003, its portfolio comprised US$1.7bn in loans outstanding and US$3.5bn in savings balances. Excess liquidity amounted to US$1.85bn. Several lessons can be drawn from BRI's experience:

- Financial sector policies work and are conducive to financial innovations.
- With attractive savings and credit products, appropriate staff incentives, and an effective system of internal regulation and supervision, rural microfinance can be highly profitable.
- The poor and near-poor can save; and rural financial institutions can mobilize their savings cost-effectively.
- If financial services are offered without a credit bias, the demand for savings deposit services effectively exceeds the demand for credit by a wide margin.
- Incentives for timely repayment work.
- Outreach of a financial institution to vast numbers of low-income people is compatible with including viability, self-reliance and financial self-sufficiency.
- Average transaction costs can be lowered, and both the profitability of a financial institution and the volume of loanable funds can be increased, by catering for both the poor and the non-poor with their demands for widely differing deposit and loan sizes.

Within a six-year period, 1984–89, the BRI unit system became a model case in Asia of the transformation of an ailing government-owned development bank into a viable and self-sufficient financial intermediary with ever-increasing financial resources and numbers of customers, competing successfully with a wide array of other local financial institutions. Further strength was added to BRI's microfinance operations during the Asian financial crisis: when the Indonesian banking system collapsed, BRI's Microbanking Division remained profitable and probably saved the bank with its loss-making corporate lending, while attracting 1.3 million new savers during the three-month peak period of the crisis. Due to the success of its Microbanking Division, there is no doubt in BRI, which went public around the turn of 2003–04, what the answer should be to the question, 'Agricultural Development Banks: Close Them or Reform Them?' (Seibel 2000)

Yet the immense success of the BRI units in terms of profitability and savings mobilization has generated a new challenge: How to reinvest their profits, on average substantially above US$100m annually since the mid-1990s, in the unit system; and how to recycle the excess liquidity, consistently between US$1bn and almost US$2bn annually over the past 10 years, in the village economies instead of siphoning it off into other areas of operation. In the long run, both better services and deeper outreach should pay off for the BRI units. Given their high profitability, there are few, if any, economic constraints to financial innovations geared to financial deepening and poverty outreach.

Discussion questions

1. The effective annual interest rate on loans from the BRI village units is 33 per cent, after deducting the 11 per cent discount for on-time repayments. The village units of BRI subsidize the mainstream operations of the Bank. Is this a well-designed and managed microfinance programme, or yet another example of the rich being subsidized by levying excessive prices on the poor?

2. BRI has received some modest but valuable technical assistance in the initial design and the development of its village unit system, but the World Bank loan was unnecessary and perhaps even damaging. Client savings are far in excess of what is needed for on-lending. What are the implications of this for donor assistance to MFIs?

3. Ten times as many people save with the BRI village units as borrow from them. Can MFIs that are unable to offer secure and accessible savings facilities really be said to be providing their customers with what they need most?

Chapter Two
Mainstreaming Grameen banking in Philippines

FABRIZIO FELLONI, HANS DIETER SEIBEL
and ANDRES CORNEJO

In many countries, Grameen replication has not fared well in terms of outreach and sustainability. There is no country where the approach of the Grameen Bank, reaching more than two million poor women in groups of five and centres of 30 in Bangladesh, has been replicated with similar success. In the Philippines, however, rural banks and NGOs turned rural banks have made Grameen banking a highly profitable product with rapidly expanding outreach to the enterprising poor and very poor, most of whom are women. How did they do it? Producers Bank may serve as an example.

Poverty in the Philippines

With an estimated average income per capita of US$1 020, the Philippines is classified as a lower-middle income country. It has a population of around 80 million (mid-2002), of whom 41 per cent live in rural areas. Throughout the 1990s the gross national income grew at an annual average of 3.3 per cent, an increase from the average 2 per cent of the 1980s. Inflation was also progressively under control at one-digit figures after the two-digit averages of the previous decade. In spite of good progress in terms of macroeconomic indicators, the country has experienced persisting poverty: the overall poverty rate was about 28.1 per cent in 1997 and, virtually unchanged, at 28.4 per cent in 2000.[1]

A highly differentiated financial sector

The formal financial sector in the Philippines is highly segmented, comprising commercial banks, thrift banks, rural banks and non-bank financial institutions. In June 2003, there were 906 banks – including 42 commercial banks, 93 thrift banks and 771 rural banks – and 5486 non-bank financial institutions. Thrift banks (or private development banks) serve small- and medium-scale enterprises outside the national capital region and are privately owned. Rural banks are small local banks, originally conceived (1952) as unit banks, with lower capital requirements than thrift banks, and only recently allowed to open branches. Rural banks are either privately or co-operatively owned. Among the banking institutions, commercial banks accounted for 56.3 per cent of the total number of bank offices and 90.3 per cent of assets, thrift banks for 17 per cent of offices and 7.3 per cent of assets, and rural banks for 25.7 per cent of offices and a mere 2.4 per cent of assets. All Philippine banking institutions are subject to prudential regulation and supervision by the Central Bank, *Bangko Sentral ng Pilipinas* (BSP). While the central bank is the supervisory body of banks, the National Credit Council, created in 1993 and located within the Department of Finance, has been the main promoter of policy reforms, particularly for microfinance.

The microfinance sub-sector: towards a more conducive policy environment

According to the National Credit Council's definition, microfinance in the Philippines is geared to:

> the viable and sustainable provision of a broad range of financial services (savings and credit), generally by the private sector to poor and low-income households engaged in livelihood and micro-enterprise activities using non-traditional and innovative methodologies and approaches (e.g. non-collateralized cash-flow based lending). The maximum individual loan amount provided for microfinance loans is P150 000 [circa US$3000].[2]

Similar to the fragmentation which characterizes the overall financial sector, microfinance institutions (MFIs) can be divided into:

> **1.** formal financial institutions, comprising rural banks and thrift banks subject to prudential regulation and central bank supervision;
> **2.** semi-formal institutions, such as co-operatives and NGOs, facing limitations to savings mobilization and some registration requirements but no special prudential regulation and supervision. Co-operatives can mobilize savings from their members but not from the public. NGOs are allowed to collect savings from their borrowers only provided that they do not exceed the outstanding balance of loans (National Credit Council Policy Paper, July 2002); and
> **3.** informal financial institutions such as the ubiquitous rotating savings and credit associations (*paluwagan*) and moneylenders, without registration, regulation and supervision requirements. However, for moneylenders, the central bank has opened an avenue to recognition and respectability: as so-called 'lending investors', which register with the central bank but are not supervised.

During the 1970s and 1980s microfinance followed the characteristic supply-led directed credit approach whereby loans were provided to rural households at below-market interest rates. Programmes proved to be financially unsustainable and frequently turned out to be biased towards relatively better-off clients. Building upon the lessons learned in the 1980s and following the creation of the National Credit Council, clearer policies and guidelines against directed credit programmes emerged. In 1999, the policies culminated with Executive Order 138, which mandated government non-financial institutions to terminate credit programmes and government financial institutions to remove caps on interest rates and adopt market-based pricing. More recently, in 2002, the National Credit Council launched a new policy for microfinance.

Parallel to the evolution in public policies, microfinance has emerged as an element of anti-poverty and community development approaches promoted by non-government organizations (NGOs). Some of them have specialized in microfinance and a few have established formal banks, thus laying the ground for more sustainable operations and showing that poor clients can be served on a commercial basis. Originally cautious towards the growth of a new industry, the Central Bank has showed a more encouraging attitude towards microfinance in recent years, for example by allowing some exemptions from regulation concerning unsecured loans, providing rural banks with more freedom to branch out and by opening a rediscounting window for microfinance (2001).

In spite of the improving policy environment, progress made by microfinance institutions by the mid-1990s was still limited. In 1989, an attempt had been made by the Agricultural Credit Policy Council (ACPC), an agency of the Department of Agriculture to replicate the Grameen methodology. A typical example of a surviving directed credit programme, it was found unsustainable in an evaluation by ACPC (1995) due to caps on interest rates and exorbitant operating costs. On the same lines, in 1996, an assessment of MFIs in eleven Asian and Pacific countries presented findings on seven MFIs in the Philippines (one co-operative bank and six NGOs) most of which had adopted the Grameen methodology. Their common traits were limited numbers of clients and weak financial performance. Outreach ranged from 1260 to 7000 clients, average loans outstanding ranged from US$30 to US$467 among the poor and from US$1500 to US$2600 among the non-poor. Operating costs per loan outstanding varied from 19 per cent to 130 per cent, and the financial self-sufficiency ratio varied from 0.07 to 1.18, with an average of 0.55 (Quiñones and Seibel 2000, 2001).

In 1997 the Asian Development Bank (ADB) and the International Fund for Agricultural Development (IFAD) launched a country-wide Grameen replication project, the Rural Micro-Enterprise Finance Project, without any interest rate restrictions. The two donors also financed a new specialized apex organization, the People's Credit and Finance Corporation (PCFC), as the national wholesaler of funds to microfinance institutions in the Philippines. PCFC is formally owned by the Land Bank of the Philippines, a government-owned financial institution. It has been refinanced by a number of donors, including IFAD, ADB, and the World Bank at concessional interest rates. In the case of the ADB-IFAD Grameen replication project, PCFC was lending at an annual interest rate of 12 per cent (with an upfront 1 per cent charge) and was refinanced by the two agencies at 5.25 per cent and 5 per cent respectively, through the Land Bank of the Philippines. When PCFC was established (1997), it was foreseen that it would be privatized a few years later but a plan for its privatization was not yet in place as of December 2003.

PCFC displayed a remarkable degree of autonomy and enforced high repayment rates from its 162 client MFIs, a heterogeneous group of rural banks (38 per cent), thrift banks (2 per cent), co-operative banks (15 per cent), multi-purpose co-operatives (15 per cent) and NGOs (14 per cent), reaching a cumulative number of 520 000 households as of December 2002.[3] Producers Rural Banking Corporation is one of the microfinance institutions refinanced by PCFC.

New rural bank in Nueva Ecija Province: the Producers Rural Banking Corporation

The province of Nueva Ecija is located within the Eastern rim of Central Luzon, some 90 km from Manila. Predominantly an agricultural area, dubbed the rice basket of 'central Luzon', with paddy and vegetables as major crops, the province is highly vulnerable to fluctuations in agricultural prices. Agricultural land tends to be concentrated in the hands of few large farmers, while smallholders and landless households rely on wage labour, seasonal labour and (seasonal) off-farm income-generating activities. In 2000, 32 per cent of households in Nueva Ecija were below the poverty line.[4]

The Producers Rural Banking Corporation (hereafter, Producers Bank) was established in 1995 in San José City (Nueva Ecija) by Andres Cornejo, a certified public accountant and owner of a pawnshop, who had retired from the position of Treasurer and Chief Financial Officer at the First Philippine Holdings Corporation. On 27 November 1995, with an investment of P5 million (approximately US$100 000), operations started in a small rented facility.

Act One: expanding by capturing untapped savings

As a small player, the newly born bank was facing competition from existing larger banks in deposit taking and lending. In search of a niche, expansion to clients ignored by formal financial institutions appeared the only avenue to survival and perhaps prosperity. After only one year of operations, Producers Bank filed a request to the central bank to open new branches, and three branches were opened in 1996.

At the centre of its strategy was a savings mobilization campaign to reach households which had never before met bank staff. The strategy included house-to-house visits on non-working days, raffles for depositors (a ticket for every P2000, or US$38, deposited); special children's deposit products; promotional fiestas when opening a new branch.

In the effort to bridge the gap between the potential demand and the actual supply of financial services, Producers Bank started testing credit products tailored for low-income clients. The first step was to offer small individual short-term loans, up to US$100 for working capital to some

500 micro-entrepreneurs: street vendors, small store and repair shop owners. Maturities were 30 to 90 days; instalments were daily, weekly or monthly, depending on the cash flow, payable either at the bank or at doorsteps combined with deposit collection. Outstanding loans almost tripled between 1996 and 1997, but a price for growth was paid in terms of deteriorating quality of the portfolio. In fact, the operational self-sufficiency ratio declined from 104.7 per cent in 1996 to 69.2 per cent in 1997.

Act Two: commercializing Grameen, from social service to financial product

In 1998 PCFC proposed that Producers Bank participate in the new Grameen replication project. Producers Bank's staff received training in Grameen lending from CARD Bank, a former NGO which had received a banking license in 1997 and was considered as a leader in the microfinance industry.[5] The exposure to this programme gave Producers Bank a standardized set of financial products which were relatively easy for the management to understand, for the field staff to sell, and for low-income clients to access. First experimented with in Bangladesh by Prof. Yunus in the mid 1970s, the Grameen banking approach consists of releasing small loans (and some limited ancillary financial services) to groups of five borrowers. Groups are federated into centres (of 20 to 50 borrowers). Credit is provided to individual members, while the repayment of loan is made through frequent (normally weekly) instalments guaranteed by the group. This technique replaces material collateral with peer pressure, since group members can receive larger loans when all the members have fully and timely repaid all their instalments.

The absence of collateral requirements reduces (although it does not completely eliminate) barriers to entry for very poor and landless households, while peer pressure reduces the usual problems connected with asymmetry of information between the lender and the borrower and leads to high repayment rates: well above 95 per cent when the approach is well implemented. Following positive feedback from a field test, Producers Bank created a special lending portfolio for Grameen clients, the Livelihood Support Programme, with separate accounts. While conventional clients had access to the standard individual loan and deposit products, the following Grameen products were available for the new microfinance clients:

- solidarity group loans, collateral-free, with six-month maturity and weekly repayments; The size of the first loan is about US$100. Upon full and timely repayment, loans increase subsequently up to a ceiling of US$500. Beyond that, Producers Bank offers larger-size individual loans to borrowers with a good track record;
- compulsory savings deposited in weekly instalments and remunerated at an annual interest rate of 2 per cent, not withdrawable before a client leaves the programme;

- an insurance package in case of accident or death of the borrower.

In addition to these standard Grameen services, Producers Bank offers its microfinance clients the following products and options.

- Grameen clients are offered individual voluntary deposits accounts according to a client's capacity, which are not part of the standard Grameen compulsory savings accounts.
- Individual loans are offered as a part of a graduation strategy to clients with good repayment to expand their business or access consumer loans. Within the traditional Grameen system, clients who intended to make relatively larger investments in fixed equipments would face opposition from other group members, unwilling to guarantee larger amounts. Moreover, weekly repayments would not have matched the typical cash flows for medium-term investments. Although only few clients have been able to-date to take larger loans, the opportunity of access to individual loans has been appreciated.
- Discount cards are non-financial products sold to Grameen clients for an annual fee of P500 (US$10), which give the right to discounts of 2 per cent to 5 per cent at local grocery, drug, hardware and spare parts stores.
- The option of staying in the Grameen system without borrowing was granted as a measure to reduce the loss of clients and lower the dropout rate, a typical problem of Grameen banking. The Grameen approach assumes that clients want to borrow increasing amount of loans. In reality, clients may not always be willing immediately to take further loans.

In many cases, the Grameen approach has been used by NGOs in community development, using credit as the main propeller of change accompanied by non-financial services. In contrast, Producers Bank turned the Grameen approach into a profitable commercial product: a contribution to the formation of social capital in microfinance, as explained at the conclusion of this chapter.

The Grameen approach has provided Producers Bank with an entry point to the market segment of poor income households which was previously inaccessible to the bank, and with a method to enforce credit discipline based on peer pressure and the commitment of groups and centre leaders. Producers Bank was initially stimulated by access to refinancing sources through PCFC; but it would have soon abandoned the approach had it not found it profitable in the first place.

It is also interesting to highlight that, while there was a transfer of knowledge and capacity from conventional banking practices to the microfinance portfolio, the process of cross-fertilization also worked in the other direction. One of the requirements to obtain funds from PCFC was that of administering means test questionnaires to applicants, in order to ensure that their household income did not exceed a ceiling of

P10 000 (US$188) per month, corresponding approximately to the national poverty threshold for a household of six members. The management learned to use the questionnaire as an instrument to acquire information on clients' cash flow, vulnerability to shocks and repayment capacity. It was used as a decision tool to distinguish between clients qualified for individual loans and other clients who would better fit into group lending. As a fringe benefit, it turned out that the exercise was instrumental to instil better practices in loan appraisal within their conventional lending programme.

The bank now considers offering a Grameen franchising or build-operate-transfer service to other financial institutions. The package, still to be tested, could consist of Producers Bank building and initially operating a new microfinance programme and then, after reaching profitability, transferring ownership to a financial institution for a commercial fee.

Act Three: focus on human resources and management information systems

High repayment rates and profitability require professionalism and commitment among staff and a monitoring system which provides timely information. Particular emphasis is given to staff selection, training and performance incentives. Account officers are entitled to 2 per cent of the principal of fully and timely repaid loans, while their area and headquarter supervisors receive 0.75 per cent and 0.25 per cent, respectively. In addition to pecuniary rewards, highly performing staff members are also offered on-the-job training and are encouraged to attend seminars at local business schools. As a result, the average outstanding portfolio per account officer increased by 112 per cent (from US$11 600 to US$24 700) between 1999 and 2003.

Effective monitoring has been one of the early concerns of the Producers Bank to spot delinquency problems, develop the bank's policies and financial products and reduce the scope for fraud by field staff. Monitoring is done through 'management by exception', that is, concentrating on delinquent accounts. Copies of collection sheets signed by the account officers are left with the Grameen centre at the closure of the meeting, while official repayment receipts are given to the borrowers at the next meeting. A computerized tracking system is used to encode transactions at the branch level; and account officers are expected to submit weekly written reports, consolidated at the branch level and sent to the headquarters to be summarized into monthly progress reports. Reporting requirements include the following indicators:

(a) outreach (number of borrowers, number of groups and centres served);
(b) loan disbursement and repayment (amount released and outstanding);

Table 2.1 *Producers Bank – Grameen operations outreach and repayment indicators*

Year	1999	2000	2001	2002	2003
No. of clients with outstanding loans	2 919	5 678	12 223	19 037	44 037
No. of clients with savings	2 919	7 699	14 463	26 332	51 358
Amount of outstanding loans (US$)	196 548	451 146	1 068 877	1 379 736	3 403 721
Amount of savings accounts (US$)	43 712	90 286	271 772	368 457	581 839
Average outstanding loan per client (US$)	67.3	79.5	87.4	72.5	77.3
Average savings per client (US$)	15.0	11.7	18.8	14.0	11.3
Collection rate [a]	98%	98%	99%	99%	99%
Past-due ratio [b]	3%	5%	1%	5%	1%

a. Percentage ratio between total loan principal collected and total principal due
b. Percentage ratio between the past due amount and the value of average outstanding loans

Source: Producers Bank (2004)

(c) overall portfolio quality (repayment rate, past-due rate, portfolio at risk);
(d) productivity (borrowers and value of outstanding loans per account officer).

Financial performance: growth without massive delinquency

From 1999, the first year of implementation of Grameen-based microfinance, to 2003, the growth of Producers Bank's financial operations has been impressive (Table 2.1). The number of microfinance clients with outstanding loans has increased from 2900 to 44 000 (+1409 per cent), the value of outstanding Grameen loans from US$196 500 to US$3.4 million (+2340 per cent) and the value of Grameen deposits from US$43 000 to US$ 580 000 (+1775 per cent). As of 2002, Grameen clients represented around 80 per cent of the bank's borrowers and 40 per cent of savers but only 12 per cent of the outstanding loans and 4 per cent of savings. The average outstanding loan of regular clients was 28 times higher than that of Grameen clients (approximately US$1430 vs. US$52) and the average savings account 15 times higher (US$215 vs. US$14). Between 1999 and 2003, the average value of outstanding loans per Grameen borrower has hovered around US$77 and the average (mainly compulsory) savings per depositor around US$14, or 7 per cent and 1 per cent, respectively, of average GDP per capita, suggesting that the target clientele has been represented by very poor households without any mission drift over five years. Collection rates have been 98 per cent and above and past-due ratios have never exceeded 5 per cent (see Table 2.1 opposite).

For Producers Bank, Grameen banking turned out to be substantially more profitable than regular banking. In 2001 and 2002, return on performing assets (ROPA) for microfinance operations was calculated at 5.6 per cent and 2.0 per cent respectively (see Table 2.2 below), compared to 1.5 per cent in 2001 and 1.7 per cent in 2002 for the whole bank (not shown).

At the same time, a price has been paid for the very fast growth, in terms of declining profitability of Grameen operations between 2001 and 2003. Main cost factors include a surge in administrative costs (staff salaries and benefits), especially between 2002 and 2003, when staff were recruited or shifted from ordinary to microfinance operations, after the tremendous expansion of the Grameen loan portfolio; declining effective interest rates due to emerging competition with other lenders; and a slight deterioration of the quality of the loan portfolio.

Table 2.2 Producers Bank - Grameen operations productivity and profitability indicators

Year	2001	2002	2003	Average 2001–03
Operating costs ratio [a]	17.8%	8.3%	17.6%	14.6%
Loan loss ratio [b]	3.3%	2.5%	3.2%	3.0%
Operational self-sufficiency (OSS) [c]	132.0%	117.2%	106%	118.4%
Return on performing assets (ROPA) [d]	5.6%	2.0%	1.1%	2.9%

a. Percentage ratio between administrative and staff costs and the value of average outstanding loans

b. Percentage ratio between loan loss provision and the value of average outstanding loans

c. Percentage ratio between financial revenue and the sum of operating costs, financial costs and loan loss provision (as interest rates paid on PCFC loans are now at market level, OSS is practically equivalent to financial self-sufficiency)

d. Percentage ratio between net financial income and assets (excluding fixed assets)

Source: Producers Bank (2004)

Maintaining profitability while facing the entry of competitors in the same market segments will be one of the major challenges in the future. Competition is likely in the medium term to bring about a reduction in effective interest rates. Grameen banking is an expensive technology. In spite of increasing competition, effective interest rates are still very high, calculating the combined effect of monthly flat interest rates of 2.5 per cent, up-front fees and compulsory savings. The effective annual interest rates paid by clients for loans of P5000 (US$94), P10 000 (US$188) and P15 000 (US$282) are around 120 per cent, 92 per cent and 77 per cent, respectively. In other areas, banks and NGOs offer micro-loans at similar and higher interests. Effective annual interest rates around 150 per cent are common among pawnshops, and they are higher still from moneylenders.

Interest rates have remained high so far, because of the quasi-monopolistic power of the bank, which has only had to face competition from pawnshops in peri-urban areas and informal moneylenders in rural ones. Certainly the bank has so far made good progress: after only seven years of operations and almost unaffected by the 1997 Asian crisis, it is ranked as the 13th rural bank in the Philippines in terms of assets and has received several awards for its financial performance, organization and management.

The clients: gender and poverty depth

The sections above have shown the growth in outreach in terms of number of clients. Beyond head counting, other dimensions of outreach may include gender and poverty depth. As women suffer from several forms of relative deprivation in many developing countries, a high proportion of female clients is normally seen as an indicator of success of microlending programmes. Grameen-based projects typically have a majority of women borrowers; this is also true in the case of Producers Bank: 99 per cent are women, as against 50 per cent among non-Grameen clients. Rural women are reportedly more inclined than men to observe the strict requirement of attending weekly centre meetings.

A third outreach dimension to be explored is the profile of the typical borrowers in terms of poverty. Most borrowers had a small grocery (*sari-sari*) shop as their main activity, followed by clients engaged in street vending and food processing. The majority of clients had more than one microenterprise activity. The usual combination was that of a typical non-agricultural micro-business as first activity, with pig or poultry raising as a secondary activity. Many clients were marginal farmers aiming at diversifying income sources and the Grameen technology was found to be better suited for non-agricultural activities with relatively steady and continuous cash inflow. The option of two or more activities, each of them with different cash-flow patterns is a risk management strategy to even out cyclical effects and help smoothing consumption.

Table 2.3 Producers Bank (PRB) financial statements, December 2002

BALANCE SHEET	PRB Microfinance 2002 US$ (000)	PRB Consolidated 2002 US$ (000)
Assets	**2 415**	**15 146**
Cash on hand and due from other banks	667	3 042
Loans and discounts (net of loan loss reserves)	1 294	11 198
Fixed & other assets (net of depreciation)	454	905
Liabilities and capital accounts	**2 415**	**15 146**
Deposit liabilities	347	8 787
Bills payable	2 004	3 843
Other liabilities	30	539
Total capital	**33**	**1 977**
INCOME STATEMENT		
Income	**266**	**1 845**
Interest income	253	1 807
Service charges & other income	13	38
Expenses	**227**	**1 606**
Interest on deposit	5	286
Interest on borrowed funds	94	228
Compensation/fringe benefits	63	483
Insurance & other expenses	27	380
Depreciation/amortization	9	101
Bad debts expenses	30	128
Net income	**39**	**239**

Source: Producers Bank (2004)

A common proxy of relative wealth of clients is the ratio of the average outstanding loan over GDP per capita. In the case of Producers Bank, the ratio has been hovering around 7 per cent between 1999 and 2003 without an appreciable increase, probably due to the raising number of clients with a small first loan but also suggesting that there has not been any substantial change in targeting strategy. This value is far lower than averages computed for both formal and informal microfinance institutions in South-East Asia. In spite of these very small loan sizes, Producers Bank finds it difficult to target the poorest segment of the population and very remote areas.

The selection of clients involves at least three stages. First, there is an implicit self-selection process, by which households decide whether to apply or not for membership in a Grameen group. Information problems are minimal as the microlending programme is widely publicized and talked about. However, households without regular income may be discouraged from borrowing by weekly instalments. Second comes the screening of loan applications, which normally requires that clients be physically healthy, have some previous experience in microbusiness, and have a regular cash flow. This is done as a precautionary measure to avoid massive delinquency problems but may lead to the exclusion of poorest households. A third important step is the peer-selection process: as in any case of joint liability, groups members may refuse access to applicants they judge unreliable even though they have passed the bank's screening.

For these reasons, the 'enterprising poor' represent the bulk of the clients. Efforts to enhance the participation of applicants with little or no micro-business experience were not successful. Lessons learned from the experience include:

1. microfinance institutions need to start with conservative targets in terms of poverty depths lest they have to face high default ratios and put their sustainability at risk;
2. micro-credit is a valid anti-poverty instrument for many but not all households: the poorest families may perhaps better benefit from appropriately developed savings products;
3. reaching progressively poorer clients requires innovative financial products.

Main benefits to clients

One of the assumptions underlying donor support to microfinance programmes is that they would significantly propel enterprise growth and household income, thereby stimulating the local economy and creating new job opportunities. This was found to apply only to few. Roughly 15 per cent to 20 per cent of the microenterprises served by Producers Bank display the potential to become small or medium-sized. The small shops, street vendors and livestock raisers are generally characterized by a low equity base and a high degree of competition. Furthermore, not all microfinance clients are business people: some are not so much interested in expanding micro-enterprises but simply in diversifying household income sources or coping with temporary liquidity problems. For this reason, Producers Bank could graduate only a small fraction of its clients to larger individual loans with lower interest rates (although this remains their ultimate objective). In terms of impact, it was observed that:

- households had a preference for diversifying horizontally rather than expanding their business;
- increases in enterprise and household income have not been dramatic, but seasonal and business cycles fluctuations have been reduced, smoothing cash flow and household consumption;
- given the fungibility of money, Grameen loans have frequently represented a support to the overall household budget rather than a targeted intervention on specific economic activities. Part of the loans have been used to face temporary illiquidity (for example, paying for school fees, unforeseen household expenses or loans from moneylenders), without leading to extensive delinquency problems. The bank's loan officers are quite pragmatic, and do not interfere too much with loan use as long as households meet their repayment requirements.

Producers Bank and the social capital of Grameen banking in the Philippines: a wider perspective

Producers Bank, as a Grameen replicator, has followed three sound practices, constituting the core social capital of the original Grameen approach:

- high moral commitment of leaders based on values enforced through training;
- peer selection and peer enforcement, to reduce information gaps on the risk profile of the clients and incentives for voluntary defaults (the 'adverse selection and moral hazard problems' in the language of the economists);
- credit discipline, including weekly instalments; rigid insistence on timely repayment; and repeat loans of growing sizes contingent upon repayment performance.

In addition, as a promising replicator, the Producers Bank added the following elements of commercialization of Grameen banking:

- (rural) bank status;
- deposit mobilization through differentiated products;
- differentiated loan and insurance products which cover all costs and yield a profit;
- client differentiation through larger-size loan and deposit products for non-poor members (generating additional loan capital) and graduation opportunities for the poor.

Future Challenges

We have presented the case of a small bank that has begun to penetrate the market of the rural poor in the Philippines in search of a competitive niche. This was inspired by the offer of a suitable financial product, namely Grameen banking, and access to a source of refinancing. While social motives were not alien to the Producers Bank, financial activities were conducted on a commercial base. The bank has experienced fast growth and has so far been able to keep credit delinquency under control and preserve profitability, although with a (perhaps temporarily) declining trend.

Its good performance notwithstanding, Producers Bank is exposed to challenges and risks. First, the bank will have to continue defending its profitability. Second, it will need to control the dropout of clients due to the rigidity of the Grameen approach and its credit bias. Producers Bank has responded to this need by graduating clients to the individual loan window and by allowing their clients to deposit savings without borrowing. In the future, however, the bank might have to introduce further innovations.

Third, the bank will presently face stronger competition. Producers Bank has for some time benefited from a local near-monopoly. But competition is emerging: from operators who offer a wider range of services, not necessarily lower interest rates. This brings about two risks: losing clients to competitors; and a deteriorating microfinance portfolio, as clients may borrow from several sources.

Four, the increasing size and complexity of microfinance operations may raise organizational challenges. Producers Bank has a separate accounting system for its microfinance portfolio but not a separate management and organizational line. In the future, a specialized divisional structure might be needed.

Five, a growing financial institution needs a further injection of capital. At present, as for most rural banks in the Philippines, Producers Bank's equity is concentrated in the hands of few stockholders, while, in the future, the bank's ownership may have to become more differentiated.

Acknowledgement

The authors wish to thank Ms. Pier Elva Mercado and the staff of Producers Rural Banking Corporation. However, the opinions expressed in this case study are those of the authors only and do not engage the responsibility of their institutions. The authors are solely responsible for any error or omission.

Discussion questions

1. Why did Producers Bank enter the microfinance market? Can microfinance be an effective niche for small locally based commercial banks which have increasingly to compete with national and even international institutions?

2. The Grameen methodology is mainly used only by institutions which are organized specifically for this purpose. Banks which want to combine microfinance with mainstream banking generally employ self-help groups or other methods. How suitable is the Grameen method for Producers Bank, and how effectively has it been integrated with the Bank's other operations?

3. The Grameen methodology is labour intensive and expensive. This demands high interest rates. How will Producers Bank be able to meet competition from lower-priced products?

Chapter Three
The Bank of Khyber, Pakistan
AMJAD ALI ARBAB

North West Frontier Province

North West Frontier Province (NWFP), where the Bank of Khyber (BoK) carries out its microfinance operation, is one of four provinces of Pakistan. With Peshawar as the capital city, the NWFP is located in north-west Pakistan and shares a long border with Afghanistan. The region has been historically and strategically important due to its proximity to Afghanistan and Central Asia. As a crossroad of history, the famous Khyber Pass, which connects Afghanistan with Pakistan, has always been a pathway of commerce, migration and invasion. The Soviet invasion of Afghanistan caused over three million Afghan refugees to flee to the NWFP.[1] The Soviet withdrawal in 1989 raised hopes that refugees would be repatriated, but renewed factional fighting has left little room for the Afghans to go back to their homeland.

With an area of 74 521 square kilometres, NWFP makes up under 10 per cent of the area of Pakistan and 13.6 per cent of its population. The province contains high barren mountains and forests and fertile valleys in the north. Wheat is the main crop and barley, sugarcane, tobacco, cotton, fruits and vegetables are also cultivated. The provincial economy is predominantly agrarian with a weak industrial base. Small and cottage industry provides most of the employment besides agriculture. Trade with Afghanistan is also important.

Pakistan ranks 136 of 174 countries in the Human Development Index. Real GDP at factor cost in 2002–03 grew by 5.1 percent, and per capita income reached US$492 in 2002–03.[2] The country's rate of inflation stands at 3.27 per cent for the year 2002–03.[3] As in much of the developing world, economic growth in Pakistan, and particularly in the NWFP, has not benefited the poor. Poverty is in fact increasing; according to the Government of Pakistan, the incidence of poverty in the country has increased from 17.3 per cent in 1988 to 32.6 per cent in 1999.[4] The population of NWFP is more than 17 million, and is growing at over 3 per cent per annum. More than 80 per cent live in rural areas, and the incidence of poverty in NWFP is 42.6 per cent.[5] More than 60 per cent of the rural population in NWFP has no access to safe drinking water and 50 per cent have no access to sanitation. Many of the men from NWFP migrate to other cities in Pakistan and the Gulf for jobs. Women have to carry more household and farming responsibilities. They are politically, economically and socially disadvantaged, especially in terms of ownership of productive assets, access to social services and decision-making within homes. Women are rarely engaged in mainstream business, and those who have small businesses have little access to formal sources of credit and other business development services. There is a large network of public sector banks, and many people have access to savings and other banking services, but very few poorer people can get loans.

There are a number of sources of informal credit in NWFP, but the credit needs of the vast majority of people are not met. Many non-governmental organizations (NGOs) are active in the NWFP, but the range of other programmes that they offer dilutes their focus on microfinance services. NGOs also lack the financial and technical expertise to initiate and manage effective microfinance programmes. The commercial banks lack interest in microfinance primarily because of the high costs of operation and lack of collateral security. The retail commercial banks cannot provide sustainable micro-credit on a large scale because their systems and procedures are incompatible with the requirements and capacities of the poor.

Microfinance in Pakistan

The three main sources of microfinance in Pakistan can be categorized as informal, semi-formal and formal institutions. Informal sources of credit dominate the microfinance industry, and are estimated to meet 83 per cent of the financial requirements of the poor. Moneylenders, shopkeepers, traders, middlemen, family and friends provide credit both for production and consumption purposes. The effective annual rates of interest in the informal sector are much higher than for formal finance and are estimated at between 50 and 120 per cent.[6]

NGOs and rural support programmes (RSPs)[7] play an important semi-formal role in providing financial services to the poor. Their outreach, despite their rapid growth in recent years, remains minimal. Out of the 20 000 or so registered NGOs in the country only a few dozen offer microfinance services. Some of the microfinance providers, including NGOs, RSPs, and specialized and commercial banks have formed a network called the Pakistan Microfinance Network (PMN). The purpose of PMN is to 'support microfinance sector so that it can effectively provide financial services to most poor people. The network places particular focus on enhancing the scale, quality, diversity and sustainability of the services provided by retail microfinance institutions.' The members are now lending to over 170 000 people, and the outstanding portfolio at the end of 2002 was about US$22 million.[8] The Government of Pakistan, with the support of the World Bank, has established the Pakistan Poverty Alleviation Fund (PPAF) as an apex institution providing wholesale credit for microfinance institutions.

Among the formal sources of finance, Khushali Bank, established in 2000, is the lead microfinance institution (MFI) in the country. First Microfinance Bank Limited (FMFBL), sponsored by the Aga Khan Foundation and the International Finance Corporation (IFC), was established in 2001 and is the first private-sector microfinance bank in Pakistan. In addition, some commercial banks have also ventured into microfinance activity. The Bank of Khyber (BoK) is the most active

Table 3.1 Annual reach of commercial banks, MFIs and NGOs during 2002

Organizations	Annual Borrowers	
Commercial Banks and MFIs (including BoK and Khushali Bank)		242 166
NGOs		
Punjab Rural Support Programme (PRSP)	42 928	
KASHF Foundation	36 103	
National Rural Support Programme (NRSP)	28 768	
Aga Khan Rural Support Programme (AKRSP)	12 232	
NGO others	19 677	
NGOs total		139 708
Grand total		381 874
Source: Pakistan Microfinance Network (PMN), December 2003		

commercial bank in the field of microfinance. Table 3.1 (see above) shows the annual outreach of key players in the microfinance sector for the year 2002.

There are about 45 million poor people in Pakistan.[9] If MFIs are reaching only 380 000 of them, even assuming that only a quarter of them need credit, MFIs in Pakistan are now reaching only about 3.4 per cent of the poor who need credit. Most demand for microfinance is in rural areas where the poor need to invest in farming, livestock and microenterprises. The demand for microfinance in urban areas is from vendors, small traders and microenterprises, as well as wage earners. Assuming an average loan of US$175[10,11], the potential demand for microfinance services in Pakistan is around US$2 billion per annum.

As in many other countries, access to microfinance is considered an effective tool for poverty alleviation in Pakistan. Although institutional microfinance is a recent development in the country, the government has taken a number of steps to create a legal, supervisory and regulatory framework for the development of the microfinance industry. Notable government measures include promulgation of the Microfinance Ordinance in 2001 subsequent to which the FMFB was created, the microfinance Prudential Regulations in 2002, and the establishment of the government owned Khushali Bank. These developments show that policy makers are interested in enhancing the effective provision of microfinance to the poor in Pakistan. Although these developments constitute a major step forward, yet the sector is still in its nascent stage compared to other countries of the region.

The Bank of Khyber

The Government of NWFP established the Bank of Khyber (BoK) in 1991 under an Act of the Provincial Legislative Assembly. The provincial government is the major shareholder with 87 per cent of the shares, and the balance is held by DEG, a German development agency. BoK was established in response to the long-standing demand of the business community of the region. They felt that NWFP needed its own commercial bank, with its head office and roots in the province. At the time it was established, the major objective of the bank was to generate deposits from within the province for investment within the NWFP in industry, agriculture and trade. BoK has a total of 426 officers and 133 support staff. As at 31 December 2003, the total number of account holders was 101 375 and the total deposit base nearly US$400m. The Bank had a net loan portfolio of US$94.4m by the end of 2003, and made a net profit of US$5.34m during the year.

BoK started as a provincial commercial bank but attained the status of a Scheduled Bank within four years, at which point it came under the regulatory framework of the central bank, the State Bank of Pakistan. This allowed the bank to open branches outside NWFP, to become a member of the clearing house and to engage in trade and finance activities directly. BoK has a total of 29 branches, of which 23 are located within NWFP and six are located in other major cities of Pakistan. Of the 23 branches in NWFP, the head office and eight branches are located in the provincial capital Peshawar, while the remaining 15 branches are dispersed across the Province

Although the BoK was established as a commercial bank it was given a strong developmental mandate by the government of NWFP. Soon after establishment, it started commercial banking activities by developing a network of branches, generating deposits and finding sound commercial avenues for the application of funds. Parallel with its general banking activities, in the fourth year of its establishment BoK also started exploring ways and means to bring a new set of clients into its fold who were considered either un-bankable or high risk by other commercial banks. This decision to enter the micro- and small business segment and to scale down the commercial banking operations primarily came from the top management, some of whom had rich experience and orientation in agriculture and development financing prior to joining BoK. They wanted to develop effective banking mechanisms and accompanying products and services for more disadvantaged micro- and small entrepreneurs at the grassroots.

BoK administers its microfinance operation through a separate division at the Bank's head office called Microfinance Unit (MFU). MFU credit officers at 16 (general banking) branches in NWFP manage the microfinance loan portfolio. Microfinance services are offered by all the branches in NWFP, apart from Peshawar, where the micro-loan portfolio is consolidated into three of the eight branches. In the urban branches the microfinance portfolio's contribution to profitability is

Table 3.2 Major differences in BoK's microfinance loans and general banking loans

Characteristics	General banking	Microfinance
Clients' status	Individuals, partnerships, corporate bodies, etc.	Individuals and informal groups
Clients' social standing	Affluent with good net worth	Low-income with very few assets
Clients' business profile	Preferably small, medium and large scale	Only micro-businesses and personal finance
Clients' security/collateral	Collateral is a must. Preferably mortgage of landed properties	Collateral not necessary Personal guarantees and social collateral
Clients' track record	Need minimum banking relationship terms with BoK	No previous banking history/record required
Loan size (average)	US$9192	US$841
Loan term	May be up to 7 years	Must not be beyond 2 years
Loan repayment	Quarterly repayment of interest only	Frequent/monthly instalments
Loan type	Fund/non-fund Cash credit and demand finance type	Demand finance only

insignificant. However, the microfinance operation is a major source of income for the branches outside the city. The credit officers approve and disburse loans at their branches and inform the MFU so it can enter data on its loan tracking system. Loans beyond the credit officers' sanctioning powers are forwarded to the MFU for approval and subsequent disbursement at respective branches. Loan collections are made at the branches and a statement of monthly recoveries is submitted to MFU. The features of loan products offered under the microfinance operation and those offered under the general banking schemes are quite different.

No specific saving products were introduced for microfinance clientele as BoK's main commercial banking channels and credit lines from multilateral institutions provided sufficient funds for microfinance lending. However, it does encourage savings amongst rural communities where microfinance clientele can make use of BoK's general savings products. For instance, in order to accommodate small savers, BoK brought down its minimum account-opening limit to US$1.75 as against US$8.8.

Phase I: downscaling of commercial individual loans

BoK launched its micro-business development programme in 1995. It was actually the downscaling of conventional commercial bank lending through existing staff members involved in general banking. Lending at this stage was focused on individual small and medium enterprises with average loan size around US$3650. The loan amounts ranged from US$877 to US$52 600. BoK started with a single microenterprise loan characterized by a wide rage of loan size and terms, and a loosely defined target market. Microenterprise loans were provided to individual clients both for existing and new business to meet their financial needs for fixed or working capital. There was little awareness in BoK about microfinance practices at that time but a solid step had been taken towards developing a mechanism for reaching out to the lower levels of economic activity.

BoK was planning to gear its institutional set up to meet the needs of the large majority of small businesses under the specific economic realities of the region. However, it was felt that commercial bankers did not appreciate the requirements of micro- and small entrepreneurs whose major qualification for acquiring a loan was their credibility and goodwill rather than their cash flow and collateral. Operating the micro-business development programme through commercial banking staff was not very successful, and only 97 loans amounting to US$305 263 had been disbursed by the end of 1996.

To overcome this problem, in 1997 a team of young professionals were hired from outside the commercial banking field, primarily those who had worked in foreign-funded development projects. This led to major growth in the microfinance portfolio in a short time. By the end of 1997, 400 loans had been disbursed, with a cumulative value of US$1.1m. BoK, at this stage, focused on microfinance for selected sectors, such as woodwork and light engineering. These two activities were selected because BoK was able to develop strategic alliances with development projects whose trained entrepreneurs needed small amounts of money to expand or establish their new businesses. BoK's products and services were much appreciated by both the clientele and the provincial government. This resulted in increased goodwill and publicity for the microfinance functions of the Bank.

Phase II: collaboration with RSPs and NGOs

BoK at this stage felt that a large potential market in the rural areas was still uncovered. It started looking for collaboration with several cluster associations, NGOs and RSPs to use their services as facilitators in extending microfinance. Multilateral institutions, such as the Asian Development Bank (ADB) and the International Fund for Agriculture Development (IFAD) also started approaching BoK to seek its assistance in channeling funds for the rural financial services components of the bilateral area development projects of the Government of NWFP

Box 3.1 *Roles of the facilitator, community and BoK*

Facilitator's role

▶ Grassroots awareness and mobilization of rural communities
▶ Organize and develop communities
▶ Introduce and link organized communities to financial institutions
▶ Assist BoK in evaluating social maturity level of communities
▶ Assist communities in assessing their needs and endorse credit requests for processing by BoK
▶ Facilitate BoK interaction with COs

Communities' role

▶ Assume responsibility for credit progamme along with BoK
▶ Develop social organizations capable of representing communities and assuming responsibility
▶ Establish sustainable saving schemes as part of social collateral
▶ Carry out social activities for common welfare
▶ Assess and prioritize credit needs
▶ Guarantee for loans and ensure regular repayment.

BoK's role

▶ Provide credit orientation to facilitators' staff and COs
▶ Provide banking channels to facilitators and COs
▶ Assist COs and facilitators in credit-need assessment
▶ Design and implement credit progammes that are responsive to communities' needs
▶ Strengthen credit delivery systems through training and orientation
▶ Encourage saving schemes

(GoNWFP). 1997 was a turning point in the history of BoK and a watershed year in the microfinance history of Pakistan, since it was the first time that a commercial bank entered into rural finance by collaborating with facilitators. The main feature of this phase was to draw upon the social capital developed by facilitators to provide group loans to members of community organizations (COs). The roles and responsibilities of the facilitator, BoK and the community were clearly delineated. (see Box 3.1, above).

'Group loans' were introduced as a product for the rural market which was provided to members of COs both, men and women. The unique aspect of group lending for a commercial bank was that no tangible security was required from the borrower. They had to have a coherent CO structure, regular meetings and savings and awareness of the community's problems. This product was both for development and working capital requirements of new and existing micro- and agro-based businesses. The fundamental strength of group lending was derived from principles of community empowerment. Social collateral was the driving force behind the concept of group lending. Some of the salient features of group loans were specified as follows:

- CO members had to constitute groups of at least three but not more than five members.
- The maximum loan was US$877 per member. First loans could not exceed US$526. (The average loan is US$400.)
- Loan period was fixed at one year for agricultural inputs and three years for other micro-businesses.
- Except for agro-based enterprises, all loans were recoverable in equal monthly installments.
- The borrowing community groups had to deposit 10 per cent of the loan amount with BoK to qualify for loan.

Collaboration with facilitators provided BoK with an entry point into the rural market and a quantum increase in the number of clients, including female borrowers. In a short period of time, BoK thus became a conduit to channel funds from multilateral organizations to the poor and disadvantaged segments of the rural population. The funds are provided as loans to BoK through the Government of NWFP.

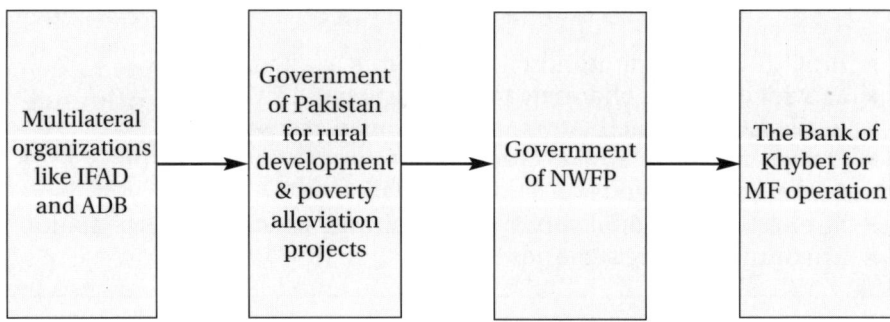

Within two-and-a-half years of starting group lending BoK was able, by the end of 1999, to disburse US$680 702 through 1532 loans averaging around US$444. Aggregate average loan size at this stage was US$1835; cumulative loans disbursed reached US$5.1m, to 2797 borrowers. The outstanding loan portfolio at this stage was around US$3.7m. This group lending was confined to specific project areas financed by ADB.

Developing productive working relationships with the facilitators was challenging and several issues had to be dealt with. Over a period of time, some facilitators also ventured into micro-lending in the same geographic area and thus an element of competition rather than co-operation began to set in. Another problem was that groups formed by facilitators frequently lacked financial focus as they were formed for village development rather than credit and savings. Similarly groups' 'loyalty' remained with facilitators as their patron institutions. Moreover, the disintegration of the COs after the withdrawal of facilitators at the termination of the project left BoK with no effective platform to render its microfinance services.

Another issue in area development projects is the involvement of credit lines from multilateral organizations that are passed on to BoK through subsidiary loan agreements between BoK and the government. Due to government's limited awareness of microfinance, it makes no distinction between corporate and microfinance lending methodologies. Therefore, problems arise when the government dictates terms and conditions that hamper smooth operations and the financial viability of microfinance programmes. The most important issue relates to the interest rates at which funds are borrowed from the government and the subsequent on-lending rate. GoNWFP sets a limit to this, which leaves a very thin margin for BoK to cover its costs. Problems also arise because area development projects may overlap with areas where BoK is operating.

Until 29 April 2003, BoK borrowed from the GoNWFP at a rate of 9 per cent per annum for on-lending to microfinance clients. Interest rates have declined over the last two years. As a result, BoK's cost of funds has fallen below the level at which it was borrowing from GoNWFP. Therefore, BoK has proposed to GoNWFP to return the loans and to on-lend its own resources. GoNWFP has agreed to the proposal and ADB's concurrence is awaited.

Phase III: establishing financial viability of the microfinance operation

Encouraged by its growing experience and expertise in microfinance, at the end of 1999 BoK established a separate Microfinance Unit (MFU) to consolidate its micro-lending activities in a coherent way and to establish its commercial viability. More operational autonomy and decentralization of loan sanctioning were achieved with the creation of this unit. This was a new era in the evolution of BoK's microfinance operations and major restructuring was carried out, which included hiring additional staff and building their capacity, standardizing operational procedures and developing a strong loan tracking system. Microfinance loans, which were previously part of the loan portfolio of respective branches, were transferred and consolidated in the MFU. This was followed by introduction of new loan products and revision of the existing ones.

The learning process continued and understanding of international best practices improved at BoK. It was realized that the range of financial products offered was too wide and a strategic decision was made to narrow them down. BoK made conscious efforts to reduce average loan sizes, to limit loan terms and to decentralize loan-sanctioning power to the branches. The maximum loan limit for 'Microenterprise loans' was

Table 3.3 Comparison of loan portfolio 1999 and 2000

	Jan. to Dec. 1999	Jan. to Dec. 2000
Number of clients		
Number of new clients during the year	1 424	3 232
Cumulative number of clients	2 797	6 142
Loans disbursed (US$)		
Amount of loans during the year	2 005 105	2 117 107
Total (cumulative) amount of loans disbursed	5 133 850	7 065 333
Average loan size		
During the year	1 408	655
Cumulative	1 835	1 150
Outstanding portfolio	3 744 270	4 358 051

brought down to US$8772. There was no lower loan limit particularly for loans to women. The maximum loan term was reduced from five to three years. The interest rate for smaller group loans in remote areas was increased above the commercial rate. These measures not only injected a fresh life into the loan portfolio but also brought it in line with international best practices in microfinance. Table 3.3 (see above) compares the growth of new loans and average loan size during 1999 and 2000.

Product innovation and development was given serious thought after the establishment of MFU when awareness regarding financial self-sufficiency was growing. A third loan product, the 'Self Employment Scheme' loan, similar in characteristics to the microenterprise loan, was launched on the advice of the Government of Pakistan. In a country where there is no effective institutional mechanism of meeting multifarious financial needs, it was necessary to launch a loan product for consumption purposes. Consequently, BoK introduced the 'domestic consumption loan' under institutional guarantee for the salaried class. Although this product represents only 6 per cent of the portfolio, it helped in diversifying risks, broadening the revenue base and reducing the gap between credit demand and supply. Besides, innovation in loan products is a consistent feature. The characteristics of the microenterprise loan product during the various phases of the microfinance operation are presented in Table 3.4 for comparison.

Opposition to greater autonomy in financial and operational matters after the creation of MFU started emerging within BoK during early

Table 3.4 *Comparison of changes in microenterprise loan product over the last eight years*

Characteristics	1995–1999	2000–2003	Current (2004)
Per person loan limit	US$52 632	US$8 772	US$877
Maximum loan term	60 months	36 months	24 months
Rate of mark-up	18% per annum (diminishing balance)	13–18% (diminishing balance)	12% (flat)
Repayment mode	Monthly, quarterly, lump sum	Monthly, quarterly, lump sum	Monthly
Security	Ranging from personal guarantee to mortgage of property	Ranging from personal guarantee to mortgage of property	Personal guarantees

2001. The cost of the microfinance operation is always higher than the commercial banking activities, and in mid-2001 management concluded that the microfinance portfolio was a losing operation. They therefore decided to bring it under the strict supervision of the branch managers, which meant reverting back to the centralized system. Senior management and the board of directors believed that microfinance involved high costs and they felt that it had emerged as 'a bank within the bank'. The microfinance unit was therefore brought under the umbrella of the Credit Division of the commercial banking operation. The loan portfolio was transferred back to respective commercial branches and the credit officers dealing with microfinance were placed under the administrative control of respective branch managers. The branch managers did not assume ownership of the programme, as they still understood very little about the dynamics of microfinance. Similarly, loan-sanctioning powers previously given to MFU were withdrawn and all loan proposals, regardless of the amount of loan, were sent to head office for approval. This not only created doubts about the future of the microfinance programme in BoK, but it also demoralized the staff, and the microfinance programme's income and loan portfolio both decreased during 2002. However, this situation did not last very long, as in 2003 there were changes in the top management of BoK. This created a much more favourable environment for the microfinance programme as indicated by the figures in Table 3.5 (overleaf).

Financial impact of BoK's microfinance operation
Research studies worldwide show that MFIs cannot make a real impact on poverty unless they are operationally and financially sustainable. It

Table 3.5 Yearly performance of MFU operations for last three years

Years	2001	2002	2003
Number of clients			
During the year	4 136	2 168	4 715
Cumulative	10 534	12 903	17 494
Loans disbursed (US$)			
During the year	3 165 508	1 491 669	2 760 600
Cumulative	10 232 152	11 733 444	14 440 201
Average loan size			
During the year	765	688	579
Cumulative	971	909	825
Outstanding portfolio	5 273 215	4 238 959	4 298 440

has also been reported that there are very few financially sustainable MFIs around the world. There are reports, for example, that a number of reputable African MFIs have achieved significant depth of outreach, but could cover only 30 to 40 per cent of their operating expenses. Working in harsh socio-economic conditions and geographically isolated communities, financial self-sufficiency is still a very difficult proposition for South Asian MFIs.[12]

BoK had never given serious consideration to the financial results of its microfinance operations, for two reasons. First, microfinance was part of the integrated profit and loss account of the bank and other commercial products were subsidizing its operations. Second, there was little realization of the importance of financial sustainability for microfinance.

The establishment of MFU as a profit centre in November 1999 meant that it had to cover all its costs from the income of its lending operation. MFU's loan portfolio is its only source of earnings and is replenished by either borrowing from GoNWFP against credit lines, and/or borrowing from BoK's head office at commercial rates. The funds borrowed are thus deployed in microfinance operation for generating revenues. The establishment of MFU made it possible for the first time to segregate its expenses and produce a separate profit and loss account.

As shown in Table 3.6 opposite, it is encouraging to note that BoK has been able to cover more than 90 per cent of its cost including the cost of operation, cost of funds and loans loss provision. However, it will take 12–18 months before MFU can generate enough revenues to operate without subsidy. The profit and loss position of the micro-

Table 3.6 *Operational and financial indicators of BoK's microfinance operation*

Indicators	Jan–Dec 2000	Jan–Dec 2001	Jan–Dec 2002	Jan–Dec 2003
Financial sustainability				
Return on outstanding portfolio	12.1%	16.4%	13.7%	12.8%
Financial cost ratio	10.3%	10.1%	9.1%	6.1%
Operating cost ratio	5.3%	6.1%	5.4%	8.4%
Loan loss provision ratio	0.0%	0.5%	0.0%	2.0%
Financial self sufficiency ratio	77%	98%	94%	77%
Operating efficiency				
Cost per unit of money lent (US$)	0.10	0.09	0.17	0.13
Cost per borrower (US$)	66	73	119	76
Average loan size per borrower (US$)	655	767	688	579
Number of loans made per credit officer	135	179	83	163
Number of active borrowers per credit officer	216	368	299	298

finance operations is calculated on a full-cost basis and all costs related to it at branch-level are included.

BoK is uniquely positioned to take advantage of its strength in microfinance. Despite some internal and external issues, MFU foresees microfinance playing an important role in the overall operations of the bank in the coming years. It also believes that this is the right time to scale up its operations for achieving financial viability through economies of scale. The three year business plan of microfinance commencing from 2004 foresees scaling up of credit operations through around 30 per cent annual growth, by reaching out to even smaller clients and attaining break-even position by 2005. Although the microfinance services of BoK may still remain a small component of its overall credit portfolio for some years to come, BoK will become the largest microfinance provider in the province, in terms of volume and geographical coverage. BoK's balance sheet and profit and loss accounts for the year 2003 are shown in Tables 3.7 and 3.8 (overleaf).

Phase IV: New Lending Methodology

Operating from 16 branches in NWFP, BoK reached 17 500 clients, including more than 14 per cent women, by the end of 2003. With

Table 3.7 *BoK's balance sheet as at 31 December 2003*

	Total (US$)	Microfinance services (US$)	General banking services (US$)
Assets			
Cash and due from banks	17 396 281	–	17 396 281
Reserve in central bank	14 865 596	–	14 865 596
Short term financial assets	146 683 158	–	146 683 158
Net loan portfolio	94 426 561	4 051 607	90 374 954
Interest receivable	17 202 509	–	17 202 509
Accounts receivable and other assets	11 781 105	–	11 781 105
Long term financial assets	42 677 018	–	42 677 018
Net fixed assets	2 280 737	–	2 280 737
Total assets	**347 312 965**	**4 051 607**	**343 261 358**
Liabilities			
Demand deposits	146 471 947	–	146 471 947
Time deposits	123 121 754	–	123 121 754
Borrowings	18 555 456	4 298 440	14 257 016
Interest payable	2 880 947	–	2 880 947
Accounts payable and other liabilities	21 959 281	–	21 959 281
Total liabilities	**312 989 386**	**4 298 440**	**308 690 946**
Equity			
Paid up capital	18 421 053	–	18 421 053
Retained earnings	109 930	(246 833)	356 763
Reserves	8 883 965	–	8 883 965
Other equity accounts	6 908 632	–	6 908 632
Total equity	**34 323 579**	**(246 833)**	**34 570 412**
Total liabilities and equity	**347 312 965**	**4 051 607**	**343 261 358**

aggregate lending of US$14.439m, it has an active client base of 8648 borrowers and outstanding loan portfolio of US$4.3m. Although BoK's capacity to reach out to more microfinance clients has improved, it must scale up its operation in order to attain financial viability. In its efforts

Table 3.8 Profit and loss for the year 2003

	Total (US$)	Microfinance services (US$)	General banking services (US$)
Account title			
Financial revenue	28 350 105	545 371	27 804 735
Financial expenses	11 785 526	262 656	11 522 871
Net financial income	16 564 579	282 715	16 281 864
Net loan loss provision expenses	3 963 789	87 439	3 876 351
Gross financial income	12 600 789	195 276	12 405 513
Operating expenses	5 634 526	358 277	5 276 250
Net income (before taxes and donations)	6 966 263	(163 000)	7 129 264
Taxes	1 622 789	–	1 622 789
Net income (after taxes and before donations)	5 343 474	(163 000)	5 506 474

to achieve financial self-reliance, BoK has made strategic decision regarding its lending methodology and the system of repayments. The strategic move has been based on the lessons learned from previous phases. For instance, commercial banks cannot go to the grassroots because of their corporate structure, human resource policies and regulatory framework. BoK, therefore, has to collaborate with focused, unregulated partners who can reach out to the poor cost-effectively.

Until recently, BoK used to lend to individuals and groups that were formed by facilitators. By lending to individuals it faced the problem of reduced outreach. The problems in lending to groups formed by facilitators have been mentioned earlier. BoK has therefore made a paradigm shift, and has changed its outreach methodology by forming its own specific credit groups that are **not** to be jointly responsible for loan repayments. The reason for forming groups is to cost-effectively increase outreach and collect instalments from groups rather than from individuals. Groups formed by BoK will have a specific focus on microfinance and will not only be cost-effective but also in line with the international best practices. Similarly, a new tier of regional monitors will be introduced to act as a link between the field and the head office with a view to ensure strict supervision of the loan portfolio. The new phase began in late 2003 on a pilot basis in three branches. The groups attend meetings regularly during the formation stage and the respective field officers are required to be present in these meetings.

Table 3.9 Features of the revised lending methodology

Target group	Micro-entrepreneurs and low income households
Target area	Enterprises and houses in close proximity, trade clusters at manageable distances from branches
Outreach mechanism	Formation of credit groups by BoK, starting from nearest clusters with sequential expansion
Credit group features	5-8 members per group with homogeneous income level, focused on credit and without cross-guarantees Group leader selected/elected by members, has to keep liaison with BoK, has to assist in reporting on members' credit worthiness and facilitate meetings with members
Credit assessment	Informal credit assessment with minimal documentation All credit group members apply through one proforma
Approval schedule	Decentralized sanctioning, standardized repayment
Recovery	Monthly recovery through credit group leader, recovery date and time to be specified, recovery pass books updated, zero tolerance of arrears
Loan size	Fresh loans of US$211 in rural and US$351 in urban centres, increment of US$140 in rural and US$175 in urban loans, maximum loan limit is US$877
Loan term	12 months up to US$351 loan, 18 months up to US$877 loan, 24 months up to US$1754

Loan size and tenure have been further reduced under the new approach that will result in improved quality of the loan portfolio. Besides simplifications in the credit assessment and documentation process, sanctioning power for fresh loans up to US$526 and repeat loans up to US$877 has once again been decentralized. This should scale up the lending operation. Table 3.9 (above) shows the principal features of the revised methodology.

The new loan product under the revised methodology ranges from US$211 to US$1754. Loans up to US$877 are provided against two personal guarantees, however, additional securities may be required for loans exceeding this limit. Loan tenure for first loan shall be 12 months and this shall not extend beyond 24 months in subsequent loans. All loans are repayable in equal monthly installments whereas repayment in lump sum is considered in specific business situations and sectors.

Major challenges

The biggest challenge facing BoK's microfinance operations is the need to demonstrate that it can be sustainable without cross-subsidy from other operations of the bank. Although it almost reached break-even position in the year 2000, this progress could not be maintained as changes at BoK's top management brought new uncertainties that had negative impact on the microfinance operation. This attitude towards microfinance stems primarily from lack of awareness about microfinance as a separate activity that has little in common with conventional credit techniques. Therefore microfinance is looked at with suspicion within BoK. Although the creation of Khushali Bank and FMFBL showed that microfinance needs to be institutionalized, the level of acceptance has yet to create a genuinely enabling environment.

The initial response of commercial banking staff to microfinance was generally negative, as they considered it to be a social service rather than a financially viable credit programme. Therefore both at the head office and branch levels there was little ownership for this new initiative. Even the executives at the head office saw it as an experiment by those who want to carve out something for themselves, and as something that had little relevance to commercial banking. This impression even was shared by junior employees. The support of the branch staff, particularly the manager, was vital as in the initial stages a loan proposal could not be processed and forwarded for approval to the head office without his approval. Branch managers saw no reward in doing this additional work as their performance is evaluated on deposit mobilization and profitability. In order to address this it was decided to provide some autonomy to the microfinance field staff. They could recommend loans on their own without the involvement of the branch manager and could undertake field activities independently. At head office, the microfinance department was authorized to modify its systems and procedures, train manpower and post them anywhere to suit the operational requirements of MFU.

Although several meetings were held with the commercial banking executives and officers to emphasize the importance and role of microfinance, this had little effect on their mindset. However, as the portfolio grew, the branch managers saw the microfinance portfolio as a source of income for the branch. Although their level of awareness and acceptability is still inadequate, the working relationship between the commercial banking and the microfinance staff has greatly improved. The confusion regarding the future of microfinance stems primarily from a lack of recognition that microfinance is a separate lending methodology.

In order to compete with non-regulated MFIs and achieve a quantum increase in the loan portfolio, loan documentation must be substantially simplified. BoK is a regulated institution, and there are certain minimum requirements to be fulfilled before a loan is disbursed. This includes obtaining a demand promissory note, a letter of guarantee, a letter of set-off, and hypothecation of stock. Since all these formalities have to be completed at the branch, it delays disbursement, increases borrowers' costs and reduces productivity.

The academic profile and status of commercial bankers does not necessarily suit the requirements of microfinance. Banks in general require higher educational qualification and pay their employees more than most other professions, whereas microfinance needs ordinary graduates or even less qualified personnel who are ready to work for low salaries and can relate socially to their clients. As the credit portfolio expands, there is a need to hire additional staff to handle the increased workload, and the recruitment policy of the bank does not allow any special dispensation for microfinance staff.

Finally, in the near future the provincial government is planning to convert BoK into an Islamic Bank. This would entail a major exercise of adapting Islamic banking systems and procedures to the bank, and the microfinance operation would also have to be made Shariah compliant.[13] This would pose a major challenge for the future of microfinance in BoK, since profit-sharing banking on Islamic principles is generally easier for mainstream banking than for microfinance.

Discussion Questions

1. The Bank of Khyber's microfinance programme started as a donor-assisted project, with finance from the Asian Development Bank. How did this affect the evolution of the Bank's microfinance operations, and how might the donor's interventions have been modified to facilitate the 'mainstreaming' of microfinance in the Bank?

2. Sometimes the Bank's microfinance operations were managed from the branch level, while at other times microfinance was run as a separate division, centrally managed. Which approach most successfully balanced the need to offer suitably designed products with the need to integrate microfinance into branch operations?

3. The Bank of Khyber's microfinance operation was frequently misunderstood, and even actively opposed, by management at the head office and the branch level. How might the operation's proponents have more successfully 'sold' the concept within the Bank?

Chapter Four
Wholesale microfinance: Sonali Bank, Bangladesh

M. ABDUL AWAL and ABUL KALAM AZAD

Bangladesh is a densely populated country of only 150 000 km^2 with a population of around 140 million. The country consists mainly of a flat delta plain. In addition to its very high population density, the country has few natural resources and is subject to regular natural disasters such as floods and cyclones. This has led to low economic growth and a high incidence of poverty; according to the World Bank indicators, around 36 per cent of the population live on the equivalent of less than US$1 a day.

The economy of Bangladesh is predominantly based on agriculture. About 74 per cent of the population live in rural areas. Unemployment and poverty are high, productivity and literacy are low, and the people suffer from overpopulation and malnutrition. Agriculture and the non-farm sector are pivotal to future development. Like other developing economies, the burden of poverty falls disproportionately on women. They are the most vulnerable members of society, and they have limited access to opportunities for gainful employment. The rising incidence of landlessness, and the decline in home-based economic activities has exposed women in particular to serious economic pressure. Nevertheless, agriculture and related activities still play a dominant role in the national economy. One quarter of GDP and about half the country's export earnings come from agriculture.

Bangladesh is still one of the poorest countries in the world, outside of Africa, but the country has made notable progress in reducing poverty since independence. Between 1991 and 2000, the incidence of poverty declined from 58.8 to 49.8 per cent, although there was more success in urban than in rural areas. However, the rural areas did make better progress in reducing the depth and severity of poverty.

Microfinance in Bangladesh

Bangladesh is often considered to be the birthplace of 'modern' microfinance. The Grameen Bank started operations here in 1976, and the group and centre-based system which was pioneered by Grameen is still very widely used, in Bangladesh and in some 50 other countries. Precise figures are not available, but it is likely that a higher proportion of the market, the people who need microfinancial services, is being reached in Bangladesh than in almost any other country. Microfinance in Bangladesh can be classified into three sectors: formal, semi-formal and informal. The formal sector includes banks and other regulated financial institutions. The semi-formal sector includes microfinance institutions (MFIs) and their programmes, which were mostly initiated and in many cases are still operated by non-governmental organizations (NGOs). There are also some government organizations which operate microfinance programmes, such as Swanirvar Bangladesh and the Bangladesh Rural Development Board (BRDB), an apex organization working with formal co-operatives. These are quasi-government organizations that are answerable to their line ministries in the government, and are not regulated by the Central Bank. The informal sector includes private transactions which fall outside the regulated banking framework, such as moneylenders, traders and dealers in agricultural markets, shopkeepers, landlords, friends and relatives.

The informal sector

Informal lenders continue to be active and the lender of the last resort for many. Households without access to formal sources, or those whose credit from public sector financial institutions and MFIs is rationed, turn to informal sources. The informal credit sector functions efficiently with low defaults and low transaction cost. Personalized transactions alleviate information problems in screening and monitoring borrowers; geographical proximity makes lenders more accessible; flexibility in terms and conditions allows loans to be customized for borrowers' needs and the threat of monetary and social sanction creates strong disincentives to default.

Informal loans are generally believed to be used mainly for non-commercial purposes, such as consumption, marriage and other social expenses, and medical costs or other emergencies. The sources of loans are widely diversified; most are from neighbours (37 per cent), relatives (16 per cent), friends (26 per cent), and the rest (21 per cent) from professional moneylenders. Interest rates range from zero in the case of relatives, friends and neighbours to 10 per cent a month or more for credit from moneylenders.

Government microfinance programmes

Many countries implemented heavily subsidized credit programmes in the past, usually through specialized development finance institutions but often, as in India, using the commercial banks as distribution channels. These programmes have usually failed, and 'new paradigm' MFIs have subsequently come into the market and have demonstrated the merits of their radically different approach. Bangladesh is unusual in that a number of government departments have introduced their own public-sector microfinance programmes, subsequent to the success of the MFIs.

These government programmes are usually focused on particular issues and institutions, and they have not been implemented through commercial banks. Table 4.1 (see opposite) shows the extent and the performance of some of the more important government microfinance programmes.

Table 4.1 Bangladesh government microfinance programmes, as at December 2002

Sl. No	Government department	Total no. of beneficiaries — Male	Total no. of beneficiaries — Female	Cumulative disbursement (US$m)	Total loan outstanding (US$m)	Recovery rate (%)
1	Bangladesh Rural Development Board (BRDB)	2 554 000	1 080 000	465	80	87.67
3	Department of Youth Development	317 000	231 643	85	8	89
4	*Palli Daridro Bimochon Foundation (PDBF)*	34 000	327 000	165	17	97

Source: CDF MF Statistics, Volume 15, 2002

There are also some smaller government programmes, lending to a few thousand or even a few hundred people. These government programmes are generally donor-funded projects, with a fixed duration, usually between five and ten years. They are staffed by government personnel who are attached to them for the life of the project, at attractive salaries. MFIs, on the other hand, are permanent institutions with a long-term commitment to their clients. Their interest rates are usually higher than those of the government projects, because they have to be sustainable.

MFIs

The Grameen Bank is Bangladesh's largest MFI, and it is the only MFI which is a registered bank. All the others are NGOs/MFIs. Some of the biggest and best known are BRAC, PROSHIKA, ASA, BURO Tangail and Shakti Foundation. The largest five organizations – Grameen Bank, BRAC, and three others – account for almost 93 per cent of the total amount disbursed.

There are, however, many hundreds of other MFIs. The Credit and Development Forum (CDF), a network of MFIs, estimates that in addition to its own members there are about 1000 NGOs that are not CDF-members but are offering microfinancial services. Whatever the number, the MFIs have achieved remarkable success in outreach and the quality of services provided to their clients, and in their contributions towards long-term poverty alleviation.

Most MFIs use the Grameen Bank model of group lending. The peer monitoring and joint liability structure of this credit-delivery mechanism

Table 4.2 Analysis of CDF membership at December 2002

Total active members	16 160 615
Active male members	2 017 000
Active female members	13 327 000
Total staff	104 000
Staff dedicated to credit	55 000
Number of active borrowers	12 762 000
Net savings	US$435 790 000
Cumulative disbursement	US$6 416 830 000
Outstanding loans	US$522 390 000
Total loan funds available	US$ 884 000 000
Sources of loan fund (RLF) (US$m)	
Members savings	398 (48%)
PKSF	146 (17.5%)
Loans from local banks	**60 (7%)**
International NGOs	4 (0.5%)
International official donors	99 (12%)
Surplus from service charges	118 (14%)
	Source: CDF MF Statistics, Volume 15, December 2002

overcomes the screening and enforcement problems of the traditional banking system. Strong leadership, functional autonomy, freedom from political pressure, rational and economic interest rates, diversified portfolios, regular savings, well trained staff, performance-based incentives and mandatory loan insurance are all key elements in the success of MFIs in Bangladesh.

The CDF microfinance statistics show that, according to the borrowers, 45 per cent of the total disbursements goes to petty trading. A further 18 per cent is used to purchase livestock, 13 per cent for farming, 5 per cent each for fisheries and food processing. The balance is spent on small industries, transport vehicles such as rickshaws and auto-taxis, housing, health, education and other uses.

Table 4.2 (above) summarizes the achievements and the funds sources of the 657 MFIs which are members of CDF, including the Grameen Bank, as at December 2002.

The figures for the sources of funds show that clients' and members' savings are the most important single source. Only the Grameen Bank, which was given a banking license in 1983 under a special ordinance, is legally permitted to mobilize savings. Grameen's savings obligations to its members amount to around a quarter of the above figure of some US$400m, and the legal position of the other MFIs as deposit takers is unclear.

PKSF is a special revolving fund which was set up by the Government as a channel through which its own and foreign donor funds could reach MFIs, and could then be recycled and on-lent again to other MFIs. Some donors would rather lend direct, and some MFIs prefer not to borrow from PKSF, as the figure of about US$100 million from international donors demonstrates. The accumulated surplus from interest, service charges and other income is also growing, as more MFIs attain sustainability and are able to plough back their profits into their own operations.

The figure of some US$60m which has been borrowed from local commercial banks is growing even more rapidly, as the NGO/MFIs come to realize that they must diversify their sources of funds, and the commercial banks see that they are missing out on a major and potentially profitable credit market.

Formal financial institutions in Bangladesh

There are both public and private financial institutions in Bangladesh. The public sector comprises the state-owned commercial banks, a number of specialized banks including two agricultural development banks, the Industrial Development Bank and other development finance institutions. The private sector comprises privately-owned commercial banks, foreign banks and some private development finance institutions. The microfinance activities of Bangladesh's second-largest NGO/MFI, BRAC, have been constituted into a private bank, known as BRAC Bank. Table 4.3 (overleaf) summarizes the numbers and deposit and advances profile of the formal institutions.

Given that some 74 per cent of the population of Bangladesh live in rural areas, these figures illustrate the very strong urban bias of the commercial banks and other formal financial institutions. While rural deposits are about a fifth of the total, loans in rural areas are only just over a tenth of the total.

The banks have recognized this problem, and a number of them have entered the microfinance market themselves. Some have started their own retail microfinance operations, such as the Islami Bank which has developed a substantial business with self-help groups, based on Islamic banking principles. Others, such as the privately-owned BASIC Bank, have decided to enter the market as wholesalers, using the existing MFIs as distribution channels, and in the process helping the MFIs to overcome their own shortage of funds.

PKSF is one of the major sources of finance for MFIs, but has rather rigid lending criteria. Its procedures are closely linked to the Grameen Bank method, which is the dominant methodology in Bangladesh. Commercial banks have been able to assist MFIs, which do not fit

Table 4.3 *Formal financial institutions in Bangladesh*

State-run commercial banks	4
Specialized banks	5
Private commercial bank (including BRAC Bank)	30
Foreign private banks	11
Other specialized financial institutions – privately and publicly owned	27
Total deposits in the formal sector as of December 2002	US$17.17 billion
Total loans and advances	US$14.18 billion
Loans and advances, public sector share	62%
Loans and advances, private sector share	38%
Ratio of rural to urban deposits	19:81
Ratio of rural to urban loans and advances	12:88

PKSF's criteria, and this has helped to broaden the range of micro-financial products on offer in Bangladesh.

Table 4.4 (opposite) summarizes the microfinance operations of those commercial banks which have become involved. The table includes both wholesale and direct microfinance, and the majority of the operations are through government-sponsored schemes.

Sonali Bank

Table 4.4 (opposite) shows that Sonali Bank has the largest stake in microfinance of any of the commercial banks. This is to be expected, since Sonali is the largest bank in Bangladesh. The Bank is 100 per cent owned by the State. It was formed in 1972 through a merger of the branches of the then National Bank of Pakistan, the Bank of Bahawalpur and Premier Bank, which had been functioning in what was at that time the Pakistani province of East Pakistan. In 1971 the Province became the independent state of Bangladesh.

The microfinance savings (see Table 4.5, page 62) are deposits by Sonali Bank's partner MFIs in various Sonali branches. One condition of Sonali Bank's finance to MFIs is that they should deposit their own and their members' savings only in Sonali Bank.

Sonali Bank has seven directors, all nominated by the government. The non-executive chairman is appointed from among the directors by the government and heads the board. The directors are responsible for setting the overall policy of the Bank. The Bank has 376 rural branches, and 808 urban branches, including one in the UK and one in the USA.

Table 4.4 Microcredit operations of commercial banks, excluding Grameen Bank (as at December 2002)

Sl. No	Name of bank	Total no. of customers Male	Total no. of customers Female	Cumulative disbursement (US$m)*	Total loan outstanding (US$m)*	Recovery rate (%)
1	Agrani Bank	454 600	50 500	227.67	86.67	80
2	Bangladesh Krishi Bank (BKB)	632 000	658 000	147.51	51.59	83
3	BASIC Bank Limited	50 000	60 000	8.53	3.16	98
4	Islami Bank Bangladesh Limited	5 700	83 000	34.40		99
5	Janata Bank	315 000	220 000	283.55	95.93	80
6	Rajshahi Krishi Unnayan Bank	78 400	95 800	26.06	8.51	89
7	Rupali Bank Limited	3 000	300	0.45	0.29	87
8	Social Investment Bank Limited (SIBL)	1 300	4 700	3.12	0.95	92
9	**Sonali Bank**	1 359 700	3 125 900	659.52	354.15	72
10	The Trust Bank Limited	23 000	–	12.33	7.40	70
	Grand total	3 042 050	6 662 112	1403.14	608.65	86

* These figures include both retail and wholesale microfinance operations. Islami Bank is the only one which is engaged solely in retail microfinance; all the others have both.

It employs just under 25 000 people, and the Bank made a profit of about US$10m in the year ending 31 March 2003.

As a public sector bank, Sonali is responsible for providing all types of banking services to the people. The Bank also participates in various social and development programmes and helps to implement government's policies and commitments. As Bangladesh's largest public sector bank, Sonali has played a significant role in the economic development of the country. The main business of the Bank includes deposit mobilization, and providing funds for investment in productive and priority activities The Bank also performs a wide range of treasury functions all over the country and acts for the Central Bank in areas where it has no branches.

Sonali Bank has operated a number of 'old paradigm' micro-credit services since its establishment. These were mainly for crop production

Table 4.5 Sonali Bank, as at 31 December 2003

Total savings balance	US$3 806 000 000
Total number of borrowers	3 126 000
Loans and advances	US$2 629 000 000
Microfinance loans outstanding	US$354 000 000
% of microfinance savings to total savings	1.31 %
% of microfinance loans to total loans	13.19 %
Disbursement in NGO linkage	US$9 930 000

and self-employment, and were offered as a social obligation, rather than on a business basis. Initially, the main focus was on crop loans. As time went by, this was broadened to include both on-farm and off-farm activities, as a means to create jobs and reduce poverty. Self-employment came to be seen as more effective, both in order to generate jobs and to make profit for the Bank. In this way, micro-credit and microfinance became part of Sonali Bank's activities.

The Bank has implemented a number of credit programmes to reduce poverty through the creation of sustainable on-farm and off-farm employment for the poor, who are defined as those owning less than half an acre land, including their homestead, or whose annual earnings are under $340.

Banking with the poor is now considered not only as a social commitment, but also as good business, particularly in terms of high repayment and large savings. Many new private banks have started in Bangladesh, and the banking sector has become more competitive. There is little scope for increasing the amount and quality of existing customers' deposits or loans. By mobilizing the savings of the poor, who are the vast majority, banks can create large numbers of reliable and regular savers. In Bangladesh, as elsewhere, the poor are better borrowers than the rich. Among the poor; women are better borrowers than men. For that reason, like most MFIs, Sonali Bank's programmes are mainly designed for women.

Sonali Bank first moved into rural lending during the 1970s, under the umbrella of the formal co-operative societies in the Integrated Rural Development Programme, which is now called the Bangladesh Rural Development Board. This was the first time a commercial bank had entered the rural finance market in Bangladesh. One other specialized agricultural bank, the Bangladesh Krishi Bank, was operating in the field, along with some insignificant government projects. Very few rural people had any access to formal financial services when Sonali Bank entered into the field in 1973. There were no NGO/MFIs at that time, and the few NGOs that were operating were mainly providing charitable social welfare services.

Sonali Bank is now offering a number of rural and microfinance products whose objectives are to increase agricultural output, to promote agro-based small and microenterprises, to facilitate agricultural support services, and to create and sustain both urban and rural employment opportunities.

NGO linkage programme

The NGO linkage programme constitutes less than 10 per cent of Sonali bank's microfinance portfolio, but it is one of the best performing programmes of Sonali Bank, both in terms of its profitability and the quality of the assets. The Swiss Agency for Development and Co-operation (SDC) encouraged Sonali Bank to get into this business, using a two-pronged approach. SDC partially guaranteed Sonali Bank's first loan, to Shakti Foundation, an NGO working for the disadvantaged women in city slums. SDC also helped to build the capacity of Sonali Bank's staff and branches in microfinance Additionally, SDC helped the Bank to use credit ratings as part of its decision-making process in approving loans to NGOs. SDC provided the services of Micro-Credit Ratings International, or M-CRIL, an Indian MFI rating agency, for this purpose. Loans to Shakti Foundation carry an interest rate of 10 per cent, which provides a reasonable profit margin over Sonali Bank's cost of funds of 7.5 per cent.

The intention of Sonali Bank's linkage programme is to supplement and not to compete with PKSF. In 2003, encouraged by Sonali Bank's initial success in lending to Shakti Foundation, the International Fund for Agricultural Development (IFAD) offered Sonali Bank two separate packages of finance for on-lending to MFIs, amounting to around US$3.4m, at the very low interest rate of 1.5 per cent. These transactions have been of great value to the MFIs, but they are also profitable for Sonali Bank.

In 1997, Sonali Bank responded to a personal request from Professor Yunus, the legendary Managing Director of Grameen Bank, and approved a loan of US$850 000 to the Grameen Krishi Foundation, an affiliate of Grameen Bank, at an interest rate of 10 per cent per annum. The MFI community regarded this quite small loan as a very important gesture. It showed them that commercial banks had the potential to provide a sustained flow of funds to the microfinance sector in Bangladesh.

At that time Sonali Bank had two enthusiasts for microfinance on its board. They met the Association of Development Agencies in Bangladesh (ADAB), a networking organization for NGOs, and PROSHIKA, one of the two largest NGOs of Bangladesh, and negotiated a set of wholesale funding guidelines whereby Sonali Bank would bulk-lend to NGOs, free of collateral, for on-lending to their groups and members. The initial stimulus for this came from the two board members and one mid-level executive of Sonali Bank. He followed up the initiative, and made it happen.

Sonali Bank now has four types of microfinance products: direct loans, loans under the ADAB agreement, loans to members of CDF, the networking organization for MFIs, and loans made from the IFAD-fund.

The first three types of loans, including the initial advances to Grameen Krishi and to Shakti Foundation, carry commercial rates of interest. Only the loans from IFAD funds are at sub-commercial rates. Under the arrangement with CDF, Sonali Bank wholesales fund to its members as CDF recommends, and CDF also guarantees repayment. The first loan to Shakti Foundation was part-guaranteed by SDC, but subsequent loans have not been guaranteed. The interest rate remains unchanged at 10 per cent.

Table 4.6 (opposite) summarizes the position of the Sonali Bank linkage-based microfinance portfolio at 31 March 2004.

Only two of the 47 MFI/NGOs to which Sonali Bank has disbursed loans have failed to repay on time. PROSHIKA is the largest defaulter, and is also one of Bangladesh's largest and best known MFIs. PROSHIKA's problems have arisen as a result of an acrimonious personal dispute between its president and other people who are well-connected with government. As a result of this, PKSF has cut off PROSHIKA's credit line, which is one of the institution's main sources of funds, and the President of PKSF has been imprisoned. When these problems first occurred a few groups lost confidence in the organization and withdrew their savings and delayed loan repayments, but this has now been corrected. The condition of the institution is said to be fundamentally sound, and the loan should eventually be recovered in full.

The other repayments which are overdue, for some US$30 000, are owed by one small MFI which is primarily involved in the financing of dairy production. Due to some confusion over the terms of its loans to milk producers, the Sonali Bank advance was wrongly scheduled. The repayments will be made in due course, but not on the time schedule that was originally agreed.

MFIs in Bangladesh have many sources of funds, but many of them are coming to realize that they cannot rely on donor and government funds for ever. They want to achieve genuine sustainability, without subsidies, and they want to build long-term business relationships with mainstream funding sources which can provide them with as much funding as they need, for as long as they need it. They realize that they must start accessing funds from commercial banks. Donors are cutting down their support for micro-credit, and PKSF funding is unsuitable for many medium and small MFIs. They have to go through many hassles to get it, and since PKSF is ultimately controlled by the government many MFIs wish to reduce their dependence on them.

As the nation's largest commercial bank, Sonali Bank's main focus is on commercial banking, but 'new paradigm' microfinance has provided a good source of profitable business. The conventional, 'old paradigm' loan portfolio under the various rural credit schemes had on-time recovery rates ranging from 52 per cent to 86 per cent. Wholesale

Sl. No	Source of funds	MFI/NGO	Disbursed at 31.03.2004	Recoveries	On time repayment rate	Interest rate	Cost of fund
01	Own funds, with partial SDC guarantee	Shakti Foundation	US$1 220 339	US$76 272	100%	10%	7.5%
02	IFAD Fund-1	PADAKHAP	US$1 777 966	US$1 776 034	100%/a	4%	1.5%
	IFAD Fund-2, 70% IFAD, 30% own funds	13 NGO/MFIs, disbursements between US$500 and US$4 000, in total	US$277 288	US$286 746	100%	IFAD 3.3%, own funds 7.5%	7.25%
03	Own fund	1. PROSHIKA 2. Grameen Krishi Foundation 3. BRAC 4. 12 other MFIs	US$ 1 694 915 US$ 1 694 915 US$ 3 389 831 Disbursements between US$170 000 and US$3000	US$ 938 983 US$ 469 390 - Recoveries all 100% except one loan for $34 000, 28% recovery	77% 100% 100%	10% 10% 10% All at 10%	7.5%
	Total		**US$7 639 834**	**US$1 785 713**			
	CDF scheme, with CDDF guarantee in total	17 NGO/MFIs, disbursements between US$5 000 and US$16 000,	US$144 918	US$238 510			

Table 4.6 *Sonali Bank's linkage-based microfinance portfolio at 31 March 2004*

microfinance has been a much better proposition. The recovery rate for the portfolio was 98.96 per cent as at September 2003, and the Mohakhali and Mohammadpur Bazar branches, through which most of the loans were operated, earned gross profits of around US$300 000 and US$100 000 from these loans. Fourteen other Sonali branches are also operating loans to MFI. The MFIs themselves choose the branches which handle their loans, although the terms and other details are arranged at head office by the specialized micro-credits division. Wholesale lending of this type is also the best way of serving the poor. NGO-linkage credit earns profit for the branches and involves very little monitoring or supervision cost. For that reason, the branch managers and staff are quite interested in this type of loan.

Sonali Bank has thus been able to integrate microfinance into its on-going portfolio by creating a separate full-fledged Micro Credit Division to take care of all microfinance business. This division is located at the head office and provides management services to the branches. The branches pay for its services, on the same basis as they pay for services from other head office divisions.

Unlike other traditional products, such as business loans, small and medium enterprises loans and major industrial loans, which have had a particularly poor repayment record, microfinance products have been very successful in terms of their track record and their profitability. This has been possible because Sonali Bank has offered good service. The MFIs monitor and supervise the final users effectively , and they and Sonali Bank's staff have built good relationships. There have been no cases of malpractice, and the MFIs have used appropriate lending methodologies to develop group cohesion, through pre-loan group promotion and capacity-building training for their prospective clients.

The main constraint to the expansion of Sonali Bank's microfinance portfolio is the mindset, attitude and commitment of its staff. The Bank has surplus liquidity, and shortage of funds has never been a constraint. A specialized linkage cell has been formed in the Micro Credit Division to focus exclusively on wholesale finance to NGOs, and the Bank's general policy is in favour of this type of business. The main problem is that many of the management staff who have to implement the policy are neither skilled in nor committed to this type of work. There is no need for further cheap funds such as the IFAD loans, nor even for guarantees such as those obtained from SDC or CDF; what is needed is management knowledge and commitment, throughout the organization.

Almost all the staff of Sonali Bank are aware of its earlier microfinance activities, since more than 800 rural branches of the Bank have been operating 'old paradigm' micro-credits, almost all of which were initiated and directed by the government. The NGO-linkage credit programme, which was innovated and developed by Sonali Bank, is less familiar because it is relatively new and it has been centrally operated.

The Bank has therefore undertaken a programme of capacity building, with support from SDC. More than 100 Sonali Bank staff drawn from senior management, operating departments and the Bank's own

Staff Training College, were oriented to 'new paradigm' microfinance. The Staff College also organized a series of training programmes to make microfinance understandable to staff at all levels. Partner organizations such as PROSHIKA and BRAC have also come forward to support Sonali Bank in its efforts to build up the capacity of its staff in 'new paradigm' microfinance.

Microfinance has contributed substantially to Sonali Bank's profits. The Bank has been a pioneer in this area, and its general reputation and image have been enhanced because of this work. The Government of Bangladesh has also praised the Bank's microfinance programme. Many other commercial banks are following Sonali Bank into this field, and ultimately this will help the microfinance sector to enter the competitive commercial market and to reduce its dependence on donors subsidies and grants.

Discussion questions

1. In the future are Sonali Bank and the other commercial banks in Bangladesh likely to become the main source of finance for on-lending by NGO/MFIs, if donor funds cease to be available? Or, is it more likely that the main NGO/MFIs will themselves become full-fledged banks, and thus be able to raise their own deposits from the public?

2. The Swiss Government assisted Sonali Bank with a loan guarantee, with ratings and with staff development. Was this package of foreign assistance well chosen, or might the Sonali Bank's entry into 'new paradigm' microfinance have been facilitated any more effectively?

3. The Bank's wholesale microfinance loans are managed centrally and are mainly disbursed through branch banks in the capital city. Is this the best approach to mainstreaming microfinance within the Bank?

Chapter Five
Microfinance through self-help groups – case study of State Bank of India

VIJAY KULKARNI

Self-help groups

A self-help group (SHG) is a group of 15 to 20 people who come together voluntarily and who are from a similar economic and social background. They are usually neighbours. The groups are often formed and guided initially by non-government organizations (NGOs) to promote mutual help and collective action. Since NGOs work mainly with the poor, SHG members are mainly poor people, and 90 per cent of their members are women. Most groups start by saving small amounts of money regularly. Once they have accumulated some savings, the members start to take small loans from their fund instead of keeping it in a bank account. They charge themselves interest on these loans, usually well below the rate they are used to paying to moneylenders. They adopt some formal rules and regulations for their meetings, their savings and their loans and repayments. After six months or a year, if members need to borrow more money than their accumulated savings will allow, they take a loan from a bank, which enables them to borrow enough money to start or expand their individual micro-enterprises.

Banks thus have a vital role to play. SHGs open savings accounts with banks as soon as they start to save. They take loans about a year after they start savings. India has more than 200 000 financial service outlets – one of the world's largest networks of banking institutions. This makes it possible for an SHG to access a bank almost anywhere in India.

The banks have realized that SHGs are a good channel through which to provide loans to the poor and unreached. NABARD (the National

Box 5.1   *Stages of development for a self-help group*

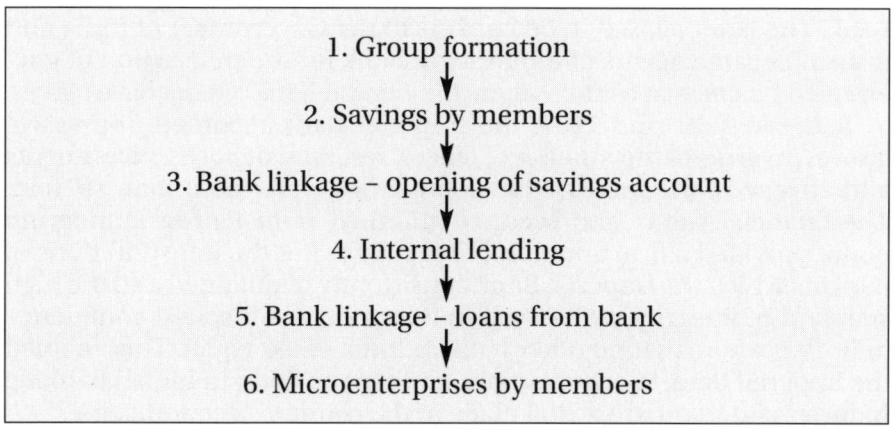

1. Group formation
2. Savings by members
3. Bank linkage – opening of savings account
4. Internal lending
5. Bank linkage – loans from bank
6. Microenterprises by members

Bank for Agriculture and Rural Development – an affiliate of the Central Bank, responsible for refinancing and promoting rural development) started the Bank Linkage programme in 1992 to motivate banks to do business with SHGs.

It took seven years to convince bankers of the potential of SHGs as a cost-effective savings and credit channel. Progress was very slow from 1992 to 1999, and only 32 995 SHGs were linked with banks during this period. Since then, however, SHG linkage has picked up significantly and, at March 2004, almost 1.1 million SHGs (with an estimated 15 million members) had taken loans from Indian banks. A still larger number have opened savings accounts but have not yet borrowed.

Since 2000/01, loans to SHGs under the linkage programme have been growing at the rate of 100 per cent annually. The SHG linkage banking movement is now considered to be the biggest microfinance programme in the world.

State Bank of India (SBI)[1]

State Bank of India (SBI) is India's largest bank. It has more than 9000 branches – the largest network of bank branches in the world.

SBI originated in the first decade of the nineteenth century with the establishment of the Bank of Calcutta in 1806. Three years later, the Bank received its charter and was re-designated as the Bank of Bengal. It was the first joint-stock bank of British India, sponsored by the Government of Bengal. The Bank of Bombay and the Bank of Madras followed in 1840 and 1843 respectively.

The three presidency banks of Bengal, Bombay and Madras, with their 70 branches, were merged in 1921 to form the Imperial Bank of India. The new bank took on the triple role of a commercial bank, a banker's bank and a banker to the government. This merger was preceded by years of deliberations on the need for a 'State Bank of India'. What eventually emerged was a 'half-way house' combining the functions of a commercial bank and a quasi-central bank.

In 1935, the establishment of the Reserve Bank of India as the central bank of the country ended the quasi-central banking role of the Imperial Bank. The latter ceased to be bankers to the Government of India and instead became agents of the Reserve Bank for the transaction of government business at centres where the Central Bank did not have offices.

Between 1921 and 1957, the Imperial Bank recorded impressive growth in terms of the number of offices, reserves, deposits, investments and advances, the increases in some cases were more than six-fold. The financial status and security inherited from its forerunners no doubt provided a firm and durable platform. But the lofty traditions of banking which the Imperial Bank consistently maintained and the high standard of integrity it observed in its operations inspired confidence in its depositors that no other bank in India could equal. This enabled the Imperial Bank to acquire a pre-eminent position in India's banking industry and to secure a vital place in the country's economic life.

Table 5.1 SBI's financial position at 31 March 2003

Number of domestic branches	9033
Number of foreign branches/offices	48
Deposits	US$65 805m
Advances	US$30 613m
Total income	US$8 184m
Total expenditure	US$7 494m
Net profit	US$690m

When India attained independence in 1947, the Imperial Bank had a capital base (including reserves) of US$2.6m, deposits and advances of US$61.1m and US$16.2m respectively and a network of 172 branches and more than 200 sub-offices extending all over the country.

In 1951, when the government launched the first Five-Year Plan, the development of rural India was given the highest priority. The commercial banks of the country, including the Imperial Bank of India, had until then confined their operations to the urban areas and were not equipped to respond to the emergent needs of economic regeneration in the rural areas.

In order, therefore, to serve the economy in general and the rural areas in particular, the All India Rural Credit Survey Committee recommended the creation of a state-partnered and state-sponsored bank by taking over the Imperial Bank of India, and integrating it with the former state-owned or state-associate banks. An Act was passed in Parliament in May 1955 and the State Bank of India was constituted on 1 July 1955. More than a quarter of the resources of the Indian banking system thus came under the direct control of the state. Later, the State Bank of India (Subsidiary Banks) Act was passed in 1959, enabling the State Bank of India to take over eight former state-associated banks as its subsidiaries (later named Associates).

The State Bank of India was born with a new sense of social purpose, aided by the 480 offices, comprising branches, sub-offices and three local head offices inherited from the Imperial Bank. Since then SBI has grown in leaps and bounds, and today it is the world's largest bank by employee and branch numbers. Although a latecomer to the use of technology, SBI is aggressively pursuing this option and already offers its customers 3700 fully computerized bank branches and 4250 ATMs. The financial position of SBI at 31 March 2003 is shown in Table 5.1.

SBI and microfinance

SBI being a 'state' bank has a social lending responsibility prescribed by the government. This social responsibility applies to all public sector

Table 5.2 SBI branch network in the northern and north-eastern states of India

State	Total no. of rural branches of commercial banks	No. of SBI branches	% of SBI branches
Bihar	1239	280	23
Orissa	845	312	37
Jharkhand	630	239	38
Chhattisgarh	303	126	42
Uttaranchal	353	202	57
Assam	427	114	27
Tripura	49	17	35
Manipur	20	11	55
Arunachal Pradesh	60	35	58
Sikkim	36	23	64
Meghalaya	84	67	80
Nagaland	33	30	91
Mizoram	16	16	100

banks in India. The Reserve Bank of India (RBI) has prescribed that 40 per cent of total lending should go to the 'priority sector', which comprises agriculture, small-scale industries, small road transport, small business, professionals and the self employed and other similar groups. At the end of March 2003, 38 per cent of SBI's loans (US$7803m) were to the priority sector. It had lent US$3527m to agriculture and US$2754m to small-scale industries.

Poverty is everywhere in India, but the north and north-east of the country are much poorer than the south and west. SBI is in a particularly strong position to reach the poorest people because it has a strong presence in these poorer areas.

Table 5.2 (above) shows that SBI is particularly well represented in Bihar, Orissa and the three new northern states of Uttaranchal, Chhattisgarh and Jharkhand, as well as in the seven north-eastern states.

Financing SHGs

SHG linkage started in 1992 at SBI on a pilot basis in a few selected branches. The results were encouraging. SBI sent a few officers to Bangladesh, Thailand, Philippines and Indonesia to study microfinance. The Bank then decided to encourage all its 6500 rural and semi-urban branches to take part in for SHG linkage. It was slow to start, but since 1997 SHG linkage has picked up in SBI. The Bank has savings bank

Table 5.3 SHG financing by SBI at March 2004

Number of SHGs with savings accounts with SBI	343 769
Cumulative number of SHGs credit linked	174 666
Deposits from SHGs	US$73m
Cumulative amount of loan provided	US$137m
SHG loans provided during 2003–04	US$59m

accounts for nearly 350 000 SHGs and has lent to 50 per cent of these groups. From a low base of 12 200 groups in March 2000, the SBI programme has expanded by 1300 per cent in four years.

While 343 769 SHGs have savings accounts with SBI, only 50 per cent of them have taken loans. While some SHGs may still be ineligible for loans, because an SHG has to complete one year of existence before taking a loan, others may not need to borrow, and some SBI branch managers may still be reluctant to make unsecured loans to groups of poor women.

Share of SBI in SHG linkage

SBI is the largest lender to SHGs of the Indian banks. As at March 2004, SBI had lent to 24 per cent of all the SHGs which had taken loans from all the 27 public sector and 21 private sector commercial banks. Market share by loan amount and number of groups is 24 per cent. Even if the 93 000 financial service co-operatives and the 15 000 regional rural bank branches are included, SBI still has 12 per cent of the total market which is well over its proportion of the total formal financial service outlets. In spite of starting slowly and rather late, SBI has shown that it can gain a major share of this new market.

Microfinance strategy at SBI

SBI is a very large bank with highly diversified portfolio. It possesses a presence all over the country and in all sectors of the economy. In such a bank any policy has to be widely accepted; no one person can induce a major policy change. This is as true for microfinance as for any other part of the business.

Although the chairman of SBI is highly committed to financing SHGs, no single individual can be quoted as the 'champion' of SHGs in the Bank. Unlike many other banks, SBI has achieved leadership in microfinance through slow and steady dissemination of successful experiences to all the branches. This is probably the only effective strategy for such a large bank. It is difficult to convince 6500 managers at one stroke. SBI has therefore focused on branches where there is scope for large-scale SHG linkage.

In fact, about 10 per cent of SBI's branches have linked the great majority of the SHGs; most branches, even in rural areas, have linked none or very few. The Bank's own staff are not generally involved in SHG formation, and only about 10 per cent of the SHGs linked by the bank have been formed by the branch staff. Identifying good NGOs and lending either through them on a wholesale basis or to their SHGs directly is the strategy followed by SBI. According to the Chief General Manager of the Development Banking Division of SBI:

> 'SHG linkage serves both financial and social commitments. The high repayment rate of SHG loans compensates for the low interest rate charged on these loans. Non-performing assets are zero when it comes to SHG loans. It makes good business sense to lend to SHGs. And since SHG loans go to the poor, they also serve the social commitment of our Bank.'

The Bank has tried to motivate its branch managers by explaining how the Bank gains from lending to SHGs using the following arguments.

1. Lending to SHGs is profitable to the bank, as the loans are repaid promptly.
2. All loans to SHGs are treated as priority sector lending.
3. The transaction costs of the banks are greatly reduced, since they have to maintain only a single account for the SHG instead of 15 to 20 individual loan accounts. Besides, the Bank's tasks of identifying borrowers, assessing individual credit needs, appraisal, sanctioning and supervision of loans are considerably reduced, as they are done by the groups. The groups also monitor their members' repayments.
4. The recovery rate is as high as 95–98 per cent on SHG loans. This leads to lower non-performing assets and speedy recycling of funds.
5. Through SHGs, small savings can be tapped at low cost.
6. Group supervision ensures that there is no misuse or diversion of funds by members.
7. Branches have problems in dealing efficiently and economically with large numbers of small borrowers. This is where SHGs can play an important role.

Another important strategy followed by SBI is to disseminate the SHG concept through training. SBI has 53 training colleges spread all over India. Every training centre conducts three days training programmes in 'SHG lending', which include lectures on the SHG concept and a field visit to SHGs. The field visits are an inspiring experience for the participants. Groups of 25 to 30 staff spread across all levels are invited for each training course. A minimum of four such programmes are held every year in every centre. This training has motivated a large number of branches to lend to SHGs.

SBI has no separate SHG cell either in the corporate office or at regional offices. Microfinance is part of the Development Banking

Division. This division looks after all priority sector loans including SHG loans. Thus, the Bank does not accord any special status to the SHG loans.

Indirect wholesale lending to SHGs

SBI also lends in bulk to SHGs through large NGOs or microfinance institutions (MFI) which are themselves engaged in financial intermediation. This qualifies as priority sector lending and, when the NGO is a substantial organization and already has strong financial systems, it makes sense to work through them rather than to try to compete.

One recent loan of this kind by SBI attracted some attention both because of its size and because the NGO in question invited bids from a large number of commercial banks, including SBI. *Shree Kshetra Dharmshthala* Rural Development Project (SKDRDP) is a large organization based in a small town near Mangalore, on the western coast of the State of Karnataka. SKDRDP is a highly reputed NGO which has promoted more than 9000 SHGs. It is a religious trust headed by Dr D. Veerendra Heggade, well known in India for his development activities.

SKDRDP informed 21 different banks that it intended to borrow more than US$3m to finance 3500 SHGs which it had promoted. SKDRDP wanted the best offer the banks could make. Many of the banks did not take up the challenge as they felt the amount was too big and the loan was too risky. But about 12 banks took the offer seriously and started working on their proposals. Some of them were very close to SKDRDP as they were already working with the NGO on other projects. They thought that they need not hurry and that SKDRDP would give them the business because of their existing relationships.

SBI's Belthangady branch took the issue very seriously. The manager immediately set up a three member group to work on the proposal. He rushed to the local head office in the State Capital of Bangalore, and then flew to Mumbai (Bombay) to get permission to quote an especially competitive interest rate. He successfully convinced corporate management, flew back to the south, prepared an offer letter of US$3.15m at 8.15 per cent annual interest, without any security, and took it by taxi to the remote village where SKDRDP is based. Dr Heggade compared the SBI offer with another dozen offers, and came to the conclusion that it was the best. He accepted it, the loan was disbursed and the loan portfolio of Belthangady branch was doubled overnight. The branch had made history, since this loan is one of the largest microfinance loans that had ever been made to an NGO in India.

This is only one of the many bulk loans that SBI has made to large NGOs and MFIs. By March 2004, these bulk loans amounted to around US$19m, and the borrowing institutions have lent this to about 22 500 SHGs. This is less than a quarter of SBI's direct microfinance business, but is an important and fast-growing part of the bank's portfolio. By acting both as a wholesaler and a retailer, SBI aims to reach the microfinance market offered by SHGs through different channels.

Conclusion

When SBI embraces microfinance more wholeheartedly, it will have a unique opportunity to contribute to poverty elimination in India. SBI has emerged as the leader in microfinance among Indian banks by steadily building appreciation for SHGs among its managers. Its 6500 branches have lent to 150 000 SHGs, but this is an average of only 24 SHGs per branch, and three-quarters of SBI's branches have not lent to SHGs at all. SBI plans to provide loans to 200 000 groups during 2004 and to one million SHGs by 2008.

Acknowledgement

In memory of Mr M.P. Deshpande, my dear friend who planned to write this case study, but passed away in a road accident.

Discussion questions

1. The Government of India requires all banks to lend to needy areas, and the State Bank of India, which is owned by the Government, must conform to the 40 per cent 'priority sector' requirement. Would it have been a good strategic move for the Bank to enter the microfinance market even if had not been compelled by government to look for such opportunities?

2. SBI's microfinance operations are very unevenly spread over its 9033 branches. What more can the Bank do to remedy this, and to use its branch network more effectively even in the poorest and most disadvantaged areas?

3. SBI is reaching the microfinance market directly, through loans to self-help groups and indirectly through bulk loans to microfinance institutions such as SKDRDP of Mangalore. Should the Bank continue to use both methods, or should it choose to focus its efforts mainly on one or the other approach?

Chapter Six
Canara Bank, Alanganallur branch, Madurai district, Tamil Nadu, India

R. SRINIVASAN

Canara Bank[1]

'Canara Bank Hindu Permanent Fund' was established by Sri Ammembal Subba Rao Paia, a philanthropist, in 1906. It evolved into a limited liability company in 1910, and this became Canara Bank after nationalization in 1969. The Government of India still owns 73 per cent of its capital. Canara is one of the biggest public sector commercial banks in the country, with its head office in Bangalore, Karnataka.

Canara Bank's foray into self-help group (SHG) financing

Stage I
The financing of SHGs was initially taken up by Canara Bank in 1993, purely as a social banking initiative and in order to respond to the directives and guidelines of Reserve Bank of India (RBI) and National Bank for Agriculture and Rural Development (NABARD). Canara Bank's branches initially started opening savings accounts for SHGs as directed by their head office. The SHGs were formed by the NGOs in their branches' areas. The branches were initially very hesitant to extend credit to SHGs, in spite of the continuing efforts of the NGOs and constant follow up from RBI and NABARD.

Stage II
RBI requires all the banks in India to lend 40 per cent of their total loans to the so-called 'priority sectors' such as agriculture, small-scale industries, and so on. Since such advances are comparatively risky, and the transaction costs of lending, follow up and recovery are very high, many banks are reluctant to involve their funds in these areas and are unable to fulfill their share of priority sector lending. In order to encourage the banks to lend to SHGs, the RBI stipulated that lending to SHGs would be counted as priority sector lending.

Because the repayment performance of the SHGs was good, Canara Bank increased their lending to SHGs to augment their lending to priority sectors. Since there are more good NGOs and good-quality SHGs in southern India, only the rural branches in South India lend to SHGs in a major way. At 31 March 2004, the total value of SHG loans outstanding to Canara Bank made up only 0.2% of their priority sector advances, and less than 0.1 per cent of all their loans. The inclusion of

Table 6.1 *Canara Bank performance highlights at 31 March 2003*

Number of branches	2 424
Deposits (in US$ @ Rs.45 per US$)	US$16 021m
Total advances (in US$)	US$8 994m
Of which to priority sector (agriculture, animal husbandry, small-scale industries, road transport operators, small business, etc)	US$3 245m
Total number of staff	47 566
Net Profit (in US$)	US$226m
Net non-performing asset ratio	3.59
Credit to deposit ratio	56%
Priority credit ratio of net credit	36%
Share capital	US$91m
Capital adequacy ratio	12.50%
Return on assets	1.24%
Number of branches in Tamil Nadu	457
Number of branches in Madurai district	34
Cumulative number of SHGs borrowing from Canara Bank throughout India at 31 March 2004	14 016
Cumulative bank loan disbursed to SHGs throughout India at 31 March 2004 (US$)	US$21m

SHG lending as part of priority sector advances did however play some part in encouraging the bank to expand their exposure to SHGs.

As the number of branches lending to SHGs increased rapidly, and the on-time repayment of SHG loans was almost 100 per cent, the bank realized that SHG business could be highly profitable.

SHG linkage by Canara Bank in Madurai district, Tamil Nadu

Madurai district is in Tamil Nadu, the southernmost state of India. Tamil Nadu is richer than much of the rest of India, but more than 20 per cent of the state's population live on less than US$1 a day. Madurai district has a population of about 2.5 million people, of whom less than half live in rural areas. Madurai district is also well-known for its very high rate of female infanticide; the social position of women is in many ways even worse than it is elsewhere in India.

Canara Bank's 25 rural and three urban branches have linked 2041 groups so far in the Madurai circle. The branches have lent more than

US$2.5m to SHGs, and just over US$1m is outstanding. Alanganallur branch is the leader, with 390 groups, followed by Kadamalai branch with 260 groups. Bodi, Vadamadurai, Athoor branches have each linked more than 200 groups, while Viruveedu and Pallapatti have each linked more than 100 groups.

Alanganallur branch profile

The Alanganallur branch of Canara Bank opened in June 1976. Alanganallur is 15 km north of Madurai, the temple city of South India. Agriculture is the mainstay of the area: paddy, sugarcane and banana are major crops, and many people are also engaged in milk production.

As Table 6.2 (overleaf) shows, SHG business constituted 48 per cent of Alanganallur branch's total loan portfolio and 10.5 per cent of their low-cost short-term deposits at the end of March 2003. The branch was also profitable during the year. SHGs usually contribute only a very small proportion of a branch's business, and most branch managers, as well as their head office colleagues, regard SHG business as a small and interesting sideline whose affect on their profits is irrelevant. There is also debate as to whether SHG business can be profitable because of the high transaction costs which are involved. The experience of Alanganallur branch, however, suggests that SHG lending is indeed profitable, since the branch has one of the highest proportions of SHG business of any commercial bank branch in India, and it still makes a profit.

Role of the SHG-promoting institutions

The rural poor are often unable to form cohesive groups on their own due to factors such as illiteracy, poverty, and inter-communal conflicts. A change agent is often necessary to sow the seeds of association and co-operation among the poor. Many NGOs have an excellent rapport with the rural poor and are familiar with their problems. Such NGOs can be very successful in forming SHGs and introducing them to banks. The following are major contributions of NGOs in the formation of SHGs:

- they motivate and organize the rural people into SHGs;
- they inculcate the idea of thrift and promote savings mobilization;
- they educate and train the group members in maintenance of accounts, conducting meetings, and managing their money;
- they facilitate interactions with banks;
- when poor women see the power of their joint efforts, through SHGs, they willingly embrace these concepts.

The role of the Dhan Foundation[2] in the promotion of SHGs

Dhan Foundation is a large and well-known NGO that was established in Madurai in 1990. The Foundation is generously supported by many

Table 6.2 Highlights of Alanganallur branch's performance

Particulars	31 March 2003 US$000s	31 March 2002 US$000s
Total short-term deposits	616 000	546 000
Total term deposits	700 000	622 000
Total deposits	1 316 000	1 168 000
Total advances	**1 373 000**	**1 202 000**
Total number of deposit accounts	7 000	6 000
Total number of loan accounts	3 000	2 600
Total income of the branch	134 000	106 000
Total expenses	113 000	85 000
Total profit of the branch	21 000	21 000
SHG details		
Number of SHG savings accounts	410	400
Number of SHG loans outstanding	378	296
Deposits in SHG savings accounts (a)	8 000	6 000
Total deposits of SHG federation (b)	56 000	46 000
Total deposits of SHGs & federation (a + b)	64 000	52 000
SHGs promoted by Dhan Foundation	349	282
SHGs promoted by other NGOs	29	14
Term loans to SHGs	472 000	377 000
Revolving credit to SHGs	186 000	95 000
Total loan outstanding to SHGs	**658 000**	**472 000**
SHGs loans outstanding as % of total loans outstanding of the branch	48%	39%
Deposits of SHGs & federation as % of total short-term deposits of the branch	**10.39%**	**9.52%**
SHG savings account as % of total deposit accounts of the branch	5.86%	6.67%

international donors, and it has built a strong reputation for its effective and innovative programme of promoting SHGs, and for assisting them to build a three-tier structure for the efficient administrative and financial management of their SHGs, by their own members.

The SHGs formed by the Dhan Foundation are given the brand name *Kalanjian*, which means 'granary' or 'storage place' in Tamil, the local language. This community banking programme focuses on women and Dhan Foundation believes that localized financial institutions owned and controlled by women are an effective strategy to impact on poverty and gender issues. The Dhan Foundation has so far promoted more than 10 000 SHGs, reaching out to nearly 0.16 million families in over 3400 villages in 20 under-developed and drought-prone districts in South India. Around 8000 SHGs have been linked to banks and have borrowed more than US$7m.

Nested institutions promoted by Dhan Foundation

Under the local administrative set up in Tamil Nadu, groups of villages form *panchayats* and a number of *panchayats* form a 'block'. In the Dhan Foundation's community banking programme, the primary unit of the community financial institution is the SHG Group, consisting of 15 to 20 poor women. The Foundation then promotes second tier organizations of 10–15 SHGs at *panchayat* level, called 'cluster-level associations' (CLAs). At the third tier 10–15 CLAs, covering around 200 SHGs, are federated at the block level and are known as 'block-level federations' (BLF).

It is critical to create people's institutions at different levels in order to address the issues of powerlessness and isolation, which are two important causes of poverty. These institutions are managed by the local community through building local leadership. The primary purpose is to prepare the community to address the issues of their own development collectively. For collective action, groups must work together and form a hierarchy of nested institutions.

SHGs are the primary members of both the CLAs and BLFs. Thus the control of both lies with the SHGs. The various levels are independent institutions with distinct identities but are interrelated and interdependent and work together for the sustainability of the whole community banking programme. All three tiers play complementary roles in ensuring access to financial services, and thus jointly address the development needs of the members of the SHGs These institutions build a strong demand system at the local level to address the issues of poverty and influence the local banks and government departments collectively.

The process of promoting nested institutions is organic and takes some time. The people involved in the promotion of these organizations need to have strong belief and confidence in people and their ability to mange. Each organization goes through different phases of growth before becoming independent.

The clusters and federations help the SHGs address other social and development needs of the members by enhancing the sustainability of these institutions. They help create linkages with banks and apex level financial institutions to meet members' credit needs, and to help them to implement civic programmes such as health and education for their members. They also provide insurance services, computer training for the children of SHG members and other services

Role of CLAs

The CLAs promote and strengthen the primary groups in neighbouring villages and assist them to attain long term sustainability. The CLAs also get loans from the BLFs to help the groups and thus their members to borrow money for their consumption needs. They raise initial membership fees from each member of the SHGs affiliated to them. This money can be used by the CLAs to meet the credit requirements of the SHGs when they cannot borrow what they need from the banks.

Role of BLFs

The function of a BLF is to build the groups' solidarity and to provide them with larger loans if their needs are not fully satisfied by the local bank branches. The BLFs mobilize bulk credit from apex level financial institutions such as the NABARD, the Small Industries Development Bank of India (SIDBI) and the Housing Development Corporation of India (HUDCO) and from major commercial banks such as Canara Bank. The loans taken by the BLFs from these apex level financial institutions are routed through the CLAs to the SHGs and from the SHGs to the individual members.

Rationale for financial intermediation by BLFs

The banks decide the loan eligibility of the SHGs based on the savings of the group. The banks generally insist that the bank loans should be utilized by the SHGs to start some income-generating economic activities and not for consumption expenditure, such as repaying loans from moneylenders or medical expenses, education, repairs to their dwelling units, getting electricity or cooking gas connections, and so on. SHGs that are only one or two years old may not be able to get loans from banks for more than one or two times of their cumulative savings. As these loan amounts may not be enough to meet their credit requirements, especially for consumption expenses, the SHGs need to access loans from the BLFs through the clusters.

The CLA committee members and the group accountants monitor the use of credit by the group members. They also ensure that the loans obtained by a member from internal loans out of the savings of the group, the bank loan obtained by the SHG and any loan mobilized by the SHGs from federation through the clusters do not exceed the repayment capacity of the members.

Cost of formation, training and management of SHGs, CLAs and BLFs

The Dhan Foundation estimates that the total cost of forming a SHG and building the capacity of its members and leaders, then forming CLAs and BLFs and training their leaders and staff members, works out

Table 6.3 Kurinji Vattara Kalanjaim *financial performance*

Income (US$)	31 March 2003	31 March 2002
Service cost on loans	7 500	151 000
Housing loans	20 500	14 700
Service	13 800	6 500
Fees	700	1 200
Bank interest and other income	2 100	600
Total	44 600	38 000
Expenditure (US$)		
Salary	8 600	5 000
Training/meeting expenses	2 700	2 300
Travelling expenses	1 800	1 400
Interest on loans	24 300	23 700
Interest on housing deposit	2 100	–
Administrative expenses	4 500	3 500
Excess of income over expenditure	600	2 100
Total	44 600	38 000
Balance Sheet (US$)		
Assets	31 March 2003	31 March 2002
Fixed assets	25 400	26 000
Current assets	54 400	28 900
Loans and advances	234 600	253 400
Total	314 400	308 300
Liabilities	31 March 2003	31 March 2002
Corpus & general fund	12 000	13 500
Members fund	43 800	36 600
Specified fund	60 000	18 600
Loan from HDFC	92 400	77 700
Loan from HUDCO	88 400	99 000
Loan from NABARD	17 800	26 700
Loan from PGB	–	36 200
Total	314 400	308 300

to between US$150 and US$200 per SHG. Thus for a federation of around 300 SHGs, the total cost for the initial two to three years, until the formation and stabilization of the SHGs, CLAs and the federation are complete, works out to approximately US$50 000.

Institutions such as the Ford Foundation (USA), the Sir Ratan Tata Trust of Mumbai and NOVIB of Netherlands have provided continued financial assistance to the Dhan Foundation for all their initiatives in their community banking programme. However, once a federation reaches take-off stage all the costs involved in maintaining the federation, the clusters and the SHGs are shared by the SHG members.

The BLFs used at one time to add a 3 per cent margin on loans given at the federation level and a further 3 per cent margin at the cluster level, in order to meet the cost of running the BLFs and CLAs, but they have recently introduced a new system. At the beginning of each year, the BLF's management calculates the total administrative cost involved in the management of the BLF, the CLAs and the SHGs – including salaries for a managing director, a community accountant and a computer operator for the BLF and a cluster associate and accountant for each CLA. At the BLF's AGM, the leaders of the SHGs agree to share these costs in proportion to the total loan outstanding at each member's level. During 2002–03, the total expenditure of one federation and its clusters worked out to US$28 890. This was shared by all the members at the rate of US$3 for each US$1000 outstanding. For the year 2003–04 the members' contribution was US$3.50/US$1000 outstanding. The increase was to cover the additional expenses involved in computerization of their operations and enhanced capacity-building training for the members, leaders and employees. The SHG members are extremely willing to contribute this quite small sum to pay for the services they get from their BLF and CLAs, and they even contribute another Rs.10 (US$0.20) per head per year towards the cost of forming new SHGs in other areas within their BLF.

Through this process, Canara Bank is spared the cost of formation, nurturing and monitoring the self-help groups. Due to the effective role played by the NGO in promoting SHGs, and in extending capacity-building training, ensuring credit linkage to the groups and periodical monitoring for proper repayment of the loans, the Canara Bank does not have to spend any time or money in managing the SHGs.

The 348 SHGs formed by Dhan Foundation in the Alanganallur area have been federated at the *panchayat* level into 16 CLAs and these have been federated in turn into a BLF called *Kurinji Vattara Kalanjaim*. The BLF has been registered under the Indian Trust Act. Table 6.3 (previous page) shows its financial performance.

Credit products offered by Alanganallur branch to SHGs

Term loans

The bank extends term loans to SHGs for four or five years depending on the purpose and the amount. The loan to each group is calculated as a multiple of the total savings of the group, irrespective of whether the savings are kept in the bank or are lent out to members. For example, if the total savings of an SHG are US$100, then, depending on the maturity level of the SHG and the branch manager's faith in their ability to repay, the loan varies from between US$100 and US$400. The repayment period is fixed in equal monthly instalments. The SHGs recovers the principal and interest from their members and repays it to the bank. This type of term loan is given to those groups which are between one and three years old. The main weakness of this type of loan for the SHGs is that they have to wait until the whole loan has been repaid before they can borrow again. This means that members who do not borrow from the first loan may have to wait some years before they can take a loan.

Revolving online credit

The other loan product is the revolving online credit (ROC). Groups that are more than three years old and have borrowed and promptly repaid once or twice already are allowed to have a cash credit or overdraft facility. The limit is fixed as a multiple of the total savings of the group.

The group takes a loan up to their limit and extends loans to its members and fixes monthly repayment schedules for them. Every month the instalments are collected by the SHG from its members and remitted to the cash credit account. As and when there is fresh demand for loan from a member of the SHG, the SHG can withdraw the necessary funds from their account and give the loan to that particular member. The bank earns more interest from ROCs than from term loans – the loan amounts outstanding are generally higher because the SHGs withdraw more frequently. At the end of the year the eligible loan limit for the SHG is re-calculated based on the increased funds of the group, including the savings they have made during that year, assuming that the account has been satisfactorily maintained.

The RBI states that cash credit accounts will be regarded as non-performing accounts if (a) the total credits in the account are not sufficient to cover the interest debited to the account during the period, or (b) the balance outstanding is more than the limit sanctioned, or (c) no payments have been made into the account for a continuous period of three months or more. Canara Bank therefore ensures that credits to SHG accounts are monitored by the cluster and federation staff to see that repayments are credited to the account when individual members' instalments are due to the SHGs. It is not enough if the interest alone is paid, and the accounts must be in credit from time to time. The ROC facility is extended only to those groups who have used their earlier term loans satisfactorily and who understand how to operate an overdraft account.

The pilot experience of providing overdrafts has been very positive, both for the SHG members and the bank. Members have got loans when they need them, repayments have been on time, and the bank's time and cost of transactions have been reduced. The overdraft facility was first tested with 20 groups in Alanganallur branch and their performance in terms of repayment and loan utilization of loan was better than with term loans. The maximum loan is US$2000 for each group, and all groups were able to revolve the funds on a regular basis to meet members' demands. This success was due to the following reasons.

- Members are confident that they can get loans at any time.
- Members can get credit when they need it.
- Members can get the amount of credit that they need.

As a result, the members and groups can now depend on one single source, that is, the bank, to meet all their credit needs.

Initiatives to ensure 100 per cent repayment

The following efforts were taken by the branch in close coordination with the BLF officials to ensure 100 per cent repayment at group level.
- The branch manager and federation executives regularly visit the groups to motivate the members and also to understand their field-level problems.
- Block level forum meetings are convened regularly to address any problems that may arise.

The following policy changes have been introduced to ensure smooth operation of the programme.

- At member level, groups can provide only one loan. Members can only take second loans after repaying the first loan.
- Groups can receive loans from only one source, either from bank or from CLAs or BLFs. The amount of the loan must be enough to meet the loan requirements of the SHG.
- In SHGs that are more than five years old, members can withdraw their savings to meet their consumption needs.

These mechanisms have enabled most groups to maintain 100 per cent repayment. In those groups which could not maintain 100 per cent repayment because of prolonged drought and wage-earners' migration for work, the following additional efforts have been initiated by the bank, the BLFs and the Dhan Foundation.

1. Rescheduling of loan instalments

One of the reasons for delayed repayment was that the period of repayment for term loans was fixed uniformly, irrespective of the amount or the purpose for which the loan was used. Some SHG members could not meet their commitments in time, mainly because of acute drought for the last three years in the Madurai area. In such cases, the bank loans, the internal loans and the federation loans were rescheduled at the member and group level. It was also decided in future to fix loan repayment periods according to the amount and the purpose, so that the instalment amounts matched the surplus income generated out of that economic activity for which the loans were used. This issue is more critical for second and third loans, which may involve amounts of more than US$2200. As a result of case-by-case analysis and initiation of corrective measures there have been considerable improvements in the recovery position of those SHGs that were earlier facing repayment problems. It has therefore not been necessary to make any provision for bad debts on these accounts.

2. Management information system

An on-line management information system (MIS) has been installed by the Dhan Foundation at the BLF and CLA levels. Special computer software, known as 'Dhanam', which means gift, has been prepared by the Foundation and supplied to the BLFs. The cluster associates and group accountants collect data in the prescribed formats from the SHGs periodically and update their data in the computer maintained at the federation office. Data relating to each member's savings, and the loan amount drawn from different sources, the loan amounts outstanding, repayment of principal and interest due for the next month, and the recovery position of each group are computerized and relevant reports are generated at the federation office. The cluster and group accountants use these reports to monitor the activities of each member and group. This has also facilitated initiation of immediate action at different levels for ensuring 100 per cent payment to the banks and other apex financial institutions by the SHGs and the Federation.

Copies of these MIS returns are also given to Bank staff. Regular interaction and review of performances of groups by the branch staff with the federation has also helped in addressing repayment problems. The cost of managing the data and its monthly analysis are included in the overall management cost of the federation and shared by all SHG members in the ratio of their total loan outstanding, as explained above.

3. Contact centres

Because of the drought and lack of agricultural income, some members have had to migrate to nearby industrial towns in search of jobs. They asked the federation and the bank to open contact centres in the towns to collect their monthly repayments. The local units of the Dhan Foundation and the local federation of SHGs near the town arranged this, and repayment improved considerably.

Experience of the branch in SHG lending

Alanganallur Branch won first prize in the Best Branch category of the Tamil Nadu State SHG Awards introduced by the Chennai (Madras) Regional office of NABARD. The experience has also provided many lessons to Canara Bank, and to Indian banks in general. These include:

- The poor need timely and adequate credit, and they need credit for consumption as well as for investment. They are less concerned with the cost of credit than its timely and adequate availability with minimum formalities.
- The SHG loans helped many poor people to escape from moneylenders. Some members were able to support existing business activities, and a few started small businesses or trade ventures. Most used their loans to meet consumption expenditure relating to health, education, social obligations, house repairs and construction, cooking gas, electricity connections, and so on.
- The SHGs and the clusters and federations have also addressed issues relating to drinking water, sanitation, street lighting, bus transport and roads, and they have also dealt with social evils such as alcoholism, mistreatment of women, and so on.

Advantages of SHG financing compared to other loans to individuals

In traditional rural individual loan accounts, the bank has to undertake pre-sanction scrutiny of the borrower, fill up loan documents, counsel the borrower, make post-sanction verification of asset creation by the borrowers, follow up repayments, and so on. This requires many visits to the borrowers' units and very high transaction costs. Compared to this, SHGs take far less time as all the above items are externalized to the representatives of the NGO and the SHGs, the clusters and the federations. Canara Bank recently announced an attractive voluntary retirement scheme for its employees and many staff seized the opportunity to retire. The staff strength in many of rural branches reduced drastically, which meant that they had even less time to deal with depositors, borrowers and administration.

In 2004 the RBI issued stringent norms relating to the classification of loan accounts, and set criteria for recognition of income only from performing assets and not from defaulted accounts and provisions for bad debts. Because many individual loan accounts of rural branches are in arrears, branches are unable to include interest from them as income, and they also have to provide for bad debts in respect of the defaulted accounts. This has forced the bank to search desperately for alternative ways of lending by their rural branches so that the branches may be able to lend more loans, with less staff and cheaper transaction costs, and also recover the loans fully at a low cost. SHG loans are performing assets for the branches, and they can include interest from these loans in their income. Additionally, there is no need to provide for bad debts in respect of these assets. SHG financing is obviously good business, and it also helps branches to build a good image among the rural poor.

Due to the combination of these direct and indirect advantages of SHG lending, Canara Bank has accepted SHG financing as a profitable banking proposition. Management has instructed all the rural branches which have good NGOs in their area to concentrate on SHG business. The role of the NGOs in SHGs promotion and nurturing and paving the way for their credit linkage with bank branches is one of the most vital reasons for the acceptance of SHGs by banks as a profitable venture.

The Alangallanur branch of Canara Bank has gained the following direct and indirect benefits from its SHG business.

- The branch mobilized US$63 600 of low-cost deposits in saving accounts. This is 10 per cent of the branch's total low-cost deposits.
- By the end of March 2003 the branch had extended loans worth more than US$657 000 at comparatively low transaction costs. The bank incurred no expenditure on the appraisal of the credit requirements of the SHGs, monitoring loan utilization, or visits to individual members' households to ensure prompt repayments, since all these tasks were dealt with by the SHG leaders and accountants, the CLA and BLF associates and employees. The cost of the SHG accountants, and cluster and federation staff are totally covered by the SHG members.
- The SHG members say that they are prepared to meet the costs of running the clusters and federations because they receive high quality services. Moreover, when compared to very high interest rates paid to moneylenders, the bank interest rates plus the maintenance cost of the clusters and federations are negligible. SHG members are well treated by the banks and enjoy facilities such as insurance, medical care and quality education through the federation. The members feel that they have been empowered economically and socially.

The only tangible cost for the branch in servicing the SHG loan accounts is the cost of keeping the savings and loan ledgers, the loan documents and a portion of the staff salary of the savings department and loans section. The branch has reserved every Tuesday between 11am and 3pm for transacting the affairs of the 400 or so SHGs that it serves. On this day, the leaders of the SHGs who transact their group's business visit the BLF office, which is just opposite the branch, and fill in all the necessary bank loan documents, and savings and loan payment vouchers. The CLA and BLF coordinators then verify all the papers to facilitate the smooth flow of work at the branch.

This arrangement has been agreed by the branch in consultation with the federation. It was felt necessary to restrict the SHG operations to a particular day in order to ensure quality service to the other individual deposit and loan customers. Previously, SHG members visited the branch on any day of the week. This caused heavy crowds and affected the quality of the service to other more affluent customers of the bank. These arrangements have made it possible to streamline the time spent on servicing SHG clients so that branch staff can attend to other existing and prospective clients of the branch.

The average cost of funds for the bank is between 5 per cent and 5.5 per cent. The bank charges an average interest rate of 11.5 per cent on loans to SHGs. The SHGs in turn lend to their members at 18 to 24 per cent depending on the purpose of the loan. The banks makes a spread of 6 per cent (11.5 per cent yield on assets less 5.5 per cent cost of funds) and only incurs a maximum cost of 1 per cent on servicing SHG loans. This 1 per cent cost includes the time spent by the officers in periodical meetings with the federation staff and occasional visits to the meetings of the SHGs, their clusters, and federation committee meetings. No special staff members are employed to attend to SHG transactions and special time sheets are maintained for attending to the SHGs' business. The 1 per cent figure was an estimate by the branch staff. The branch can be seen to make a net margin of 5 per cent on SHG lending.

Because of the failure of many non-bank finance companies that were previously accepting deposits from the public at attractive interest rates, the banks are flush with deposits that they can mobilize at quite low interest rates. Refinance from NABARD for SHG lending is available at 5.50 per cent, but since the average cost of funds to the banks is around 5–5.25 per cent, including the cost of servicing deposits, most of the major commercial banks no longer take refinance.

The Alangallanur branch of Canara Bank also makes term loans for agriculture, animal husbandry, shops and trading businesses and for consumption purposes such as education, cars and housing. The interest charged on these loans is around 11–12 per cent, which is about the same as for SHGs. The banks have heavy defaults on these loans, however, and when the principal or interest payment is in arrears for more than 90 days, the branch cannot calculate interest and take it to their profit and loss account. Canara Bank also has to provide a certain percentage of the outstanding balance on loans which are in arrears for bad debts.

For example, if the Bank lends US$100 000 to SHGs with 100 per cent repayment and the same amount is lent for agriculture and their repayment is only 70 per cent, then the Bank's net interest income under the two kinds of loan will be as follows:

It can thus be seen that the 30 per cent reduction in repayment leads to a 55 per cent reduction in the interest income of the branch.

Item	SHG lending	Agricultural loan	Explanation
Amount of loan	US$100 000	US$100 000	
On-time repayment percentage	100%	70%	
Interest income for full year at 12%	US$12 000	US$8 400	On US$70 000, as the repayment is only 70%. Interest on the balance of US$30 000 can be counted only when the principal and interest are recovered
Provision for bad debts @ 10% on the non-performing portion of the loan	Nil	US$3 000	@ 10 % on US$30 000
Net interest income	US$12 000	US$5 400	US$3 000 has to be deducted for provision out of US$8 400 earned

In the above example, it has been assumed that the transaction cost is same for SHGs as for agricultural term loan. This is not so. SHG loans are to a group and not to 15 or 20 individuals. The documentational formalities and appraisal of SHG lending are undertaken by the NGOs and federations. Hence the transaction cost is very low. Even though the SHG loans are sanctioned for a period of 36 months, the loans are usually repaid with interest within 12 to 18 months as the members want to take another larger loan.

Prompt repayment of SHG loans by poor women in villages has led to better repayment by other rural people. The SHG members have convinced many defaulters in their villages to repay their past dues to the banks so that the bankers will have a good image of the village and will be willing to lend there again.

Canara Bank managers now consider the rural poor as good credit risks who are definitely bankable. Because of the good repayment by SHGs, branch staff are willing to consider extending more loans to the rural poor and the total loan portfolio has increased considerably,

Approaches to covering the formation cost of SHGs

Developing SHGs, CLAs and BLFs and their capacity-building training programmes is expensive. Currently this cost is being funded by donor agencies, but this may not always be possible.

It is expected that banks which have benefited from SHG lending and recognized that this is the most effective, profitable and sustainable way of lending to the vast majority of the rural clientele will now started to cover the cost of forming SHGs themselves. Canara Bank has offered to pay Dhan Foundation to form around 1000 SHGs, on the condition that the savings and loan accounts of the groups will be maintained with their branches.

The SHG members of Alanganallur have shown that they are willing and able to cover the cost of running their SHGs, CLAs and BLFs, and even to pay the costs of forming new groups. This shows that SHG members are prepared to pay a price for the services that they value from the NGO. Thus the costs of forming of SHGs are shared by all the stakeholders, including the banks, government departments, NGOs and the SHG members themselves.

Discussion questions

1. Almost half the business of the Alanganallur branch of Canara Bank is with microfinance self-help groups, and the branch remains profitable. Is this experience replicable?

2. To what extent is the Alangallanur branch's success dependent on the externalization of the non-financial costs of microfinance business to the SHG federations, and can the federations be said to be sustainable in the long term?

3. Canara Bank offers the self-help groups overdraft facilities, which appear to suit both the clients and the bank much better than term loans. Such facilities are not susceptible to traditional microfinance portfolio quality measurement tools such as portfolio at risk or delinquency rates. Why are overdrafts not more commonly provided to microfinance clients, and should more institutions offer them?

Chapter Seven
Oriental Bank of Commerce's microfinance project, India

RAVINDER YADAV

In 1943 the Thapar Industrial Group of northern India established the Oriental Bank of Commerce (OBC) at Lahore, which is now in Pakistan. The head office was moved to Calcutta in 1947, and then to Delhi. When OBC was nationalized in 1980, it had 307 branches. By 2003, the Bank had 1107 offices and about US$10bn of deposits and advances.

OBC has a capital adequacy ratio of 14 per cent, return on equity of 29 per cent, and was the first bank in India to achieve zero net non-performing assets. It has the highest employee productivity of any public sector bank in India, and has made increasing profits for the last 20 years. The net profit of the bank in 2003–04 was just over US$150m. The Government sold 34 per cent of the Bank's equity to the public in 1994, but has retained majority ownership. Since nationalization, OBC has emphasized social banking and has designed its products accordingly. The Bank is actively participating in poverty-reduction programmes sponsored by various government agencies, besides implementing its own unique microfinance project in 31 selected branches.

OBC and microfinance: the beginning

OBC's microfinance programme is known as the Oriental Bank Grameen Project (OBGP). The word '*grameen*' means rural in Hindi, and it does not mean that the programme is a replication of the Bangladesh Grameen Bank. The OBGP was launched in 1995 to provide banking services to the poor at their doorstep. The aim was to assist poorer people to take decisions independently and to manage their own financial and social affairs. OBC concentrates on its core competence, which is banking, but it also facilitates access for these customers to a range of social and development agencies; they provide services to OBC's customers at no cost to OBC.

The OBGP originated from the Bank's efforts to learn from and apply the lessons of various microfinance initiatives worldwide. A general manager at the corporate level participated in a bankers' microfinance exposure visit sponsored by the Swiss Development Co-operation Agency (SDC) and organized by NABARD. He observed the success of institutions such as the Grameen Bank in Bangladesh and Bank Rakyat Indonesia (BRI). He shared his enthusiasm with another colleague at the corporate level and with a development manager who was looking for a challenging assignment in the field. The CEO of the Bank fully supported the idea, and the development manager grasped the opportunity and went on to set up a specialist 'self-help group (SHG) only' branch in the hills above Dehradun, on the edge of the Himalayas.

The Bank evolved a unique group delivery approach, which is a hybrid of the Bangladesh Grameen Bank method and the Indian SHG method. It happens also to be similar but not identical to the model used by the primary agricultural co-operative societies in Hooghly and other co-operative financial institutions in West Bengal, which are the nation's leading co-operatives in SHG linkage programmes.

The salient features of this OBC model are as follows.

- It is based on groups of five members, and the groups are themselves grouped into centres of six to eight groups. The centres often meet weekly, although some centres decided on fortnightly or monthly meetings.
- The branch manager has to promote groups himself for initial two to three months, but after this time the concept becomes well-established, and potential facilitators identify themselves from amongst the groups. The groups are serviced by these facilitators, who are paid by the groups from a centre development fund levy of 1 per cent on their loans. The facilitators are usually relatives of SHG members, with some education.
- The facilitator system externalizes much of the transaction cost burden for the Bank, which makes the Bangladesh method relatively more expensive. High transaction costs discourage most commercial banks from adopting the Bangladesh system.
- The SHGs are promoted by the staff of OBC, and eventually by the facilitators or by SHG members themselves, not by NGOs.
- The bank keeps ledger accounts for the SHGs, not for individual members. This further reduces transaction costs for the bank.
- Loan amount is based on requirement of the member and are not linked to the saving s/he has accumulated.
- Saving amounts can vary according to members' wishes, and are withdrawable.

This system has the following advantages for remote and thinly populated mountain areas such as the Himalayan foothills.

- Because of the groups' small size, they are relatively easy and quick to promote, and can be promoted by members themselves.
- The very widely scattered mountain homesteads make small groups more suitable than groups of between 15 and 20 members.
- In spite of its differences from the conventional model, NABARD have accepted this model, and can provide refinance and promotion incentives, if necessary.
- The experience of the OBC SHG-only branch demonstrates that business with these SHGs can over time reach a 1:1 credit:deposit ratio, with savings and loans of around Rs.30m each (US$0.67m) for each branch. This helps to overcome the shortage of lendable funds, which is a critical constraint for most primary agricultural co-operative societies.

Motives

All banks in India have to allocate 40 per cent of their advances to what is known as 'the priority sector', meaning farming, and within that 8 per cent to the 'weaker sections', meaning lower caste and 'tribal' people. This can be done by direct lending, such as loans to individuals or SHGs, or by wholesale loans to other institutions, which will in turn lend to the priority sector. This has always been difficult, since much of the lending has been through poorly designed, badly managed and heavily subsidized government programmes, with very low recovery rates. OBC was anxious to identify more systematic and efficient ways of doing this, which could also be profitable, and would benefit the customers. The purpose of the pilot was to prove that the poor are bankable, as had been found in other countries.

The programme was designed with the following features:

1. homogeneous groups to be formed as the medium for delivery;
2. monetary discipline to be maintained through regular savings, assured credit and timely repayment;
3. income-generation activities to be encouraged;
4. any form of subsidy to be avoided.

The project area

The pilot started in 1995 through two branches of OBC, in eight villages of Dehradun district, Uttaranchal, and Hanumangarh district, Rajasthan. Dehradun is a valley on the fringes of the Himalayas in north India, and Hanumangarh forms part of the Thar Desert in north-west India. Both are in poor areas, with low density of population, little industry and traditional, rain-fed agriculture. Poverty is widespread. In addition to the OBC branches, there is one commercial bank branch and one co-operative bank branch in each area, but they are doing very little business, with high rates of default under government-sponsored programmes. No regular microfinance services were available.

The development managers

OBC recognized that success depends on the level of commitment of the field staff. Only those who understand the poor can work with them effectively. OBC has a cadre of officers exclusively for rural finance. They are generally from rural areas and are used to working in villages. The Bank carefully selected a development manager (DM) for each of the two pilot areas, from the specialist cadre of agricultural officers. They deal with clients at the individual, group and centre level, and they also liaise with the branches and other constituents of the delivery system. OBC is crucially dependent on the DM to form and nurture the groups, to facilitate their links to the bank and generally to catalyse their empowerment.

No NGOs are involved, either as financial intermediaries or for the provision of technical inputs. However, OBC arranges skills training for group members, through government departments or with private trainers and master craftsmen; the cost of these services is met by the clients themselves, or by the government agency; there is no cost to the bank.

Facilitators

When the project expanded to a larger number of villages, particularly in Dehradun, it was no longer feasible for the one DM to meet the rising demand for his services. OBC decided to solve this problem by appointing facilitators to promote and service groups. The facilitators are generally group members, or relatives of a group member. Each facilitator looks after 12 centres every week, consisting of between 100 to 120 groups, with 500–600 individual clients. They are paid by the groups themselves, out of a 1 per cent levy on their loans, and are not employees of the bank. The facilitators have made it possible for the bank to reach 90 villages in Dehradun. This not only benefits the group members, but also provides some employment for local people.

Formation of groups

The groups are formed by the DMs or the facilitators according to the following guidelines.

1. Members should be from similar socio-economic backgrounds.
2. Preference is given to women, because they have been found to be more reliable and enthusiastic. The members are discouraged from including men and women members in the same group, and 87 per cent of the groups have only women members.
3. The Groups should not have more than one member from the same family.
4. The members should be more than 18 years old and should be poor. They are not required to be officially 'below the poverty line', since this definition is unevenly administered. In any case, people who are marginally above the poverty line often slip below it and group membership can prevent this.
5. There should be five members in each group
6. All members of a group should belong to the same village.
7. The groups are informal; they do not need any legal registration or certification.
8. If a member drops out, a new member can replace her so long as the existing members agree.

Client profile

Nobody who owns more than two hectares of land is allowed to be a member. One-third of the group members are landless, 60 per cent own up to one hectare and the rest are small farmers with up to two hectares of land. Although two-thirds of the group members own some land, they are engaged in many non-agricultural activities because their land holdings are inadequate to support the whole family. Only a quarter of the loans are used for farming as such and more than half of are used to buy cattle and goats. The balance are used for petty trading or rural crafts.

Microfinance products

Savings products

The members' incomes were very low, and they were initially reluctant to save regularly. OBC gave them wooden piggy banks to accumulate the few small coins which they saved every day. The boxes were unlocked by the group leader during the weekly meeting and the money was collected by the bank representative, and was assumed to be the member's savings. At this stage, there was no minimum savings rate. The group then opened a savings bank account, which was in itself a major step forward for people who had never before even entered a bank branch. The group members soon graduated to a minimum savings of Rs.1 a day per member. This is still the minimum rate and each client deposits Rs.7, or about US$0.15, at each weekly meeting, although they are free to deposit higher amounts if they wish. They are discouraged from withdrawing their savings (except in cases of emergencies), but their loan amounts are not dependent upon their individual savings.

As soon as the savings of a client reach Rs.1000, or just over US$20, it is converted into a term deposit, in order to earn higher interest rate and to encourage the members to save more. Many members' fixed deposits have reached over US$300. This is also a useful alternative to insurance. The banks have not been allowed to offer insurance services in the past. This is changing, and OBC is negotiating a tie-up with the Life Insurance Company of India through which it hopes to be able to offer life insurance to group members.

The members also contribute 1 per cent of their loans to a group fund. This is used for meeting emergencies and to guarantee members in case of default or the death of a group member. The facilitators' wages are also met from this fund.

Credit products

Members can borrow for any productive purpose that they wish, so long as their fellow group members agree. They can also use loans for consumption purposes when necessary. They have to save regularly for at least three months before they can borrow.

At the initial stage, only two members of a group can borrow at a time. After they have performed well for four weeks, two other members are allowed credit, and the group leader is the last to get a loan. After the first 12-month cycle has been satisfactorily completed, all the members in a group can take loans at the same time. Initially, a group's total loans cannot exceed Rs.75 000 or about US$1500, and no single member's loan can exceed US$300. This limit is gradually increased as the members' absorption capacity increases, and groups more than three years old can borrow up to about US$2750. Loans are disbursed in cash during the group meetings, and all the group members monitor each other's use of their loans.

The group's savings are not treated as collateral, and members are free to withdraw as they wish. All the group members are however liable, jointly and severally, for the loans taken by anyone in the group.

Commercial banks interest rates on loans up to Rs 200 000 (about US$4000) are regulated by the Central Bank, and are not allowed to exceed OBC's Primary Lending Rate, which is presently 11 per cent per annum. This provides a reasonable spread since OBC's cost of funds is 5.6 per cent. Most of the transaction cost of field operations is borne by the customers, through the facilitators.

Rudrapur is the only OBC branch that is wholly devoted to microfinance. The other 30 branches engaged in microfinance also do normal banking business, with only a small portion of their business pertaining to microfinance. It is not possible to separate out the profitability of the microfinance from the other business in these branches.

The Rudrapur branch made a profit during its third year of operations, which is most unusual for a rural branch. The Rudrapur branch has more business than any other rural branch of OBC in the region. All its clients are poor women, and Rudrapur is the only branch of its kind in any Indian commercial bank. After two-and-a-half years of initial losses, the branch has earned profits every year since.

The products differ from usual credit products of the bank in term of size, flexibility and delivery mechanism.

Repayment

Weekly instalments are collected during each meeting. Where an activity does not earn income every week, such as crop production, a nominal amount must still be repaid in order to maintain recovery discipline. Clients can prepay their loans with a lump sum, if they so wish. The loans are to the individual members but are made through the groups, and the members save individually also. The group's function is to guarantee repayment, to bring social pressure to bear and to make it easier for the bank worker to collect savings and repayments.

Delivery mechanism

Once a group is formed, one of its members is elected leader; this position is rotated periodically as decided by the group. The group leader is responsible for maintaining financial and functional discipline in the

Table 7.1 *Growth of business at the Rudrapur branch of OBC*

(Figures in US$)	1997-98	1998-99	1999-00	2000-01	2001-02	2002-03
Cumulative loans	71 000	222 000	433 000	777 000	1 136 000	1 446 000
Savings balances outstanding	25 000	111 000	218 000	378 000	555 000	644 000
Loan balances outstanding	40 000	131 000	24 000	411 000	560 000	645 000

group. The groups in a given village form a centre, and all the group leaders nominate one centre leader. The centre leader maintains inter-group dynamics. If the number of groups is large, they are divided into more than one centre.

The centres meet every week, on a fixed day and time, to collect savings and repayments, to disburse loans and to exchange views. A facilitator or branch official attends each centre's weekly meeting; all the banking functions are carried out in the village itself. No group or individual is required to visit the branch for any kind of banking transaction, either for depositing savings or raising loan or repayment of instalments.

Table 7.1 (above) shows the growth of the outstanding balances of both savings and loans in the Rudrapur branch from its establishment in 1997 until the end of March 2003.

After the first three years, the Rudrapur branch has made steadily increasing profits ever since 1999. Figure 7.1 (below) illustrates progress at the branch.

Figure 7.1 *Gross profitability of Rudrapur branch of OBC*

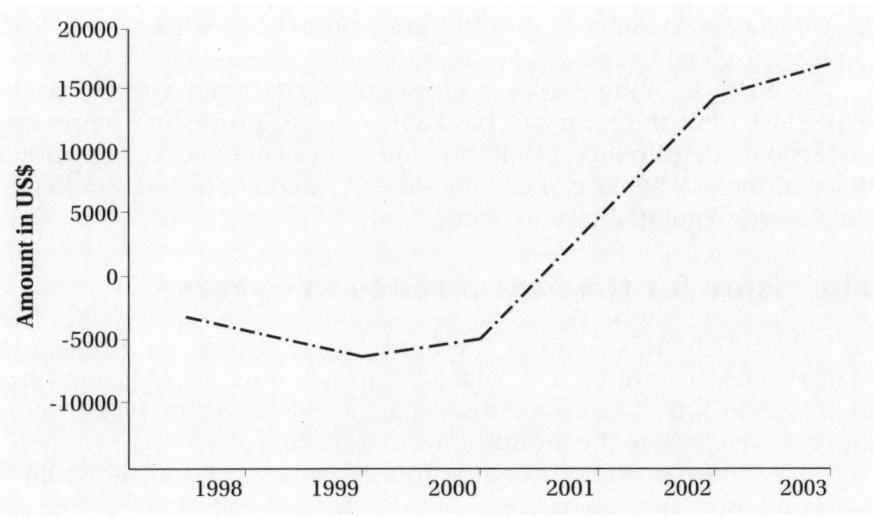

Table 7.2 *Financial performance of the Rudrapur branch of OBC*

Balance sheet as at 31 March 2003 (US$)			
Liabilities		**Assets**	
Deposits	644 400	Cash	250
Borrowings from Head Office	9 750	Current loans	645 200
Miscellaneous liabilities	1 600	Furniture and equipment	10 300
Total	**655 750**	**Total**	**655 750**
Profit and loss account for Rudrapur branch of OBC for the year ended 31 March 2003 (US$)			
Financial expense		**Financial income**	
Interest paid on deposits	48 850	Interest received on advances	79 550
Interest paid on HO borrowings	750		
Operational expenses*			
Personnel expense	9 950	Miscellaneous income	200
Administrative expense	4 550		
Total expenses	**64 100**	**Total income**	**79 750**
Gross income	**15 650**		

*The figure for operational expenses includes an allowance for head office overheads.

The 2002–03 results of the Rudrapur branch, which has only SHG clients, are given in Table 7.2 (above).

The purpose of the Bank's microfinance experiment was to test the hypothesis that the poor are bankable, and to prove that banks can undertake microfinance profitably. The experience has clearly shown that commercial banks can downscale and run microfinance profitably, even under regulated interest rates.

The vision for the next three to five years

Emboldened by this success, the Bank has expanded the project. By March 2003, it covered 185 villages and the number of groups had increased to 2406. The cumulative savings rose to Rs.29m (US$0.64m), and the advances to the groups grew to Rs110m (US$2.4m).

Table 7.3 (opposite) shows the rate of expansion and the scale of OBC's microfinance operation.

Table 7.3 Expansion of microfinance portfolio of OBC

Year end (April to March)	1996	1997	1998	1999	2000	2001	2002	2003
No. of bank branches	2	2	2	2	9	9	11	31
No. of villages	17	21	25	47	64	97	127	185
No. of groups	84	217	330	551	769	1 162	1 616	2 406
No. of clients	420	1 085	1 650	2 755	3 845	5 810	8 040	11 987
Amount advanced (US$m)	0.03	0.11	0.17	0.47	0.78	1.28	1.81	2.45
Savings mobilized (US$m)	0.002	0.03	0.05	0.14	0.24	0.38	0.52	0.64
Loan outstanding (US$m)	0.02	0.08	0.11	0.22	0.33	0.56	0.73	0.89

Portfolio at risk, defined as more than 90 days overdue, is nil.

The sums involved in the project so far are very small, in relation to the total business of the bank, but its ramifications for the Bank and the banking industry as a whole are important. The project shows clearly that the poor are bankable and that commercial banks in rural India can successfully undertake microfinance.

OBC has a network of 243 rural and 265 semi-urban branches. About 40 per cent of these branches are situated in poor regions, where there is a serious need for microfinancial services. OBC has already started to mainstream microfinance. During the first phase, the project has been extended from Rudrapur to 30 additional branches. Three specially trained officers have been posted to oversee the expansion of the project. Three branches have started to offer microfinancial services in ten or 15 villages each, and the other 27 branches are initially confining operations to one village each. At the second stage, in about two years' time, each of these 30 branches will expand its microfinance operation to more villages, and each year new branches will join the OBGP operations. It is envisaged that 100 branches will be taking part in the project by 2009.

In 2003, the manager who had managed the Rudrapur branch was appointed as Chief Executive of the Uttaranchal State Co-operative Bank. This is an apex-level institution serving nine district level co-operative banks and some 750 primary societies at the village level. Within nine months, the primary societies had promoted more than 7000 groups on the same model. It is too early to predict whether these groups will be as sustainable as those in the OBC branch, but this initial success, as well as OBC's own results in other branches, suggests that this type of groups can be effectively promoted and serviced by nonspecialist branches and does not depend on the field presence of a committed 'champion'.

Discussion questions

1. The Oriental Bank of Commerce (OBC) claims that the results of the Rudrapur branch demonstrate that a commercial bank can make microfinance profitable. How transferable is the approach, and what can be learned from it by banks that do not wish to open branches that are dedicated only to microfinance clients?

2. OBC uses an unusual hybrid between the Indian self-help group and the Bangladesh Grameen Bank delivery methodology. Is this method appropriate for other banks and clients?

3. OBC's senior management accepted and supported this innovative experiment from the outset. How can more conservative and less receptive senior managers be persuaded to look favourably on somewhat revolutionary experiments of this kind?

Chapter Eight
ICICI Bank, India

TARA NAIR, M.S. SRIRAM and VISHWANATH PRASAD

The trend and progress of the Indian microfinance sector shows slow and lopsided growth in the upscaling and outreach of micro-credit over the past decade. In 2002, Nearly US$1700m[1] was disbursed by micro-credit institutions (excluding the co-operatives) to about 12 to 15 million households. This works out to about US$120 per household. This is rapid progress from a tiny baseline, but for a country where close to 250 million people (about 50 million households) are officially considered poor, this cannot be regarded as a startlingly impressive achievement.

The overall picture of the demand for micro-credit in India as against current supply is disappointing. Demand is generally projected on the basis of average credit usage per household multiplied by the estimated number of poor households. Various studies show that the average annualized credit usage of poor households varies between US$60 and US$180. Multiplying this by 50 million, we are faced with the daunting figure of anywhere between US$3bn and US$9bn as the total demand for micro-credit.[2]

The supply of credit should be steadily increasing in order to meet this growing demand, but has in fact been doing quite the opposite, at least from the commercial banks in India. The proportion of bank loans below US$500 declined steadily from 18.3% of total commercial scheduled bank credit in 1994 to 5.3% in March 2002. The number of small borrower accounts has reduced from 55.8 million to 37.3 million.

Figure 8.1 *Trends of scheduled commercial bank advances to rural, agriculture and small loans as percentage of total advances*

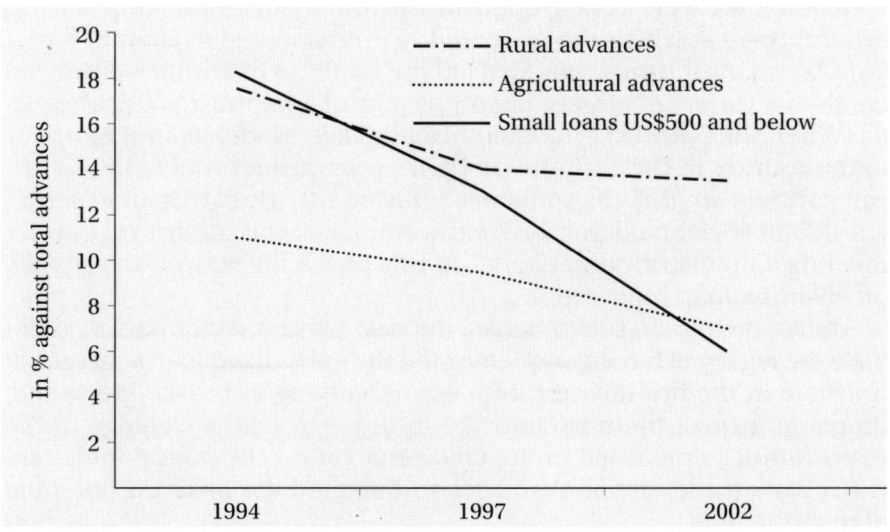

Despite the self-help group (SHG)-bank linkage effort (which has reached more than one million groups and through them, some 15 million women), the gap between demand and supply has barely begun to be bridged. In March 2003, the SHG programme had an outstanding total of around US$200m, thus meeting 2.2–6.6 per cent of the estimated demand. Microfinance institutions (MFIs) are still fledgling efforts in terms of the number of poor people reached or affected. There is a long way to go yet before the poor of India receive the credit that they need in order to manage and improve their lives and break out of the vicious cycle of poverty.

It is in this context that the few interesting innovations in recent times, that signal a progressive movement towards commercialization or integration of microfinance with mainstream financial markets, must be seen. While several NGOs are moving into commercial microfinance by establishing exclusive entities, some of the commercial banks are taking proactive steps in order to relieve the sector of its perennial bottleneck of scarcity of funds and the resultant dilemma in enhancing outreach and attaining sustainability. Some modest policy changes have given a great impetus to these initiatives. These changes include the directives of the country's Central Bank, the Reserve Bank of India (RBI), to all banks to consider lending to MFIs as part of 'priority sector' lending and to exclude unsecured advances given by banks to SHGs against a group guarantee, for the purpose of computation of prudential norms.

Commercial banks and Indian microfinance

It is untrue to say that public sector commercial banking in India has never engaged with lower-income households. However, this engagement was engineered through the means of bank nationalization, the first phase of which happened in the late 1960s. The nationalized commercial banks were called upon to assume a social banking role, to expand their reach to the unserved or underserved segments of the population. As it turned out, this led the banks to distribute subsidized credit to a variety of targets, largely as part of a populist political agenda. When the NABARD-initiated SHG linkage model gained currency in the country in the early 1990s, banks were again brought in as critical partners in the microfinance movement. Unlike in the earlier episode of social banking, where the emphasis was almost entirely on meeting loan distribution targets, in this phase the accent was equally on ensuring loan repayment.

Unlike the public sector banks, the new private sector banks do not have the legacy of having implemented the subsidized loan schemes of the State in the pre-liberalization era of banking in India. One would, therefore, expect them to innovate in order to take advantage of the opportunities unleashed in the credit market for the poor population. ICICI Bank is the first bank to have understood the business potential of microfinance.

ICICI Bank[3]

ICICI Bank is currently India's second largest bank with total assets of about US$25 000m and a network of about 450 branches and 1800 ATMs. Up until 2001, it was a subsidiary of ICICI Limited, a development finance institution launched in 1955 with the purpose of purveying medium and long-term credit to Indian businesses. Since 1998, ICICI's shareholding in the bank has been reduced to 46 per cent through a public offering of shares in India (1998), an equity offering on the New York Stock Exchange (2000) and the merger of ICICI Bank and the Bank of Madura (2001). Then in 2001 and 2002, ICICI offered secondary market sales to institutional investors. Finally, in October 2001, the Boards of Directors of ICICI and ICICI Bank approved the merger of ICICI and two of its wholly owned retail finance subsidiaries, ICICI Personal Financial Services Limited and ICICI Capital Services Limited, with ICICI Bank. The merger was approved by the Reserve Bank of India in April 2002. ICICI Bank, the entity created, integrates the ICICI group's financing and banking operations, both wholesale and retail.

Entry in to microfinance

In 2001 ICICI Bank merged with the Bank of Madura, a private sector commercial bank in the southern state of Tamil Nadu. The 57-year-old Bank of Madura, with a network of 263 branches, had assets of US$800m and deposits of US$680m.

The Bank of Madura was noted for its SHG programme. The SHG concept was part of the corporate policy of the Bank of Madura. The bank staff had received extensive training on the promotion of SHGs (forming of groups, identification of income-generating activities, monitoring) with expenditure shared by NABARD. There was no local NGO that assisted the bank in promoting these SHGs as the bank equipped itself to promote, nurture and finance the groups and managed to maintain a very good repayment rate. With its acquisition of the Bank of Madura, ICICI Bank inherited this vast SHG network and portfolio and was forced to learn this new business.

At about this time, RBI stated that microfinance could be considered as part of 'priority sector lending' – a system under which 40 per cent of loans by commercial banks should be reserved for priority sectors, and 18 per cent of this to agricultural activities.

The reverse merger of ICICI Bank with ICICI took place in April 2002, one outcome of which was a huge asset size for the bank. The financial institution (ICICI Ltd.) did not have a priority sector obligation, which meant that most of these assets were in bonds and deposits. The merged entity suddenly needed to make a much stronger effort to meet its priority sector targets and the idea was to find these rural and priority sector assets without having to open a huge number of rural branches.

The focus of ICICI Bank on microfinance thus slowly emerged and was made stronger in February 2002, with the launch of the Rural and Micro Banking Group (RMBG) within the bank. Between March 2003 and March 2004, the bank's exposure to the microfinance sector increased from less than US$28m to more than US$63m and the number of borrowers from under 66 000 to over 280 000.

The need to achieve priority sector targets was one important reason for ICICI Bank's entry into the business but, after the first pilot year, the emphasis has been to build a substantial and profitable business. As an independent effort and quite coincidentally, the bank's Social Initiatives Group, in pursuit of its own agenda within the bank, had evolved a number of new and viable ways of doing business in the microfinance sector and was able convincingly to demonstrate to the commercial groups within the bank and its insurance companies that it was possible to build a viable and substantial businesses in microfinance. A combination of these two factors is what has drawn the bank and its subsidiaries to this business in such a large manner.

There was one particular enthusiast for microfinance in ICICI Bank's senior management, but the move was well supported and encouraged by the board in general. The bank made a conscious effort to step up its entire rural and agricultural business portfolio – microfinance was a significant part of this and received as much attention as the rest.

Currently, the microfinance business is managed by the RMBG, which reports to one of the executive directors of ICICI Bank who is also a member of the bank's board. The business enjoys broad-based support within the senior management team of the bank and its board of directors. ICICI Bank has now started to gain public recognition for its work and this has helped further to strengthen its commitment to the sector.

In 2001, ICICI also made its first equity investment in an MFI, Basix, and, although the investment was small in terms of funding, it served to demonstrate the bank's view that the sector had the potential to be profitable. It was also intended to give the bank a closer view from inside a well-run MFI.

Models of microfinance delivery

The strategy of the bank has been to avoid entering the microfinance market directly. It works in partnership with institutions that provide these services to the poor and underserved. No additional branches were opened for the purpose. One reason for this could be that the expertise needed to appraise these clients and to play the role of a social intermediary already exists, and the bank (with its financial and structuring expertise) would do much better to go through existing channels than to build new ones.

A major hurdle in this process, however, was the existing regulatory framework in India for MFIs. Deficiency of capital is one of the major constraints to the growth of MFIs. Donor funds are limited, both in size and availability, and MFIs cannot rely on these exclusively if they wish to scale up their activities. The other options are for MFIs to access public deposits and equity. Existing regulation makes it very difficult for MFIs to raise public deposits – not allowed if the MFI is a non-profit organization and a strong credit rating required if the MFI is a non-bank financial institution (NBFC). The entry-level share capital requirement for an NBFC is about US$400 000, an amount that is still beyond the capacity of most MFIs wishing to transform into a regulated entity. To this day, only one MFI in India has successfully raised equity both from Indian and foreign investors. MFIs registered as not-for-profit entities dominate the Indian microfinance scene and they are still considered an unattractive investment proposition. With capital adequacy problems, unsupportive regulation and a lack of resources, MFIs in India face a tough task when it comes to scaling up operations.

It is in this context that ICICI Bank saw a clear need for an innovative approach, eventually coming up with a few unique products and channels – innovation that not only helped the bank to meet its targets for rural lending but also helped MFIs overcome their capital constraints without the need for regulatory changes. Changes in regulation will happen in due course. But the bank recognizes the need for the microfinance activity not to lose momentum in the meantime.

ICICI Bank is trying out different models of microfinance delivery with about ten NGOs/MFIs including SHARE, Basix, Asmita, Spandana, PRADAN, Dhan Foundation, Swayam Krishi Sangham, Village Welfare Society, Grameen Koota, Sanghamitra and CASHPOR.

The three models that have been piloted so far are:[4]

- **portfolio buy-out**, whereby the existing assets of the NGO/MFI are assigned in favour of the ICICI Bank in return for a purchase consideration;
- **partnership**, where the loans are originated in the books of ICICI Bank and the NGO/MFI takes up the responsibility of monitoring and recovery;
- **on-tap securitizaton** or continuous 'portfolio buyout' of loans and assignment of receivables to ICICI bank by the NGO/MFI.

Sourcing criteria and operational guidelines for the bank and NGO/MFIs are stipulated in mutually agreed arrangements.

All the models have in-built collection incentives and risk-sharing arrangements through different, mutually agreed formulae. Essentially, all the structures have two components:

1. a financing instrument for the MFI portfolio or to its clients directly;
2. credit enhancements

The financing instrument could be a portfolio buyout of the MFI or a continuous arrangement of on-tap securitization to the MFI, or loans disbursed directly to MFI clients as in the partnership model. The credit enhancement of the MFI portfolio could be provided in the form of a first loss default guarantee (FLDG) backed by one of the following.

1. An overdraft limit, as in CASHPOR

If the credit enhancement takes the form of an FLDG backed by an overdraft limit, the bank sanctions the MFI a limit to the extent of a specified percentage of the MFI receivables purchased by the bank. The overdraft limit will be drawn down only in the event of default.

2. The excess spread on the portfolio, as in Basix

Excess spread is the difference between the rate of return expected by ICICI Bank on the microfinance portfolio and what the MFI charges the final borrower. This could be as much as 12–24 per cent to account for the transaction costs incurred by the MFI in administering the portfolio. This excess spread could be trapped in a separate account and thus provide an FLDG to the bank. The amounts accumulated in the account would be paid to the MFI upon the maturity of the designated portfolio, after adjusting for losses, if any.

3. Third-party guarantee, as in SHARE, the third party guarantor being Grameen Foundation USA

The third option is to provide an FLDG to the bank in the form of cash security. In the case of SHARE, the Grameen Foundation provided 93 per cent of the cash collateral requirement of ICICI Bank.

The advantages of the above structures are as follows.[5]

- They separate the risk of the MFI from the risk of the underlying portfolio. The microfinance portfolio has exhibited negligible loss ratios. Despite this, the cost of commercial funds for MFIs has been high, due to their poor capitalization.
- The structure being scaleable in nature can provide continuous funding for MFIs that have supervision structures in place.
- The credit risk assumed by the MFI is limited to the FLDG that it provides the bank. Therefore, the capital that needs to be allocated by the MFI to this activity is dramatically reduced.
- The structure through the various FLDG options provides a mechanism to incentives MFIs to sustain performance on collection.

This would also help MFIs transcend the limitations imposed by insufficient capital and slow growth in outreach. The downside is that the MFIs' own balance sheets do not grow as rapidly and, therefore, may pose some difficulties in accessing further capital from other players in the market. As for ICICI Bank, it can extend its outreach to the hitherto untouched client segments without incurring much administrative cost, as the lion's share is borne by the MFI. It also provides the bank with an easy and less risky option to meet the priority-sector lending targets stipulated by the RBI.[6]

Portfolio buy-out

ICICI has entered into portfolio buy-out agreements with SHARE Microfin and Basix, two large MFIs based in Hyderabad, the capital of the southern Indian state of Andhra Pradesh. The deal with SHARE is worth US$4.3m, being the portfolio originating from 42 500 loans. Unlike consumer loans, the deal is not backed by assets and the business properties of the borrowers will remain unencumbered. However, there is a relaxation on provisioning and prudential norms. The RBI has stipulated that on an experimental basis such loans would be treated as secured loans for the purposes of prudential norms. This facility was initially offered for a year and has now been extended by a further year. The responsibility of collecting loans lies with SHARE. The collateral in this deal is an FLDG of 8 per cent of the total portfolio. Grameen Foundation, a non-profit entity based in the USA, has provided 93% of the collateral with SHARE bearing the rest.[7] ICICI Bank decided to purchase a branch-wide portfolio.

While the broad features of the deals are the same, the FLDG provision is 15 per cent of the portfolio in the case of Basix. This difference is largely due to the difference in the percentage of risky assets, which is about 2.5 per cent in the case of Basix and almost nil for SHARE. Other important determinants of purchase consideration are the credit ratings of the MFIs, the average period of loan maturity and the risk of 'collection'. The bank relies on the MFI's continued support to recover these loans and if for some reason the MFI does not do that, the cost of recovering these loans can be prohibitively high for the bank given the absence of a network.

The buy-out deals appear to benefit both ICICI Bank and the MFI. For the MFI, they open up a fresh and less costly source of funds. For instance, ICICI charges 9 per cent interest for the portfolio bought, which is 3–4 per cent less than the previous cost of funds. The comfort level of other banks and customers with Basix and SHARE will grow, as this is an important signal that their portfolio is real and reliable – confidence in a financial institution is a very important intangible benefit and this will signal changes in behaviour.

The guarantees are principally designed to align the incentives of the MFI with those of ICICI Bank. While the guarantee is linked to the past portfolio performance of the MFI, the extent of the guarantee would decline over successful partnership cycles. However, it is very likely that when these papers are sold in the capital markets, top-up guarantees and other arrangements such as market-making services may be needed to build a sustainable and low-cost funding source which are eventually directly accessible to mature MFIs – potentially making it unnecessary for them to access banks altogether.

ICICI Bank, once it acquires a pool of assets through deals such as those with SHARE, Basix and CASHPOR, will package the portfolio, get it rated, and sell the assets to mutual funds or other banks.[8] Being a high-quality asset, banks can safely trade it in the capital markets and hedge their own risk. Thus the mainstreaming of rural credit into formal banking systems will have beneficial effects for both the borrower and lender. ICICI Bank also believes that the potential demand for creating a large secondary market for microfinance receivables would come from more than 300 commercial and co-operative banks with substantial priority sector requirements and from mutual funds who would be attracted to the AAA ratings of the micro-credit portfolio.

Partnership model

Under the partnership model, the MFI sources loans directly in the books of ICICI Bank and continues to monitor and recover loans thus disbursed. This releases the MFIs from their capital constraint and allows them to achieve rapid increase in outreach. The NGO/MFI continues to perform the role of social intermediary, a role for which it is more than adequately equipped, while the financial intermediation and therefore the credit risk is left to the bank. This is a model that makes effective use of the strengths of both partners.

The partnership between ICICI Bank and CASHPOR Financial and Technical Services in the Chandauli district of Uttar Pradesh is one example of this. In this instance, ICICI Bank provides the necessary financial resources in terms of working-capital assistance to the partner to meet administrative costs when cash flows are inadequate, and lends directly to the CFTS borrowers, bearing the entire risk. Cashpor forms the intermediary SHGs and joint-liability groups and is also responsible for setting up and running the disbursement, monitoring and collection mechanisms and systems.

Another example is the arrangement with the NGO Micro-credit Foundation of India based in Chennai (formerly Madras), to outsource SHG development, maintenance of groups, credit linkage and recovery of loans. Under the arrangement, the Foundation facilitates formation of SHGs and helps them acquire the capability to generate income for the group. Later, it will provide finance for income-generating activities. In all these areas, ICICI Bank would back the foundation with the funds needed.

Dhan Foundation, Madurai, another partner NGO/MFI, has a target of forming 2150 groups. ICICI compensates it at the rate of US$200 per group. The total fee Dhan would receive as part of this arrangement would thus be around US$430 000. The bank expects this transaction to break-even in the third year of lending. In future, it is planned to meet the group promotion expenditure of MFIs under the partnership model by providing the MFI with a long-term loan, which it repays through a service fee charged to clients.

Since ICICI Bank maintains the books of accounts for these arrangements, it has to incur less expense on some crucial overheads. But still, it has to have a very well-managed client tracking and recovery system in order to ensure timely repayments as the arrangement involves a risk-sharing mechanism.

ICICI Bank is currently working on an arrangement with 25 MFIs, all partners of CARE India's large microfinance programme, CASHE (Credit and Savings for Household Enterprises). The bank, along with CARE, is looking to develop and devise a convergent model of partnership between large formal financial sector players and small grassroots financial intermediaries to enable sustained financial services to about 250 000 poor women clients in the three States of Andhra Pradesh, Orissa and West Bengal. This strategic tie-up is likely to be the single largest microfinance initiative to provide the poor with access to a variety of financial services, including credit, insurance and savings products. The CASHE programme, which currently facilitates credit linkages to the extent of some US$5m, should see this figure doubling within a year, through this partnership with ICICI Bank. For the bank, dealing with CARE in this manner obviates the cumbersome process of building and closing deals with 25 individual MFIs.

The partnership model, where ICICI Bank functions as a back-end provider of funds, capital and technology to MFIs on a first-loss sharing basis is expected to be the model that grows most rapidly, particularly for very poor rural households who are in their initial rounds of funding, usually under the self-help or joint liability group models. However, for repeat borrowers, asset-backed microfinance, the urban poor and the some what better off customers, the bank is also developing alternate and more direct channels such as franchisees, internet kiosks, agents (both individual and corporate) and, where necessary, even its own branches to supplement and complement the efforts of its MFI partners.

On-tap securitization

On-tap securitization is a portfolio buy-out but over an extended period, where the MFI and the bank are involved in continuous sourcing of loans and assigning of receivables to the bank. The portfolio buy-out deals are recent events so the on-tap will follow soon with at least some of these MFIs. This product can prove to be very useful given that the MFI can confidently build its assets on the strength of the continuing commitment from the bank over such an extended period.

Conclusion

Table 9.1 (see page 114) summarizes the performance of the principal components of ICICI Bank's microfinance portfolio from 2002 to 2004.

Presently, with an outstanding amount of about US$63m, the microfinance portfolio is a very small proportion of the bank's total portfolio.

The vision of the ICICI Group is to deliver a comprehensive suite of products including loans, investment products, banking services, insurance policies and derivatives to a very large customer base. While the business potential from the other, more direct, channels is still being assessed, it looks likely that the MFI channel alone will be able to

Table 8.1 Performance of ICICI Bank's microfinance portfolio

Particulars	At 31 March 2002		At 31 March 2003		At 31 March 2004	
	Number of borrowers	O/s amount US$m	Number of borrowers	O/s amount US$m	Number of borrowers	O/s amount US$m
Direct advances to SHGs	21 900	3.41	65 080	13.96	0	0
Advances under partnership with MFIs	-	-	867	0.12	197 257	38.56
Securitized microfinance portfolio	-	-	-	-	16 666	2.22
Advance to MFIs for on-lending	-	1.12	-	1.04	-	0.43
Sub-total	21 900	4.53	65 947	15.12	213 923	41.21
Individual microfinance loans*	not available	11.44	not available	13.11	68 105	21.77
Total	**21 900**	**15.97**	**65 947**	**28.23**	**282 028**	**62.98**

*includes jewel loans and farmer finance

grow to absorb almost US$4bn of credit annually. ICICI Bank expects to play a significant role in helping the MFI channel realize its full potential. The other channels, operating in a complementary manner, will perhaps do an equally large amount of business across all the products and services offered by the bank and its group of companies.

Discussion questions

1. ICICI Bank has decided to use existing MFIs as retail outlets. Many Indian MFIs are already struggling to compete with other commercial banks, which are retailing micro-financial services direct to their clients through their large branch networks. Will ICICI Bank be able to identify enough strong and effective partner MFIs to enable the Bank to achieve its ambitions?

2. Interest rates in India are falling, and microfinance customers are becoming more sophisticated in their choice of outlets, on the basis of price as well as service quality. Will ICICI Bank's partner MFIs be able to continue to charge interest rates at a level which covers their own costs and also allows the bank a reasonable margin?

3. Many multinational and national commercial banks have explicitly decided not to enter the microfinance market; they believe that they will need all their energy to survive and grow in the increasingly competitive global financial services market place. ICICI Bank also has global ambitions; does the bank risk over-diffusing its focus by becoming engaged in microfinance, even at the wholesale level?

4. Microfinance is still heavily subsidized in most countries, both directly and indirectly. ICICI Bank is a profitable, privately owned bank that cannot expect to benefit from non-commercial assistance. Can ICICI Bank hope to compete in microfinance against subsidized public sector banks and NGOs?

Chapter Nine
Microfinance at Banque du Caire, Egypt

CATHYRN CARLSON

Introduction

When Ahmed Munir El Bardai took over as Chairman of Banque du Caire (BdC) in February 2000, he became responsible for a loan portfolio including a large proportion of under- and non-performing loans – an unsurprising situation following decades of government ownership. In addition, he was also faced with another problem common to many state-owned banks around the world: a bloated, under-qualified workforce that, for legal and political reasons, could not be systematically reduced. In fact, it was this latter situation that inspired El Bardai to seek a radical solution: as part of his significant reengineering of BdC, El Bardai would establish a new loan product – the micro-loan – and attempt to transform up to 10 per cent of his 11 000-strong workforce into employees of this new business.

The macro environment

The banking sector in Egypt

Egypt's banking system comprises 62 commercial and specialized banks. Of these, 28 are commercial banks: four dominant, state-owned credit institutions and 24 smaller, private and joint venture banks. There are also 11 private and joint venture business and investment banks and 20 foreign bank branches operating in the country. While the smaller private and joint venture banks have chipped away at the state-owned banks' market share, the 'Big Four' continue to dominate the market, accounting for some 62 per cent and 67 per cent of total banking assets and deposits, respectively. These banks have tended to service public sector entities and are strong in retail banking because of their large branch networks. The four major joint-venture banks – Commercial International Bank, Misr International Bank, Nationale Societe Generale Bank, and Egyptian American Bank – are typically more profitable than their public sector counterparts and enjoy better asset quality. These joint-venture banks also attract the cream of local business and multinational corporations operating in Egypt. However, the joint-venture banks have relatively limited branch networks located exclusively in metropolitan areas. The government-owned banks are fighting back by improving the quality of their services and diversifying their product lines. Over the course of the past few years, two specialized banks (Agricultural Bank and the Housing Development Bank) have been granted commercial banking licenses. The Agricultural Bank has by far the largest branch network with 1012 outlets. This should further intensify competition for loans and deposits.

A brief history of Banque du Caire[1]

Banque du Caire was established in May 1952 as a private joint stock company. In 1957, it acquired the local operations of two of the most important French banks in Egypt, Comptoire Nationale d'Escompte de Paris (established in 1869) and Credit Lyonnais (established in 1875). BdC was nationalized in 1961, and is currently 100 per cent State-owned, operating under the auspices of the Ministry of Finance. In the 1970s, BdC was given a mandate to specialize in financing the state-owned construction and services sectors. However, deregulation in the early 1990s prompted BdC to offer a full range of commercial and investment banking services to both public and private sector companies.

With total assets of around US$9bn as of December 2002, BdC is the third largest of the four state-owned banks with an approximate 8 per cent share of total bank assets. It operates through a broad network of 228 domestic outlets (127 branches and 101 units) and 156 ATMs. The Bank also maintains five branches in the United Arab Emirates and holds equity stakes in several joint venture banks operating in Egypt as well as in three foreign banks: Saudi American Bank in Saudi Arabia (2.3 per cent), Cairo Amman Bank in Jordan (12 per cent), and Cairo International Bank in Uganda (44 per cent).

While the BdC enjoys the strong support of the Government and benefits from a large customer deposit base, several years ago it suffered a major setback in asset quality due to problems with several large customers. In 2001, in order to rectify the situation and to prepare the bank for eventual privatization, the chairman appointed several new senior managers with long track records in international private sector commercial banking. El Bardai himself was formerly with Arab African International Bank and, prior to that, served as Egypt Country Manager for Citibank.

Microenterprise in the Egyptian economy

With a population of approximately 66 million, and per capita gross national income of US$1500 in 2002 (according to World Bank statistics), Egypt is classified as a middle-income country. Nonetheless, it is estimated that around 16 per cent of the population (as of 1999–2000) remains below the poverty line. In recent years, national policy has promoted the development of the small and microenterprise sector which constitutes up to 98 per cent of the total number of all non-agricultural private businesses in Egypt. At present, approximately 94 per cent of credit goes to 2 per cent of the companies operating in Egypt (the biggest corporations) while the remaining 6 per cent goes to the other 98 per cent. The United States Agency for International

Development (USAID) has been trying to address this situation by providing assistance to the microenterprise sector since 1988. The team of the National Cooperative Business Association (NCBA) of the USA and Environmental Quality International (EQI), a privately owned, Egyptian development consulting firm, has won three separate contracts from USAID/Egypt to provide technical assistance to institutions interested in micro-credit. The current USAID programme, Small and Emerging Businesses (SEB), also offers access to guarantee facilities through the Credit Guarantee Corporation (CGC), an Egyptian institution partially funded by USAID. USAID has recently renewed its support for the SEB· program until 2007, and it is in the process of tendering the associated technical assistance contract once again.

BdC's entry into micro-credit

Through contacts with Dr Mounir Neamatallah, President of EQI, El Bardai realized that, by implementing a micro-credit programme, he could not only re-engineer his workforce (as loan officers for microfinance), but also expand his customer base for the future. He thus found a way to make use of BdC's large branch network that would support the image of BdC as a bank for the people.

Thus began the excellent cooperation between BdC and NCBA/EQI/USAID. The NCBA/EQI consortium has been providing technical assistance to BdC for three years. NCBA's efforts have been led by William Tucker who has been providing short-term consultancy since 1988 and has been based in Cairo since 1998. Including BdC, there are now 11 participating microfinance institutions benefiting from technical assistance under the SEB programme.

Demand and supply: the market for microfinance in Egypt

BdC estimates the total market for micro-credit, defined as microentrepreneurs with existing small businesses, in Egypt at around 2.4 million potential borrowers. Assuming a labor force equal to 34 per cent of the total population (growing at around 2 per cent per annum), approximately 11 per cent of the total is estimated to be in need of microfinance products. BdC estimates that only 7 per cent of the 2.4 million, or about 170 000 small entrepreneurs, currently have access to microfinance through providers other than itself. Of the remaining 93 per cent, it is thought that 1 per cent have some kind of existing relationship with a bank (although maybe not a loan) while the remaining 99 per cent, or 2.2 million small businesspersons, have no access to bank loans or to MFIs. However, they may in fact receive supplier credits or be members of ROSCAs.

Donor-funded NGOs – including the Alexandria Business Association (ABA) and other programmes financed by organizations such as USAID, CIDA (Canadian International Development Agency), KfW (the German development bank), UNICEF, CARE, and Save the

Children – served as the catalyst for the introduction of microfinance in Egypt at a time when banks were uninterested. In addition, the Social Fund (with support from the World Bank) has tried to promote micro-lending through banks by means of subsidized interest rates.

Compared to the other ten institutions tracked and supported by NCBA/EQI, BdC, with more than 50 000 loans, is by far the largest in terms of the number of current individual borrowers. Closest in size to BdC is ABA, which has been in existence for 15 years and has approximately 28 000 borrowers excluding group lending (as of November 2003). The total number of borrowers from all 11 institutions is around 140 000 excluding group lending, and 202 000 including group lending. After only two-and-a-half years of micro-lending operations, BdC thus represents around 36 per cent and 25 per cent of the respective totals. In terms of current outstanding portfolio, BdC again leads the group with around EGP100m (US$17m) in outstanding loans. Excluding group lending, its closest competitor, ABA, holds a portfolio of EGP52m (US$8.5m) compared to the group as a whole with a total of EGP276m (US$45m). Including group lending, ABA's portfolio totals EGP55m (US$9m) and that of the group as a whole stands at EGP287m (US$47m). BdC has clearly outstripped the other institutions tracked and supported by NCBA/EQI/USAID in terms of the speed and extent of its outreach.

In terms of commercial bank competitors, one of the other state-owned banks provides micro-loans at five of its branches. Also, the National Bank for Development, a private sector bank, has been actively engaged in providing micro-loans for the past seven or eight years with support from USAID.

Based on this market analysis, in the coming years BdC aims to reach one million borrowers (more than 40 per cent of the total market).

The micro solution

Implementation – the commitment of management

The key factor for any bank in the successful development of a new business line – in addition to capital, access to necessary infrastructure and knowledge of international best practice – is the acceptance and support of management. In the case of BdC, the Bank's new Chairman, El Bardai, took the lead in promoting the micro-lending product, while Gamil Salem, General Manager and board member of BdC, was chosen actually to execute the bank's move into microfinance. Salem is an information communication technology (ICT) specialist and 20-year veteran of Citibank. Before joining BdC, he was in charge of the development of Citibank's worldwide ICT network for emerging market small and medium enterprises (defined as those with a turnover of US$5 000 to US$50m).

Salem began the roll out of the micro-credit project in several branches in Upper Egypt, a relatively poor region of Egypt compared to

Cairo and other major urban areas. He figured, correctly, that if he could make micro-credit work in these branches, he could make it work nationwide. But first, Salem would have to overcome a major obstacle. When formulating the original business plan, BdC had expected to obtain a guarantee from CGC. A memorandum of understanding was signed between USAID, BdC and CGC under which CGC would provide a guarantee for up to 90 per cent of BdC's micro-credit portfolio. However, after months of negotiations, the deal was never concluded and, due to the lack of this guarantee, BdC's chairman was reluctant to start on the new business plan. However, Salem managed to persuade the board to allocate him a much reduced capital amount of US$1m to prove his case for micro-credit on a test basis – with the expectation that the guarantee would eventually be put in place and he would then be able to expand the business.

Microfinance operations began in July 2001. As the programme succeeded, Salem was able to persuade the board gradually to increase the capital allocation. Because of the absence of the guarantee and the resulting delay in start-up and expansion of the micro-credit business, today's portfolio is less than originally projected. However, the very low default rates illustrate that the guarantee was in fact unnecessary. So, although the risk of micro-credit business is perceived to be high, based on three years of data it is clear that it has made better sense for BdC to be self-insured in the form of adequate loan-loss provisions than it would have made to take advantage of the guarantee.

Another obstacle Salem faced in implementing the new micro-loan business was the need to persuade employees, from branch manager level down, that this was not simply an underhand plot to reduce staff. Employees were wary at first; they had never seen a senior level executive from head office, let alone interacted with one. The problem of motivating older employees – mostly men in their 40s and 50s – was tackled by a strategy of positive motivation. Those employees deemed qualified by their branch managers would take part in a training programme developed with the assistance of EQI. The best performers would then be invited to become team managers and eventually trainers. In spite of this opportunity, approximately 20 per cent of the employees selected were not interested in going into the micro-lending business. Loan officers were meant to spend most of their time outside the bank in the local communities (potential customers) in which they lived and their remuneration would be linked to their success. Such a strategy was radical in that, traditionally, bank employees enjoyed the prestige associated with office jobs as well as their relatively high, fixed salaries. Branch managers were also sceptical at first, but were given monetary incentives to undertake micro-lending and to expand the customer base as outlined below. Salem tried another new method in convening an annual meeting in Cairo of all staff involved in micro-credit. The Chairman of BdC presented awards to outstanding employees.

After setting up the programme, Salem hired Amro Abouesh to take over responsibility for micro-lending. Abouesh began his career as a consultant to the *Friedrich Ebert Stiftung* (FES) in Cairo in SME entrepreneurship, development, and training. He later worked as a consultant with AFPA (*Association Francaise pour la Formation Professionnelle des Adultes*) on the establishment of new enterprises before becoming Assistant for SME Affairs to the Minister of Economy and Foreign Trade. After completing his MSc at the University of Reading, Abouesh returned to the ministry as a short-term consultant. It was here that he was approached by El Bardai.

The Executive Committee, which directs BdC's ongoing operations, reports directly to the bank's board. In line with the importance of the micro-credit business in the overall strategy of the bank, Abouesh is a member of this committee. The Committee's Vice Chairman, Mrs Mona Fahmy Yassine (also formerly with Citibank and Chase for more than 20 years), is increasingly devoting her attention to micro-credit as its significance for BdC increases.

Figure 9.1 (opposite) shows an abbreviated diagram of the present management structure of the micro-credit product at BdC.

The software – staff organization and training

As national product manager, Abouesh oversees the implementation and management of the micro-credit business. At the outset, branch managers were asked to identify field specialists and their potential supervisors from their current branch staff. Field specialists, called loan extension officers, report to a supervisor who, in turn, reports to the branch manager. About 8 per cent of BdC's workforce, around 720 people, are dedicated to the micro-lending business. Specific jobs include: branch manager, supervisor, loan extension officer, branch accountant (reporting to the branch manager), and internal controller (reporting to the branch manager and to the external audit department) who conducts unannounced reviews of accounting, loans and incentive payments. The external audit department reports to Abouesh and to the board of directors and carries out periodic, unannounced reviews of branch procedures and internal controls on a random basis. Branch managers, branch accountants, and internal controllers devote only a portion of their time to the micro-credit business.

The emphasis placed on thorough staff training was instrumental to the success of the micro-credit product at BdC. The first step in the process was a one-day orientation for branch managers in order to gain their commitment to the new product and to prepare them to identify initial supervisors and loan extension officers. The staff were selected to participate in the 10-day EQI training which comprised classroom and field exercises covering credit, marketing and communication techniques, as well as instruction on the loan tracking system. USAID and the bank (head office) paid all the related expenses, including travel to Cairo and lodging costs of trainees. Later, supervisors, together with one computer specialist from each branch, participated in a one-week training course on the loan tracking system. As additional field staff are

Figure 9.1 Micro-credit management at BdC

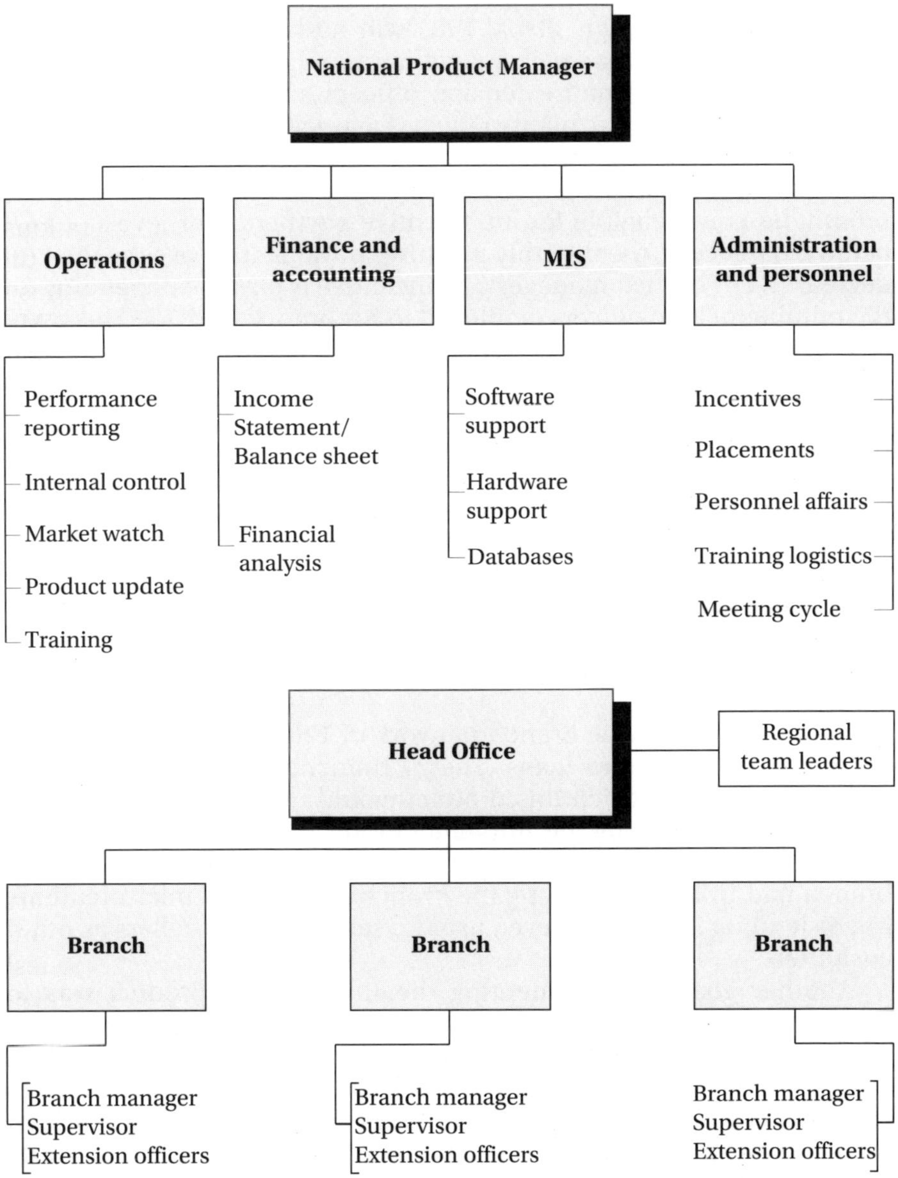

```
                     National Product Manager
                              |
     ┌────────────┬───────────┴──────────┬──────────────┐
 Operations   Finance and              MIS         Administration
              accounting                            and personnel

 Performance    Income            Software          Incentives
 reporting      Statement/        support
                Balance sheet                       Placements
 Internal control                 Hardware
                                  support           Personnel affairs
 Market watch   Financial
                analysis          Databases         Training logistics
 Product update
                                                    Meeting cycle
 Training
```

```
                    Head Office ─────── Regional
                         |              team leaders
       ┌─────────────────┼─────────────────┐
     Branch            Branch            Branch

 Branch manager    Branch manager    Branch manager
 Supervisor        Supervisor        Supervisor
 Extension officers Extension officers Extension officers
```

added, they are trained on-the-job by existing officers. More recently, a training of trainers programme was implemented and 14 of the best supervisors and field officers were promoted to regional team leaders and became the micro-credit training team within the bank.

Initial projections were based on ten loan extension officers and one supervisor per branch. However, due to the slow rollout, the bank did not meet the original numbers of employees, borrowers or loans.

There is now an average of three or four loan extension officers in most branches, with up to seven in the most active branches in Cairo. As part of its further expansion plans, BdC will add more loan officers in branches where the market is not yet saturated.

Remuneration of loan extension officers and their supervisors is based on an incentive structure which is a function of both the number of loans disbursed and the portfolio at risk (PAR) attributed to an individual officer. If an officer's PAR is greater than 3.5 per cent in any given month, he is not eligible for an incentive payment. For levels of PAR below 3.5 per cent, the monthly incentive payable increases as the PAR decreases. For branch managers, an incentive is payable depending on the number of loan officers employed in his branch, provided his overall PAR is less than 3.5 per cent. The incentive scheme has been designed to allow participants to maximize their bonuses by generating high-quality loan portfolios based on large numbers of borrowers. Branch managers and supervisors can increase their bonuses by assigning more staff to this loan product. In addition to monetary incentives, employees are also eligible to receive non-monetary awards such as recognition for 'Most Revenue per Employee' or 'Most Borrowers', and to participate in special activities such as periodic meetings with the bank's chairman.

The hardware – the underlying infrastructure

BdC owns a nationwide branch network of 120 branches of which 96 presently provide micro-loans. The 24 branches not active in micro-credit are those in which this product would not make sense (tourist areas, etc.). As part of the implementation process, an appropriate space – convenient to customers and not overly intimidating – in each branch had to be allocated by the branch manager to micro-lending. Micro-lending clients, however, use the same cashiers/tellers as other customers.

Another goal in implementing the micro-credit product was to avoid crowding in branches. To ensure efficiency, paperwork is kept to a minimum. EQI has developed and installed a loan tracking system on a stand-alone computer in each branch. These computers are linked to each branch's main computer and to the head-office network. The loan tracking system and daily reconciliation ensures accuracy and a proper degree of internal control and is consistent with work processes of tellers and accounting policies and procedures.

There is a plan to reorganize personnel in the micro-credit business into three teams each managed by a team manager, who will have six managers reporting to him/her. Each of these managers will, in turn, have six branches under his/her supervision. Each team manager will, therefore, be responsible for the performance of 36 branches under the new system. At the same time, branch managers continue to be involved with the micro-loan product. EQI is in the final stages of elaborating another management tool to be used to compare the performance of the three teams, and each of the branches, supervisors, and loan officers. It will be open to everyone and therefore transparent. Initially, six items will be monitored monthly including: revenue generated per employee, number of active borrowers, number of employees, portfolio at risk, amount of outstanding portfolio, and average debt of all borrowers. These items will be tracked for each branch and the system will allow a comparison between branches as well as a comparison to the average. Finally, all branches will be ranked according to gross revenue less loan loss provisions generated per dedicated employee. Ultimately, branches will be ranked according to the micro-loan product's contribution to overall bank profitability.

USAID covered much of the cost of staff training, as well as the costs of all technical assistance provided by NCBA/EQI. USAID also underwrote the development of the loan tracking system over a period of several years and provided the system free of charge to BdC. Total monetary costs of USAID assistance, however, were minor. BdC invested in all other necessary equipment and is also supporting the costs of the new management team, software licenses, staff incentives, and the designated office space in each of the branches. Finally, BdC has allocated the capital necessary to establish and expand the micro-loan portfolio from its own resources on a commercial basis.

The product

BdC presently only offers micro-loans at all its branches. However, three branches are experimenting with savings. There are no particular features specific to very small savings accounts; there is no minimum balance to open a savings account, although stamp duty of about US$3 is payable, and savings can be withdrawn on demand. Savings products are the same as those that were available before micro-banking was established, although previously the minimum balance necessary to open an account was decided by the branch manager. Micro-savings clients are served by the same staff at the same counters as other customers.

Loan size ranges from EGP3000–10 000 with summary terms and conditions as shown on Table 9.1 (overleaf, page 126).

The interest rate of 16 per cent flat is based on proven market acceptance and desire for product profitability as originally estimated by EQI. There are no additional fees. Inflation in Egypt is estimated at around 3 per cent.

The basic premise on which BdC's micro-loan business is based is that anybody is bankable as long as they have an ID (by law, everyone in Egypt must have an ID and this is increasingly the case) and fulfill certain other requirements. Target clients are those with a business that has been in existence for a minimum of one year. This business should be a service, manufacturing or commercial activity and family income should be derived primarily from this business. There are no poverty criteria *per se* and no attempt is made to track the success of a

Table 9.1 BdC loan terms and conditions

Clients	Self-employed individuals
Loan size	Up to EGP3000 (US$490) for first loan Up to EGP4500 (US$735) for the second loan, and so on
Loan use	Working capital/fixed assets
Interest rate	16% flat p.a. (no declining balance) (26–28% APR depending on term)
Term	Four–12 months at client's discretion
Repayment	Equal monthly instalments
Documentation	Photocopy of ID, electricity receipt (if available) and registration certificate of business (if registered)
Security	Promissory notes for each instalment plus guarantee cheque for total loan amount
Guarantee	Signature of relative (usually spouse) as guarantor for total amount
Pre-payment	Yes, but must wait until expiration of original term in order to receive new loan
Approval authority	Loan extension officer and supervisor

particular business or employment generated once a loan has been made. Farming activities do not qualify for loans. Marketing is carried out through word-of-mouth and direct visits by loan extension officers to small businesses in their areas of coverage. There has been no formal advertising campaign, although a product brochure is in development.

Micro-entrepreneurs, in general, do not keep accounting records and 99 per cent of clients have no formal credit history. Credit risk for initial loans is reduced by starting with low loan amounts and by providing a proper orientation to the customer. The initial lending decision depends primarily on the reputation and character of the potential borrower as assessed by the loan extension officer and his supervisor based on discussions with the applicant's suppliers and neighbours. The borrower must pledge on the application form that the loan is for business purposes. Although there are no physical collateral requirements, each client must provide BdC with post-dated cheques (promissory notes as opposed to conventional cheques) in the amount of each repayment as well as a cheque for the entire loan amount. The client actually signs for twice the loan amount as the cheque for the full amount would allow the bank to collect the full outstanding balance at any point in time. Each borrower is also required to have a guarantor for his/her loan, usually his spouse or another close relative, who also signs the loan agreement and must promise to pay if the borrower fails to do so. In Egyptian society, personal reputation is very important and social cohesion is strong. It is prestigious to borrow from a bank. This means that a person will go to great lengths to avoid defaulting on a loan and promissory notes are taken extremely seriously. If presented to the police, an immediate gaol term of six to 12 months is the norm. In BdC's experience, there has so far been no need to send anyone to gaol although several arrests have been made. Instances of default over 120 days have been extremely rare.

A standard one-page loan application/contract has been developed. This document is generated by the loan tracking system and is thus automatically linked to the bank's accounting system and ICT network. This standardization also saves substantially on legal costs. Approval for repeat loans is automatic and can be processed within ten minutes, but the bank must be prepared to meet this expectation. The sole criterion to obtain a new loan is timely repayment of the previous loan and clients can only move up in steps by repaying one loan and then taking another. The average loan size is around US$300. BdC's client retention rate is about 80 per cent. Experience indicates that, by means of continued emphasis on this simple policy, about 80 per cent of borrowers pay monthly instalments on time and of the remaining 20 per cent, 19 per cent pay one or two days late. Loan extension officers can concentrate on the final 1 per cent who do not repay their loans on schedule. In practice, a customer is required to make one visit to the bank, when he receives his initial loan. Following disbursement, he can send someone else to the bank with the loan instalments if he is too busy to attend in person. BdC is now considering hiring a professional collection agency whose fees would be paid by the borrower in order to further facilitate loan collection.

Once the customer has built a solid relationship with BdC, future services, such as consumer and small business loans, can be considered.

The results

Financial impact
BdC's micro-lending is expected to reach EGP300m or US$50m by 2005, compared to the present total of EGP100m (US$17m). The value of the micro-loan portfolio in US dollar terms would have been greater had the Egyptian pound not devalued from 3.78EGP/US$ in July 2001 to 6.13EGP/US$ in Dececember 2003 (the exchange rate was floated in January 2003 after a decade of being fixed to the US$). On a cumulative basis, BdC has served more than 65 000 borrowers with around 100 000 loans amounting to a total of nearly EGP300m or US$50m. In terms of absolute size, the micro-loan portfolio is not significant; as at 30 June 2002, BdC's total loan portfolio stood at EGP26bn or US$4.2bn and deposits at EGP32bn or US$5.2bn. In terms of number of loans, the micro-lending portfolio stands at around 50 000 while the bank as a whole holds around 1.6 million loans and savings accounts.

BdC is not in a position to release detailed financial figures. However, according to Abouesh, the average micro-lending yield of 26–28 per cent per annum more than covers the product's direct costs including the cost of capital estimated at 10 per cent per annum (BdC pays an average interest rate of 8 per cent on deposits compared to a rate for corporate borrowing of around 13 per cent), notional loan loss provisions of 2 per cent and direct costs of around 10 per cent. Direct costs are higher than they would be if a completely new, younger staff was recruited from the market today. Also, as the majority of staff members have only started working in this area in the past six months, their productivity is not yet at maximum levels. A typical branch with three employees dedicated to micro-lending will reach break-even within nine months. Direct costs of around 10 per cent per annum are expected to decrease to around 3 per cent as loan extension officers mature (expected loan portfolio of EGP275 000–300 000 or US$50 000 per officer). For the planned new branches (see below), it is expected that staff costs will be around one third of those experienced at existing branches.

In addition, while the profit margin exceeds that achieved by most other products offered by BdC, overhead costs have not yet been apportioned. Their inclusion would add significantly to total product costs as BdC's overheads are inflated by its excess labour force (those employees who cannot or do not wish to be retrained for micro-lending and/or do not wish to accept early retirement packages). Overheads are also higher due to the bank's past policy of owning its own premises. Efforts are underway to correct this situation and to thus increase the bank's cost competitiveness.

In spite of the relatively high direct costs and the fact that overhead costs have not yet been allocated, Abouesh believes micro-credit to be the bank's highest yielding product in terms of return on assets and return on equity. Overall, BdC's return on average assets was 1.7 per cent per annum for the fiscal year ending 30 June 2002 and return on shareholders' equity was 4.13 per cent per annum for this same period. These figures reflect the significant problems of loan quality inherited by the new management. In contrast, the quality of the micro-loan portfolio is excellent with current PAR >3 days of 0.49 per cent, PAR>30 days of 0.2 per cent, and PAR >90 days at 0.05 per cent. The maximum PAR >90 days experienced by BdC since the commencement of the micro-lending activity is 0.1 per cent. In order to adopt a more conventional commercial banking approach, the present system of provisioning (PAR 3–30 days 10 per cent of loan amount, PAR 30–60 days 25 per cent, PAR 60–90 days 50 per cent, and PAR >90 days 100 per cent) is likely to be revised in order to maintain an overall loan-loss provision of between 1–2 per cent of the total micro-loan portfolio in any given year.

Personal impact
The experiences of three customers of a typical branch office in Cairo illustrate the impact of BdC's micro-credit product on the lives and livelihoods of the bank's target customer base. While these examples are all male, approximately 23 per cent of BdC's borrowers are women and a greater proportion of women entrepreneurs are active in rural areas compared to large capital cities.

Moatsan Ahmed is a small-scale clothing retailer and is repaying his second loan from BdC. Ahmed has been in business since 1988, and is married with one child. Before becoming a customer of the bank, he financed his business with loans from relatives and credit granted by wholesalers (his suppliers). However, this latter source of credit became unavailable due to difficult economic circumstances. Ahmed was approached by the local BdC extension officer. According to Ahmed, had he not had the possibility of taking a loan from BdC, he would not have been able to purchase inventory for his business without selling some of his assets and his revenue would have declined substantially. Over time, he aspires to borrow the maximum amount available from BdC and to move beyond the micro-lending product (into the SME lending bracket) in order to eventually have his own factory.

Naser Moustafa is another customer of BdC. He owns an eyeglass shop, and fabricates lenses based on a prescription from a registered doctor. The business was founded by his father in the 1950s; he took over in 1990. Moustafa has two children and his son eventually plans to run the business in his turn. Moustafa is in the process of repaying his first loan from BdC. He was previously a customer of one of the micro-credit foundations from which he had taken eight successive loans. A BdC loan extension officer approached him and, after comparing terms, Moustafa decided to take a loan from the bank. He explains that the bank was faster in disbursing the loan than the foundation from which he used to borrow. At BdC, processing of the first loan takes a maximum of five days and took only three days in his case while he had to wait weeks when dealing with the foundation. Also, at 16 per cent flat per annum, the interest rate charged by BdC is less than that charged by the foundation (20 per cent flat). He is pleased with the service he receives from the bank and plans to borrow increasing amounts that he says will eventually exceed the maximum loan available from the foundation. He employs two people in his shop, not including himself, and also has a workshop in which he employs five people to make glass for other shops. He would like to buy more advanced equipment in order to be able to increase the range of products he can offer. With a larger loan, he would also be able to buy glass more cheaply in bulk and would then be able to sell his products more cheaply and, presumably, in greater quantity.

Finally, Hameda Hafez is a car mechanic. Hafez is repaying his second loan from BdC. With his loans, he has been able to purchase the new tools necessary to repair cars built with increasingly sophisticated technology. In the past, without the new tools, Hafez had to turn away business. He also would like to take further loans from the bank. Hafez wants to buy a crane in order to be able to lift heavy car parts, such as the engine block and he wants to hire an assistant. He also wants to renovate his simple workplace, to add lights so that he will be able to work at night and to make it more attractive to his customers. He is grateful to BdC and to the loan extension officer who approached him at his workplace; the bank has helped him to get his business going.

The way forward

Based on its success to date, BdC is planning to expand the outreach of its micro-lending product by creating 150 new branches or 'bureaux' dedicated solely to micro-credit. Currently, while the market leader in terms of the number of borrowers on a national scale, BdC is always second in non-urban areas behind the more locally concentrated NGOs present in particular regions. This is not surprising given that the vast majority of BdC's branches are in Egypt's cities. By setting up dedicated bureaux in more rural areas, BdC will be able to reach significantly more of its target market. To this end, BdC considered setting up a joint venture with the national Post Office in order to benefit from its extensive branch network. However, for various reasons, it was concluded that the most feasible solution would be to set up entirely new bureaux.

The establishment of these new bureaux is a radical departure from previous policy with regard to micro-lending in that the impact so far on the total salary bill of the bank has been nil. With the setting up of new bureaux, the salary bill will necessarily increase; it is planned to take on as many as 1000 new employees. By hiring these new people, BdC will be able to change the cost structure of its micro-loan product because the younger employees the bank is looking to recruit will be considerably less expensive than those presently employed in the business, and will be more willing to adapt to current market practice instead of expecting to be rewarded on the basis of seniority. As part of its expansion strategy, BdC also plans to hire more women loan extension officers in order to reach out to more female borrowers, who currently make up only 20–25 per cent of its outstanding customer base.

In terms of new products, BdC plans to introduce new small and medium-size business loans and to cross-sell other bank products for SMEs including micro-savings. Micro-lending is also regarded as a platform for the development of retail banking, a target sector for expansion within BdC.

There are also plans to embed insurance in the micro-loan product from the second quarter of this year – at no charge to the borrower – by tying up with a large domestic insurance provider. It is extremely important for BdC to maintain its policy of 'no hidden charges' so that the client receives the face value of the loan he is contracting for with no extra amounts subtracted. This insurance will repay the remaining loan balance including interest should the borrower die or become permanently disabled during the term of his loan. BdC is also thinking of introducing an additional micro-insurance product to be paid for by the borrower and is currently negotiating a package deal that will be very inexpensive on an individual basis, due to the large customer base that the bank can bring to the table. Under such a policy, in the event of the death of the borrower, his heirs would receive in cash the amount of the original loan already repaid by the borrower and would not be required to make further repayments of principal or interest. It is possible that this same type of strategy, BdC acting as agent and making use of large-scale group negotiating power, can be employed with regard to the purchase of other items, such as mobile phones, by BdC's micro-borrowers.

Other ideas under discussion include the expansion of micro-lending abroad to BdC-owned branches in Uganda and possibly to those owned by joint venture partners in other countries in the Middle East and Asia.

Finally, with the help of USAID, Banque du Caire is contributing to the establishment of a credit bureau in Egypt.

Conclusion

The experience of BdC in the establishment and development of a commercially viable micro-lending business illustrates both the successes and the difficulties that can be encountered by a commercial bank in entering a domain once reserved for donor-funded NGOs. The speed with which significant scale of outreach and loan volume (according to microfinance standards) can be achieved provided certain conditions are met – supportive and motivated management, access to the necessary infrastructure and ICT systems, availability of capital, and knowledge of international best practice – has been convincingly demonstrated by the example of BdC. With regard to profitability, return on assets and return on equity in the micro-lending business have proven in this case to be greater than those earned by more traditional commercial banking products. However, profits from the micro-credit product are still comparatively small scale in absolute terms.

Finally, the experience of BdC has shown that partnerships between public entities such as USAID and private commercial enterprises can work to the benefit of all concerned as long as each of these institutions can bring to bear its comparative advantages without compromising the commercial viability of the micro-loan product in any way.

Sources:
1. Banque du Caire, Business Plan, June 2001.
2. EQI, Consolidated Lending Information, November 2003.
3. Abouesh, Amro, Presentation of Opinion on the Future of Microfinance in Egypt, November 2002.
4. Capital Intelligence, Banque du Caire Bank Report, September 2003.
5. Moody's Investors Service, Banque du Caire SAE Analysis, September 2003.
6. Banque du Caire, Annual Report 50 Years Golden Jubilee, 2002.

Acknowledgement

Special thanks to William Tucker of NCBA and Amro Abouesh, Gamil Salem, and other staff members of BdC.

Discussion questions

1. Although the financial contribution by USAID was very small, would the Banque du Caire's micro-finance initiative have taken place without USAID's assistance? Was there genuine 'additionality'?

2. Was the bank's entry into the microfinance market a strategic corporate decision, or was it the result of one or two 'product champions'? How can microfinance be introduced to banks which do not have such champions ?

3. BdC proposes setting up special bureaux to service microfinance clients. Will this promote or hinder the integration of microfinance, and its customers, into the Bank's mainstream operations?

Chapter Ten
Strategic partnerships in microfinance: the case of the Commercial Bank of Zimbabwe

KENNETH RUFASHA

Background and introduction

Commercial Bank of Zimbabwe (CBZ) is a commercial bank in Zimbabwe, a country in southern Africa with a population of 11.6 million people. Seventy-five percent of the population lives below the poverty line and most of them on less than US$1 per day. Gross domestic product (GDP) grew by 3.7 per cent in 1997 but has been declining since then, registering a fall of 7.3 per cent in 2003. Inflation is rampant, fluctuating within a range of 100–600 per cent over the period from 2001 to 2003.

The fast shrinkage of the employment market is forcing most former employees into the burgeoning informal sector. There are now an estimated 3 million people in the informal sector out of a total labour force of 5.5 million. Unemployment currently stands at 60 per cent. Sixty-six per cent of Zimbabwe's labour force works in agriculture, 24 per cent in services and 10 per cent in industry. Micro-entrepreneurs are engaged in all fields, including agriculture, mining, manufacturing, clothing, shoe making, cross-border trading, tourism, crafts and the general retail trade.

An estimated 90 per cent of informal sector entrepreneurs have no access to bank credit or formal financial services. There are about 60 licensed microfinance operators in the country, but less than ten have a significant presence in the informal sector and of these only two are commercial banks. Most other microfinance institutions offer consumer credit and target salaried employees.

Barclays Bank was the first financial institution to enter the small- and medium-enterprise credit market in 1988, with the help of funding from the World Bank. In 1996 CBZ followed the example of Barclays Bank, targeting informal and micro-enterprises. By 2003 there were 14 commercial banks in Zimbabwe, only two of which offered microfinance services. In 2000 Kingdom Bank entered this market, targeting CBZ's market and offering individual loans backed by a guarantee of a salaried relative through its subsidiary, Micro-King. Their portfolio performance is yet to be established.

A report by Bannock (2000) summarized the problems encountered in the microfinance sector as high bad debts; lack of staff capacity to assess, monitor and track debts; high staff turnover; poor systems and procedures; unavailability of management information systems; exhaustion of capital budgets to continue financing new loans.

A brief history of the bank

CBZ was born out of the collapsed Bank of Credit and Commerce International (BCCI) in 1991. BCCI owned 51 percent of the Bank of Credit and Commerce of Zimbabwe (BCCZ) and the balance was owned by the Government of Zimbabwe. Upon the demise of BCCI in 1991, the Government took up the entire shareholding of the bank and renamed the institution as CBZ.

A blaze of publicity accompanied the collapse of BCCI in 1991, after it was discovered the bank had disguised losses and was insolvent. CBZ experienced a run on deposits. By 1994, the bank was sinking under heavy losses and faced imminent collapse. The bank was technically insolvent, and all important links with the international community, including those with correspondent banks, had been severed. With a market share of 5 per cent in 1995 and occupying the fifth and last position in a market of five commercial banks, revival looked less likely than closure. Nevertheless, in 1997, the CBZ was successfully re-capitalized through a private placement in partnership with the International Finance Corporation (IFC), an affiliate of the World Bank, and ABSA Banking Group of South Africa, the largest banking group in sub-Saharan Africa. The due diligence process focused particularly on the nature and quality of the new relationships the bank had lately forged; the link with international development agencies was clearly helpful. IFC and ABSA took up 15 per cent and 26 per cent equity stakes respectively in the bank and both undertook to provide technical support. CBZ is now a listed company and the current shareholders include ABSA Banking Group [S.A.] (25.9 per cent); Libyan Arab Foreign Bank (12.4 per cent); the government (17.3 per cent). The rest of the shares are in the hands of companies and private individuals. CBZ is now the country's third largest bank in terms of deposits.

Changes at the top and CBZ's entry into microfinance

A new chief executive officer was appointed in 1995. He soon assembled a new management team. They defined their strategic task as being to design and implement a turnaround strategy to achieve profitability, solvency, and market leadership within five years. Their vision was 'to be the jewel of the banking industry before the year 2000'. (CBZ Strategic Planning Document, 1995). The management team realized that, as an underlying dimension of their strategy, they not only had to reshape their institution, but to redefine the boundaries of the banking industry at the same time.

Meanwhile, the Department for International Development (DFID) of the UK Government, was seeking to deliver microfinance services to the economically active poor. In 1995, CARE floated a proposal on behalf of DFID to all the commercial banks seeking a partner in the provision of microfinance to the informal sector. Only CBZ responded as it identified this as an opportunity to reverse the bank's fortunes.

CBZ's community banking model

Funding and the loan guarantee fund

DFID funded the initial costs of establishing and running the microfinance project and provided a fund-backed guarantee to the bank. Because the project was in a bank, it had to conform to the Central Bank's statutory requirements on loan security: 80 per cent of all loans had to be secured by immovable property or blocked funds.

At the start of the project, DFID placed US$750 000 in an account at CBZ, managed by CARE, to cover the bank against non-collectable microfinance loans. The guarantee covered 80 per cent of losses due to non-collectable first loans, and 60 per cent of second loans. In all subsequent loans after the second, the guarantee does not apply. The guarantee allayed concerns at CBZ about lending without security.

CARE was appointed by DFID to:

- manage the loan guarantee fund;
- process and reimburse guarantee claims;
- submit periodic performance reports;
- provide technical assistance to develop staff capacity and build systems and procedures

Target market, conditions, and safeguards

The microfinance facility targets existing and new micro-entrepreneurs. They are organized into self-selected groups of five to ten members which is in itself a risk-management mechanism in the form of beneficiary-facilitated screening. The initial requirements for the group to be eligible for borrowing are that each member opens an individual savings account and that they collectively also open a group savings account. The required minimum deposit of US$15 is below that for mainstream savings accounts of US$25, and is refundable upon closure of the account. By contrast, some NGO microfinance project's demand up to US$5 as a non-refundable joining fee.

CBZ borrowers qualify for initial loans ranging from US$85 to US$1300 repayable over three to six months. In subsequent borrowings, clients could be eligible for loans of up to US$1720 for repayment periods of six to 18 months. Like all other clients of the bank, the microfinance clients do not enjoy any grace period on the loans.

The individual loan limit is partly determined by considering the viability of the business and the business requirements, the individual account turnover and savings balance. The capacity of the group to guarantee, the total indebtedness of the group members and the group's integrity are other factors that influence loan sanctioning decisions.

The micro-loans are principally secured by cross-member joint and several liability guarantees. Clients may also pledge any moveable assets such as household effects and business equipment in order further to secure their personal borrowings and back up their guarantees on the other members' borrowings. The absence of such tangible assets does not necessarily mean rejection In any case, all pledged belongings remain in the possession of the owner or the borrower until a claim for restitution is made by either the bank or the guarantors.

Team cohesion within the groups acts as a powerful source of social control over the members to enforce loan repayments through normative influence and peer pressure. By defaulting, a member risks losing the pledged property and also jeopardizes long-standing social ties.

As an additional safeguard, each borrower maintains a minimum of 20 per cent of the initial loan value[1] in the savings account which is non-withdrawable until the loan of the member and those of the other group members are fully settled. Group members are only eligible for repeat loans if all the members have discharged their previous loans.

The bank invoked the group guarantees in less than 4 per cent of the loans disbursed so far and, more often than not, the individuals eventually turn up to settle the loan in full. In some cases, CBZ may never become aware of individual members' difficulties, which are resolved either by assistance from members or by peer pressure. In other cases, loan arrears are fully settled by the bank pooling the members' 20 per cent retained savings and the group's savings account. To date, there has not been a single instance where the bank has had to fall back on pledged assets to recover debt.

Starting in January 2002, the bank took additional protection to reduce risk on micro-loans. All microfinance and other mainstream banking borrowers compulsorily subscribe to a loan and funeral insurance product. This insurance package covers: loan arrears in the event of an absconding defaulter and outstanding loan balances and funeral costs upon the client's death or, if included in the cover, the funeral costs on the death of the client's dependants.

Deposit-taking as the source of loan funding

The microfinance loans are financed by deposits collected from the microfinance clients, the growth of which is driven by a number of factors:

- a prospective microfinance client of CBZ is required to operate an individual savings account for at least a month in order to be eligible for borrowing;
- customers have to maintain a minimum deposit of 20 per cent of their loan size in the individual savings;
- there are always customers who hold deposits with the bank and are subject to a waiting period while they undergo a four-week orientation programme run by the loan officers and while their applications are being processed.

This deposit-taking process taps into the special functions of clearing banks to create money. This is because the loan disbursement involves a book transfer between the individual loan and the individual savings account both in the name of the same client and is rarely accompanied by instant and full withdrawal by the borrower. This creates capacity for the bank to enter into another lending cycle from the higher deposit platform. Clients only part-withdraw loan proceeds, leaving a significant part as savings deposits, which raises the previous deposit base.

Further, the half-yearly interest payments to savings accounts raises the bank's microfinance savings deposits, which in turn technically raises the bank's lending capacity. Customer withdrawals are also recycled as deposits in the form of increased sales turnover after utilizing the microfinance loans.

The marketing function

The bank's microfinance products and services mainly comprise loans, savings and insurance products. These are targeted at micro-entrepreneurs within the 18 to 65 year-old age group. Generally they earn less than US$35 per month before taking bank support. The project aims to have a minimum of 80 per cent of women clients of this type

To reach this target group, CBZ employs a mix of marketing methods, although direct marketing has been the major vehicle for raising market awareness. The officers regularly visit clients in the field and connect with civic organizations; social groups and business associations such as housing cooperatives; burial societies; informal traders' associations; church associations and rotating credit associations. They also attend mass meetings convened by local municipalities and district councils.

In addition, videotapes of CBZ's microfinance facilities and stories of successful microfinance clients are played daily in the banking halls. This is complemented by leaflets and framed wallcharts distributed in the branches during field-marketing errands and at business meetings by mainstream and micro-banking staff.

The bank conducts annual events that attract wide press coverage. One such event, run in conjunction with one of the national weekly newspapers, is an 'Entrepreneur of the Year Award for the Informal Sector' ceremony. The event attracts press and television publicity at national level. The microfinance services are also marketed at national trade exhibitions such as the annual international trade fair, as well as the agricultural shows that are held in every city. CBZ's mainstream and microfinance staff jointly organize and participate in such events.

At selected points on national highways and in urban areas, the microfinance facilities and other banking products feature on the bank's billboards. In addition, the bank's website (www.cbz.co.zw) is regularly updated.

Delivery channels

The bank's branch network is the principal service delivery channel for all microfinance services. Unlike NGO microfinance projects, from the beginning, CBZ's microfinance initiative used the advantages which the bank's branch network provided.

Piloted first at Highfield branch in Harare in 1996, the project was subsequently rolled out to Bulawayo (1997), Chitungwiza (1997) and Mutare (1998) – cities with high micro-enterprise concentration and a combined population of 3.6 million. At Highfield and Chitungwiza, sub-branches of the two branches, threatened with closure due to lack of viability, were converted into savings centres. More than half the customers at these sub-branches are microfinance customers. Like all sub-branches, they are headed by a manager who reports to the overall branch manager stationed at the main branch in the same town. Sub-branches provide core banking services such as counter service and account opening facilities. Microfinance units operate as departments within the sub-branches. Sub-branches are part of the main branch for all practical purposes and are only meant to ease operational congestion at the main branches and to have service points closer to the market.

In addition to these 'bricks-and-mortar' delivery channels, microfinance savings and insurance products can be accessed by customers through internet-banking and PC-banking facilities. Most microfinance customers do not use these, but 85 per cent of customers have debit cards for ATM cash withdrawals and point-of-sales purchases.

Market-based pricing

CBZ's microfinance loans bear an interest rate of 7 per cent above the bank's prime lending rates plus a flat 1 per cent fee. All balances in arrears attract a surcharge of 10 per cent over and above the normal interest rate. These are the same rates levied on the bank's secured medium risk loans and the rates are still lower than those on consumer loans. In keeping with standard banking practice, the rates applicable to microfinance loans are market-linked and the bank's prime lending rate has been fluctuating between 49 per cent and 100 per cent per annum over the period from 1998 to 2003. However, temporary self-correcting market fluctuations have seen the bank's prime lending rate soar to more than 500 per cent in January 2004, only to fall to just over 100 per cent by February. NGO microfinance loans usually attract a flat rate upon disbursement which translates to an industry average of 90 per cent per annum. The bank's interest rates have been above this only for brief periods when market rates rose above 90 per cent per annum in late 2003. Since the microfinance project started, the prime lending rate has been well below 70 per cent, which makes the bank's loans cheaper than those from other sources.

Operations management, human resources and MIS

The head of microfinance is in charge of the microfinance portfolio. He is stationed at the head office and reports to the general manager of the credit division.

The service delivery cycle
At branch level, the microfinance project is administered by 16 loan officers, distributed across the four branches. The officers at each branch are assimilated into the branch or sub-branch as the community banking department.

The loan officers take batches of ten to 40 new customers through a four-week orientation and induction programme. This allows them to understand the project concept and the officers can start establishing personal relationships with the new customers; this is critical for the project. The loan officers also train customers on basic management techniques, with an emphasis on cash-flow management and how to account for personal expenses as drawings, which are separate from business expenses, in order to be able to sustain loan repayments and operational viability.

The loan officers have a lead officer at branch level who reports to the head of microfinance who, in turn, is ultimately accountable to top management for the entire project

The service delivery tasks are divided between the head office, the branch manager and mainstream staff at the branches.

1. Loan officers
- opening of micro-savings accounts
- customer induction and training
- loan application appraisals
- security documentation
- loan disbursement
- monitoring of loan repayments and follow-ups on defaulters

2. Head of microfinance
- loan approval/rejection

3. Branch manager
- as with all other accounts, the manager approves the opening of the savings account if the bank's normal conditions and the special condition on minimum deposit are satisfied
- co-signs loan approvals, with the head of microfinance
- co-signs the offer letter on the approval of the loan, with the loan officer

4. Branch staff (mainstream)
- deliver cash deposit/withdrawal services
- provide services such as balance and transaction information

These actors all have mutually supportive and interactive roles in the delivery of loan products.

In assessing the loan applications, officers visit prospective borrowers at their homes and businesses. They also consult with clients' business associates and neighbours to ascertain their social and economic status.

Loan applications and appraisal reports are sent to head office and are normally processed and returned to the branches within 48 hours.

Upon return of the documents, in accordance with CBZ's policy of dual control and accountability, the branch manager co-signs all loans approved by the head of microfinance. An offer letter, detailing the amount and conditions of the loan is issued to the client. If the client accepts, a copy remains with the client and two copies are sent to the bank. Each group member signs a joint and several liability guarantee.

All security documentation, completed by the loan officers and co-witnessed by the branch manager, is placed under the dual custodianship of the lead loan officer and the branch manager.

Another special feature of the loans being bank-administered is that the bank has spot access to all group members' and joint group accounts. This makes it possible for the bank to settle due loan repayments by instant auto-processed book transfers across the matching savings and loan accounts, an advantage which NGO microfinance institutions do not have. This reduces the incidence of loan defaults and related transaction costs as well as avoiding the need for the bank staff to visit the customer on every repayment date.

The bank's training department regularly includes microfinance staff in on-going in-house training programmes such as credit management, product knowledge and customer care. Such approaches ease staff integration challenges and facilitate collaboration.

Human resources issues

Although the project staff's costs are largely covered by DFID, both management and staff are to all intents and purposes bank employees. As such they are subject to the Banking Undertaking Act, which governs employee–employer relations, as well as the bank's human resources policy as applied to all employees and administered by the bank's human resources department. Similarly they have the same salaries and benefits as mainstream employees of similar grades. The bank is responsible for recruiting, disciplining and disengaging microfinance employees as with any other bank employee. The salary scales and benefits, and the sense of job security and pride associated with working for a bank, are way ahead of those in microfinance institutions run by non-banking organizations. This has helped to attract and retain good staff from academic and professional backgrounds with an interest in social work, including some from NGO microfinance projects.

High staff turnover has been a major challenge afflicting the microfinance sector. CBZ remains competitive in the microfinance industry with a staff turnover rate averaging below 0.5 per cent per annum since the project started, largely owing to the factors cited above.

A contentious issue is that all the microfinance staff join the bank at officer level and there is no lower grade. This sharply contrasts with the entry point in mainstream banking which is a clerical grade; mainstream employees have to earn promotion to officer grade over years of meritorious service. On the other hand, there is no higher level beyond the entry level within the community banking departments at branches and the absence of a clear-cut career path may be a problem. The perception of microfinance as a donor project within the bank is shared by some branch managers and mainstream employees.

Another challenge, which has been alleviated by the involvement of the donor, has been in staff development for microfinance employees. This is central to the project, given that the bank lacked competence in micro-lending, group management and transacting with the informal sector. CARE develops the bank's capabilities in best practices of microfinance and in the principles of group-based lending as well as training customers to manage their businesses.

Outcomes

Profitability

By March 2000, within four years of start-up, the CBZ microfinance project was achieving an operating self-sufficiency ratio of 105 per cent. Table 10.1 (below) shows the income and expenditure statement for the project for the years 2001 to 2003, after factoring out the donor's subsidy.

Table 10.1 shows that despite the decline in national aggregate demand, the Bank's microfinance operations continue to be profitable even without subsidy.

Table 10.1 *Income and expenditure statement for the years 2001–2003 (US$m)*

	2001	2002	2003
Interest income	0.2	0.06	0.09
Interest expense	(0.03)	(0.005)	(0.01)
Net interest income	0.17	0.055	0.08
Non-interest income	0.04	0.005	0.008
Total income	**0.21**	**0.06**	**0.088**
Provision for bad debts	(0.03)	(0.003)	(0.001)
Operating income	0.18	0.057	0.087
Operating expenditure	(0.08)	(0.037)	(0.037)
Operating profit (loss)	0.1	0.02	0.05
Subsidy	0.006	0.02	n.a.
Profit after subsidy	**0.106**	**0.04**	**0.05**

Table 10.2 *CBZ microfinance and bank profits (US$m)*

	2001	2002	2003
Microfinance profit (loss)	0.1	0.02	0.05
Bank profit (loss)	14.69	48.95	7.96
Profitability of microfinance portfolio as a percentage of overall profitability (%)	0.68	0.04	0.6

The sharp drop in bank-wide profits for 2003 is due to hyperinflation, which reached 600 per cent in that year.

Asset quality

Non-performing loans have averaged 1.5 per cent of the loan portfolio. This compares favourably with the bank's overall non-performing loan portfolio which averages 15 per cent, and that of NGO microfinance institutions which average over 12 per cent. Despite this, CBZ has now set up a loan-loss provisions account for 5 per cent of outstanding loans. By 2003, only US$2100 had been claimed from the loan guarantee fund for non-collectable debts

As a result, the guarantee fund has largely served as a letter of comfort to the bank and in 2000, by consensual agreement, its size was reduced to US$300 000.

Microfinance deposits and loan portfolio

There are few sustainable sources of loanable funds for NGO microfinance institutions as they cannot legally collect deposits from the market.

In 1998 and 1999, the deposits to loan ratios for CBZ's microfinance operation were 108.4 per cent and 119.3 per cent respectively. This indicates that deposits more than adequately funded the loan portfolio. Table 10.3 (below) shows the deposits, loans and the deposit to loan ratios for the last four years.

Table 10.3 *Deposit to loan ratios (US$m)*

Year	Deposits	Loans	Deposits to loans ratio
2000	0.3	0.54	56%
2001	1	0.6	167%
2002	0.3	0.11	273%
2003	1.1	0.3	367%

The bank's microfinance savings deposits reached 6.4 per cent of the bank's total savings deposits at the end of 2003. Savings deposits constituted 6.1 per cent of the bank's total deposit base of US$277 273 058 in November 2003. It is important to note that savings deposits are rated, after current account deposits, as the cheapest deposits for commercial banks. During the period 1999 to 2003, reflecting these relative cost differentials, interest rates on savings deposits have been fluctuating between 12 per cent and 20 per cent; current accounts earn between 5 per cent and 10 per cent whilst money market deposits fluctuated between 50 per cent and 90 per cent during the same period. Moreover, savings are generally the most stable form of deposits.

The microfinance loan portfolio of US$241 426 in November 2003 constituted 1.2 per cent of the bank's non-corporate loans. Microfinance loans are about four times covered by microfinance deposits. This leaves the excess savings deposits for investment across the bank's mainstream activities. All these figures seem small in US dollar terms because the rates of exchange that have evolved in Zimbabwe's hyperinflationary situation do not reflect day-to-day purchasing values. The Zimbabwe dollar to US dollar rate moved from around 40:1 in 2001 to more than 800:1 in 2003, and is still falling.

Microfinance deposits constitute the primary source of funding for microfinance loans within the bank. This positions CBZ's initiative ahead of similar NGO projects that are no larger than the size of their respective internal budget allotments. Their capital budgets are quickly exhausted leading to periodic suspension of lending. Two leading NGO microfinance institutions, ZWIFT and Zambuko Trust, have had to cope with frequent capital budget exhaustion. By contrast, when microfinance deposits were at one time exhausted in the bank in 2000, the deposit to loan ratio having fallen to 55.56 per cent, the funding gap was made good by funding from mainstream banking, which is always available when needed.

Some efficiency indicators

Comparative performance measures for CBZ and Zambuko Trust, an NGO microfinance institution, suggest that CBZ's staff are extremely productive and transaction costs are very efficient, because the microfinance operations are embedded within the bank.

Table 10.4 Performance measures' comparison between CBZ Microfinance and Zambuko Trust

	CBZ Microfinance	**Zambuko Trust**
Loans per officer	195	86
Cost per US$1 lent	US$0.009	US$0.018
Average loan size	US$135	US$78

Table 10.5 Summary project statistics (December 2003)

Number of loans disbursed to date (cumulative)	11 822
Number of loans outstanding	3 120
Number of savings deposit accounts	11 691
Percentage of female borrowers	70%
Jobs created (cumulative)	10 796

With regard to Table 10.4 (see previous page), the industry norm for loans per officer is 300, which suggests that there is scope for scale economies within the bank's growing microfinance operations.

Social and economic outcomes

The over-arching objective of the bank's partners reflects the belief that poverty can be sustainably alleviated among the economically active poor, through income generation and job creation.

Table 10.5 (above) shows how CBZ contributed towards meeting such objectives.

The proportion of women beneficiaries has fluctuated between 70 per cent and 82 per cent. Before taking loans, individual client's earnings are as low as US$35 per month. Thereafter, their earnings move up to an average of US$170 per month.

Furthermore, the bank's involvement in microfinance has had a significant impact on the status of micro-entrepreneurs in the economy of Zimbabwe:

> *A very important development was that dealing with the bank lifted our image in the informal sector ... in society and within government institutions. We got new support and, most importantly, we were legitimised.* (Mr Rusinamwana: entrepreneur and winner of Top Company of the Year Award, 2001)

The bank's dealings with the informal sector underscored a new direction for national policy. By 2000, the Zimbabwean Government had created a Ministry of Small to Medium Scale Enterprises.

The central bank took similar cues from CBZ and announced:

> *Monetary authorities acknowledge and recognise the existence of the informal sector as a major source of sustenance for many.*
> (Reserve Bank of Zimbabwe, 2002)

The following case study captures some real experiences of an entrepreneur who is in the process of migrating from the micro- to mainstream banking.

Mr Rusinamwana is a micro-entrepreneur who for nine years failed to expand his business for want of capital and had long suffered the then negative stigma attached to the informal sector. He started embroidery manufacturing in 1987. Since 1996, Rusinamwana has borrowed through CBZ's microfinance project on a number of separate occasions, starting with US$444 then US$730, then US$1050 and thereafter several times more. In 2003, he received the largest loan of US$2427 outside the group guarantee support.

Starting with five sewing machines and five employees, he now has 14 machines and 22 employees. After obtaining the first loan, he expanded production and started exporting to Namibia. Exports contribute 60 per cent of total sales. From ploughed-back profits and proceeds from successive borrowings, Rusinamwana diversified into transport and now operates a 7-tonne haulage truck and two taxis.

In 2001 he bought a house. In the same year, he won the Top Company of the Year Award in the informal sector. Previously without a bank account, he now has a savings account, a loan account, credit insurance, funeral insurance, a cheque account, a cheque guarantee card and a debit card. He adds,

'I discussed with the Bank, I am not afraid of moving to mainstream banking. I am fully informed ... I now need bigger loans ... I registered my company in 2000.'

A number of prospective borrowers have however failed to access loans because they have failed to be part of a group. This is for many reasons, including poor social integration, perceived low credit rating by prospective colleagues or perceived low project viability. The members discuss their projects and in most cases already know them. It is not uncommon for members to regroup, admitting new members in a process of self-renewal to sustain and enhance the group's ability to repay the bank.

Those who are members of groups that help them to borrow and, in some cases, to co-manage enterprises, have had very revealing experiences. They meet at least once every two weeks, and some of them can be termed as virtual entrepreneurship teams in that they operate like one business housing a constellation of independently owned micro-ventures. The group members share management and operational responsibilities. They exchange business advice; cross-market the other group members' products/services and, when needed, assist one another with soft loans to repay the bank or refinance the business. The bonded network not only enables them to access finance but also provides links to new markets, suppliers and information. This insulates the micro-ventures from competition. Most of them are not only new and without institutional credibility and resources, but also have to compete with established large organizations for resources and customers in the same markets.

A second case study provides a typical instance of one such virtual entrepreneurship team.

Formed by four women in 2002, Takunda is a soap-making group. Although the group members jointly work on production, output is shared among members on the basis of the members' relative raw material contributions. They jointly own production equipment and also share marketing activities, usually bidding for large tenders jointly.

In 2002, the group members were granted their first individual loans ranging from US$363 to US$410 per member. The members have borrowed twice more since then. Although their last loans were higher than before in domestic currency terms, they only averaged US$90 per individual. They could not meet the increased working capital requirements because of the impact of currency devaluation on input costs resulting in the members losing a combined order of US$7281.

Borrowings facilitated the group's bulk procurement of raw materials for volume discounts.

In one instance, a member misappropriated loan proceeds and failed to repay the bank. The other members paid for her. The member had to work for the group without receiving payment for a period and was then assisted to get another loan in the next round.

In 2003, to cope with growing business operations, the group decided to split between the founder members and four of their children who had by then joined them as workers. They became Takunda 1 (founders) and Takunda 2. Takunda 1 then introduced Takunda 2 to the bank and they started getting loans.

Each member of the newer group has increased her income by an average of US$120 per month. The founder group has just bought an embroidery machine to diversify income sources and minimize idle time when raw material supplies for soap-making are unavailable.

Future directions

The high level of microfinance deposits, which now cover borrowings about fourfold, means that the bank has an obligation to develop additional financial products for these customers. The Bank is actively exploring possibilities for new products such as pension and credit cards for microfinance customers.

Eight in every ten borrowers who outgrow the microfinance facility still cannot meet the bank's requirement for collateral within mainstream banking. This leaves most of those who would have graduated from microfinance and would then be managing small businesses in a 'no man's land' as far as the provision of bank credit is concerned. In a very few cases, good personal relationships between microfinance and mainstream staff have helped such people to become mainstream customers by waiving some traditional banking requirements such as adequate collateral security. CBZ is now exploring the opportunity to develop an individual-based credit line for this segment of the market.

The low incidence of bad debts, which are more than adequately covered by the standard loan loss provision of 5 per cent, suggests that the loan guarantee fund may have outlived its purpose. The bank now plans to take this up with the Reserve Bank of Zimbabwe in order to lobby for a policy change to the effect that such guarantees, or the normal security equivalents, could be done away with for this class of advances.

Given that the microfinance operations within the bank have been financially self-sustaining, the subsidies, which were critical for the initial establishment and capacity-building in the bank, may not be necessary in the latter phases of the project's evolution. There are many areas where the blending of specialist capabilities has made the project more efficient and effective than other microfinance institutions. The bank's management of the project has freed CARE's and DFID's time for other areas, and has allowed them to build specialist capabilities within the bank, including managing borrowing groups. The bank's expertise in such areas as credit administration; risk assessment; accounting; auditing; marketing and deposit collection are of a specialist nature. Many microfinance projects managed by non-banking institutions have failed because of shortcomings in these areas.

The bank's staff are now fairly well grounded in microfinance. CARE and DFID may in future shift their focus towards new areas, such as product development and research, or the extension of the project to other areas such as the sparsely-populated rural parts of Zimbabwe where the bank may be reluctant to start. A new research-based model may be needed.

The prospect of separating and running microfinance operations as a stand-alone subsidiary of the bank in line with practices elsewhere has been discussed from time to time by management at various levels. Such discussions may reshape the future strategic directions of microfinance operations within the bank. Any such changes would affect the synergies of the current set-up.

Continuing challenges of staff integration and career paths, which result in part from the donors' intensive involvement in the project, are now receiving management attention.

Many donor-funded projects do not survive donor withdrawal, not because the beneficiaries are unwilling but because they lack the management skills to run the projects unaided. The CBZ project has survived one long period of uncertainty when the donors were considering the case for extending project tenure. The bank did not suspend the project in the interim despite the many problems involved in doing business with semi-literate clients who have never before managed anything more complex than short-term ROSCAs. The project has posed many problems for the bank but its success thus far suggests that it can become a permanent and integral part of CBZ's operations.

Acknowledgements

The author gratefully acknowledges the support of Mr L. Loader, Executive Director; Mr N. Makuvise, Managing Director and Chief Executive Director; Mr D. Mandivenga, Head of Microfinance; and other CBZ staff.

Discussion questions

1. CBZ quite deliberately used the microfinance project as part of its corporate renewal strategy. Was the primary motive to remerchandize the bank's image as a good corporate citizen, or to build a new and profitable customer base?

2. Zimbabwe has been suffering severe economic problems for almost the whole of the project's life. Has the project assisted CBZ to weather the storm in any way, and is it likely that CBZ will continue its microfinance activity when DFID's support is withdrawn and the economy returns to normal?

3. How effectively has CBZ managed the challenge of integrating microfinance into its mainstream operations while at the same time addressing the needs of the new client group?

4. Hyper-inflation and economic stress can severely damage both MFIs and commercial banks. Has CBZ's microfinance project been more or less severely affected by Zimbabwe's problems than an MFI serving similar clients under the same conditions?

Chapter Eleven
Equity Building Society's market-led approach to microfinance in Kenya

GRAHAM A.N. WRIGHT and JAMES MWANGI

Background[1]

Kenya's economic performance in the last decade has been weak and poverty continues to increase. GDP increased by 2 per cent per annum between 1990 and 1997, but the average population growth was around 2.6 per cent per annum over the same period. There has been a decline in GDP per capita to US$289. In 1992, 45 per cent of Kenyans were living in poverty, by 1997 this figure had increased to 53 per cent (Government of Kenya, 2000), and by 2002 it had reached 56 per cent at national level and 62 per cent in rural areas. Among the weaknesses in the Kenyan economy, the lack of a strong financial sector remains a key constraint. While exhibiting greater financial depth than other economies in the region and much of sub-Saharan Africa, the sector is characterized by over-concentration, inefficiency and poor asset quality.

Economic liberalization has been nominally underway since the first structural adjustment programme in 1980. However, progress has been patchy. In 1991, financial liberalization commenced with the removal of interest rate controls. In 1993, exchange-rate controls were finally abandoned. However, the government remains heavily involved both directly and through regulation with a number of key sectors. While the basic legal and regulatory framework is largely supportive of a liberalized market, two of the four largest banks remain state owned, notably including the largest – the Kenya Commercial Bank (KCB).[2]

The 4.5 million Kenyans served by Savings and Credit Cooperatives (SACCOs), the 1.8 million served by the Post Office Savings Bank (KPOSB) and the 0.4 million served by microfinance institutions (MFIs) are either under-banked or poorly banked since limited financial services are offered to them. A population of 6.7 million under-banked or poorly banked Kenyans requires comprehensive financial services that include savings, credit and money transfers, as well as insurance services. According to official estimates[3], out of the 11 million potential customers, 8.6 million Kenyans enjoy at least some rudimentary financial services (see Table 11.1, opposite). Many of these services are very basic and, on the credit side, severely rationed.

An entrepreneurial vision of the potential demand for financial services in the under-served, low-income section of the Kenyan market was the inspiration behind the foundation of Equity. Five friends pooled their resources to capitalize Equity and to drive its operations in order to maximize returns on their investment. In 1984 Equity opened as a registered building society. The choice of the legal form was a function of what was available at the time and what could be afforded in

Table 11.1 Basic analysis of the Kenyan market for financial services (Ksh.78 = US$1)

Class	No. of savings clients	Deposits	No. of borrowers	Outstanding portfolio
Banks	1.9 million	US$4 705m	538 000	US$2 346m
SACCOs	4.5 million	US$1 000m	2.1 million	US$833m
KPOSB	1.8 million	US$90m	0	0
MFIs, not including Equity	400 000	0	380 000	US$35m

terms of licence fees and capitalization. At the end of 2003, Equity operated through 15 branches and 24 outlets served by mobile units, had more than 252 000 depositors with deposits of US$41.0m (average savings account balance US$163), and a loan portfolio of 66 000 borrowers, worth US$20.6m (average loan size US$312). Equity was fully computerized, and had more than 360 staff members, eight directors and 2469 shareholders – of which only AfriCap was a 'social' investor.

Equity's entry into microfinance

Between 1984 and 1993, Equity operated through five branches in Nairobi and Central Province but experienced a stagnant deposit base, stagnant loan base, a deteriorating loan portfolio and continuing losses. As at 31 December 1993, Equity received a Central Bank of Kenya (CBK) rating as technically insolvent. The rating noted that supervision by the board was poor, management control was inadequate, asset quality was unsatisfactory, Equity's capital was fully eroded by accumulated losses, and that deposits were being used to meet operating expenses. A decision was made to refocus the institution and to turn Equity around.

The building society legislation had influenced Equity towards offering savings services and mortgage loans. However, Equity realized that it was servicing a microfinance market and that the loans were rarely used for housing. From 1994, Equity began to transform into an institution that focused on 'the mobilization of savings, term deposits and other funds to promptly and efficiently provide loan facilities to the microfinance sector in order to generate sufficient and sustainable profits for the welfare of all stakeholders'. In essence, the result was a complete refocusing of the institution. Since then, Equity has experienced consistent growth of 40–50 per cent per year in terms of profitability, deposit base, loan portfolio investment portfolio and asset base.

Equity received no external donor assistance until 1999. Since then it has received the grants, loans and equity as outlined in Table 11.2; success brings many friends. These grants have not affected Equity's mission but have assisted it to increase its outreach significantly.

Table 11.2 *External assistance received by Equity Building Society 1999–date*

Donor/Agency	Amount (US$)	Instrument	Purpose
European Union	1 million	Loan	Loan capital
European Union	40 000	Grant	Staff development
European Union	50 000	Grant	Business training for clients
Swiss contact		Technical assistance (TA)	Market research Policies & procedures documentation Human resource concept development Change management
MicroSave		TA	Market research Costing & pricing New product development Policies & procedures documentation Process mapping Strategic and product marketing Customer service Branding and corporate identity
UNDP-MicroStart	150 000	Grant	Strategic plan development MIS development
DFID-Financial Deepening Challenge Fund	400 000	Grant	Mobile banking systems' development
DFID	850 000	Grant for TA	Design of staff incentive schemes Credit management ITC and e-banking systems' development Institutional transformation
AfriCap[4]	1.54 million	Equity	'Social' share capital investment
AfriCap	244 000	Grant for TA	Operations development Credit management

These investments, combined with the commitment of Equity's board, management and staff to a market-led, client-focused approach to microfinance has brought massive growth in the past two to three years. Although it does serve some corporate and relatively well-off clients, Equity's core business remains microfinance. Indeed, in 2002 seeing the huge opportunities offered by going further down-market,

Table 11.3 Growth in numbers of staff at different levels in Equity, 1995–2003 (alternate years)

	1995	1997	1999	2001	2003
Board level	3	3	3	7	8
Executive management	2	2	2	2	3
Branch/assistant branch managers	6	10	15	22	30
Senior managers at head office	2	2	1	3	7
Administrative support staff	4	1	5	7	22
Credit staff	6	10	16	36	51
Savings' staff	25	31	72	81	205
Management information systems' staff	1		1	3	8
Finance/accounting staff	3	1	1	6	11
Marketing staff	–	–	–	5	12
Internal audit staff	–	–	–	2	5
Total	**50**	**60**	**116**	**176**	**360**

Equity decided to offer loans to even lower income clients using cash-flow and credit scoring-based technologies. These loan products are currently under development and will be rolled out in 2004–05.

Equity's mission is to 'Mobilize resources to maximize value and economically empower the microfinance clients and other stakeholders by offering customer-focused quality financial services and solutions'. Equity's vision is 'To be the leading and preferred microfinance services provider'. In pursuit of these, Equity's 2003 strategic plan calls for:

- maintaining the focus on the low-income market and deepening outreach on credit side
- conversion from a building society into a commercial bank
- using technology to optimize the quality and minimize the costs of service
- open three or four new branches each year for the next three years
- US$81m deposits mobilized from 450 000 clients by end 2006
- US$57m lent to 88 000 borrowers by end 2006
- return on assets (after income tax) of 4.69 per cent
- return on equity (after income tax) of 34.01 per cent

Equity seems likely to meet, and in some cases exceed, these targets.

The staff and the customers

To make the transition, Equity needed both to acquire relevant human resources and train and reorient the existing ones. Thereafter, the growth in the number and capacity of the staff was driven by growth of the business and changes in technology (see Table 11.3, opposite).

Equity has a tradition of recruiting young people with little or no experience at entry points. A recruitment committee, comprising senior managers in the Nairobi branches and at head office, interviews and selects suitable candidate for a position. The emphasis in Equity is on inculcating the corporate culture, as many newcomers are young but well educated. In a way, the selection of staff at entry/junior level is not so much aimed at bringing skills into the institution, but to mould inexperienced graduates to its operational norms and customer focus. This has worked very well, and is reflected in the work ethic and culture emanating from the activities of the entire staff complement.

Equity prefers to fill management positions from within. However, in the last two years it has needed to recruit some experienced people from outside the Society for senior management positions – particularly for finance, marketing, human resources, ITC, credit and operations. This has been done by headhunting from outside the banking industry. Perhaps as a consequence of never having served low-income clients, traditional bankers have often proved unable to absorb Equity Building Society's corporate culture and operational norms.

Equity does not 'target', it has no poverty criteria for client selection. It seeks to serve low-income people from all walks of life. The vast majority of its clients are small-scale tea and coffee farmers, low salary earners (for example, teachers, workers at Nairobi City Council and so on), and small business people and petty traders. Equity also offers its services to higher income people and operates 'corporate' banking halls/teller stations to ensure that higher value clients receive appropriately high quality services. Table 11.4 shows how the vast majority of Equity's depositors have a net deposit on account of less than US$50.

Table 11.4 Range of savings accounts as of March 31, 2004

Range ($)	No. of depositors	Total value of deposits in range(US$m)	Average value of net deposit per account
Less than 668	283 493	13.33	US$47
668–1 333	6 471	6.06	US$936
1 334–6 667	5 087	12.89	US$2 534
1 668–13 334	406	3.63	US$8 945
Above 13 335	230	14.34	US$62 327

Table 11.5 Equity customers analysed in the survey, July 2001

	Total	Farmers	%	Salaried	%	SME	%
Total	47 695	25 102	53	8 101	17	14 105	30

A 2001 market research survey analysed Equity's records from the eight branches: a total of over 47 000 active customers consisting of more than 95 per cent ordinary savings and remittance account holders, and 5 per cent business savings accounts. Table 11.5 (above) shows that smallholder farmers are the majority in these branches, accounting for 53 per cent of all accounts. Salaried employees held 17 per cent of the accounts, while small and medium scale entrepreneurs accounted for 30 per cent.

The responsiveness of Equity to its recommendations has meant that CBK has been very supportive of its activities. Indeed, CBK has developed respect for Equity as a 'financial institution that has touched many Kenyans in a special way'. Equity's success has also begun to alert other commercial banks to the potential of the low-income market and Equity is beginning to experience competition, particularly at the upper end of its market, from Cooperative Bank, KCB and even Barclays Bank. This trend is being accelerated by the current Treasury bill rate in Kenya, which was hovering around 1 per cent for all of 2003.

The products

As part of its commitment to client service, Equity Building Society offers a range of products as shown in Tables 11.6 and 11.7 (below, opposite and overleaf).

Table 11.6 Savings product range

Product	No. sold at end 2003	Purpose	Features
Ordinary savings account	205 790	To provide a medium for remittance processing and savings	Operating balance of US$5.13 No ledger fees No opening balance No limit on amount and frequency of withdrawals US$0.38 withdrawal charges No charges on deposit Annual interest credit (2003 rate = 2.5% p.a.) Free photo card

Product	No. sold at end 2003	Purpose	Features
Business savings	23 394	To provide a medium for business transactions and savings	Minimum balance of US$12.82 (or US$64.10 for corporate branch) No ledger fees No limit on withdrawals US$0.38 withdrawal fee Annual interest credit (2003 rate = 2.5% p.a.) Free photo card
Jijenge savings account	4 366	To provide a medium for contractual savings	Disciplines clients to save Flexibility for clients to fix their own savings plans Earns bonus interest (2003 rate = 3% p.a.) Fast access to loans of up to 90% of deposits at low-interest rates No ledger fees
Call and fixed deposits	3 774	To provide a premium interest earning investment opportunity	Low minimum deposits Competitive interest rates (2003 rates = 3.25% p.a.) No penalties or loss of interest for premature withdrawal of deposits
Super junior investment	2 293	To provide a medium for investing in a dependant's future	No opening balance Minimum operating balance of US$0.13 No ledger fees Free bankers' cheque No transaction charges for deposits Interest 2.5% p.a.
Mobile savings account	12 569	To bring banking services closer to the people	Operating balance of US$5.13 No ledger fees No opening balance No limit on withdrawals Banking services offered once a week US$0.38 withdrawal charges Monthly fee of US$0.64 No charges on deposit Annual interest credit (2003 rate = 2.5% p.a.) Free photo card
Total accounts	**252 286**		

Table 11.7 Loan product range

Product	No. sold at end 2003	Purpose	Features
Business loan	7 972	To provide financial solutions for investing in business	Affordable low interest rates of 1.5% per month Small application fee of 5% (minimum US$3.85) Available for terms up to 12 months
Salary advance	25 228	To support customers to meet unexpected socio-economic needs	Available to all active salaried clients Loan of up to 4 times the average monthly net salary Affordable low interest rate of 1.4% per month Small application fee of 5% (minimum US$3.85)
Farm input advance	28 178	To support customers to carry out various farming activities	Affordable low interest rate of 1.4% per month Small application fee of 5% (minimum US$3.85) Available for terms up to 12 months
Medical loan	265	To support customers meet healthcare needs	Affordable low interest rate of 1% per month. No loan application fee Available for terms up to 12 months
Development loan	1 847	To provide support for acquisition of durable assets	Affordable low interest rate of 1.5% Small application fee of 5% (minimum US$3.85) No hidden charges Available for terms of up to 36 months Interest discounts
Education loan	1 655	To provide solutions for investing in education	Affordable low interest rate of 1.2% Small application fee of 5% (minimum US$3.85) Available for terms up to 12 months No guarantors
Total number of loans	**66 022**		

Growing with Equity, the 'Listening, Caring Financial Partner': a client's story

I started banking with Equity back in 1992, when I was still a housewife. I had only a little money, which I had always kept in the house for any emergencies. I believe, even without banking, that women can control their finances much better than men: my case is an example. Then, Equity was still a small bank and I knew that I would not be looked down upon with my little savings and irregular deposits.

By 1993 due to having an account, I had strong belief in the Swahili adage *haba na haba hujaza kibaba* ('little by little, the coins fill in a large bowl'). It was a struggle to maintain the Ksh.300 minimum deposit. For the sake of my children, I had to cut on expenses so as to save from the money I got from my husband, which was only enough for daily survival.

I used to see people queuing at the credit counter and I was jealous and pitied myself because if I borrowed what would I pay with? I knew if I showed some initiative of some business I could seek help on a better ground. I consulted my husband about the sort of business I could open and at the time the most appealing was a kiosk. It was good because it was next to my house, which I could still watch over as I worked and take care of the children too.

My first loan, which I remember to this day, was for Ksh.20 000 (about US$670 at the time), which helped in stocking the business. The small neighbourhood shop had now gained frequent customers. I bought more sugar and flour and all the little things, which make it called a 'big' shop. I ran this shop until 1995 where it had grown some bit and had enough stock.

In 1996, I went for a very big loan of Ksh.50 000 (US$1450) with which I was to expand my business. I had already chosen a stall at the nearby centre where I could rent a room and at least be more open to customers from all over, especially because it was a busy area near the road.

By 1997, my next-door business colleague was seeking to get out of the mini-market buisness he was running. I saw this as a golden opportunity. It is good that my husband and my bank were a strong support to my growth. I acquired another loan and, this time, my manager gave me tips on investing the money wisely. This was one of the best pieces of advice I got. He saw I was determined and told me to go for it. With the help of yet another loan, which this time I secured with a fixed deposit, I managed to buy out the mini-market and moved my shop there.

In 1999, business was very slow and the bank almost repossessed my securities except that it is a bank which listens to your problems. I was able to reschedule my repayments to a much more stress-free plan. I was happy and fully concentrated on the growing shop so that I could clear my debts. I am happy they had a chance to believe in me, which is not usual because most people do not listen to your financial worries, especially the big banks.

Just last year, 2003, I began plans to upgrade my mini-market into a supermarket, though not as big as *Uchumi* supermarket, but it will serve my neighbourhood well. You never know in years to come, with the help of Equity, I might grow to *Uchumi*-size! Right now, I have even taken a school fees loan and a medical loan for my ageing mother. I have no worries of repayment, as I know that the shop will take care of all that. I am more independent – never having to ask my husband for small monies and also my financial literacy has improved.

My advice especially for women who sit at home thinking that they cannot make it in life – you are failing yourself. Even others and I have shown you that housewives can be good money mangers. For the small, 'Equity is our kind of bank.'

Figure 11.1 *All new savings accounts opened in 2003–04, by month*

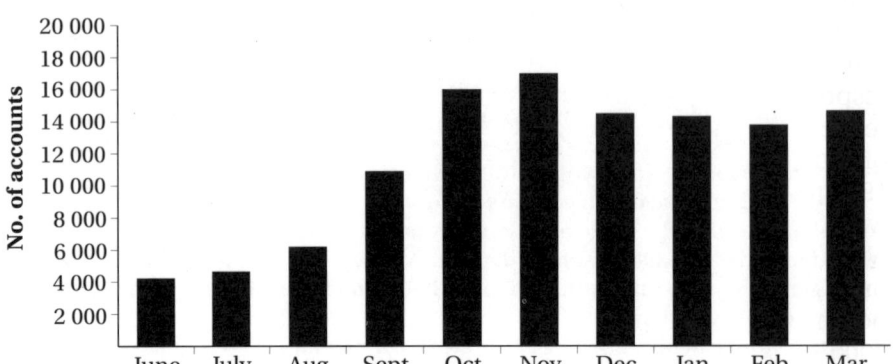

In August 2003, the marketing and public relations efforts conducted on the basis of Equity's 20th Anniversary of 'Providing Financial Solutions to Kenyans' yielded spectacular results with the number of new savings accounts rising dramatically as a result (Figure 12.1, above).

As a result of this rapid growth, many of Equity's branches are increasingly congested. In response, Equity has conducted a detailed process mapping exercise to optimize the speed and efficiency of customer service within the branches, introduced floor managers to assist and direct customers to the correct counters and is examining opportunities for deploying ATMs.

The portfolio at risk for Equity has grown rapidly with the explosive growth in volume of borrowers and volume of loans. The rate of portfolio at risk over the past three years had gone down from 21 per cent to 8 per cent. However, during 2003 the portfolio at risk rose again to 19.2 per cent. While a significant proportion of this portfolio at risk is secured by high quality collateral, Equity devoted 2004 to strengthening credit management through a comprehensive review of the methodology of appraisal, follow up and staff training. The results of the first half of 2004 have shown a significantly improving portfolio at risk. In addition, in recognition of the high risk associated with lending to high value corporate clients (which account for around 80 per cent of the PAR), Equity is reorienting its credit portfolio to concentrate more on the low-end clients through salary/remittance-based lending and cash flow-based micro-credit products to finance education, emergencies and small-scale business development.

The financial impact on the bank

Equity has been extremely successful in its efforts to provide microfinance services. It has identified a significant market niche, designed products and delivery systems that respond to and satisfy the needs of that niche and is now making significant returns on its investment. But it was not ever thus.

As it faced insolvency in 1993, Equity reoriented itself towards microfinance. Following this mission shift from mortgage financing to microfinance in 1994, Equity has gradually evolved from a product-driven through a selling-driven and social-marketing to a full-fledged, client-responsive market-led approach[5]. This evolution has been clearly reflected in the organization's results over time. Until 1994, Equity was product-driven and sustaining regular and debilitating losses. From 1994 to around 1997, Equity tried hard selling its products in the market with a modicum of success. In the period 1998–2000, Equity focused on what they called 'social marketing' efforts, such as the presentation of prizes to the best farmers and sponsoring carefully selected, high-potential children through college. In 2000 Equity installed the Bank 2000 software, which greatly improved the productivity of their staff. The following year, Equity started working with MicroSave on a market-led approach[6] that started with market research to understand what clients wanted and then sought to amend products and delivery systems to reflect those client needs and preferences. For example, following some market research that indicated that customers were confused by their prices, Equity re-priced their products consolidating a series of fees into the interest rates. The result was that new account openings rose ten-fold – without any significant marketing efforts.

Figure 11.2 shows the growing profitability of the institution as it shifted its approach and orientation from product-driven to market-led.

Subsequent work with MicroSave has involved new product development, product marketing, process mapping to optimize delivery systems, institutional and product risk analysis, and the improvement of customer service and staff incentive schemes. In addition, Equity institutionalized product- and branch-based cost analysis so that these are now an integral part of its management reporting system, thus allowing it a clear understanding of the revenue streams and cost drivers.

The results of moving to a market-led approach have been startling – indeed Equity has had to move fast to implement more comprehensive systems and to recruit an almost entirely new senior management team to handle the resultant rapid expansion.

Figure 11.2 Equity's profits 1986–2003 (millions of Ksh.)

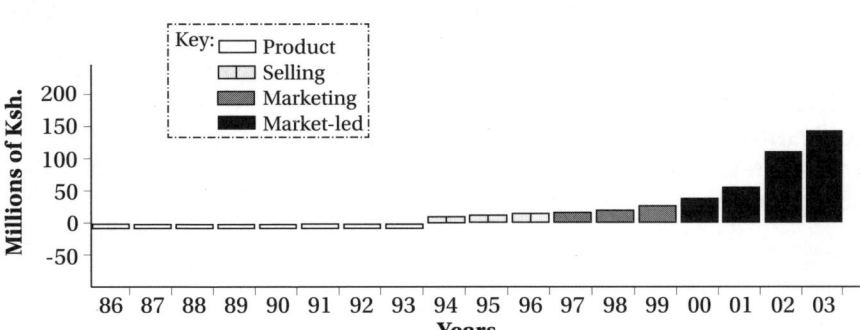

Figure 11.3 *Number of savings' clients: 1994–March 2004 ('000s)*

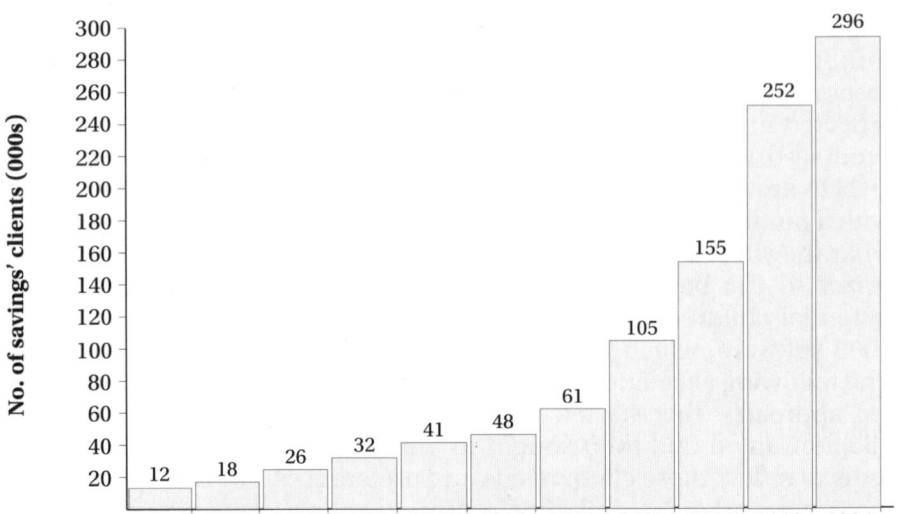

The number of savings clients has risen by more than 140 per cent in the two years 2002 and 2003. As noted above, this growth has been particularly marked in the last half of 2003, after the public relations' and marketing exercise in August of that year. At one stage, some branches were opening 500–1000 accounts a day, and even in the month of January 2004, around 15 000 accounts were opened despite an almost complete shut down of marketing efforts by Equity. In an environment where 58 per cent of clients learn about services at microfinance institutions through word of mouth (Wright et al., 2003), it is perhaps not too surprising to see the effects of the August 2003 marketing campaign persisting some time after the campaign closed.

The rise in the value of deposits has been commensurate with the increase in the number of savers. Equity now has deposit liabilities that are 113 per cent greater than they were at the end of 2001. And in January 2004, a notoriously bad month for deposit mobilization because rent, school costs and other household expenses fall due at this time, Equity's clients made another Ksh.200m (US$2.56m) net deposits.

This rise was recorded despite the fact that in the last half of 2003, Equity moved to introduce a withdrawal fee on their most popular Ordinary Savings Account (and indeed other accounts). Perhaps as a result of the on-going focus on customer service, this new fee has not significantly affected clients' behaviour and is yielding a valuable fee income stream. This is despite a very competitive market (see Table 11.8, opposite).

Figure 11.4 *Value of deposits: 1994–Mar 2004 (Ksh.m)*

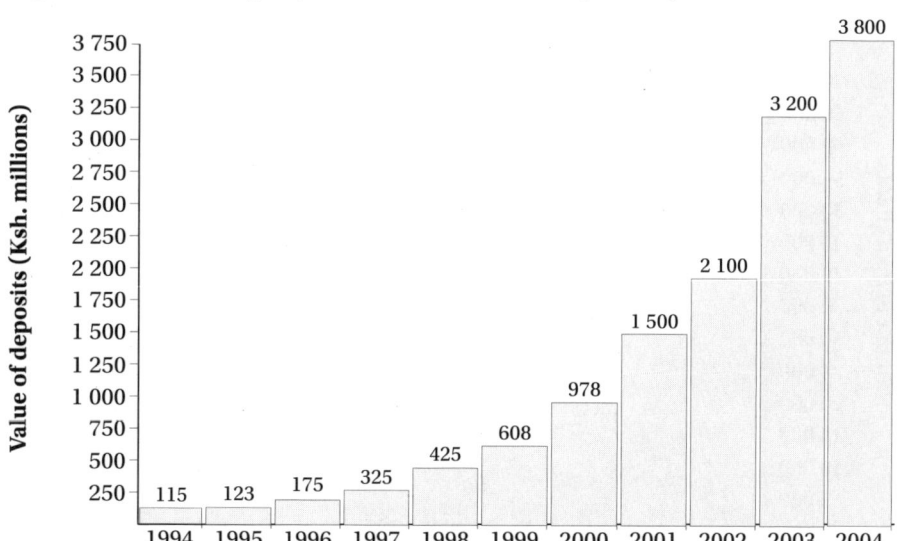

Table 11.8 Deposit account fees and charges in the Kenyan banking sector, as at 31 March 2004

	Minimum opening balance		Minimum balance		Ledger Fees	Withdrawal Charge
	Savings	Current	Savings	Current		
Equity Building Society	0	0	400	1 000	0	50
Barclays Bank	20 000	20 000	20 000	30 000	750	30 (ATM) 370 (counter)
K-Rep Bank	500	2 000	500	0	0	20
Family Finance Building Society	0	500	500	0	100	40
Kenya Post Office Savings Bank	500	500	500	500	0	30
Kenya Commercial Bank	20 000	10 000	Nil	Nil	200	25 (ATM)
East Africa Building Society	1 000	2 000	2 000	2 000	100 monthly	300 (in branch)
All figures in Kenyan shillings (Ksh): US$1 = Ksh. 78						

Figure 11.5 Number of loan clients: 1994–March 2004

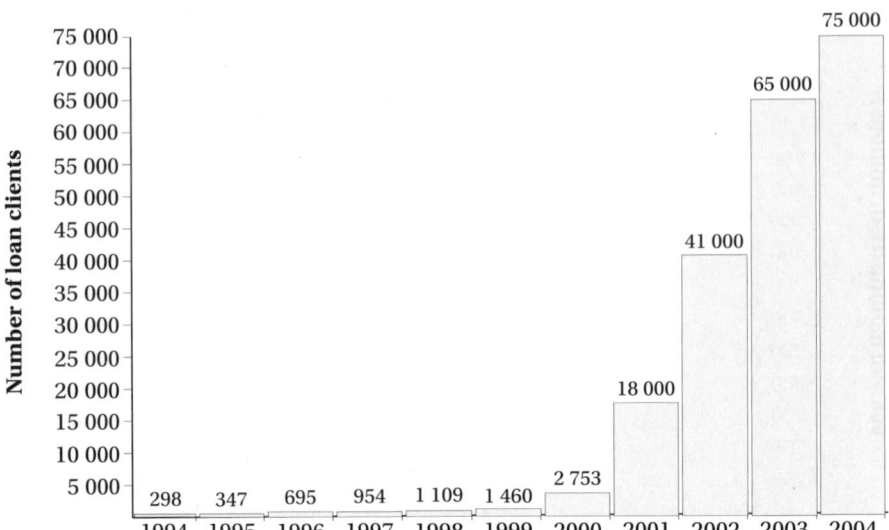

Equity has seen a similarly phenomenal rise in the number of loan clients in the same period. As the value of deposits has risen, so the need to lend and the opportunities to do so have increased. In early 2003, the T-bill rate in Kenya fell beneath 1 per cent and looks likely to remain low for the foreseeable future. As a result, all the banks and building societies are looking for opportunities to lend where they have not needed to before. Equity is continuing to focus on its core business of lending against salaries and tea/coffee remittances but has begun to pilot-test a cash-flow based, individual lending microcredit product. Perhaps the biggest challenge facing Equity comes from the pressure (from both balance sheet and clients) to lend – a pressure that is testing Equity's staff, management and systems like never before.

The value of loans outstanding has risen with the number of loan clients (see Figure 11.6, opposite). The value of loans outstanding at the end of 2003 was marginally less than double that of the value at the end of 2001. When compared to the rise in the number and value of savings accounts and net deposits, this represents a relatively modest increase. The limited increase reflects Equity's need to rein in and control the loan portfolio while it puts more rigorous systems in place in preparation for a massive expansion of lending in line with the liability side of its balance sheet. The average outstanding loan size as of December 2003 was Ksh. 24 333 (US$312).

Financial statements to 31 December 2003

As a result of the above, despite the problems with its portfolio, Equity Building Society has a robust balance sheet and continues to grow its profits (see Tables 11.9 and 11.10, opposite and overleaf).

Figure 11.6 Loans outstanding: 1994–March 2004 (Ksh.m)

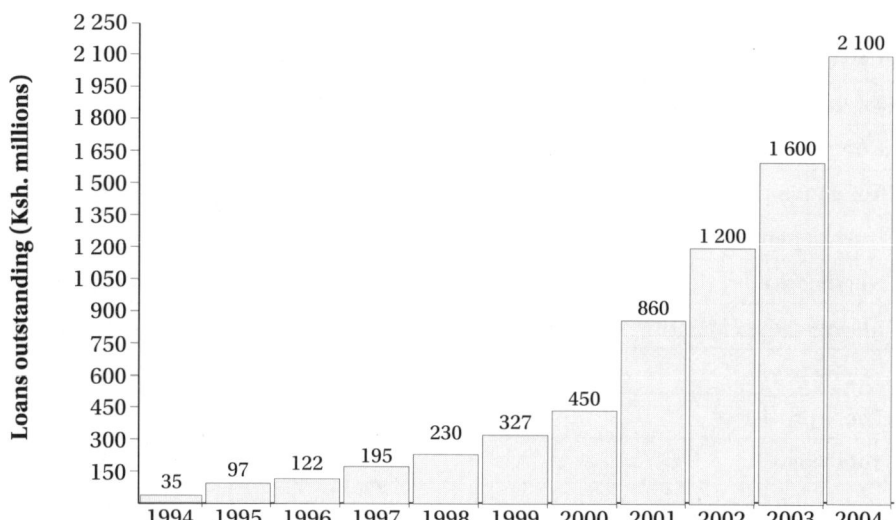

Conclusion

Equity's focus on its microfinance customers must be regarded as an important factor in its success since 1995. This focus, which is embodied in the mission of the Building Society, drives most of the activities of Equity. It is clear when interacting with any staff member that they have internalized this focus – it is a key part of the Equity culture. This committed attention to client service is one of the most important aspects of Equity's success story.

For over 16 years, Equity survived under the difficulties of a manual information system, difficulties which were amplified at every level of growth. Both customers and staff members felt the strain of the manual

Table 11.9 Equity Building Society's balance sheet, as at December 2003 (figures are in thousands of Kenyan shillings)

Assets (Ksh. '000s)		Liabilities (Ksh. '000s)	
Cash	451 469	Customer deposits	3 368 589
Deposits with banks	702 984	Short-term liabilities	77 156
Treasury bonds	870 086	Subscribers' capital	478 201
Other assets	41 548		
Loans & advances	1 06 723		
Fixed assets	251 136		
Total assets	**3 923 946**	**Total liabilities**	**3 923 946**

Table 11.10 *Equity Building Society's profit and loss for the period ended December 2003 (in '000s of Kenyan shillings)*

Particulars	Ksh. '000s
Interest earned	324 428
Commission and other income	306 429
Total income	**630 857**
Interest paid on deposits	(67 855)
Net income	**563 002**
Management expenses	319 049
Depreciation	50 711
Loans provision	50 585
Total costs	**420 345**
Profit before tax	**142 657**
Tax	(45 344)
Net profit	**97 313**
Proposed dividend	(18 859)
Retained profit for the year	**78 454**
US$1 = Ksh. 78	

system as Equity expanded its volume of business over the years. Equity launched its computerized management information system in June 2000, completing the process of computerization in a record four months. Equity's efficiency in collecting and giving data and its service delivery to customers improved greatly thereafter. With the new system Equity managed to improve its customer turnaround time at the counter from 30–40 minutes to about five minutes . This counter time has now been further reduced by the process mapping exercise, which allowed Equity to streamline the related front- and back-office operations. Although Equity's growth is partly attributed to its marketing and customer-focused efforts, it is clear from the high growth spurt in the 2001 figures that the new computerized system has also been a major contributing factor. This, of course, demonstrates the importance of harnessing technology in banking in general – and high volume, low-value microfinance in particular.

The future looks bright for Equity – indeed its most significant and pressing challenge is that of managing the rapid growth that has resulted from its success. With a return on equity of 29.8 per cent and a return on assets of 3.6 per cent in 2003, Equity has demonstrated a successful business model for microfinance. The model is driven by a market-led approach and meticulous attention to clients' perceptions and customer care linked to charging for this high-quality service – on both the savings and loan accounts. Equity is exciting proof of the profitability of high-quality microfinance activities tailored for the low-income market, and that this market will happily pay for such services.

Discussion questions

1. Equity has demonstrated quite convincingly that smaller poorer clients are more profitable than larger ones. Is this conclusion a function of the history of Equity and its business model and culture, or can more traditional commercial banks draw the same conclusions?

2. Equity is not a bank, it is a building society. Has its legal form constrained its growth and its success, and what are the implications for banking regulators and other microfinance institutions that aspire to banking status?

3. Equity is mobilizing twice as much money in deposits as it is lending. What conclusions might prospective domestic or foreign wholesale lenders draw from this?

Chapter Twelve
Finadev SA:
the first commercial bank for microfinance in Benin

LATÉ LAWSON and HERMAN MESSAN

Background

Overview of Benin

Benin is located in sub-Saharan Africa between Togo and Nigeria and, with a gross domestic product (GDP) per capita of US$360, is one of the poorest countries in the world. The population of Benin was estimated at 6.3 million inhabitants in 2001, of which 51 per cent were women (World Bank data). Average population growth is 2.8 per cent and population density is relatively low at 56 people per square kilometre. However, 25 per cent of the population lives along the coast in the southern half of the country, where the density reaches 340 people per square kilometre, one of the highest densities in Africa. Nearly 60 per cent of the population live in rural areas on subsistence agriculture and the cultivation of cotton. In terms of infrastructure, Benin has yet to develop a modern road system, heavy industry or reliable sources of energy. Manufacturing activity is still small-scale and, apart from the construction materials industry, is confined to the processing of primary products for export. Benin enjoys a high level of political stability.

In the late 1980s, Benin experienced great economic difficulties associated with an overvalued currency, weak primary commodity prices, and mismanagement of public finances. Under a structural adjustment programme started in 1991 and guided by the IMF and World Bank, real GDP growth averaged 2.4 per cent a year in the period 1980–92, and picked up above 4 per cent in the early 1990s. It increased to 5 per cent after the CFA Franc devaluation in 1994, and averaged 5.3 per cent in 1995 to 2002. However, GDP increases were partially offset by a high annual rate of population growth of 3 per cent. Inflation remained low at an average of 1.9 per cent during the period 1990–93, rose to 38.5 per cent in 1994 following the devaluation of the currency that year, but subsided gradually in 1995 and has remained below 5 per cent since 1996 (IMF statistics). In 2002, GDP grew by 6 percent, in line with growth in recent years, reflecting a bumper cotton crop, and increased investment in manufacturing and public works. Inflation as measured by the consumer price index (CPI), registered low at a 2.3 per cent year-on-year rate in July 2003.

The economy of Benin was once highly dependent on subsistence agriculture and on cotton production. In recent years, however, the share of the agricultural sector in Benin's economy has been falling.

Value-added in agriculture accounts for 37 per cent of GDP, while agriculture employs about 40 per cent of the active labour force.

Trade and migration across the border are important sources of income in Benin due to its role as a trade corridor for landlocked West Africa Economy and Monetary Union (WAEMU) countries and as a link to Nigeria. Commercial and transport activities, which make up a large part of GDP, remain vulnerable to developments in Nigeria, particularly fuel shortages.

The illiteracy rate in Benin is 60 per cent, which is 15 per cent higher than in other similar West African countries. Less than half the male population and less than a quarter of the female population can read and write. Life expectancy in Benin is only 53 years. Poor education standards undoubtedly reduce the economic opportunities available to the poor, and also shrink the pool of available human resources for all sectors of the economy. Thirty-three per cent of the rural and 23 per cent of the urban population are poor.

The financial sector and the market for microfinance in Benin

Benin is a member of the Franc Zone, which controls its monetary policy, currency and trading regulations. At the end of 2003, the financial sector in Benin consisted of eight commercial banks, two non-bank financial institutions and more than 600 microfinance and savings and loans initiatives including primary structures and branches. About 20 institutions are authorized by the Ministry of Finance and Economy in Benin as Microfinance Institutions.

Commercial banks operate in major urban areas and have limited or no branches in rural areas. Today, the financial sector in Benin remains shallow, with a ratio of 15.22 per cent to GDP for a total outstanding loan of about US$683m, indicating that the size of formal financial intermediation is small compared to the size of the economy. However, financial deepening in Benin remains slightly higher than the average ratio of 25 per cent in sub-Saharan Africa.

Credit to the private sector represented 11 per cent of GDP in 1999. Demand for financial services from poor households is not satisfied by the banking sector, as access to bank loans is restricted to a few large, established firms, mostly involved with commerce.

Only the microfinance industry is able to achieve broader and deeper outreach and to provide financial services to clients who lack access to the formal banking sector. However, by the end of 2000, credit from MFIs represented only 8 per cent of total financial sector credit and 6.1 per cent of all financial sector deposits were held by MFIs. Despite its relatively small size, Benin remains the country with the largest number of MFIs in the WAEMU region and with a comparable diverse array of institutions. The Ministry of Finance estimated that, as of 31 December 2002, the MFI industry in Benin had over 600 microfinance institutions including primary structures and around 700 000 clients, US$66m in savings deposits, and US$144m in loans outstanding. Organizations

Table 12.1 *Evolution of formal MFIs in Benin from 1995 to 1998*

Year	1995	1997	1998
Number of credit unions	12	11	7
No. of credit-only institutions	2	3	3
Number of donors' projects	11	16	6
Total	**25**	**30**	**16**
		Source: *Banque de données sur les SFD*, UMOA	

engaged in microfinance in Benin and the rest of WAEMU are formally classified into three main categories: (i) credit unions, (ii) credit-only MFIs, and (iii) donor projects with a microfinance component.

Credit unions
Credit unions dominate the microfinance industry in Benin. The reason for this is closely related to the evolution of the formal financial sector. The large number of credit unions in Benin today are the result of a rehabilitation of the *Caisse Nationale de Crédit Agricole*, a parastatal organization engaged in agricultural credit, after its collapse at the end of 1980s. To restore the savings and loans system to its original mutualist principles, the Government withdrew from the management of the co-operatives and replaced them with credit unions or *caisses locales de crédit agricole mutuel*, which organized into the largest credit union network in Benin, the *Fédération des Caisses d'Epargne et de Crédit Mutuel* (FECECAM). By the end of 2002, FECECAM completely dominated the microfinance industry in Benin with 94.2 per cent of savings deposits of the industry and 42 per cent of total loans outstanding.

Credit-only institutions
Credit-only institutions are the second biggest players in the microfinance industry in Benin, each with more than US$1.3m in total loans outstanding in 2002. They are: (i) FINADEV, a microfinance outlet of a commercial bank with US$5.66m loans outstanding; (ii) PADME (*Programme d'Appui au Développement des Micro Entreprises*) with loans outstanding of US$14.8m; and (iii) PAPME (*Programme d'appui aux Petites et Moyennes Entreprises*), aimed at providing financial services to micro-entrepreneurs as well as small and medium scale enterprises, and outstanding loan portfolio of US$18.6m. Both PADME and PAPME were World Bank and *Agence Canadienne de Développement International* (ACDI) supported projects. By the end of 2002, credit-only institutions provided 52 per cent of all loans in microfinance.

Donor projects
Donor projects with a microfinance component are numerous. Small non-governmental organizations (NGOs), some of them organized as

Table 12.2 Portfolio data on the leading MFIs in Benin in 2002

Organization name	FECECAM	PADME	PAPME	FINADEV
Outstanding loan portfolio in US$m	28.1	14.8	18.6	5.66
Number of loans	56 000	30 780	22 905	12 000
Average loan size in US$	500	481	792	472

credit unions, including FENACREP, ASSEF, CBDIBA, GRAPAD, etc. are supported by donors. In rural areas, MFIs are structured as financial service associations and are supported by IFAD and other donors. Loans outstanding in these projects represents less than 6 per cent of the microfinance market.

In addition to the formal microfinance market, there are a large number of informal microfinance organizations in Benin including money-keepers, moneylenders and rotating savings and credit associations (ROSCAs) or tontines, particularly in urban markets but also in many rural areas.

Microfinance instituions in Benin are organized into a professional association known as Consortium ALAFIA, which has a membership of 26 MFIs. ALAFIA's main objective is to play an active advocacy role for improving the environment for the expansion and the sustainability of the sector.

The whole sector is regulated by the PARMEC law. Legislation to implement the PARMEC law (*Project d'Appui à la Reéglementation des Mutuelles d'Epargne et de Crédit*) was enacted in Benin in August 1997, and is very close to the regional model law. Under the PARMEC law, only credit unions and their network federation can be granted a full-fledged licence. Other MFIs are permitted to operate within the rules defined by a convention-cadre signed with the Ministry of Finance for five years and renewable by mutual consent. MFIs in this category can collect savings if they wish to, but this must be stated in the agreement.

Prudential regulation of financial institutions involves definition of detailed standards for financial structure, accounting policies, and other important dimensions of an institution's business. Key prudential standards have been defined for licensed MFIs under separate *Banque Centrale des Etats de l'Afrique de l'Ouest* (BCEAO), the Central Bank of Benin, instructions related to the PARMEC law. Prudential guidelines and ratios are defined with respect to loan classification and provisioning, reserve requirement, liquidity adequacy, single borrower limit, ceiling on loans to management and conflict of interest rule. The PARMEC law is currently under review in order to take into account all the constraints faced by MFIs in the WAEMU member countries.

Context of FINADEV's entry into microfinance

Motivation of FINADEV initiative

The FINADEV initiative was motivated by many reasons but the most important was the vision of the CEO of the Financial Bank (FBB) group. In the mid-1990s he realized that microfinance is essential to the development of the entire financial system for clients who are neglected by the traditional commercial banks. Through the development of microfinance, commercial banks could, by working in close co-operation with MFIs (risk sharing arrangements, technical skills, etc.), reach areas outside their field of competence. Since the sector is very dynamic, has great growth potential, and many MFIs face difficulties in medium-term lending, commercial banks could engage in their refinancing and play a significant role in the monitoring of their development and at the same time make profit.

In 1995, in response to that vision, FBB introduced a 'social loan' – a product designed for groups of workers who wanted to borrow for housing improvements or the purchase of small plots of land, but who could not access commercial banks on a purely individual basis. It also helped PADME (the second most important MFI in Benin) implement its activities as an elected member of the board and through active partnership (training of PADME staff within the bank, technical assistance, utilization of bank facilities by PADME clients for loan collection and repayment, etc.). Those experiences provided many lessons to FBB and placed it in a leadership position in the support of microfinance development in Benin as the first commercial bank to enter the field.

On the basis of the reality of Benin (huge market, emerging microfinance sector, political stability and economic growth), lessons learned and experiences acquired by working closely with PADME, FBB decided to open a microfinance window within the bank.

Statistics on Financial Bank are presented in Table 12.3 below:

Table 12.3 *Statistics of Financial Bank (in US$)*

	31 Dec 2001	31 Dec 2002	31 Dec 2003
Outstanding loan	70 864 000	77 287 000	77 655 000
Outstanding savings	49 023 000	47 371 000	48 706 000
Number of borrowers	578	677	442
Number of savings' account holders	5 610	5 841	6 045
Number of staff	152	160	155
Number of agencies	9	9	9

Note: A flat rate of US$1=530 F CFA is used.

FINADEV at the beginning

FINADEV began in November 1998 as a microfinance window integrated into the Financial Bank and delivered through its agencies. FINADEV first specialized in the refinancing of other microfinance institutions on behalf of the bank. A line of credit of 5 million euro received by Financial Bank Benin from the European Investment Bank of Luxembourg was passed on to FINADEV in the form of an overdraft at a rate of 7 per cent excluding taxes. This funding was used by FINADEV to continue the refinancing of MFIs and a large part of it was also used to finance the micro-entrepreneur credit, known as TPE. These resources allowed to effectively launch the direct micro-lending activities of the window, but they soon proved to be insufficient to meet the customers' need, as the number grew.

Since micro-lending requires different skills, close follow-up, and a higher interest rate to be able to sustain the initiative (up to 27 per cent as per the usury law for the microfinance sector, against 18 per cent maximum for a commercial bank), and based on the experience gained so far, FBB's idea for the two-and-half-year pilot phase was not for the window to become a permanent entity within the bank, but rather for it to be transformed as rapidly as possible into a separate legal entity. Thus Financial Bank Benin prepared to launch FINADEV, as the first fully fledged private microfinance limited company in West African French-speaking countries

By 2001 FINADEV had become the fourth largest microfinance organization in Benin with more than US$9.6m total loans outstanding at the end of 2003. Currently, FINADEV has more than 14 000 active clients and more than 32 000 people have benefited from its services since its creation. It operates through seven branches across the country: three in Cotonou (South Benin), one in Parakou (North Benin), one in Porto-Novo (South East), one in Lokossa (South West), and one in Natitingou (North West). Around 50 per cent of its clients are located in Cotonou, the economic capital of the country. FINADEV's main clientele is made up of micro-entrepreneurs, urban women with small-scale commercial activities or those who are managing very small-scale and informal enterprises, and salaried workers. The average loan size is US$434, the minimum loan size being US$94.

The limited company was created in July 2000 but had to obtain permission from the relevant authorities to be able to operate under this legal form. As a direct credit institution, FINADEV has to secure a five-year renewable authorization from the Ministry of Finance and Economy. By end 2001, the fully subscribed capital of FINADEV was US$1.8m and its shareholders include the International Finance Corporation (25%), Dutch FMO (25%), Financial Bank Benin (25%), Financial Bank Holding (15%) and Lafayette Participations/Horus Group (10%). This allowed FINADEV to receive an authorization for its activities but not for the full five years. This was because FBB and Financial Bank Holding are considered as the same entity, and as such should not exceed a certain percentage in the share structure of the limited company according to the banking law of the WAEMU zone. FINADEV has yet to regularize this issue.

At this stage, FINADEV did not opt for savings mobilization. The Ministry of Finance and Economy considers a risky activity and so the requirements are difficult to comply with. Since the FINADEV model is very new in the sector and is struggling to secure a full authorization, it strategically opted only to provide loans to its customer, along with other social services such as education and business counselling. But as time goes on clients are asking for savings services and FINADEV is planning to introduce these once it resolves the authorization issue with the Ministry of Finance. It will then need to put in place the required facility and personnel and to amend its authorization.

Since its creation as a microfinance window, FINADEV has given innovative and lasting banking responses to the many problems encountered by microfinance institutions, such as the limitation on their financing sources, the inflexibility of loans management, the lack of innovation and adaptation to riskier and more demanding proposals, the weaknesses of their MIS and their governance difficulties.

Actual relationship between FINADEV and FBB

FINADEV is presently a separate entity from FBB even though they share the same premises in some locations. FINADEV also has its own premises in areas where there are no FBB facilities. However, there is some complementarity between the two institutions. When a customer does not meet the conditions of the bank because FBB cannot handle the constraints of profitability and administrative unwieldiness of small loans (less than US$9500), FBB directs him or her to FINADEV. Likewise, when the volume of a customer's business becomes quite high, FINADEV has a policy to direct the customer to the bank. However, most customers who are directed to FBB by FINADEV prefer to keep their relations with the MFI due to their personal relationship and proximity.

The role of the regulation authorities

During the process of the creation of FINADEV SA, the central authorities in charge of sector regulation have played an important role. Indeed, it was the first time a commercial bank has taken advantage of the PARMEC law to go down market into microfinance. After the creation of FINADEV SA, the microfinance window continued to function for an additional year until FINADEV signed its agreement with the Ministry of Finance and Economy. On 4 July 2001, the agreement was signed with the Ministry, and this allowed FINADEV to begin operating as an entirely autonomous limited company.

Limited company status was chosen for FINADEV because of the special nature of microfinance operations. FBB made a strategic choice to spin if off early in order to attract new shareholders and enhance the image of FBB as the first commercial bank in microfinance in the region. There were many advantages, including clear governance, rapid decision-making and a well-defined and controlled plan for growth. On the other hand, because of that status, the institution's business is treated on the same basis as a private commercial company, without any tax exemption, which makes it more expensive for the company, since there are no subsidies or preferential lines of credit.

Impact on staff, customers and other actors

Staff response to the initiative

At the start, the bank staff was reluctant. The microfinance idea was associated with a crowd of strange customers whose behaviour is quite opposite to the standards of traditional customers of the bank. This feeling was strengthened by the first experiences; the initial staff were sceptical especially as the turnover at the beginning was insignificant.

Today, with the unprecedented development of FINADEV with more than 14 000 active clients in less than three years, the perception of the initiative has really changed. FINADEV contributes up to 80 per cent of the volume of some branches that it shares with the FBB, such as the Dantokpa branch. The FINADEV staff are envied by the bank employers, many of whom wish to join FINADEV.

There are currently 70 staff members and the average age is 30 years. The personnel of FINADEV are independent from the FBB. Apart from the general manager and the deputy general manager who are employed by FBB and assigned to FINADEV – the general manager on a part-time basis and the deputy manager on a full-time basis – all other members of staff are full-time employees of FINADEV and are hired directly by it.

FINADEV has developed partnerships with organizations such as CARE International and other organizations in order to train its new staff, who had no previous banking or microfinance experience. Most of them are university or high school graduates.

The clients' reaction

Today, FINADEV has more than 14 000 active clients, of whom more than 80 per cent are women. They borrow from a diversified range of products, ranging from group-based and individual loans of working capital to fixed-asset loans. A typical client of FINADEV is a market woman without previous access to a bank. She is a trader in different types of products such as clothes, materials, food and so on. An October 2003 satisfaction survey of FINADEV's customers showed that 70 per cent of the customers were satisfied with the varied range of products offered by FINADEV. However, some customers still want FINADEV to increase the amount of the loans granted, and develop new products such as home-purchase loans.

Speaking of how they first came to the institution, 90 per cent of the surveyed clients say they got to know FINADEV through relatives or friends, 5 per cent mentioned the media and the remaining 5 per cent came through other means.

Generally, the majority of FINADEV's clients admit that they have experienced both personal and business changes since taking advantage of FINADEV loans. Many were able to use their profit to make a personal investment such as the purchase of a plot of land or a car. Women have acquired some independence from their husbands, and the welfare of their children has improved. Some 77 per cent say the turnover of their business has increased.

Impact on other actors

Commercial banks
At the start, the banks did not respond to the initiative, as they considered micro-finance customers to be down-market clients. Today their perception has changed and, even though none of them has really committed itself as deeply as the FBB, all the commercial banks have begun to introduce social loans in their product range, like FBB used to do. Several banks have also started refinancing activities for the most important MFIs in Benin (PADME, PAPME, VITAL FINANCE, etc.).

FINADEV has also been able to negotiate collaboration with other commercial banks such as Bank of Africa, which granted a line of credit of about US$2m with the same conditions as FBB, that is 7 per cent interest, excluding taxes. Some contacts have also been made with other banks and the Post Office for financial relations. FBB is very comfortable with this diversification of FINADEV's financial partners, because it does not have the capacity to respond to all its needs, and the law does limit the risk a bank should take with a given client. For Bank of Africa, the deal with FINADEV is not the first experience; the bank has made a strategic choice to partner MFIs through financing the instituions.

FINADEV is also an active member of the professional association of the Microfinance Institutions of Benin, known as the Consortium ALAFIA, and expects to contribute to the advocacy strategy of the network in order to reduce the legal constraints that hinder the smooth development of microfinance in Benin.

Other microfinance institutions
At the start, the other MFIs felt threatened by the creation of FINADEV because of its professionalism and its ability to receive funding from FBB for its activities. But, progressively, this situation changed because many understood that there is room in the market for all the MFIs, and that FINADEV, in view of its legal status, represents a unique model in the sector as a private commercial entity that may serve as an example for the whole sector. In addition, FINADEV succeeded in launching the credit bureau initiative with support from CARE International and

PlaNet Finance with three other microfinance institutions (PADME, VITAL FINANCE, CFAD) to exchange information on the portfolio on a regular basis. Today, about 12 MFIs are members of the credit bureau.

Staff and clients

As stated earlier, there is a problem of interpretation with respect to the distribution of FINADEV shares, which prevents the company from obtaining a long-term licence from the authorities. In fact the Central Bank considers that since the Financial Bank Group and FBB are effectively the same entity, their joint holding of 40 per cent of the shares contravenes the banking law, which sets a participation limit of 25 per cent. The microfinance unit of the Central Bank and the Ministry of Finance and Economy and the other parties do not have the same interpretation, and for this reason FINADEV has a short-term licence which it has to renew regularly. This dispute must be resolved. It affects the staff because their contracts are short-term contracts. It might also affect the quality of the portfolio if the clients are aware of the dispute, but this has not happened yet.

Products offered by FINADEV and the financial situation of the institution

Financial transactions volume

As at 31 December 2003, the total amount of loan disbursed by FINADEV is more than US$28m for a total number of 42 648 loans disbursed since inception. Out of that total amount, US$20m is lent to women organized into groups. The function of the groups is to provide collateral: each member is identified by FINADEV in its books, but in case of default, the group is responsible for repaying the loan. The women run different economic activities such as small trading shops, services and small restaurants. The remaining US$8m serves to finance small enterprises and salaried workers, with no guarantees.

Financial services and products offered

Different products are offered by FINADEV. Each product is designed for a specific clientele. Table 12.4 (opposite) describes the five main products. None of them is similar to FBB's products, in term of size of the loan, target group, or procedures. However, some of FINADEV products are similar to other MFIs' products in terms of speed of processing, education required, interest rate, and so on. FINADEV requires every client to have an ID card. This is not difficult to get and helps to identify clients. Most MFIs working in the capital city also require this. FINADEV is in the process of deciding on the use of the guarantee fund. For the time being, its only use is to pay back loans if a client dies. This avoids putting pressure on the family.

Products	Akuwe Kleun	Akuwe Djreme	Individual credit	Social credit	TPE credit
People	Women in petty trade	Good Akuwe Kleun customers that have repaid over US$943	Salaried workers who have an account at FBB	Groups of salaried workers	Small-scale enterprises, traders and economic operators with medium-scale activities
Conditions	Groups of non-pregnant women of different families	Groups of non-pregnant women of different families			To have an account at FBB
Minimum/Max. amount	US$94 to US$943	Minimum US$1 037	Variable depending on salary	Variable, around US$943	US$ 943 to US$5 660
Interest rate	12% per year of the outstanding balance	1% per month 12% per year	15% of the outstanding balance	11% of the outstanding balance	15% of the outstanding balance
Guarantee fund	1% per month up to the 5th month, 5% for more than 5 months	5% for amount below US$1 500, 2.5% for more than US$1 500	2%	2%	2%
Duration	From 3 to 10 months	From 1 to 10 months	24 months	Up to 5 years	Up to 2 years
Minimum deposit	20% of the loan	20% for loans less than US$1 500, and 25% for loans over US$1 500		Long-term deposit of 3.5% of loan amount	
Statement fees	1% of loan amount	1% of loan if less than US$1 500, 0.5% if not	US$20	1% of loan amount	US$20
Documents	ID Card photocopy	ID Card photocopy	Payslip	Payslip	
Guarantees	Solidarity caution	Solidarity caution	Insurance account at FBB	Death insurance policy	Landowner's certificate Death insurance policy
Age requirement	Between 22 and 55	Between 22 and 55	Between 22 and 55	No limit	No limit

Table 12.4 FINADEV's main products

The profitability of the initiative

In July 2003, FINADEV reached an operational self-sufficiency ratio of 114 per cent. Financial self-sufficiency has yet to be achieved, and was 96 per cent for the same period. This was caused by an adjustment suggested by the Microfinance Information Exchange in its publication of July 2003 – in order to reflect inflation and subsidy-in-kind in the financial statements. The nominal return on the loan portfolio was 13.47 per cent for the same period, and the adjusted financial income over total assets amounted to 10.9 per cent.

In terms of loan portfolio quality, FINADEV's portfolio overdue more than 30 days as at 30 July 2003 was 0.2 per cent, and the ratio of adjusted personnel costs to the loan portfolio was 2.6 per cent. The portfolio at risk ratio had increased to 1.02 per cent at the end of the fiscal year (December 2003). FINADEV had a good performance in terms of loan management, and FINADEV made a profit in the year ending 31 December 2003, as shown by the simplified balance sheet and profit and loss account in Tables 12.5 and 12.6 (below and opposite).

Future vision of FINADEV

FINADEV's ambition is to become a very large private microfinance institution covering the whole of Benin, especially in the urban and

Table 12.5 Simplified profit and loss account as at 31 December 2003 (US$ '000)

Interest earned on current loans	975
Other interest & commissions	178
Total financial income	**1 153**
Interest paid on loans	-243
Other commissions paid on loans	-7
Net income	**903**
Other operational income	108
Operating costs	-419
Personnel cost	-327
Depreciation	-44
Total costs	**-790**
Profit before tax	**221**
Tax	-86
Net profit	**135**
Note: US$1 = 530 F CFA	

Table 12.6 Simplified balance sheet as at 31 December 2003 (US$ '000)

Assets		Liabilities	
Cash	414	Deposits	1 275
Current Loans	9 685	Short term loans	4 473
Other assets	87	Other short term liabilities	267
Equipment	206	Long term loans	1 602
		Equity and quasi-equity	2 775
Total assets	**10 392**	**Total liabilities**	**10 392**
Note: US$1 = 530 F CFA			

rural areas with high potential. To be able to do that, FINADEV plans to open its equity base to other interested shareholders and to diversify its financial partners in order to increase its financial basis and to respond to the increasing demand from current and potential clients.

Based on lessons learned from the current experience, Financial Bank Group is intending to replicate the experience of FINADEV in other countries such as Togo, Gabon and Guinea, and to consolidate the experience already started in Chad.

Lessons learned from the experience

- To create a private microfinance institution like FINADEV, it is important to have strategic partnerships with a commercial bank and other institutions. The commercial bank will play a critical role in launching the microfinance institution by providing loan funds, competent staff and all physical facilities needed such as its infrastructure. Other institutions will provide necessary shares and adequate support for official recognition of the initiative from the competent authority.

- An initiative such as the one set up by FBB in collaboration with other shareholders can be profitable, if adequate funding is mobilized at the inception to respond to clients' needs and if it is well managed by professional staff.

- It is important to conduct market research at the inception in order to assure that the microfinance products developed by the institution are responsive to clients' needs.

- It is good to attach bank staff to a microfinance programme since this helps to professionalize the management. The attached staff brought banking professionalism and expertise to microfinance, and they adapted it to the special requirements of microfinance.

- The recruitment of microfinance staff from outside the bank, especially young university graduates with little, if any, banking experience made them more receptive to the special mission and practices of the microfinance programme.

- Sharing bank facilities at the beginning of the FINADEV initiative has helped to expand and reach out to potential microfinance clients at low cost. However, it is important for the microfinance programme management to build a good independent image for the new institution, to plan for separation and to diversify partners when appropriate.

- It is important for government to encourage other microfinance programmes to convert into fully fledged banking or non-banking microfinance institutions with adequate legal status in order to be able to mobilize funding to respond to clients needs and to achieve sustainability. Government should put in place a conducive environment, including tax relief for a period of time, and rapid licensing when necessary.

Conclusion

A microfinance programme can be introduced by a commercial bank. One way to do this is to set up a separate entity with various shareholders and appropriate governance to run the programme. A fully private microfinance programme without any subsidy from a donor can be profitable if it is well-managed, with professional staff committed to the mission of the institution.

Discussion questions

1. The Financial Bank Group decided from the outset to set up a separate institution for microfinance, and the microfinance window was only a transitional step towards this. Was this the optimum policy, or might the microfinance become more firmly embedded in the bank and in society, if it was integrated into the bank itself?

2. Financial Bank started by wholesaling bulk funds to MFIs, and then moved into direct financing. Was this necessary, might it have been possible and more efficient to develop microfinance by assisting some of the existing MFIs to grow into more substantial and sustainable institutions?

3. The bank's staff felt initially that microfinance clients were socially inferior to their traditional banking clients and that their presence in the bank's premises would offend their existing clients. This is a common if usually unspoken issue; how can banks overcome it, without necessarily opening separate branches for micro-clients?

Chapter Thirteen
Banco Solidario, Ecuador

MELITA SAWYER and MARÍA SOLEDAD JARRÍN

Introduction

Banco Solidario is a microfinance bank, headquartered in Quito, Ecuador, that provides financial services to a section of the population traditionally excluded from the financial sector. In contrast to many microfinance institutions (MFIs), Banco Solidario was born as a private bank with a social mission, not as an NGO and, since its inception in 1995, has balanced the twin goals of financial and social profitability. While the bank always emphasizes social profitability, it can never ignore financial returns or rely upon donations. In order to compete with the traditional banking sector for savings and deposits, Banco Solidario has invested heavily in the research and development of innovative products tailored to the needs of its target clientele.

Vision and mission

Banco Solidario strives to be the leader in the financial sector with a social mission. The bank's philosophy is to 'believe in people for who they are, not for what they own.'

Banco Solidario focuses on poverty reduction by satisfying the needs of the market segment that lacks access to credit through the traditional financial system. The bank emphasizes customer loyalty by offering quality and innovative financial products and services. It aims to reward the trust of its depositors, investors, shareholders and collaborators with financial and social gains resulting from an efficient administration by a qualified and happy team of people, who make Banco Solidario's mission a part of their life's purpose.

'Living Solidarity' (*Vivir Solidario*)

Banco Solidario is unique because of the dedication of its staff to the bank's mission and institutional spirit of 'Living Solidarity'. 'Living Solidarity' is more than simply a motto; it means being happy in the knowledge that our work has a new significance, looking beyond one's own personal interests, and positively affecting the lives of others. This spirit permeates the bank at every level, and guides the daily behaviour of personnel as well as the overall strategy of the bank. A 2003 human resources survey reported that the bank's personnel identify closely with *Vivir Solidario* and with the bank's corporate values of 'ethics, prudence, enthusiasm, solidarity, quality service, social responsibility, and helping not judging'. Achieving social profitability along with financial profitability is at the centre of Banco Solidario's activities, and the bank's staff search for ways to maximize both indicators.

Overview of the Ecuadorian economy and the microenterprise sector

The Ecuadorian economy has performed poorly in the past decade, and the country experienced the worst financial and economic crisis in its history in 1999. Overall growth has been negative and production has stagnated. GDP per capita remains at 1970s levels (currently US$1450) while poverty continues to grow. Difficulties peaked in the crisis of 1999, as instability caused by factors including the El Niño phenomenon, repercussions of the Asian and Brazilian financial crises, unstable oil prices, poor governance, and crisis in the financial sector led to devaluation of the Sucre, rapid inflation, capital flight, and a massive reduction in government spending. The percentage of the population living below the poverty level rose from 50 per cent in 1995 to 69 per cent in 1999.[1] GDP plummeted 7.3 per cent and 20 banks closed, representing 45 per cent of the financial system.[2] The inflation rate reached 30 per cent in 2001, but has since stabilized at 6.07 per cent in 2003, and is projected to be approximately 4 per cent in 2004. However, Banco Solidario posted profits even in the toughest years of the crisis; the bank's success during a time when many financial institutions failed was closely linked to its focus on the micro-entrepreneurial sector and will be examined more closely later in this case study.

In 1999 and 2000, several structural changes to the framework of the economy resulted from the crisis, including dollarization of the Ecuadorian economy, a vast reduction in formal employment, and the migration of approximately 400 000 Ecuadorians to other countries. One of the most profound legacies was rapid growth of the microenterprise sector due to the drop in formal employment. There currently exist around 1.3 million microenterprises in Ecuador that generate 2.5 million jobs (60 per cent of the economically active population is involved in this sector[4]), sustain at least 5.2 million people (40 per cent of the total population), and contribute 15 per cent of GDP.[5] Additionally, the sector creates 75 per cent of the country's new jobs at a much lower cost than job creation in the formal sector.[6] Although the microenterprise sector is vitally important to the overall economy and the people involved in it, it still suffers from poor access to financing and other important non-financial services.

At the time Banco Solidario was founded in 1995, 70 per cent of the economically active population was without recourse to the traditional financial sector.[7] While certain organizations, including governmental organizations, NGOs and credit unions were serving the micro-entrepeneurial sector, Banco Solidario was the first private bank in Ecuador to focus on microfinance. The bank now offers products directed to any person without access to the formal financial sector, such as 'Pot of Gold' loans, housing loans, and savings products; however, the focus and volume of the bank's business remains on micro-business owners. Although the informal sector is now better attended than at any time previously, and microenterprise loan portfolios are growing rapidly,

MFIs in Ecuador have achieved only limited geographic reach and market penetration. The majority of micro-entrepreneurs still do not have access to formal sources of financing; for example, only an estimated 20 per cent of urban micro-entrepreneurs have access to formal loans.[8] The lack of formal coverage is seen by the continued dominance of informal lenders who charge interest rates of 10 per cent to 15 per cent per month but continue to control 23 per cent of the market.[9]

Banco Solidario: origins and history

The bank's founding

Banco Solidario was created in 1995, as the first financial institution in Latin America financed with private capital to focus on those without access to the traditional banking sector. Initially investment came from private investors; today 49 per cent of the bank's shares are owned by international organizations.

The bank's motivation in entering the micro-financial sector was two-fold: first, to be a leader in the financial sector by offering services and products to the market segment that lacks access to traditional financial institutions; and second, to provide a trustworthy channel through which international investors can direct funds towards the poorest sections of the Ecuadorian population.

In 1991, the Bank's founders, Santiago Ribadeneira Troya and Mónica Hernández (respectively the bank's current Executive President and Executive Vice President) began to work towards their goal of creating a financial institution focused on microenterprises with the creation of *Fundación Alternativa*. This is the social promoter of Banco Solidario and a shareholder in the bank. The foundation is the bank's centre for both internal and third party training, and develops other financial and social projects. In 1995, their project, promoted by *Fundación Alternativa*, became a reality when private local investors purchased an existing financial company.

In 1996, Banco Solidario absorbed another financial company and converted into a regulated bank with the help of international investors, including PROFUND, ACCION International, Seed Capital, and CARE (USAID-funding enabled Seed Capital and CARE to become shareholders). Banco Solidario could then offer savings and checking services to its customers. Through the discipline and transparency that followed from regulation, Banco Solidario became even more attractive to international investors who became shareholders or provided lines of credit.

Currently, both private and institutional investors own the bank's shares, with 49 per cent of shares in the hands of the international organizations ProFund (with support of IADB, CAF, World Bank), SEED Capital (with support of USAID), CAF, SwissContact, ACCION Gateway, ACCION Investments, Martin Conell, CARE, Oikocredit,

SIDI, *Stichting Hivos-Triodos Fonds* and *Stichting Triodos-Doen*. The remaining 51 per cent of shares are owned by 90 socially minded Ecuadorian investors.

Entry into microfinance

The bank's founders established a specific department for microfinance activities, because they require different methodologies and more involved management. Since microenterprise lending is unique – small loans, a market niche requiring different credit technology, and long-term profitability – the bank chose not to liquidate the conventional portfolio of small and medium enterprises inherited from the purchased financial companies immediately, but rather to manage this portfolio to subsidize the growth of the micro-credit portfolio. The approach was successful, and the results generated by the old portfolio helped back the development and consolidation of microfinance activities in the early years of the bank. At the time the bank was founded, there were no specific Central Bank regulations for microfinance; indeed Banco Solidario was the first regulated bank in Ecuador to focus on the micro-entrepreneurial sector. However, the microenterprise portfolio of regulated institutions grew 176 per cent between October 2002 and October 2003, and the *Superintendencia de Bancos* has recently instituted regulations intended to strengthen and monitor the concession of micro-loans, for example requiring micro-credit methodology to be elaborated in the manuals of regulated financial institutions.

In the first few years, Banco Solidario faced significant challenges, especially with regard to initial investment. For example, at the time there did not exist adequate information systems tailored to microfinance, compelling the bank to invest substantially in the development of such a system. Similarly, the hiring and thorough training of personnel in the methodology of micro-credit represented a large, but clearly essential, investment.

The Bank has grown rapidly from a single office in Quito and an office inherited from the absorbed financial company in Ambato, and now has 23 points-of-sale in six provinces, including 13 agency offices.

International investors

Banco Solidario's strong relationships with a variety of international organizations has always been one of its strengths. One of its founding objectives was to become a trustworthy channel for international investors who wanted to support the poor in Ecuador. It captured the attention of international organizations involved in microfinance or development, including multilateral development banks and bilateral aid agencies. These organizations have provided technical assistance in the development of adequate methodologies, product development and institutional build up. Many have been primary lenders and share-

Figure 13.1 Banco Solidario's international funds (US$m)

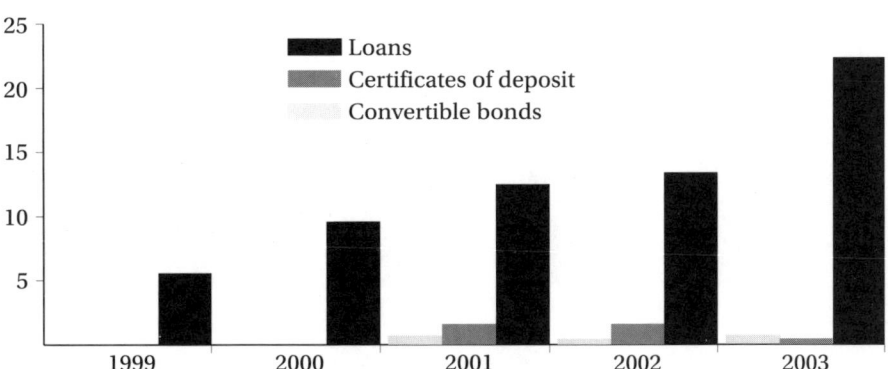

holders, participating actively on the board of directors, and have been an integral part of the strategies followed by the bank.

During the crisis in 1999, Banco Solidario's international shareholders and investors played an especially vital role through their technical, strategic and financial support, providing not only much needed liquidity but also strengthening the bank's credibility in the face of foreign and national investors who were withdrawing funds from Ecuador. As a result, Banco Solidario was the only private Ecuadorian bank to receive funds during a time when international credit lines for the Ecuadorian financial system had been cut off.

Clients and products

The majority of Banco Solidario's niche clients are urban micro-entrepreneurs in the highland regions of Ecuador, although the bank is actively expanding its services in rural and coastal areas. Services are marketed equally to men and women, with the primary requirement for a micro-loan being that the client possesses a productive enterprise which generates sufficient income both to cover the household's expenses and repay the loan. While there is not a poverty requirement to solicit a loan, 75 per cent of the bank's clients belong to the country's lowest income strata.[10]

Initially, the bank offered two products to its microfinance clientele, urban solidarity group loans and individual loans, under the prevailing methodology of the time. However, since its founding the bank has been driven by the demands of the market and has prioritized the research and development of diverse products tailored specifically to clients' needs, rather than implementing technology developed by other institutions.

The largest of the bank's niche products in terms of both financial volume and number of clients is urban microenterprise loans. This portfolio continues to grow rapidly, with approximately 10 per cent of the microenterprise portfolio composed of solidarity group loans.

Figure 13.2 *Average micro-loan amounts (US$)*

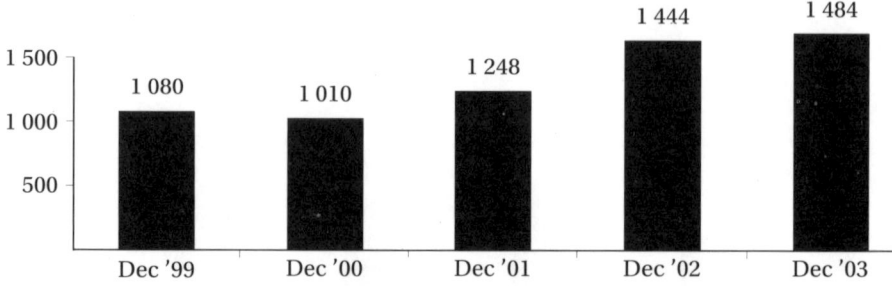

Solidarity groups are composed of three to eight people, and members are selected by the clients themselves. The group provides a solidarity guarantee for the loan, and the credit officer consolidates the group, assuring that the group is composed of clients who know each other, who have businesses of similar types and sizes, and who understand the commitment of participating in a solidarity group. Over the years, the average size of the bank's microenterprise loans has gradually increased, as is shown in Figure 13.2. (Note: the drop in average loan size in 2000 is due to the dollarization of the Ecuadorian economy and the subsequent switch from Sucres to dollars.)

The bank's innovation in product development is demonstrated in its social housing, emigrant, *Chauchera* Card, and 'Pot of Gold' (*Olla de Oro*) products. These are both financial and non-financial products that were developed as the bank broadened its focus and coverage beyond micro-entrepreneurs to serve others who do not have access to the financial system, as well as to offer original products to its micro-entrepreneur clients. This innovation has required high investment, and this is reflected in the bank's high operating costs. However, the bank views this development as a worthwhile cost, and its innovation has had an industry-wide impact.

The 'Pot of Gold' is a pawn-loan product that provides an immediate loan guaranteed by gold jewellery. This is a personal consumption loan and is accessible to any client, not only to micro-entrepreneurs. The *Chauchera* Card (*Chauchera* is a popular term used for a money purse) is an 'electronic purse' in the form of a debit and credit card that allows micro-entrepreneurs access to large industries in order to purchase their raw materials and inputs at wholesale cost. Given their small size, micro-businesses usually do not have access to wholesale vendors. To address this need, the bank has reached an agreement with wholesale providers, giving clients access to their goods and services through the *Chauchera*. The *Chauchera* has an interest rate of 18.7 per cent and the cost of funds is 10 per cent. The *Chauchera* has proved to be popular and by December 2003, more than 14 774 clients were using this product.

The Bank's social housing products are targeted towards the strong demand for affordable and quality housing. As at December 2003, more than 3500 homes had been financed, creating more than 40 000 temporary jobs, with a portfolio value of US$12.4m.

Banco Solidario has also developed the 'My Family, My Country, My Return' programme (*Mi Familia, Mi País, Mi Regreso*) to meet the needs of Ecuadorian emigrants and their families, whose numbers have grown rapidly in recent years. This programme aims to channel emigrants' effort and sacrifice abroad towards building a foundation for their return. It provides a safe method of transferring remittances and allows the income generated by emigrants abroad to be invested in a home or business, a project with a return, and not simply directed towards unproductive expenses. Clients who maintain a minimum amount in their savings account may realize remittances for free. Banco Solidario has established a network of banks in Spain and Italy from which transfers may be sent, and has formed a similar network in Ecuador so that family members may withdraw the transfer at a financial institution close to where they live, often in rural areas. As at November 2003, there had been 13 239 transfers representing US$25.7m, and more than 200 homes sold.

The bank has also begun to focus on the rural sector and to expand its services there. In 2001, Banco Solidario and *Fundación Alternativa* launched a rural group loan product with the help and funding of Belgian Technical Cooperation and technical assistance from ACCION. In that year alone, the project disbursed US$1m in rural group loans. The bank now offers rural solidarity group and individual loans.

Table 13.1 below shows the volume and coverage of specific niche products:

Financial impact

Banco Solidario is the leader in the microenterprise finance market in Ecuador. The bank has grown quite rapidly from a portfolio of less than US$30m in 1997 to more than US$130m in December 2003. Growth is not happening without regard to quality; across the board, the bank's

Table 13.1 Coverage of Banco Solidario niche products at December 2003

Product	Number of clients	Portfolio value (US$m)(US$)	Average per client
Microenterprise loans	42 617	57.08	1 342
Pot of Gold	42 800	16.5	388
Social housing	1 520	12.4	11 100
Rural credit	3 921	5.37	1 371

Table 13.2 *Financial data for Banco Solidario, 2002 and 2003*

	Dec 2002	**Dec 2003**
Total number of clients	72 777	96 823
Total portfolio (US$ '000)[11]	105 081	130 067
Micro-credit portfolio (US$ '000)	69 863	92 085
Number of micro-credit clients	66 877	91 109
Total assets (US$ '000)	158 163	181 582
(Portfolio at risk)/total portfolio[12]	5.3%	4.54%
(Micro-credit portfolio at risk)/total microcredit portfolio	7.6%	4.27%
Total deposits (US$ '000)[13]	105 572	126 600
Savings deposits (US$ '000)	9 930	13 861
Checking accounts (US$ '000)	9 773	10 163
Net return on assets (ROA)	1.90%	1.85%
Net return on equity (ROE)	30.22%	24.61%
Liquidity: available funds/short term deposits	9.06%	14.66%

Source: Banco Solidario's financial control area

financial indicators have been steadily improving. While the volume of the total portfolio and the microenterprise portfolio grew significantly in 2003, the percentages of both total portfolio at risk and microenterprise portfolio at risk dropped continuously throughout the year (see Table 13.2, above).

In spite of the difficult economic environment in Ecuador during recent years, the bank has been able to post ever-increasing profits. The bank earned a profit even during the crisis years of 1999 and 2000, posting ROA and ROE of 1.33 per cent and 12.24 per cent respectively in 1999 and 0.88 per cent and 6.53 per cent in 2000 (profit of approximately US$1m each year).

Tables 13.3 and 13.5 (opposite and overleaf) show Banco Solidario's balance sheet and profit and loss statement for 2003.

Role of microfinance in Banco Solidario

The focus of the bank is strongly on the niche market of those who previously were without access to the financial sector, not only in terms of philosophy and goals, but also in number of clients and volume of portfolio. This focus has proved profitable. Table 13.4 (see opposite) demonstrates the profitability of key niche products; 'Other revenue' includes the product's commissions and service costs.

Table 13.3 Banco Solidario Balance Sheet at 31 December 2003 (expressed in US$)

Assets		Liabilities and capital	
Available funds	16 817 237	Obligations with the public	126 632 164
Investments	20 753 456	Immediate obligations	732 350
Loan portfolio	122 524 450	Accounts payable	4 836 517
Accounts receivable	2 285 335	Financial obligations	31 037 488
Realizable current assets, allocated by payment from commercial leases not used by institution	630 223	Convertible bonds	777 350
Property and equipment	4 154 837	Other liabilities	576 002
Other assets	14 417 151	Equity	16 990 818
Total assets	**181 582 689**	**Total liabilities**	**181 582 689**

The bank's success in surviving the 1999 Ecuadorian financial crisis was largely due to its involvement in microfinance, and has led the bank to re-double its efforts in this sector. Some 94 per cent of the bank's clients are micro-product clients. Figures 13.3 and 13.4 (overleaf) demonstrate the significant focus of the bank on the niche market, in terms of overall volume of niche portfolio, as a percentage of total portfolio, and in number and percentage of niche clients.

Microfinance in unstable times: Banco Solidario and Ecuador's 1999 Crisis

During the crisis of 1999, some 45 per cent of Ecuador's financial system closed its doors, as Government withdrawals, a lack of confidence in the banking system, the drying up of external funds to Ecuador, and a fall in clients' cash flow brought the system's liquidity and solvency

Table 13.4 Profitability of niche products

Products	Interest rate	Other revenue	Costs	Net profit	Risk	Liquidity
Microenterprise loans	14.34%	32.50%	-24.38%	22.45%	Low	High
Pot of Gold	17.82%	28.57%	-20.03%	26.37%	Low	High
Social Housing	15.41%	2.34%	-16.07%	1.68%	Low	High
Chauchera Card	18.70%	15.64%	-23.83%	10.51%	Low	High

Table 13.5 Banco Solidario profit and loss statement for the year ending 31 December 2003 (expressed in US$)

Financial income		
Earned interest	17 864 248	
Earned commissions	5 297 095	
Financial gains	4 152 827	
Income from services	12 867 107	
Total income		40 181 277
Financial expenditure		
Incurred interest	-10 184 000	
Incurred commissions	-1 013 810	
Financial losses	-3 147 770	
Total expenditure		-14 345 580
Gross financial margin		25 835 697
Other operational income		627 694
Operational expenses	-20 525 084	
Other operational losses	-113 617	
Total operational costs		-20 638 701
Operational margin before provisions depreciations and amortizations		5 824 690
Provisions, depreciations and amortizations		
Provisions	-334 424	
Depreciations	-599 554	
Amortizations	-1 077 014	
Total provisions, depreciations and amortizations		-2 010 992
Net operating margin		3 813 698
Non-operational receipts and expenditures, net		357 660
Profit before taxes and profit sharing		4 171 358
The Fund for Infant Development (FODINFA)	-36 164	
Employee profit sharing	-319 095	
Tax on revenue	-460 389	
Net profit for 2003		3 355 710

under pressure. However, Banco Solidario, the only private bank in Ecuador focused on microfinance, was able to not only remain open but even to post modest profits.

The bank's focus on its niche clientele was not a liability during the crisis; indeed, it was the liquidity of its microenterprise portfolio and the recognition of the bank as a unique entity that enabled it to weather the difficult times. The problems of micro-entrepreneurs, such as failure and bad debts, take longer to impact on an entity like Banco Solidario, because the risks are shared out over so many small loans. Moreover, the bank's diverse products, in particular social housing savings, helped prevent a massive run on deposits. However, the devaluation of the Sucre caused a drop in the value of assets and equity, in dollar terms.

The bank's focus during the crisis was how best to protect its clients. To this end, the bank solicited advice from MFIs in Peru and Bolivia who had successfully weathered crisis times. The bank lowered average loan amounts and shortened terms, and identified types of businesses that were particularly at risk. Through these adaptations, it was able to continue serving its clientele.

In turn, the microenterprise clients trusted the bank and honored their obligations. Although they tend to suffer from the same shocks as large companies, microenterprises are less exposed to external shocks, given that they make use of local inputs to meet local demand; micro-entrepreneurs also often have multiple sources of income and are creative and flexible when faced with a crisis. Upon reopening the bank after the week-long national bank holiday, Banco Solidario had micro-entrepreneurs queuing to pay their debts rather than withdraw money.

While the quality of the bank's portfolio did deteriorate during the crisis, this deterioration was largely in the bank's commercial loans. Meanwhile, the quality of the microenterprise portfolio did not fall but remained steady, as demonstrated in Figure 13.5 (overleaf).

Figure 13.3 Banco Solidario's niche market portfolio vs. total portfolio

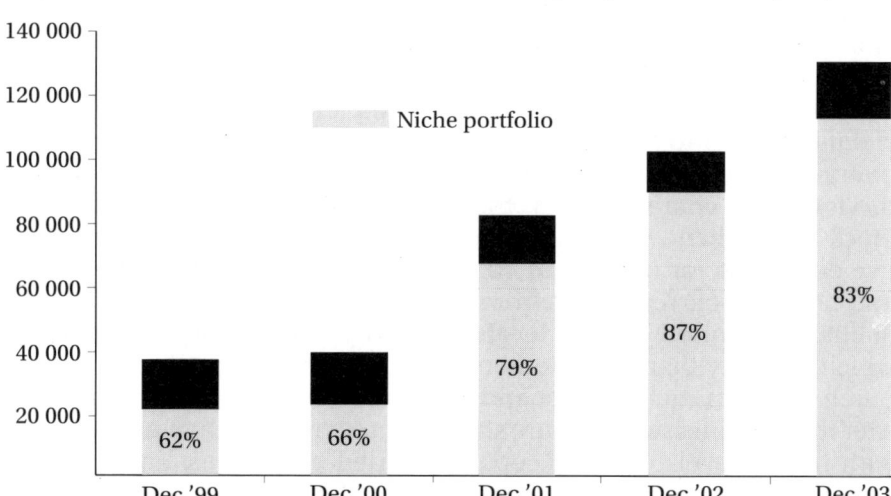

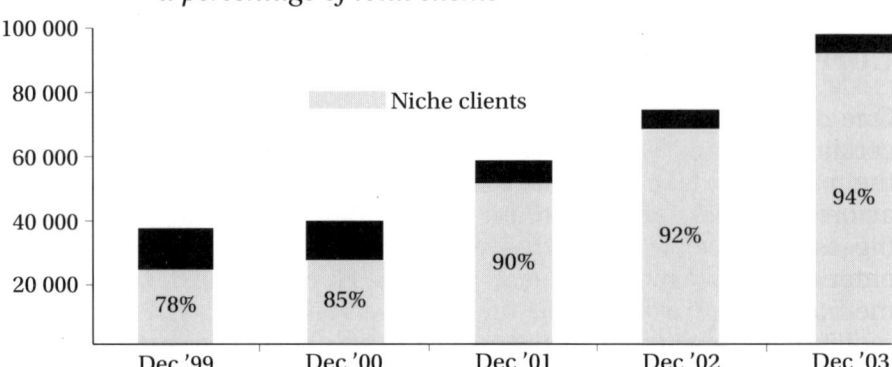

Figure 13.4 *Evolution of Banco Solidario's niche market clients as a percentage of total clients*

At the beginning of 1999, international organizations owned 26.26 per cent of Banco Solidario's shares and participated actively both in strategic decision-making and in the financing that allowed Banco Solidario to survive the crisis. The bank's ability to keep capturing diverse sources of financing was key to maintaining its credibility and liquidity.

Social impact

While the financial profitability that the bank has achieved is essential, it represents only one half of Banco Solidario's goals. Additionally and importantly, the bank's products have achieved social returns.

An impact study, produced in 2002 and funded by HIVOS and conducted by CDR-ULA (Free University of Amsterdam) and *Fundación Alternativa* demonstrated that the bank's micro-loans not only benefit clients' microenterprises, but that their households' standards of living improve as well. The study was commissioned in order to measure the impact of micro-loans issued by HIVOS' counterparts Banco Solidario and Caja los Andes, and to analyse the extent to which their financial products were helping to accomplish HIVOS' overall goal of poverty alleviation. Strict criteria were employed in the selection of 'non-clients' in order to achieve an appropriate comparison. For each client interviewed, a corresponding non-client was interviewed according to the following characteristics: the non-client had to live in the same block as the client, work in the same sector, have possessed a productive enterprise for more than 12 months, not be a salaried employee, and not have current loans from any formal source. Clients of Banco Solidario reported higher levels of food security than non-clients, which is to say that they are better able to avoid food scarcity and to purchase items such as meat and chicken. Additionally, clients administer their businesses in a more sophisticated manner than non-clients, with higher levels of bookkeeping, salaried employees, and a better understanding of which products bring them the greatest profit.[15]

Table 13.6 (see overleaf) displays the results of several key variables examined in the study.

Current and future challenges

One of the greatest challenges that the bank currently faces and will certainly continue to face is competition. Each day, competition within the microfinance industry in Ecuador becomes more intense, as new actors enter the industry and current actors expand their services. The biggest threat to the bank is not losing market share, but that actors entering the market without using proper micro-credit technology and methodology could potentially over-indebt the sector. Microfinance requires in-depth analysis of clients' financial situations, examining income and expenses of both the business and home; those institutions that grant loans without conducting proper analysis threaten the health of the sector for all MFIs and their clients.

The development of an adequate regulatory framework for the micro-financial sector in Ecuador is another current challenge. As the sector grows rapidly, it is becoming increasingly imperative that there is well-defined regulation and a responsible monitoring body. These elements, however, are still in their early stages of development. An additional regulatory threat is that the Government will intervene to control interest rates, distorting the market.

An ongoing challenge for Banco Solidario is ensuring that its members of staff are thoroughly trained and adhere to the institution's methodology. Credit officers with inadequate preparation and training, or who deviate from the established technology, can significantly increase the risks facing the bank. Therefore, the bank is constantly investing in

Figure 13.4 *Portfolio quality during the crisis: microenterprise vs. total Banco Solidario*[14]

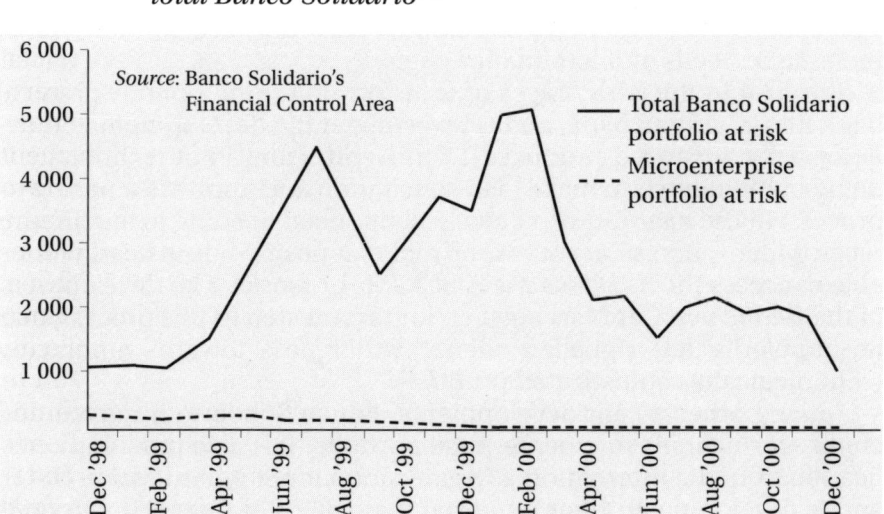

Figure 13.4 Results of survey of livelihood impacts on Banco Solidario clients

Indicator	Client of Banco Solidario	Non-client
Homeowner	72.7%	62.4%
Home improvements >US$500**	26.3%	15.6%
Expansion of business*	79.6%	65.4%
Higher sales figures*	38.8%	26.9%
Sales in a new market*	57.1%	30.8%
Have a savings account	70.7%	35.6%
* within the last year; ** within the last two years		

training and re-training, especially as it expands into new markets and increases the numbers of its officers.

Conclusion and perspectives on the future

The bank's dedication to serving clients who traditionally have been excluded from the financial sector has not waned, and microfinance will continue to constitute the majority of the bank's activities for the foreseeable future.

However, while the focus of the bank's activities will remain unchanged, the form of those activities is changing. In response to customer demand over the last few years, the bank's microenterprise portfolio is becoming increasingly concentrated in individual loans and moving away from group loans. Further, the bank is continuing its development as a microfinance bank through increased diversification of its products and the expansion of savings and checking accounts. The bank is currently designing new savings products to better meet the unique needs of microfinance clients.

It is also in the early stages of transforming from a purely physical bank into a 'virtual' bank, and is investing in the development of technologically advanced products. To this end, Palm Pilot technology is being implemented to make loan solicitation and approval a paperless process. In the near future, clients will not need to come to an office to receive loans, access accounts, or make deposits, but instead will be able to access the bank's services at ATMs or kiosks. The development of the *Chauchera* Card has been an important step in this process, and its popularity has signalled clients' willingness towards embracing technologically sophisticated products.

Among other recent developments, Banco Solidario implemented credit scoring in its microenterprise portfolio. It is also pursuing certification from the International Organization for Standardization (ISO), and is developing an Internet portal that will offer financial and non-financial services to credit unions, NGOs, governmental organizations, international organizations and private businesses.

As Banco Solidario has experienced: given strong human resources and leadership, and a dedicated focus on the niche market, microfinance can be both a financially and socially profitable business. The bank will continue to keep niche market clients as the basis of its decision-making process, innovating and expanding to best serve those who are still unattended financially.

Acknowledgements

This case study was made possible through the contribution and cooperation of many people, especially Mónica Hernández, Soledad Burbano and Natasha Cruz, as well as Banco Solidario's International Affairs Office, the Office of the Vice-Presidency, the Microfinance Department, and the Financial Control Department.

Discussion questions

1. Banco Solidario and its investors have both social and commercial goals; such a mixture would normally be expected to constrain profitable growth. How has the bank's choice of apparently unattractive market segments affected their financial performance?

2. The bank survived the national financial crisis better than the purely profit-seeking institutions Why was this, and what are the lessons of this experience for other banks, for investors and for the bank regulators?

3. The bank's portfolio mix is moving towards individual versus group clients, and they are also working towards electronic banking. Does this indicate the beginnings of a drift away from more needy clients, and how can such a drift be avoided?

Chapter Fourteen
Bancafé, Guatemala[1]

JOB BLIJDENSTEIN

Guatemala

Guatemala is a small Central American country with some 12 million inhabitants, 60 per cent of whom live in rural areas. A large part of the population is indigenous, especially in the north and west. Per capita income stands at US$1750, and 56 per cent of the population lives below the poverty line. Social indicators of health, education and distribution of wealth are among the worst in the continent. Approximately 36 per cent of the working population depends on the informal sector for their livelihoods.

For 2003, the gross internal product was some US$19bn; exports had a value of US$2371m and imports US$6223m, leaving a commercial deficit of US$3850m. Foreign currency is earned mainly from coffee, tourism and some non-traditional products, while the remittances migrants send from abroad have grown explosively and now exceed US$2100m per annum. During the last few years, annual economic growth has been little more than 2 per cent per year, less than population growth. The macro-economic picture is stable: annual inflation rates have been between 5 and 10 per cent, and the exchange rate between the US dollar and the Quetzal was 7.75 during 2000 and now stands at 8.00.

Until 1986, Guatemala mainly had military governments, but since then it has held various democratic presidential and congressional elections, resulting in civil presidencies. A 30-year-long guerrilla war ended in 1996.

Since the 1980s, the financial sector has grown considerably: more than 30 banks were active in 1997. However, since 1998, various mergers have taken place, and during the last five years the authorities have had to intervene in the affairs of various banks which were eventually closed and liquidated.

Since 1986, the government, various NGOs and the State-owned Agricultural Development Bank (BANDESA) – later transformed with mixed capital into the Rural Development Bank (BANRURAL) – have started programmes to bring financial services, mainly loans, to the microenterprise sector. These efforts received strong support from the international community.

A history of Bancafé

Bancafé (Banco del Café or 'Coffee Bank') started operations in 1978, as a result of an initiative by a group of Guatemalan entrepreneurs, who were convinced that the existing banking sector did not meet the requirements of a growing and dynamic economy. The banking sector

Table 14.1 Basic indicators for Bancafé and the Guatemalan banking system, 2003. All figures in US$m unless stated.

Indicator	Bancafé	Banking system	Bancafé as % of total system
Number of branches	170	1 284	13.2
Number of employees	2 081	17 007	12.2
Total assets	849	8 392	10.1
Loan portfolio	292	3 749	7.8
Float (*encaje legal*) 14.6%	195	1 226	10.1
Investments	300	2 770	10.8
Deposits	752	6 084	12.4
Capital	45	465	9.6
Income from interest	73	715	10.1
Costs of finance	32	340	9.3
Gross operational margin	47	447	10.5
Administrative expenses	40	347	11.5
Gross profit	8	47	17.0
Loan portfolio/Assets (%)	34.3	44.5	
Deposits /Assets (%)	88.5	72.5	
Return on assets (%)	0.9	0.1	
Return on equity (%)	16.6	1.0	
Source: *Superintendencia de Bancos de Guatemala*			

was conservative, served a limited amount of clients and provided slow and impersonal service with short opening hours. Access to credit was based mainly on guarantees, and credit was concentrated amongst a select group of clients and economic sectors.

In line with its mission and philosophy of corporate social responsibility, Bancafé was the first bank to radically extend opening hours and to establish branches outside the major cities.

Bancafé also quickly diversified and, by 1995, the *Grupo Financiero del País* was unveiled as one business group. The group now consists of 13 financial service companies and is supervised as a financial group according to the recently approved banking laws and regulations.

In 1999, Bancafé merged with Multibanco – the first successful bank merger in Guatemala's history. The two banks complemented each other perfectly, since Multibanco had many small branches in the capital, Guatamala City, while Bancafé distinguishes itself by its presence in less populated rural areas.

Bancafé now is smaller only than BANRURAL in terms of branch offices and clients, growing from 516 000 clients to more than 850 000 deposit holders and borrowers. Only two banks have more total assets and deposits than Bancafé, but they serve a clearly different market.

Entry into the micro-, small and medium business market

In November 1999, Bancafé entered the micro, small and medium enterprise (MSME) market segment. The decision to do so was taken at the highest level of the company and group, and was based on strategic considerations as well as the bank's social philosophy. A feasibility study was produced, and clear targets for profitability and growth were established.

The study emphasized two important and favourable factors:

- the network of branch offices, as a result of merger with Multibanco;
- the highly recognized brand name: in market research, Bancafé consistently scores highest in terms of name recognition.

At the time, many microfinancial institutions (MFIs) already existed. This competition includes: BANRURAL, which is an important actor in rural microfinance; the foundation 'Genesis Empresarial'; various large NGOs, and some credit and savings co-operatives active in more urban areas. Two other private banks entered the market but did not manage to establish a permanent presence: one was closed, the other withdrew from the MSME sector.

In 1999, Bancafé introduced its product *Bancafé Comunitario*, 'Community Bancafé' or BCC. In 2001, the MSME department became the business unit responsible for the development of this sector. Bancafé quickly introduced new products were for groups as well as individuals.

By 2003, MSME loans were available in more than half of the 170 branch offices, and in 16 of Guatemala's 22 departments. The main emphasis is on the southern, eastern and northern regions, which include some of the poorest regions of the country. During 2002, the bank became active in the metropolitan area around Guatemala City, where almost 25 per cent of the population lives. Table 14.2 (overleaf) highlights this expansion.

Clearly, the accelerated growth of the portfolio, and increase in average loan size are due mainly to the introduction of individual credit products, but Bancafé´s portfolio of more than 400 community banks is still larger than that of any competitor.

By December 2003, the MSME loan portfolio of US$16.9 represented 6 per cent of the bank's total portfolio.

Loans are used mainly for informal businesses in commerce (70 per cent), services (17 per cent) and industry (13 per cent); clients engage

Table 14.2 Growth indicators of MSME banking, figures at 31 December each year

	1999	2000	2001	2002	2003
Outstanding loan portfolio (US$)	20 000	200 000	900 000	7 000 000	16 900 000
Portfolio Community Bancafés (%)	100	100	90	30	12
Portfolio individual loans (%)	–	–	10	70	88
No. of BCC members	150	1 658	8 500	9 000	10 000
No. of individual borrowers	–	–	178	1 757	1 700
Total no. of MSME clients	150	1 658	8 678	10 757	11 700
Average loan per client (US$)	125	120	104	650	1 500

in production and selling of tortillas, which is the local staple food, the sale of fruit and vegetables, and clothing in local markets, and so on. 64 per cent of the clients are women.

MSME portfolio quality has been high, and compares favourably with banking industry standards. Despite the difficult economic situation, portfolio at risk (PAR) has never been above 2.5 per cent, and now stands at 0.5 per cent, while the bank as a whole reports a PAR of 2.9 per cent. Through loan supervision and collection of arrears, it has become clear that many of the problem cases results from the emigration of borrowers to the USA.

Products and product development for MSME

Community-based products

Bancafé started out with the Bancafé Community Bank model, known as BCC. A BCC is a group of between 15 and 40 men and women – people with very low incomes, who make a living in commerce or services, with a high rotation of capital, and belonging to the same community.

In the formation phase of establishing a BCC, the promoters hold four meetings with prospective members, during which they promote group solidarity and train them in their responsibilities. The BCC then selects its members and its board.

At the end of this process, BCC receives a loan from Bancafé, which it distributes amongst its members. Group members have a collective responsibility to repay the loan they receive from the bank. They also have to deposit a minimum of 10 per cent of the loan they ask for, as 'programmed' saving, that is administered by the BCC. These savings are deposited by the BCC as a collective account with Bancafé.

During a loan cycle, which lasts between four and 12 months, the group holds periodic meetings to pay quotas and collect savings. At the end of each cycle, loans are repaid and a new cycle may start. The loan amount increases as the BCC and its members show their repayment capacity and increase their savings.

The interest rate that Bancafé charges the BCC, and the BCC charges its members, is 4.5 per cent per month on the outstanding loan balance. This rate appears high, but is competitive in this market, since most competitors charge flat rates of 4 per cent per month over the original amount of the loan. For example, a client of the competition who borrows Q1000 for four months, would pay Q40 a month (4 per cent of the loan amount) in interest, or a total of Q160 over four months. The Bancafé client pays a total of Q112 in interest, which averages to Q28 per month. This 'implicit rate' of 2.8 per cent should be used to compare it with the flat rate charged by other institutions. Payment of principal and interest is always once or twice a month.

Bancafé works with three types of BCC: copper, silver and gold. The characteristics of the three groups are shown in Table 14.3 (below).

In order to become a Silver BCC, a Copper BCC has to have gone through at least four cycles. A Silver BCC that wants to become Gold, must have passed through four six-month cycles and maintained a perfect payment record. Many existing BCC have gone through nine cycles or 36 months and most of them have reached gold status.

Individual loans

The MSME department also offers these individual credit products:

1. Bancafé Short Term   Up to US$70
2. Bancafé Mutual Support   US$130–US$ 700
3. Bancafé 'Prestaprem'   US$130–US$2 600
4. Bancafé Fiduciary   US$130–US$2 600
5. Bancafé Guaranteed   US$520–US$5 200
6. Bancafé Relative (mortgage)   US$ 5 200–US$70 000

Table 14.3 Conditions for three types of BCC

BCC title	Minimum amount per member	Maximum amount per member	Payments per month	Cycle duration
Copper	US$125	US$250	4 months	2
Silver	US$250	US$500	6 months	1
Gold	US$500	US$900	8–12 months	1

To determine the loan amount, payment schedule and interest rate, the bank takes into account payment capacity, guarantees and use of the money (working capital or investment). The loans are usually paid back within 12 months, and the interest rate does not exceed 2.5 per cent per month.

When analysing loan requests, Bancafé takes into account the person's character when loans are small, but, as these amounts increase, financial results and guarantees become more important. The bank has introduced some important innovations regarding non-traditional guarantees, such as accepting merchandise and equipment as collateral, real but not officially registered guarantees, and the mutual support mechanism, under which two borrowers guarantee each other's loans.

Because the analysis of and by the clients indicates that Bancafé already provides ample product variety, it has decided against introducing the solidarity group model, under which smaller groups of five to seven people borrow money from a bank, administer the loan and distribute it amongst group members.

Other products and services

Bancafé promotes the savings habit, partly in order to insure payment and partly as a social responsibility. Members of a BCC must save the equivalent of 10 per cent of the loan quota, while individual borrowers open an account with Bancafé. This is usually a savings account, in which loan disbursements are registered, and to which each credit payment is debited automatically. Some clients prefer a checking account or debit card.

An insurance policy covers the outstanding loan amount: should a borrower die, he or she does not pass the debt to the BCC, family or friends who guaranteed the loan.

Organizational and financial aspects

Organizational structure

Bancafé's business is divided into four business units, reporting to the Vice President of Business Development: personal banking, private and corporate banking, MSME, and insurance.

The MSME department has the following personnel:

- a director
- three managers
- five supervisors in charge of business development
- 20 promoters in charge of development, supervision and support
- 60 advisers who serve individual clients and are assisted by 55 junior advisers (one per office), whose main tasks are to assist clients in the branch office and data processing

The MSME business unit's operations are integrated into the bank's physical and technological infrastructure.

The business unit has a decentralized system for loan approval and disbursement. The promoters and branch managers, who report to the operations department, make decisions on loan requests for up to US$3000, supervisors can approve up to US$10 000, and managers up to US$20 000. The process is quick, and most requests for loans are processed within 72 hours.

The MSME business unit coordinates closely with the staff of the risk-analysis department, while the internal auditors have incorporated some innovative methods to control the non-traditional operations of the MSME department.

Human resources

When it set up its microfinance business, the Bank made major changes in the way it hires, inducts and trains MSME personnel, since they must be highly motivated to work with this sector. For example, Jose Antonio Balanyá, supervisor in the metropolitan area, joined the department after a few years as corporate investment officer at head office, but feels far more fulfilled working with small enterprises.

New personnel at the field level are carefully selected. Bancafé has developed a profile for a successful candidate and conducts a range of tests and requests references to make sure the candidate has the right attitudes, motivation and capacity to learn and develop.

The people who are selected to join MSME usually already live in the communities they will work in and know their clients personally. They are usually university graduates. The bank rarely hires people away from other microfinance institutions

Human development is emphasized at the first stage of personnel training; it includes deeper orientation as to the expected role of the promoter or adviser, and presentations about the role of the bank in microfinance. The emphasis is on identification with the clients, their growth, and the benefits the programme may bring them, but it is made clear that the bank is a for-profit financial intermediary.

Training for personnel that pass this stage emphasizes techniques used in assessing various types of loans, knowledge of microfinance, and how the MSME department operates.

Additional training takes place often. Bancafé spends 13 per cent of its training budget on MSME personnel. Whenever an employee distinguishes himself because of high productivity, the bank facilitates promotion and further personal development. Staff turnover is low, and most personnel changes are related to internal strategies or policies.

Incentives

Each promoter or adviser manages his own clientele and receives remuneration that includes a basic salary of US$400, plus additional

Box 15.1: *Where it started: a visit to Bancafé in Asunción Mita*

The city of Asunción Mita, is located in Jutiapa, south-east Guatemala, 140 km from Guatemala City. It has a population of 63 384 and borders El Salvador, which is one reason for the city's dynamic economy. Bancafé's branch office is located downtown and is very active and profitable.

The start of the MSME programme in the region
Asunción Mita, together with El Progreso, Atescatempa and Jutiapa, was selected by Bancafé to start the first BCC programme. Bancafé has a branch in each town, where the MSME programme and staff are located.

Mauricio Contreras, who is still with the Bank in Asunción Mita, became the supervisor in charge of the programme in this region. Along with other staff, he received intensive training in microfinance.

A promoter was assigned to cover each of the four towns, and most of them still remain with Bancafé and the BCC programme. In those early days, each promoter was expected to serve an average of ten BCCs.

Evolution of the *Bancafé Comunitarios*
In 1999, the first seven BCCs opened. The new clients had never before belonged to a formal bank, either because they lacked collateral, or because they mistrusted banks and, in some cases, because they lacked self-confidence.

At first, all BCC cycles lasted four months, the loan averaged US$140 per member, and periodic payments included principal, interests and programmed savings. BCC meetings took place every two weeks and, during the meeting, each member was called on, in public, to make his or her payment to the treasurer. All payments were deposited later into the BCC account with Bancafé.

The first groups that were established tended to be rather heterogeneous, as members had different economic activities with different patterns of rotation of capital, different initial desires and expectations regarding loan amounts and capacity to assume bigger loans. A few members would have real guarantees. Experience has made it clear that the BCC programme serves several levels of clients:

1. At the highest level, a few members who have understood the function of financial institutions and their services have moved on to other opportunities. They outgrew the BCC, which became too small to accommodate their expectations and potential, and meetings tended to take too much time.
2. Many members have continued to be members of BCC and have suggested changes in the methodology and products that are in line with the nature of their business and their growth. As a result, a variety of changes in policies, norms and regulations, such as duration of the cycles, payment schedules in line with business cash flows, increasing loan amounts, frequency of meetings, were implemented.
3. Some members withdraw from the group for one or more cycles, or remain as members but do not increase the size of their loans or savings, which would indicate their business is stagnant or irregular.
4. At the lowest level, there are members who have withdrawn because the profits and cash flows of their economic activities are insufficient to keep up with the rhythm of other members of the BCC.

As a consequence, some groups disappeared; other groups merged into groups that reflect the desire of clients to form more integrated groups. As a result of the suggestions of their clients and different situations that were encountered, Bancafé now manages three categories of BCC: copper, silver and gold. Yet, the principles of the community bank methodology still apply. In fact, Asunción Mita has been a living laboratory to improve the application of BCC concepts and adapt procedures to local realities, giving the product its own dynamics.

The results
BCC loan portfolio
The BCC loan portfolio in Asunción Mita now consists of 23 BCCs – 13 in urban areas and 10 in rural areas – with a total of some 350 members. The outstanding portfolio is US$101 500, which means an average of US$4 400 per group and US$190 per group member.

The four municipalities Mauricio Contreras manages represent a BCC loan portfolio that stands at US$1 386 750, and has no cases of default or arrears. It is made up of 251 BCCs: 12 Copper, 44 Silver and 195 Gold, illustrating the maturity of this portfolio.

Portfolio of individual loans
Bancafé's branch in Asunción Mita provides individual loans to small businesses. These are used by a different segment of the population, and most clients can and do offer more traditional guarantees. Sixty-three borrowers share an outstanding portfolio of US$305 000. Although the individual loan products include a variety of innovations, such as mutual guarantees, most BCC members are not yet eligible for them. The experience with bigger clients was fundamental in the design of individual credit products.

What the members of BCC say
Representatives of five of the oldest BCCs in Asunción Mita, each with some four years and ten cycles of experience, expressed the following opinions about their experiences with their BCC.

Motivations
Access to money without offering tangible and officially registered guarantees is the most fundamental aspect of the programme. All members always try hard to keep a perfect record with their BCC, because this has given them all the opportunity to receive bigger and better loans.

Changes in memberships
All groups have had changes in membership. 'We divided because some of us wanted bigger amounts to run our business,' Doña Lilian Perez says about BCC La Asunción and the BCC La Libertad. These changes, by and large, are not seen as negative, but rather a part of the natural development of peoples' needs. 'Our group now is nice, healthy and united', she concludes.

Satisfaction with the service and the possibility to participate in its design
Members emphasize the support of Bancafé, the frequent presence of its personnel, the stability and the transparency of their actions. 'Don Ludwin, the promoter, has been very attentive, he is always present in our meetings, he arrives on time, listens, and has time for us when we come to his office ...' says Doña Chús; she is happy that Don Ludwin asks for their opinions so that he can improve the services.

Doña Carmen Ramirez, who sells wash basins, says that they have always received their loans on the agreed dates, and BCC has kept its promises to have more funds available as long as the group fulfils its obligations

Jorge Pérez says that other MFI's are more expensive than his BCC. As for the local informal money lender, 'He charges too much and gossips about who has loans with him.'

The chance for a husband and wife to take part in a group, and for both to have their own loans with which they can complement each other's business, has helped their businesses to grow. 'Four years ago, I had a stand near the park where I sold 'tacos'; then my husband also became a member, and now we have a restaurant, a pick-up truck and we're going to build a second floor in the house, so we can put more tables ...' Doña Lilian explained, smiling enthusiastically.

(continued overleaf)

> **Box 15.1:** *The results*
> *(continued from previous page)*
>
> Doña Lucero Martinez explains that she identifies and manages the annual highs and lows of their business and matches her needs for credit accordingly. 'In my bookshop, business is great from November to January because of the holiday season. It is when the school-year starts again that I need money most.'
>
> **Programmed and voluntary savings**
> Saving with the BCC is seen as positive. Bank personnel and group members consider that the programmed savings represent insurance: the last payment or the ticket to enter a BCC. 'The Bank says we better save two quotas, so we can always pay in time.' Savings do not really grow much, but they are insurance and they gather some interest. Doña Lucero also has her personal saving accounts. She shows her Bancafé booklet, which, she says, is more confidential and gives her flexibility to use the money.
>
> **'The little expectation'**
> Doña Maria Rodriguez, owner of a typing school, wants to buy some computers to modernize her business and help it grow. 'As members of BCC, we have always believed that we will get the chance for bigger loans. Our credit history will give us credibility and it will serve as a guarantee for us, so we can get an individual loan.'
>
> **Pending matters**
> Socorro Rodriguez, on a cautious note, says that some things are pending such as training on how to improve their business management skills. Also, she would like to receive a bigger loan.

benefits that are greater than statutory requirements. They also receive a performance bonus, the amount of which depends on three factors:

- the number of clients
- net growth of the portfolio
- arrears rate – the most important single factor

The value of this bonus can reach US$400 per month, but with this bonus promoters and advisers are expected to cover the costs, such as transport and occasional meals, they incur when visiting clients. Since the distance between the branch offices and clients is never more than 20 kilometres, these costs are not very high.

Technological support and decentralization

Modern technological infrastructure makes it possible for all information, from the first contact with clients, through the preparation of the legal loan documents, to loan disbursement, to be processed automatically.

Access to the bank's intranet system provides personnel with the right procedures, and enables them to give prompt attention to their clients. As a first step, the junior advisers obtain references from credit bureaux through the system, then they register credit information and guarantees and use the system to authorize applications, following established norms and policies, and control the loan portfolio and credit operations. This support also makes the decentralized portfolio management system viable, and clients are served quickly and can reduce the time of group meetings, the risk of theft, and so on.

The data produced by the management information system does not yet include data that can measure impact, client's incomes, or the outreach and depth of the portfolio.

External support and co-ordination

Bancafé is a shareholder in CREDIREF – the Credit Reference Corporation – that provides a database used by various MFI's to check the credit references of prospective clients. It also participates in the National Advisory Committee, which assists the Ministry of Economy in developing policies for the MSME sector.

The bank has received loans for micro-lending, but these resources are not of vital importance to the programme's growth, since it has been so successful in mobilizing deposits. External credit is usually more costly than Bancafé's average cost of deposits of around 4 per cent. The main advantage is that these loans are long term.

During the first years, Inter-American Development Bank, AID and UNDP provided significant support for the training and technical advice to microfinance personnel, covering a wide range of activities, such as product development, training in credit procedures, human relations and loan administration. At present however, the bank receives no significant subsidized finance or technical assistance programmes.

Financial results

The MSME transactions are fully integrated into Bancafé's operations, so the amount of overhead that should be attributed to the MSME product lines is not yet clearly determined. MSME personnel costs and the bank's costs of finance, however, are known. Table 14.4 (below) gives provisional figures for 2003, which seem to indicate that, as a whole, the department has been profitable.

Table 14.4 Estimates of MSME incomes and costs for 2003

Indicator	2003
Average interest on MSME loans	28%
Average MSME portfolio	US$11 800 000
MSME financial products (incomes)	US$3 300 000
Costs of finance (weighted interest on deposits) 4 %	US$450 000
Personnel costs: salaries, benefits, bonuses	US$1 250 000
Difference between income and costs of personnel and finance	US$1 600 000

The cost of loan write-offs should be low, since the PAR stands at 0.5 per cent. The difference between incomes and direct expenses is considered enough to cover these costs, as well as indirect costs, even when considering that the cost of using the bank's extensive modern technological infrastructure may be rather high.

Conclusions

Key factors

According to Bancafé, the success of its MSME banking activities depends on the following factors.

- Bancafé has provided its brand name, branch offices that are close to the clients, and the necessary funding for the loans.
- The MSME department is an independent business unit that possesses its own personal channel of distribution to the clients.
- Modern technology and infrastructure provide support for the various MSME products, the information system and decentralized decision making.
- The credit products are adapted to clients' needs and supported by the savings facilities and insurance that covers the outstanding loan in case a client dies.
- Careful selection, incentive systems and constant training help motivate field personnel.

The following additional factors are also important.

- Bancafé has been able to interpret the changes in its client's demands and capacities quickly, and the MSME business unit constantly modifies its products and procedures; this is done hand-in-hand with the clients, using client focus-group discussions in an intensive and honest way.
- The key consideration when facing competition is to maintain and improve customer satisfaction and loyalty to the bank's services.
- Personnel productivity continues to increase. A BCC promoter, for example, used to serve ten BCCs, but now manages 20 on average.
- The development of homogeneous groups in terms of business cycles and economic and entrepreneurial capacity is fundamental for the success of the BCC methodology, but the BCC, to its members, is a means to acquire greater access to financial services.

Plans and perspectives

Bancafé is optimistic about its competitive position and potential for growth, although the main competitors such as BANRURAL, NGOs and financial co-operatives, as well as informal money lenders, are very aggressive and increasingly efficient in channelling finance to the sector.

However, in the metropolitan area, as well as more rural areas, the competition does not offer the quality of service and product diversity that Bancafé can provide.

It is felt that the market is not yet saturated, and the vision for the next five years is to build up a loan portfolio of US$50m, which would make the MSME portfolio an important generator of revenues and profit.

To this end, the bank plans to reach virtual national coverage through all its branch offices both in the metropolitan and rural areas.

Challenges

In general, it will be necessary to maintain a fast but well-controlled expansion, responding to increasing demand but applying all the new banking laws, rules and regulations that were recently put into effect – the exact effect of which on microfinance is not yet clear.

Rural expansion
By the end of 2004, Bancafé hopes to serve all areas of the country with market potential, even if it does not yet have an office there.

Trust of the clients
It remains a challenge to convince other potential clients that Bancafé supplies credit and is not merely a place for savings; on the other hand, many small-business people still distrust the 'formality' of the banking sector.

Transition from group loans to individual lending
The BCCs have been the window through which many people have done business with a bank for the first time. But the proven members of BCCs expect bigger loans, and want to 'graduate'. To provide service to BCCs is also costly. Does this mean that those members who are able to should move on to individual loans, and thus let their stagnating BCC die? Or should the successful members of unsuccessful BCCs be integrated into other BCCs? The adaptation of individual credit products should improve the level of service to those BCC members who have shown their credibility and capacity to grow.

Product diversification
- Credit innovations that are being considered include loans to young entrepreneurs and for eco-tourism.
- In the near future, new savings products will be designed and introduced to appeal especially to micro- and small-business people.
- In insurance, Bancafé plans to extend its coverage and product range, in order to diminish its vulnerability. Proposals include insurance for funeral services, robbery and fire damage.

- Bancafé wants to expand its business in the remittance market, and promote the best use of these resources by recipients, designing appropriate and innovative products.

Sales force development
To reach these goals will require an institutional effort to develop the MSME staff into a truly professional sales and market development force, including integral incentives and control systems, as well as extensive training.

Discussion questions

1. The smallest borrowers pay interest to Bancafé at 4.5 per cent a month, or 54 per cent a year. This is lower than the MFI competition, but are such high rates of interest sustainable for other than petty traders or others with high turnover micro-enterprises?

2. A certain number of Bancafé clients drop out of their BCC groups because they cannot afford the regular savings that are required. Should the bank monitor the numbers and reasons for these dropouts, and what, if anything, should be done to assist them?

3. Like many banks and MFIs, Bancafé is developing new products and services for microfinance clients who want to graduate from microfinance to larger individual loans and other services. Should such clients be encouraged to move to other banks, so that Bancafé can concentrate its attention on the smallest, most numerous and most needy clients?

Chapter Fifteen
The service company model: Sogesol in Haiti[1]

ELISABETH RHYNE

The challenge: long term commitment of commercial banks to microfinance

During the past few years, commercial banks have become increasingly important in the development of microfinance services. Banks that enter microfinance can offer low-income customers a full range of financial services, including credit, savings and fee-based services. With their extensive physical, financial and human resources, banks can launch and expand microfinance services relatively inexpensively. If commercial banks become serious players in microfinance, they can offer very strong competition to traditional microfinance institutions. However, there is a perception within the microfinance community that commercial bank entry into microfinance will be short-lived or shallow. These perceptions have been fuelled by example.

In view of the very significant advantages commercial banks can potentially bring to microfinance, ACCION International, a US non-profit organization devoted to microfinance, has developed relationships with several commercial banks to launch and expand microfinance operations. In most of these cases, ACCION and its partners are using an approach known as the service company model, which shows early promise as a workable method to establish a long-lived microfinance operation through a commercial bank.

This chapter describes how the service company model addresses the key issues in commercial bank entry into microfinance, using as a case study one of ACCION's partner microfinance service companies, Sogesol, a part of the Sogebank Group in Haiti. Early results suggest that the service company model represents a significant breakthrough in enabling commercial banks to enter and stay in microfinance.[2]

The Haitian context

To understand and interpret the experience of Sogebank and Sogesol, it is important to recognize the unique Haitian context in which they operate. With a 2002 per capita GDP of US$433, Haiti is the poorest country in the Western Hemisphere.[3] As many as 80 per cent of its 6.8 million people live below the poverty line. Literacy levels are very low (50 per cent), life expectancy is only 53 years, and infant mortality is 81 per 1000 live births. Haiti's underdeveloped economy is the result of decades of political instability. The country has suffered severe political unrest during most of the past 15 years, further crippling its chronically weak economy. A wave of political unrest and violence, culminating in the resignation in February 2004 of President Aristide, caused further significant damage and deterioration to the economy and the situation continues to be unstable.

The Haitian economy remains primarily rural. Many Haitian families depend on remittances from Haitians living abroad. In 1994 the budding sub-component industry collapsed in the wake of a United Nations' embargo imposed on Haiti following political problems. In the absence of a strong formal sector, a large urban self-employed sector has emerged. Many of the country's adult population are prospective clients for microfinance.

Haitian banks and other formal businesses face a difficult operating environment. Mountainous terrain and a weak government mean that infrastructure is poor, while the island economy means that Haiti depends on high-cost imports. During 2002 and 2003 inflation has been high (40 per cent from July 2002 through June 2003) and the local currency, the Gourde, has devalued by 57 per cent. Interest rates have stayed below inflation, with the prime rate fluctuating between 20 and 34 per cent.

Sogebank

Within this difficult setting, Sogebank is the largest commercial bank in Haiti. It was formed in 1986, when a group of Haitian business people purchased the local affiliate of Royal Bank of Canada at a time when foreign businesses were leaving the country. With total assets of almost G14bn (US$333m) at September 2003, Sogebank claims a 24 per cent market share in the Haitian financial sector. Loans outstanding totalled G5bn (US$118m). With 30 branches, Sogebank offers the most extensive banking infrastructure in the country. It is Haiti's only provider of ATM services and has over half of the credit-card market. Sogebank operates special lines of business through six subsidiary companies, such as SogeExpress, its remittances arm, and Sogebel, its housing subsidiary, in addition to Sogesol, the microfinance service company.

The service company model

A service company is a non-financial company that provides loan origination and credit administration services to a bank. In the Sogebank/Sogesol model, the microfinance service company does all the work of promoting, evaluating, approving, tracking and collecting loans, but the loans themselves are on the books of the bank. In return for providing these credit administration services, the service company is paid a fee (and vice versa, when the bank provides services to the service company). The fee is contingent on adequate risk-management as measured by portfolio quality. The service company employs the loan officers and other microfinance programme staff, while the bank furnishes services to the service company, which includes teller support, human resources and information communication technology. The service company can be a wholly-owned subsidiary of the bank, but in this case it involves additional investors.

Legally, a service company is a non-financial subsidiary. As a non-financial company, it does not require a separate banking licence, is not separately supervised by the banking authorities, and does not require a large equity base. It is thus relatively easy and inexpensive to launch from a legal and regulatory point of view.

The service company model establishes a long-lived structure with its own governance and staffing that gives the microfinance operation space to operate. Because transactions are between legally separate entities, a service company provides a transparent framework for operation. In this way, it is an attractive structure for involving technical partners as investors and participants in governance. Yet, as an entity that exclusively serves a single bank, the service company can take full advantage of the benefits the bank has to offer and can save overhead costs because the parent bank can handle processes that do not require specialized microfinance knowledge.

Service companies must negotiate detailed agreements with the parent bank that assign cost, risk, responsibility and return to each party in an effective way. Good agreements must align incentives to promote the overall interests of the institution, particularly if external investors are involved. We shall look more closely at how Sogebank and Sogesol structured their agreement.

Creation of Sogesol

Sogebank's involvement in microfinance followed a common pattern for banks in the sector. A senior manager at Sogebank, Pierre-Marie Boisson, the bank's chief economist, became interested in microfinance after observing successful experiences in other countries. He believed that microfinance offered Sogebank an opportunity to achieve both social and business objectives, and he convinced the other key decision-makers at the bank to explore the possibilities. Sogebank created a project team and launched a feasibility study, carried out by Bannock Consulting and financed by a grant from the Multilateral Investment Fund of the Inter-American Development Bank.

Market research conducted for the feasibility study revealed that the market for microfinance services was quite large and dramatically under served, with fewer than 50 000 active micro-loans in total. A few credit co-operatives and NGOs operated, but these were judged to be weak in human and financial resources. One bank, *Banque de l'Union Haitien*, had launched a microfinance programme with 2500 active loans, while another, Unibank, had just set up an independent finance company, Micro Credit National, in partnership with International Project Consult (IPC), a German microfinance firm. The banks were suddenly becoming aware of the market opportunity in microfinance, and Sogebank felt a sense of urgency to act quickly while the field remained open.

Even though Sogebank was an experienced retail bank, its managers recognized that building an effective microfinance operation would require expertise they did not have in-house. The shift into microfinance – products, delivery systems and especially clients – required both experience and orientation that they, as a traditional bank, lacked. They selected ACCION International to join the project as technical advisers and investors. Initial planning and design of operations involved a team of four ACCION consultants, including two residents, and three senior Sogebank managers assigned full time to the new institution. Sogesol was created in August 2000, with three main shareholders: Sogebank (35 per cent), ACCION (20 per cent) and ProFund, an investment fund focused on Latin American microfinance (21 per cent). The remaining 24 per cent of the capital came from 33 individuals, mostly associated with Sogebank. All the investors bought into the deal on commercial terms. ACCION and Profund are socially responsible investors, seeking both financial returns and social impact as a result of the investment. Sogesol has a five-member board, including three Sogebank representatives and one each from ACCION and ProFund. Pierre-Marie Boisson, Sogebank's 'internal champion' chairs the Sogesol board.

Mr Boisson played a key role in shaping an agreement between Sogesol and Sogebank that suited the context of Haiti and Sogebank. To avoid moral hazard and provide a strong performance incentive to management, Sogesol's long-term contract with Sogebank includes the following provisions.

- Sogesol receives all interest revenue from client loans. Its operating expenses and profit come from these revenues, less payments to Sogebank for:
    a. cost of funds
    b. transactions services by Sogebank to Sogesol customers
    c. special services provided by Sogebank to Sogesol (marketing, accounting, legal, etc.)
    d. a portion of the cost of provisions

- The cost of funds Sogebank charges Sogesol is based on the cost of funds in the Haitian market.

- Sogesol pays Sogebank a transaction fee, calculated as a predetermined percentage of the average portfolio, when its clients use Sogebank branches, as they do for all disbursements and repayments.

- An agreed provisioning formula determines how credit risk is shared between Sogebank and Sogesol. It is based on the higher of provisions calculated on the ACCION CAMEL[4] standards and a maximum percentage of 3.5 per cent of the outstanding portfolio. (If it exceeds 3.5 per cent, Sogesol and Sogebank evenly split the remaining provisioning expense.) In the face of recent political unrest, Sogesol has tightened its provisioning approach even more: provisioning all loans more than 30 days late at 100 per cent.

Sogesol's income is subject to significant variation depending on fluctuations in funding costs, risk in the portfolio and operating costs. Incentives are strong for Sogesol to be efficient while maintaining a high-quality portfolio. ACCION also has an option (a put) to exit that can require the other shareholders in Sogesol to purchase ACCION's shares at a certain multiple of book value. This option reduces the risk ACCION might face as a minority shareholder. It reflects ACCION's role in maintaining microfinance orientation, at least until the microfinance operation can show reliable profitability to assure that the bank will have a permanent commitment to the microenterprise sector.

Sogesol operations

Microfinance operations at Sogesol are very similar to microfinance operations at other commercial microfinance institutions in ACCION's network, such as BancoSol in Bolivia, Mibanco in Peru and Banco Solidario in Ecuador in terms of product, clientele, and delivery systems.

Product

The main – and for the first two years the only – product is a working capital loan provided individually (no group lending). Clients are micro-entrepreneurs who have been in business for at least one year and operate from a fixed location, even though the location may be little more than a regular spot on the pavement. The loans are secured by a co-signer and by non-traditional collateral: household and business assets. Cosigners are evaluated in much the same way as borrowers, and so are essentially the peers of borrowers. The average term of these loans is between four and five months, and the interest rate is 4.5 per cent flat per month, with an annual effective rate of about 87 per cent including loan processing fees, which is competitive with other microfinance providers.

Clients

Sogesol serves microenterprises and small enterprises, with the emphasis overwhelmingly on the micro-level. Many of its clients occupy the market stalls in the crowded informal markets that line the streets of downtown Port au Prince, Haiti's capital. Market clients include jewellery makers, cobblers, and vendors of toiletries, music tapes and CDs, clothing, flowers and food. In less densely populated neighborhoods, clients include corner grocers and home-based businesses such as tailoring. In short, Sogesol clients offer the gamut of goods and services found in the informal sector.

The vast majority of clients are in commerce (86 per cent), while 8 per cent are in manufacturing and 5 per cent are in the service sector. The average age of clients is 39, and 61 per cent are women. The income level of Sogesol's clients reflects the income distribution of the Haitian population in general, with 37 per cent of the clients below the nationally established poverty line, and 50 per cent below the international US$2-per-day poverty line. A small proportion, 16 per cent, fall into the extreme poverty classification. Although the Sogesol clients are poor, they are on the whole somewhat better educated than the general population. Most have a primary-school education but very few have any post-secondary training.[5]

Delivery of services

Like other individual microenterprise lending operations, Sogesol is driven by the loan officer corps, who have responsibility for client relationships from the initial presentations they give, through loan approval, to collection. Loan officers are organized into geographic zones, and spend much of their time in the field conducting credit evaluations and following up on late payment. Credit evaluations take into account the enterprise and household situation of clients, focusing on willingness and ability to repay. In order to achieve a highly productive staff, Sogesol offers loan officers and their supervisors incentives based on volume and quality of portfolio. Specific monetary incentives are given per active client and per amount of portfolio and per net increase in number of clients, while monetary disincentives are levied for number of clients and amount of portfolio delinquent. Like other microenterprise lenders, Sogesol believes in immediate personal follow-up of late payments as a cornerstone of its methods.

The Sogesol-Sogebank interface

From the beginning, starting microfinance operations with Sogesol had significant advantages. Banking operation costs are extremely high in Haiti due to poor infrastructure, limited power supply and security problems. To begin banking operations requires large investments in private communications, power generators and security. The relationship with Sogebank allows Sogesol to put its branches near or inside Sogebank branches, reducing these costs. At the same time, arranging a smooth interface between the bank and the microfinance operations has at times proved challenging and created internal tensions. Some of these tensions are ongoing.

Branding

As is clear from its name, Sogesol is marketed as a distinct brand within the overall Sogebank family. This linked branding aims to accomplish the following:

1. the link to the bank enhances credibility;
2. the distinct identity welcomes low-income clients who may be intimidated by a bank;
3. the main branding of the traditional bank is undisturbed. Sogesol has its own logo and distinct marketing materials.

Transactions processing

Sogesol customers carry out all their transactions through Sogebank tellers. On receiving a loan from Sogesol, customers must go next door to the Sogebank branch to obtain their cash and later to make repayments. This relationship has made it easy to offer Sogesol customers savings accounts at Sogebank. It has been one of the more difficult challenges to solve, however, because of the sheer number of transactions microfinance generates. At times there are more Sogesol clients than standard Sogebank clients in the Sogebank branch. This volume of transactions poses challenges for management of traffic flow and waiting times in the branches and for the information technology communications systems, all of which have a direct impact on customer service quality. Staff must also be trained in appropriate treatment of customers, as customer service norms in Haiti are not high, particularly with low-income customers. Sogesol and Sogebank are still working out optimal solutions in this area.

Information communications technology (ICT)

Sogesol has its own management information system, covering the loan approval process and delinquency tracking. This system interfaces with the main Sogebank system, where all financial transactions take place. Developing a separate but smoothly connected ICT system was one of the most challenging aspects of launching Sogesol, and glitches still emerge from time to time.

Use of bank headquarters' staff

Bank expertise in the areas of information communications technology, human resources, marketing, legal issues, internal audit and financial management have reduced the need for Sogesol to develop full-fledged departments in these areas, substantially reducing costs. Issues arising in this area include:

1. the need to develop specialized microfinance knowledge by bank staff in these departments;
2. the low level of priority often given to microfinance by these departments in the main bank; and
3. transparency of payment for services between the departments and the microfinance operation through clear agreements.

Table 15.1 Sogesol: growth in loans and portfolio: end of year status

	2000	2001	2002	2003
Active loans	640	3 546	6 364	7 070
Portfolio (US$)	159 051	1 166 122	2 721 568	4 841 720
Average loan	249	329	428	685

On an ongoing basis, the issue of the priority given to microfinance remains perhaps the most difficult to resolve, as bank staff naturally tend to give priority to the needs of the main bank.

Results

Sogesol began lending in August 2000. After just two years of operation, it reached full profitability in 2002, and first broke even on a monthly basis in its twentieth month. By the end of 2003, Sogesol had seven branches, including three outside Port-au-Prince (Cap Haitien, Gonaives and Port au Paix), and was the largest regulated microfinance institution in Haiti in terms of number of clients. This growth was achieved in spite of the deep economic and social crisis in Haiti, which became particularly severe in late 2003. Growth has been lower than originally projected, as it has been more difficult than expected to achieve targeted levels of productivity from loan officers.

Average loan size has increased every year partly as a natural consequence of several risk-reducing elements of the lending methodology, which mean that clients receive smaller loans at first and then increase their loan sizes as they prove to be strong repayers. In addition, Sogesol has introduced a small business sub-product within its main working capital loan, aimed at a slightly more advanced clientele, and this sub-product features higher loan sizes.

Table 15.2 Summary results for Sogesol (December 2003)

Active loans	7 070
Portfolio (US$)	$4 841 720
Average loan size (US$)	$685
Portfolio at risk over 30 days	7.4 per cent
Number of branches	7
Total personnel	115
Number of loan officers (incl. 9 in training)	52
Clients per loan officer	136
Portfolio per loan officer (US$)	$93 110

Table 15.3 Sogesol balance sheet (as of fiscal year end, 30 September 2003)

	Haitian Gourdes	US$
Assets		
Liquid assets	68 013 562	1 700 339
Net fixed assets	14 195 917	354 898
Amortized start-up costs	6 455 724	161 393
Other assets	5 880 304	147 008
Total assets	94 545 507	2 363 638
Liabilities and capital		
Accounts payable to Sogebank	64 755 449	1 618 886
Other liabilities	5 084 183	127 105
Total liabilities	74 839 632	1 870 991
Total capital	19 705 875	492 647
Total liabilities and capital	94 545 507	2 363 638

Note: As at 30 September 2003, US$1 = 40 Gourdes.

Toward the end of 2003, the portfolio at risk rate at Sogesol rose from a level just below 3 per cent – where it had been throughout its life – to a high of 7.4 per cent, largely as a result of severe political disturbances which made it difficult for businesses of all kinds to operate in a normal fashion, and thus affected both the bank and its clients.

Prospects for the future

Sogesol holds a strong market position as competition in the microenterprise lending market begins to increase. Overall, the number of clients being served in the country is growing very slowly, while the number of providers has actually been shrinking, in part as a result of the growth of a handful of competent, commercially oriented providers. There are several microfinance operations in Haiti of roughly comparable size to Sogesol. The IPC finance company, MCN, had a portfolio of US$7.4m in late 2003, significantly larger than Sogesol's, but since MCN targets larger loans, its client outreach was well below Sogesol's at 4300. Fonkoze, an NGO, targets a much lower income market, with average loans of about US$60, has more presence in rural areas and a total clientele of about 8000. Fonkoze may convert into a financial institution. Another NGO, ACME, also shows strong growth, and also targets a lower level clientele than Sogesol. Other banks remain at the edges of microfinance, but none have yet built significant scale. The total number of outstanding loans to microenterprises in Haiti remains relatively

Table 15.4 Sogesol income and expense statement
(fiscal year ended 30 September 2003)

	Haitian Gourdes	US$
Interest income on loans*	62 782 821	1 569 571
Other interest income	4 800 482	120 012
Interest expense	(3 261 852)	(81 546)
Other revenues	1 979 091	49 477
Net interest income	**66 300 542**	**1 657 514**
Expenses		
Salaries and personnel	(20 761 652)	(519 041)
Other costs	(31 092 250)	(777 306)
Revenue before tax	**14 446 640**	**361 166**
Taxes	(4 612 300)	(115 308)
Net revenue	**9 834 340**	**245 859**

*Net after payment to Sogebank

small, at 62 000, and a total portfolio of roughly US$20m. Recent market research revealed that most micro-entrepreneurs still have never obtained a loan, showing that the market potential remains large. As competition increases, the lack of a credit bureau in Haiti will become an issue for all the microfinance providers. At present, an informal bad payer list circulates among microfinance lenders, managed by a USAID project. Plans are under discussion among some players to set up a simple credit bureau that will provide more detailed information than the bad payer list.

Sogesol's plans for the future include continuing to add branches and increase scale, while seeking ways to reduce operating expenses. Several of the issues noted above will continue to absorb management attention: smoothing out glitches in the information system interface between Sogebank and Sogesol, managing clients in the Sogebank branches, and improving customer service. Sogesol is adding new products, including a fixed asset loan, a home improvement loan, and a consumption loan for salaried workers. It is also examining ways to link remittances with microfinance services. Sogesol aims to reach 11 500 clients by the end of 2004.

Lessons from Sogesol's experience with the service company model

The support of a commercial bank has allowed Sogesol to focus on perfecting credit methodology without worrying about obtaining funds or opening full-fledged branches. However, problems with customer service, general resistance to change, and competing priorities have slowed the growth of these operations. ACCION is continuing to work to perfect the model based on experience to date and seeks to replicate it in bigger markets.

An important early result from the service company experience is that commercial banks getting into microfinance are not necessarily moving up-market. Sogesol's average loan sizes are comparable to the specialized banks in the ACCION network. Because Sogebank already serves clients demanding larger loans, there is relatively little pressure for Sogesol to move up-market. Low cost structures allow Sogesol to operate profitably at lower average loan sizes.

Another result with important implications is the relatively small external subsidy needed to launch the operation. Sogesol received total grant funding from pre-feasibility through maturity of less than US$500 000. Most of the grant funds supported pre-project planning by Bannock, and specialized technical assistance and training from ACCION. Sogebank carried most of the project costs in the form of its own staff time, payment of a significant share of the technical assistance costs, and by providing the equity, loan capital and infrastructure. From a donor perspective, this cost is substantially lower than the total grant funds needed to launch brand new microfinance operations in either an NGO or start-up financial institution, costs which often run into the millions of dollars. From a banking perspective, it suggests that for banks willing to put their own funds into launching a microfinance operation, it is not overly difficult to find donors willing to assist with some of costs of planning and acquiring technical know-how.

Among the specific lessons that have emerged from the service company experience are the following.

Choose the right bank

Not all banks are equally prepared to launch microfinance services. The right partner is a bank with a strategic vision to become a major retail bank. Important features include a network of branches in the relevant markets and a range of products already reaching the consumer level, such as savings, consumer lending and payment services. These features reduce start-up costs for microfinance operations and result in lower long-term operating costs, distributed among a portfolio of services.

Find an internal 'champion'

The chances of successfully creating and maintaining a microfinance service company are greatly increased with the personal support of an influential member of the bank's management team. This person can serve as a liaison between the bank and the service company and can help define the roles of each in the relationship. In Sogesol's case, the original impetus for microfinance came from within: Pierre-Marie Boisson, Sogebank's internal champion, sought out a way to make microfinance happen in his bank, and this led him first to Bannock and then to ACCION for advice and assistance.

Obtain experienced technical advice

Banks that attempt to develop microfinance services without an experienced technical assistance provider often miss essential steps in creating a successful microfinance operation. From the outside, it may look 'easy' to do microfinance, but there are many aspects of microfinance that are difficult for banks to internalize – for example, those associated with the very different corporate culture microfinance requires. The presence of experienced, committed technical partners can help overcome those difficulties.

Allocate tasks to the best-qualified entity

Banks should do what they do best, including treasury, accounting and legal functions. The microfinance unit should focus on its own comparative strengths, such as credit methodology and operations at the branch level. Some areas will require intensive co-ordination, particularly human resources and information systems. In these areas, both sides can be brought together to complement one another.

Anticipate standard problems

One of the most common difficulties in bank downscaling, which Sogesol's model addresses but does not fully eliminate, involves internal competition because service companies must compete for services with other subsidiaries or divisions of the bank. An internal negative perception can mean that the service company does not receive priority attention when it experiences problems. Another standard problem is the conflict between the high volume of customer transactions microfinance generates and the desire of mainstream banks to provide good customer service to their larger clients. This dilemma now centres on the Sogebank tellers who are the face of the bank to most customers. Sogesol and Sogebank are still working to find better solutions: in a few years, the means of handling microfinance transactions (disbursements and repayments) will undoubtedly have changed.

Create effective agreements

Service companies are dependent on the parent bank, which provides capital and holds the portfolio. Under this arrangement, the service company cannot easily access alternative sources of funding or services and thus cannot pressurize the bank to reduce the cost of funds or increase the quality of services. Dependency creates a 'moral hazard' since, once the institution starts to operate, it is costly to change strategic partners. This problem is most relevant for the external investors in a service company, who must seek protection through long-term contracts that specify all relationships and transactions transparently.

Discussion questions

1. One major advantage of commercial banks in microfinance, as opposed to MFIs, is that there is no need to build new institutions. The service company model does require a new institution. Is this a problem?

2. The service company has to pay the bank for carrying out transactions such as receiving or disbursing cash which are normally 'bundled' within a complete banking product. Many commercial banks find it difficult to allocate costs to specific transactions. How can this issue be dealt with?

3. Is it likely that the service company will eventually merge with the commercial bank, or that the two entities will slowly move further apart so that the service company might even itself become a bank? Or will the present partnership continue? Which outcome would be best for micro-clients?

4. How, if at all, has the political instability in Haiti affected Sogesol's performance?

Chapter Sixteen
The American Bank of Kosovo

VERONICA GILBERT and ROSHIKA SINGH

Background

Kosovo is part of the former Yugoslavia and has a mixed population of which the majority is ethnic Albanian. The largest minority is Serbian and other ethnic groups include Bosnians, Roma and Turks. Kosovo enjoyed a high degree of autonomy within the former Yugoslavia until 1989, when the Serbian leader Slobodan Milosevic removed its autonomy and brought it under the direct control of Belgrade, the capital of Serbia. The Kosovar Albanians opposed this and conflict between Serbian and Kosovar Albanian forces broke out. Kosovo suffered from a decade of discrimination and neglect and was further ravaged in 1999 by the Serb occupation and ethnic cleansing.

In March 1999, after many unsuccessful international efforts to find a peaceful solution to the conflict, NATO intervened and commenced air strikes that lasted until June 1999 to put an end to Milosevic's forces' attacks on Kosovar Albanians. On 10 June 1999, a UN Security Council resolution authorized the UN Secretary-General to establish an interim international civilian administration led by the UN in Kosovo. As a result, the UN Interim Administration Mission in Kosovo (UNMIK) was established.

The conflict resulted in the deaths of over 1500 Kosovar Albanians and forced approximately 400 000 to flee their homes. Most medium and large businesses were forced to cease working and significant damage was inflicted on infrastructure and industrial capacity. In addition to the general devastation of assets and property, there was no access to capital or modern banking services, and insufficient credit to support the recovery of private enterprises.

Kosovo has begun to recover, but the damage has made rebuilding its economy a long and arduous process. Extensive efforts from the international community have sought to establish a sound macro-economic policy environment and to put in place a market-oriented framework of commercial law necessary to support economic recovery. Programmes are also underway to support the reconstruction of the business sector.

By 2001, small and micro-lending programmes had been established in response to the need for credit in Kosovo, but they focused on short-term lending to micro and small businesses, and loan disbursements were small (under US$3m in total). The Kosovo Business Finance (KBF) project was designed to strike at the root of the severe economic problems facing Kosovo. UNMIK, as the province's *de facto* government, had succeeded in restoring a reasonable degree of stability and developed a coherent legal framework. Stability and the rule of law, however, are necessary but not sufficient conditions for rebuilding Kosovo's shattered economy. The province's small and medium-sized enterprises (SMEs), which generated about 75 per cent of private sector GDP and included manufacturing, farming and trading businesses, lacked a financial infrastructure and access to important business development services. These factors, combined with years of systematic exclusion of ethnic Albanians from the formal economy and the collapse of the State-owned enterprise sector, left Kosovo with an unemployment rate exceeding 50 per cent. The economic status of Kosovo at the start of the KBF project is summarized below:[1]

- GDP was US$1.4bn.
- The population was estimated to be 1.9 million and was mainly rural.
- Exports were negligible and 85 per cent of products consumed were imported.
- Remittances were 40 per cent of GDP.
- Ninety per cent of funds in the economy were deemed 'mattress money'. (Kosovar Albanians had lost any savings in banks during the civil war, as they were no longer able to travel to Belgrade and retrieve their money. The resulting distrust in banks led the Kosovar Albanians to save their money in hard currency in their homes under their beds, hence the term 'mattress money'.)
- There was little or no banking experience in Kosovo. Kosovar Albanians were neglected and not many had previously worked in banks in the former Yugoslavia.
- Only 14 669 businesses were formally registered, with about 3000 considered SMEs and 11 000 microenterprises. Loan demand was unmet with most lending programmemes targeted at the low end of the market – up to US$18 000; while most SMEs needed credit in excess of US$23 000.
- About 84 per cent of businesses saw the access to credit as their overriding constraint in developing their full market potential.
- The vast majority of business transactions were made in trade or cash barter, reflecting the lack of access to finance for commercial activities.
- Only 22 per cent of enterprises had bank accounts, all of which were abroad.
- Only 3 per cent had outstanding loan balances.
- Most businesses were operating outside the formal sector.

With the youngest population in Europe (50 per cent of the population was under the age of 22 at the start of the KBF project), Kosovo had a large but virtually untapped reservoir of human capital and entrepreneurial talent that could potentially fuel a vibrant, robust economy. However, Kosovo's economic potential was stifled by the lack of financial infrastructure on the one hand, and a lack of business and managerial skills on the other.

Introduction

The purpose of the KBF project was to 'establish a sustainable source of financing for small and medium enterprises and to establish a permanent indigenous financial institution in Kosovo to provide financial services and mobilize deposits.' The KBF project was designed to support the USAID/Kosovo objective of contributing towards the establishment of market-oriented economic policy and institutional framework. The explicit focus of the project was on stimulating employment and increasing private investment in the SME sector, thereby supporting the rapid and sustainable recovery of living standards for Kosovo's population.

The scope and structure of the KBF project were carefully designed to respond to the financial needs of Kosovo's SMEs, as identified by a detailed market assessment that USAID had conducted in 2000.[2] The assessment team had examined both the demand for and the supply of credit among SMEs – and identified substantial gaps between the two. First, there was a vast gap in absolute terms: annual demand for credit among Kosovo's SMEs could be in the order of US$200m[3], but aggregate loan disbursement by the Micro Enterprise Bank (MEB) and other lending programmes in Kosovo so far totalled only about US$4m – only about 2 per cent of potential demand.[4] Second, there was a mismatch of loan size and terms. This assessment found that 60 per cent of surveyed SMEs required loans above US$23 000 and more than 84 per cent identified the 'difficulty of obtaining long-term credit' as their single most severe financial constraint. However, MEB's average loan size was less than US$5500 and both MEB and other active lenders in Kosovo, such as FINCA, tended to offer only short-term loans. Overall, there were certain positive and negative factors in place with regards to establishing an SME financing institution and these are listed below.

Positive factors
- A well-educated and profit motivated entrepreneurial sector was already in existence.
- Kosovars were familiar with, and had positive attitudes towards, western commercial banking due to their experience while abroad and the experience of their relatives still living abroad.
- The euro conversion requirement due on 31 December 2001 would force a large influx of currency into the banking system.
- A Deutsche Mark denominated currency was in use prior to the introduction of the euro, reducing the devaluation risk that other local soft currencies in transitional economies may have.
- The unique situation of Kosovo being administered by UNMIK contributed towards the establishment of a stable legal and regulatory banking environment.

Negative factors
- Potential borrowers had little or no credit history.
- Valuation of collateral was an issue, mainly due to inconsistencies

in registry/property titling systems and poor quality of available information.
- Kosovars had distrust in the local banking system as a result of losing all their savings kept in the previous local banks.

As noted above, the KBF programme had the explicit purpose of establishing a permanent, indigenous financial institution in Kosovo to mobilize deposits and recycle them into loans to local businesses. Second, it was to develop an innovative approach to SME-lending that addressed the unique challenges of lending to largely informal businesses in a post-conflict society with limited legal protection, by drawing on the lessons of micro-credit and specialized SME-lending programmes in other transitional economies.

There was not an exclusive focus on SMEs however, and it was also part of the plan to establish a bank that would offer ordinary banking services and products such as current and checking accounts, overdrafts, foreign exchange, provide cash, and so forth and be bankers to the government and private sector.

On 10 May 2001, USAID awarded Deloitte Touche Tohmatsu Emerging Markets, Ltd. (Deloitte) a contract by for the implementation of the KBF.

The original purpose of the KBF project was to:

1. support the recovery and revitalization of SMEs in Kosovo by providing a quick response SME credit facility (the loan production unit or LPU);
2. establish a full-service bank to mobilize deposits and provide other financial services to SMEs in Kosovo; and
3. provide technical assistance to develop the financial analysis and management capability of bank professionals locally to assure post-project sustainability.

Programmes had already been underway in Kosovo to support the rebuilding of the business sector. Small- and micro-lending programmes had been established to respond to the need for credit, but they focused on short-term lending to micro and small businesses, and loan disbursements were small (under $3 million in total). These existing programmes did not become part of KBF, and the KBF project differed in that it had the express purpose of building a sustainable business bank to provide credit, as well as to mobilize deposits and recycle them as loans, while also providing critical banking services. To do this, the project would aggressively employ micro- and SME-loan analysis and administration techniques and processes that had proven successful in other transitional and developing economies. Realizing the challenges in lending to SMEs, the use of microfinance approaches in the lending methodology was considered. While the microfinance model could not be imported wholesale into a SME-focused lending programme, specific approaches were successfully employed in Kosovo, such as:

- extensive outreach and loan marketing;
- innovative product design and lending approach;
- streamlined cost-effective credit assessment and approval;
- proactive loan monitoring and loss prevention.

The project team accomplished the requirements under the KBF project under budget and ahead of schedule. Specifically, a lending facility was established; a full service commercial bank, the American Bank of Kosovo (ABK) was created into which the lending facility was integrated; training and capacity building was provided to Kosovars hired to work in the bank; and the bank was sold to a foreign investor (Raiffeisen Bank of Austria). This case study presents the ABK during 2001–2003, prior to the sale of all its shares to Raifeissen and while still part of the KBF project. It focuses particularly on the incorporation of microfinance lending techniques in its operations. Box 16.1 (below) gives an implementation timeline of the KBF project and the ABK.

At the start of the KBF project, there was only one other bank in Kosovo, MEB. As noted previously, its client base was limited, as were its services. ABK was created to respond to a pent up demand for loans, financing and general bank services.

Under the KBF project, ABK was actually the second stage of an SME lending programme. The Kosovo Business Finance Fund (KBFF) was established under the KBF project as a non-profit organization to help in the reconstruction and economic development in Kosovo by encouraging lending activities, particularly to small- or medium-size businesses. The creation of this lending facility was necessary in order to channel grant funds from USAID to borrowers in Kosovo. It operated at the discretion of USAID and the KBFF directors. The integration of the KBFF into the bank began in November 2001 when part of the KBFF loan portfolio was used as capital for bank set-up (and continued in January 2002 with the placement of the KBFF loan unit inside the physical premises of ABK). Senior bank staff members became part of the KBFF credit committee and, as of April 2002, KBFF was integrated as the lending department of ABK, with all staff becoming part of ABK and

Box 16.1 *KBF Project implementation timeline*

Phase I: Start up (May–December 2001)
Annual work-plan completed; KBFF office set up; lending officers trained; ABK incorporated; credit manual written; lending activities commenced; staff trained; bank premises set up; banking licence received; deposit activities commenced; systems implemented.

Phase II: Sustainable operations (January 2002–July 2003)
Euro conversion; KBFF merged with ABK; ABK branching strategy drafted and implemented; 76 per cent of shares sold to RIB; local management integrated; name changed to RBKO; new products launched; remaining 24 per cent of shares sold; KBF staff demobilized.

all existing performing loans transferred to ABK. By 30 April 2003, ABK's deposit level had increased to US$62.9m and, since project inception, the credit committee had approved 1866 loans for a total outstanding portfolio of US$29.8m. A total of US$47.1 million had been disbursed to borrowers.

As set out in the original plan, a loan unit was created to address the needs in the early post-war situation that then became part of a functioning bank as a banking culture emerged again. As the KBFF had worked on extending loans to SMEs in Kosovo during June–October 2001, other members of the KBF project team worked in parallel to create the physical and legal infrastructure necessary to establish ABK. As with the creation of the KBFF, the team:

- delineated and created a bank shareholding and management structure, charter and by-laws;
- worked with USAID and the Banking and Payments Authority of Kosovo (BPK) (the BPK was essentially the Central Bank in Kosovo) to clarify bank capitalization requirements and funding arrangements (such as setting up escrow account for bank pre-operating expenses);
- drafted bank policies and procedures;
- completed necessary legal and regulatory forms;
- identified, leased, and oversaw the building of bank premises;
- procured bank accounting systems;
- recruited, hired and trained Kosovars to staff the bank and assume bank operations. Members of the Kosovar diaspora began to return, including Kosovars who had worked at banks in Switzerland, New York, Germany and so forth.

Within six months of the start of the KBF project (by November 2001), the ABK building was fully equipped and compliant with the security requirements of the BPK. ABK was incorporated as a joint stock company under UNMIK regulation 2001/6 on 14 August 2001 and registered with UNMIK as a joint-stock company on 15 August 2001. It received its bank licence on 8 November 2001, which was granted under UNMIK regulation 1999/21. The initial capital requirement for the bank licence was US$1.37m. This initial bank capital was provided by USAID via KBFF with a token amount from Rabo International Advisory Services, who were KBF project consortium members.

ABK branches

The first ABK branch was located in Pristina, the largest city in Kosovo and also site of the bank headquarters. ABK had prioritized expanding its services through the expansion of a branch network. At the start of May 2002, the ABK/RBKO[5] team was awarded the BPK competitive tender for six branches and five sub-branches. The tender was part of the BPK plan to extract itself from performing non-central bank core functions such as payment of state employee salaries and pensions. After opening all of the acquired BPK branches and leasing a few other locations, ABK/RBKO had a network of 17 branches throughout Kosovo, including in the Serb territories. Along with its network of branches, the ABK/RBKO operated ten ATMs throughout Kosovo.

Deposits mobilized by ABK

There was rapid growth in deposits initially in 2002 when the currency was converted, but the level of deposits levelled off after this, as more banks entered the market. In an interesting development, by June 2003 ABK/RBKO was experiencing a steady increase in deposits, despite the presence of other banks in the market, demonstrating that there was a growing customer base.

Loans disbursed by ABK

The lending team at ABK maintained an active pipeline in SME lending. The team approved over 2400 loans and approximately US$74m was disbursed to ABK borrowers from the beginning of the KBF project until USAID and Deloitte divested themselves of the banking and lending components under the project on 10 July 2003. Further disbursements of approved loans occurred on a daily basis as the team at RBKO took over full operation and management of the SME lending programme.

Delinquencies

According to the credit administration team, the portfolio was good, but increasing at a very fast pace and so were past dues. Of the total outstanding portfolio, 2.60 per cent of the loans were reported as being more than 30 days past due on all or a portion of their payments.

The estimated value of collateral that was pledged and filed on the loans in arrears was four to 18 times greater than the loan amount. Therefore, the loans appeared to be adequately secured. There were no unsecured loans for SMEs. However, the security position is only relevant to the extent that the Municipal Courts recognize contractual rights to acquire the property through foreclosure actions. The attitude of the courts differs by municipality, with some courts being very understanding of contractual rights and others appearing to be obstructive. Legal action was taken against all borrowers that defaulted on their loans during USAID and Deloitte's involvement with ABK. Because of this aggressive action, the arrears rate remained below 3 per cent.

Products offered by ABK

With the success of the SME loan programme in the first two years of the KBF project, the lending team developed several new loan products to release in the Kosovar market. These included direct deposits for payroll, different lending services, and ATM and debit card services. ABK offered a full range of deposit products, money transfer services, pension payments, welfare payments, payroll processing services and a basic cash management system to larger companies that did business throughout Kosovo. ABK also had an active SME lending programme and was the only bank in Kosovo that allowed customers to maintain accounts in four currencies. ABK also offered a basic cash management/payroll system for the largest entities in Kosovo, a branded debit card with an overdraft facility on it for qualified customer employees and several retail loan products. A product pricing committee systematically reviewed all ABK financial products to determine whether product prices were competitive in the marketplace and profitable for the bank to offer.

The use of microfinance techniques in ABK lending

While the microfinance model obviously could not be imported wholesale into an SME-focused lending programme, there are specific MFI approaches that were successfully employed by KBF. The design of the project was largely driven by the assumption that the processes and technologies used in microfinance are also applicable to financing SMEs. The microfinance best practices employed spanned the entire lending process, not just credit approval. Some of the specific microfinance approaches that the Deloitte team built into KBF included the following:

Extensive outreach and loan marketing
- Leveraging existing networks and institutions that the Deloitte team worked with, such as the University of Pristina, Mercy Corps and so forth, to identify (and gather information on) potential borrowers.
- Maintaining a presence in local communities and conducting outreach programme at the grassroots level.
- Providing hands-on assistance to borrowers in completing applications and preparing business plans.

Innovative product design and lending approach
- Starting small and then increasing loan amounts as borrowers demonstrate credit-worthiness (step loans).
- Offering standardized, simple products tailored to the specific needs of target customer groups.
- Utilizing non-traditional forms of collateral such as compulsory savings and third-party guarantees.

Streamlined, cost-effective credit assessment and approval
- Using standardized, streamlined application forms for standard loan sizes and types (organized into tiers).

- Maintaining a low overhead cost structure and an efficient, fast assessment and approval process.
- Basing lending decisions primarily on character by leveraging sources of in-depth local knowledge.

Proactive loan monitoring and loss prevention
- Continuing frequent interaction with and monitoring of borrowers after loans have been disbursed.
- Providing incentives for prompt repayment, such as quick approval of new loans and reduced rates.
- Offering fee-based business support services to active borrowers (in our case, through KBS).

In essence, the ABK lending approach reflected the following microfinance principles.

- The most important evaluation criteria are the potential client's character and business acumen.
- Reliance on financials is based more on interviews and discussions with potential clients and reviews of their operations than on formal financial statements.
- Clients make their loan repayments when their reputation and family home is at stake and when they are receiving frequent visits by loan officers.
- Larger loans and longer maturities are only extended after the clients have developed a good record of servicing smaller loans.

ABK customers and staff and microfinance lending techniques

ABK client base

In accordance with the project goals for employment generation and economic stimulation, the lending priority was to finance businesses engaged in labor-intensive manufacturing and production activities. Consistent with this objective, approximately 10 per cent of the loans granted during the project period were for agriculture. Of the 2408 loan applications that were approved by the project to July 2003, 52 per cent were in the manufacturing and production industries, 15.8 per cent were in the service industry and 32.2 per cent were engaged in trade. A detailed breakdown of the loan portfolio by industry sector is shown in Table 16.1 (overleaf).

The lending team focused on visiting clients within Pristina as well as throughout Kosovo, including the Serbian enclaves. Of the 2408 loans approved, 16.6 per cent are to borrowers within the Pristina municipality, 14 per cent in Prizren, 8.3 per cent in Ferizaj, and 4.5 per cent in Mitrovica municipality.

Table 16.1 Industry concentration at 10 July 2003

Industry/ sector	Amount (US$)	Amount %	No. of Loans	% of Loans
Manufacturing and production	39 090 000	53.2	1 252	52.0
Trade	26 660 000	36.3	776	32.2
Services	7 750 000	10.5	380	15.8
Total	73 500 000	100.0	2 408	100.0

ABK customer profile

Table 16.1 outlines the profile of ABK's customer base. BAST (Bajram Abdullahu and Sylejman Topanica) was among the first of 2405 businesses to obtain a loan from ABK. BAST, a plastics manufacturer based in Pristina, signed a one-year loan agreement to cover 80 per cent of the cost of new equipment. As good credit customers, BAST has been promised full support with investments in the future. The BAST owners update equipment and product lines as consumer trends change. With the loan, they purchased new equipment necessary to produce updated plastic bottles to meet consumer demands, and added four more employees to help supply the growing demand for their plastics.

Many businesses like BAST had previously looked for capital but found only personal lenders willing to lend surplus cash. Without loans, BAST could not add equipment needed to produce the kinds of plastics in demand. Thanks to ABK, business owners could formally receive loans and build credit, something that previously did not exist.

Training ABK employees in microfinance techniques and SME-lending practices

New recruits were provided with extensive training through formal classroom training, seminars and workshops and continuous on-the-job training. Training was on small and micro lending techniques as well as other areas such as credit risk management, SME business risk evaluation, cash flow analysis, collateral evaluation, loan restructuring and so forth. The ABK lending staff received training on all the products and services offered by ABK and the sales process, so that they could effectively grow client relationships and increase deposits. The ABK credit staff received both formal credit training and on-the-job skill development training. The Training Schedule Report (Table 16.2, opposite) provides a snapshot of 12 formal credit training courses that were conducted from May 2001–May 2002. Ongoing job training also occurred each work day, as local employees worked directly with either a loan officer or a senior credit manager in the activities of originating, disbursing and monitoring KBFF's loan portfolio.

Table 16.2 *Training Schedule Report (May 2002)*

Date	Title	Description
17 July 2001	Small and Micro Lending Techniques	Short course to KBFF management on how small and micro lending techniques could be used in the KBFF lending process.
15 August 2001	Credit File Structure	An electronic filing system allows KBFF 2001 staff to access approved lending documents and store business communication and lending documents in an electronic filing system.
15 August 2001	Central Calendar Loan Info System	A central calendar was implemented to assist with scheduling client meetings and gives KBFF managers the ability to supervise employee activities.
15 August 2001	Credit Manual	The KBFF Credit Manual containing the policies and procedures that govern all aspects of loan delivery and recovery.
21–22 August 2001	Basic Accounting	Basics of how to construct the balance sheet and cash flow statement and how these financial statements apply to credit analysis and lending decisions.
27–31 August 2001	Credit Risk Management	Week-long session which contained eight modules covering financial statement analysis, cash flow analysis and projections, SME business risk-evaluation, business planning, client interaction, collateral valuation and loan monitoring.
17–19 September 2001	Small and Micro Lending Techniques	How small and micro lending techniques are utilized in the KBFF lending process and their applicability to Kosovo environment.
19 September 2001	Lending Processes	Approach and format for completing the Loan Recommendation form and other loan file documents.
20–22 November 2001	Credit Risk	Basic double-entry bookkeeping, financial analysis techniques and critical case-study review of KBFF loan recommendations.
11–14 March 2002	Accounting	Accounting review: balance sheet, amortization, accounts payable, accounts receivable, bookkeeping.
21 March 2002	KBFF Credit Process	Review of KBFF lending approach and loan recommendation package.
24–29 April 2002	Deposit Mobilization	Discussion on deposits mobilization, characteristics that make deposits attractive to depositors and strategies for selling ABK deposits and other financial products.

Participation in ABK's employee development programme resulted in local employees being promoted to the position of junior loan officer. This is a management position which supervised the work of lending associates. In addition, local employees were promoted to full loan officer responsibilities, supervising a team of up to six lending associates. Staff from the lending unit were able to move over to bank operations/ supervision as needed. The staff members recruited earlier (about 12) received in-depth and theoretical training. The later lenders (about 20) received only a few days of theoretical training and more practical training about how to evaluate the client, to complete the documents required and process the loans. The formal training was about four days a year for these individuals and the practical training was ongoing.

ABK credit manual

An important tool in staff development and training was the drafting and use of a credit manual covering the basics of credit operating policies and procedures, which was issued in August 2001. After that, credit policies and procedures were updated as necessary to clarify all phases of credit operations, and to meet the requirements of the BPK for banking institutions after the integration of the lending unit into the ABK. In addition, improvements were made in standardizing the loan recommendation form and supporting credit documents that are provided to USAID for each loan approved. The KBF project continued to refine credit operating procedures that promote sound lending standards.

Financial performance of ABK

Although much progress had been made in the areas of operations and controls at ABK, the financial performance was initially not quite at the level that was projected in the original budget. This was due, in part, to unforeseen delays in the release of new products and services and the overall declining deposit trends seen in the banking industry to date. This, in turn, resulted in relatively high operating expenses in relation to current and future revenue generation.

By May 2003, the net interest income of the bank was US$6.91m, but high staff and administrative expenses resulted in an overall loss of US$1.19m. Cost-cutting measures were put in place and expenses were reduced by 20 per cent in three months, with plans for further reductions. ABK introduced an account management fee for customers, which brought in a further US$14 113 per month, and implemented upfront loan fees that generated US$70 566. Development and launch of new products, home improvement loans, payroll overdraft for cards, and trade finance products and installing ten ATMs helped improve uptake. The bank planned to continue its credit activity through all the branches and to speed up the disbursement process.

The bank had completed and passed two audits by the first quarter of 2003. The net outstanding deposit figure from customers totalled

US$65m and the outstanding loan portfolio was US$32m. The loan portfolio was strong, with a problem loan exposure of only 2.97 per cent. The number of retail bank customers was 77 299 and retail loans were started in August 2003. The highlight of the retail banking report was that, despite the newly introduced loan origination fee, ABK was able to increase SME loans to 50 per week. The average size and term of the SME loans had increased from less than US$47 044 over one year to US$64 685 over 13 months. The bank broke even by December 2003, and the management team continued its efforts to achieve profitability.

Summary of KBF/ABK impact and results

By many accounts, the KBF project, and ABK in particular, was one of the successful examples of public–private collaboration in the history of USAID's economic governance work. In addition to having achieved a successful exit and the return of a substantial portion of its development capital as programme income, ABK had a marked impact on the economy and the perception of the public towards credit and the banking environment at large. Through the lending and banking components of the project, the ABK realized tangible results

Tangible results

- It was revealed through surveys of loan applicants that 5348 new direct jobs were created, or one job for approximately every US$13 109 of loan volume.
- More than US$74m was loaned to 2400 SMEs.
- Loans had an exceptional default rate: less than 3 per cent.
- US$65m in deposits were mobilized.
- ABK is the leading province-wide bank with 17 branches and an extensive ATM network.
- ABK assumed the central bank's commercial operations.
- ABK employed and trained over 300 Kosovars in banking.
- USAID made a successful exit through a strategic sale to a major regional bank.

Economic
- ABK fostered public confidence and catalysed a flow of savings from 'the mattress' to the formal economy.
- Through a systematic programme of deposit mobilization, it channeled domestic savings to productive investment for the creation of new jobs.
- The rapid delivery of new credit to entrepreneurs stimulated financial intermediation and helped to construct a ready-made customer book. This in turn provided new funds for on-lending.
- As a new competitor to the market, ABK facilitated competitive tension among a handful of existing foreign-owned banks (there were no banks that operated before the civil war still functioning

in Kosovo), and had a strong impact on the price structure and quality of services provided. New products and sponsorships were used to generate public awareness of a market-oriented system.
- The Central Bank was able to shed all of its branches and non-traditional core functions, such as social security and pension payments.
- USAID capital was successfully allocated to induce private sector investment in the Kosovo financial system.

Social
- By employing individuals from the Central Bank, the ABK project provided a transitional employment strategy and compensated for lack of a social safety net.
- The project hired and trained at least 300 people, more than 50 per cent of whom were women; the majority of the staff were under the age of 30.
- Through the lending programme, the ABK project constructed and contributed to the revitalization of 16 local markets.
- It re-instilled trust and confidence in the banking sector and reestablished a credit culture.

There are many factors we have identified as key to ABK's success, and among these was the incorporation of micro-lending techniques to the lending process. Most importantly, the project and bank fostered the co-operation and involvement of both Albanian and Serb groups. The project team made an effort to reach out to include both ethnic groups in the set-up and operations of the bank, and Albanians as well as Serbs were among the 300 Kosovars trained during the course of the KBF project. The resulting legacy is the development of the indigenous banking and lending capacity in Kosovo, which bodes very well for future economic development.

The bank continues to operate 18 branches in Kosovo, with a plan to have 21 by the end of 2004. As RBKO, the bank retained a number of the KBF project staff and currently has three expatriates who previously worked on the project serving as the CEO, the head of finance and the head of retail banking.

This case study demonstrates a successful business model for a commercial investor as, despite political and other risks being high, ABK's successful level of deposits and resulting loan portfolio allowed KBFF to sell the shares of ABK to an established international bank. It is a unique project with a successful exit strategy that clearly demonstrates that a development project can develop a sustainable business. The transformation of this project to a privatized, sustainable business was an achievement that will continue to create jobs and provide lending to support the economy.

Discussion questions

1. ABK applied microfinance methods to the design of services for medium-sized businesses, and to the evolution of a complete full-service commercial bank. The usual approach is to trade 'down', from traditional banking to microfinance. How successful was the ABK approach, and how can more conventional MFIs learn from it?

2. The original mission of ABK was to serve SMEs, but the bank focused only on banking and did not provide business development services. Was this the correct strategy?

3. The whole process of creating the bank and then selling it off to a private foreign investor took only 26 months. Was this too hasty?

Chapter Seventeen
Commercial banks in microfinance in Georgia

TEONA MIKADZE and GUILLEMETTE JAFFRIN[1]

Background

Georgia has 4.4 million inhabitants[2] in a geographical area of nearly 70 000 square kilometres. Georgia borders the Russian Federation, Azerbaijan, Armenia, Turkey and the Black Sea, and is strategically located as a trade and transit corridor in the Caucasus, between Europe and Asia.

Georgia ranks 88 in the UNDP's *Human Development Report 2003*, but it ranks 121 in term of GDP per capita. Georgia is one of the poorest members of the Commonwealth of Independent States (CIS).

Georgia gained independence from the Soviet Union in 1991. This independence was followed by a brief civil war and by massive economic disruption due to the break-up of the Soviet Union. As a result, GDP fell by an average of 20 per cent per year between 1990 and 1995 and poverty and income inequality increased substantially.[3] The World Bank's 'Georgia Poverty Update' reported that poverty increased sharply over the period 1997–2000, rising from 50–63 per cent of the population when using the Georgian poverty line of US$4.30 a day; or from 14–24 per cent using the more conservative poverty line of the World Bank for the Former Soviet Union (US$2.15 a day).[4]

In addition, Georgia suffers from the existence of separatist movements, in particular in the north-east (Abhkazia) and in the north (South Ossetia) of the country. The separatist movement in Chechnya (which borders Georgia) is also a source of instability. Finally, Georgia has recently faced some political turmoil with the overthrow of its long-serving president, Eduard Shevardnadze, in November 2003. A new president, Mikhael Saakashvili, was elected on 4 January 2004.

Economic situation

The informal economy accounts for 64 per cent of GDP and 30 per cent of total employment. It is estimated that there are about 360 000 micro, small and medium enterprises, however only 65 000 are registered. Microenterprises (with one to nine employees) account for 82 per cent. Around 50 per cent of these enterprises are located in the national capital, Tbilisi.[5] Microenterprises are typically composed of one self-employed person, with a few employees, engaged in trading or services activities. Most of the microenterprises are new and have emerged since Georgia became independent.

The Georgian business culture, inherited from the former Soviet Union, is characterized by a distrust of government institutions. As a

Table 17.1 Socioeconomic indicators for Georgia

	1999	2000	2001	2002	2003
GDP (US$bn.)	2.8	3.0	3.1	3.4	4.0
Population (million)	4.46	4.43	4.40	4.37	4.35
GDP per capita (US$)	628	677	705	778	920
Real GDP growth (%)	3.0	1.9	4.7	5.6	8.0
Consumer price inflation (av. %)	19.2	4.0	4.7	5.6	4.5
Exchange rate (av.) Lari (GEL):US$	2.02	1.98	2.07	2.20	2.15

Source: Country Report, Georgia, *The Economist* Intelligence Unit, November 2003

result, businesses strive to operate with minimum visibility and rely on personal connections. According to a World Bank study[6], among countries of the former Soviet Union, Georgian businesses (especially micro and small businesses) pay the highest proportion of their revenues as bribes. Businesses also suffer from arbitrary tax collection, the absence of reliable property registries, administrative corruption, onerous licensing requirements, and a lack of reliable recourse in the judicial system.[7]

The banking sector

Following a process of consolidation, Georgia's banking sector currently consists of 24 commercial banks. The EBRD notes that, during the past five years, the management of the larger, former State banks – as well as of some of the newly established banks – has improved significantly.[8] However, poor management, corporate governance deficiencies and weak loan portfolios in several banks have undermined the Georgian financial sector and three banks ran into insolvency in 2001 and 2002.

Bank failures and the hyperinflation of the early 1990s that wiped out the value of deposits have ruined public confidence in the banking system. As a result, the EBRD reports that financial intermediation is very thin: only 3 to 4 per cent of Georgians have a bank account. As at the end of 2003, the leading banks in Georgia are TBC Bank, Bank of Georgia, United Georgian Bank, and ProCredit Bank (the former Microfinance Bank of Georgia), as highlighted by Table 17.2 (opposite).

Microfinance sector

According to a recent review[10] commissioned by the CGAP on microfinance in Central and Eastern Europe and the New Independent States, Georgia has a reasonably well-developed microfinance sector, with the two largest microfinance institutions (in term of number of clients) of the region, in addition to several small and medium-sized microfinance institutions. The microfinance market is now in a phase

Table 17.2 Major Georgian banks in terms of assets (at 31 December 2003)

Bank	Assets (US$m)[9]
TBC Bank	122.72
Bank of Georgia	106.99
United Georgian Bank	78.93
ProCredit Bank	59.49
	Source: National Bank of Georgia

of consolidation, following the strong growth that characterized previous years. The volume of outstanding micro-loans (less than US$10 000) is estimated at US$30m, with around 30 000 clients.

The largest microfinance provider, by number of active clients, is ProCredit Bank with over 32 000 clients (at December 2003). Constanta is the second largest MFI by this measure, with over 16 000 clients.

The CGAP review identified other sources of financial services to micro and rural clients, such as:

- The Agro Business Bank of Georgia, established in early 2000 to provide rural financial services (with an average size of loan disbursed of US$16 000).
- 79 credit unions affiliated to the Credit Union Development Centre (9000 members, US$1m in member shares and savings).
- 18 rural credit unions supported by UMCOR and six farmer credit associations supported by ACDI/VOCA.
- Moneylenders (with monthly rates up to 15 per cent) and traders.
- In addition, commercial banks provide a range of financial services to micro and rural clients, such as micro and small enterprises loans, consumer loans and pawnshop loans.

Commercial banks involved in microfinance

Georgia is a particularly interesting case, considering the number of commercial banks involved in microfinance. In this section, we shall discuss the experience of three commercial banks in microfinance: one microfinance bank and two commercial banks that have downscaled.

A microfinance bank: ProCredit Bank[11]

Donors and investors have shown increasing interest in microfinance in Georgia because of its fast-growing informal economy and the initial success of microfinance institutions (such as Constanta and FINCA).

The Microfinance Bank of Georgia (which was in September 2003 renamed as ProCredit Bank) was established in 1999 by international

Table 17.3 ProCredit Bank ownership structure

Institution	Ownership percentage
Internationale Micro Investments (IMI)	39%
German State Development Bank (KFW)	10%
International Finance Corporation (IFC)	16%
Commerzbank	3%
European Bank for Reconstruction and Development (EBRD)	20%
Internationale Projekt Consult (IPC)	12%

financial organizations. Four Georgian banks (Tbilcom Bank, Tblicredit Bank, TBC Bank and Intellect Bank) were among shareholders as well. IPC, a German consultancy company, was appointed to manage the newly established bank.

ProCredit Bank is part of a network of microfinance banks set up by IMI (Internationale Micro Investments). IMI was founded in 1998 by IPC in partnership with other investors and is the origin of the microfinance bank model. IPC usually provides management services to the microfinance banks during their creation and early operation.[12] As at September 2003, IMI had invested in 18 microfinance banks around

Table 17.4 ProCredit Bank key indicators (US$m), at 31 December 2003

		Note
Total assets	59.49	2
Outstanding loans (volume)	47.51	1
Outstanding loans (number)	28 494	1
Deposits (volume)	17.58	1
Share capital	9.30	2
Average outstanding loan size	US$1 667	1
Branches	7	1
Outlets	11	1
Number of staff	440	1
Profit/loss	+ 1.5	2
Note 1: *source*: ProCredit Bank		
Note 2: *source*: National Bank of Georgia		

Figure 17.1 Loan portfolio (in volume and number) and deposits (in volume)

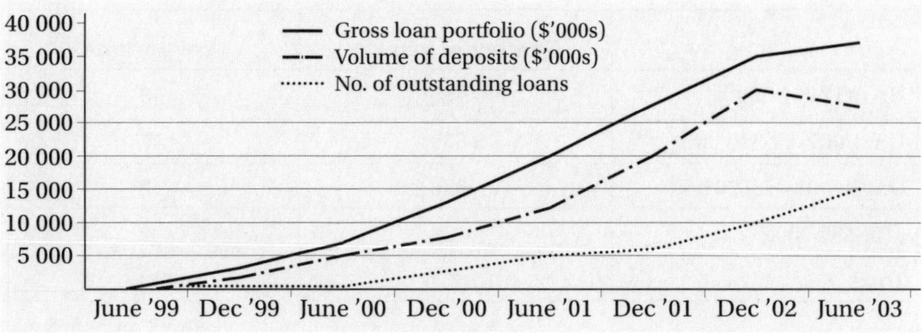

```
40 000 ┬
35 000 ┤    ─── Gross loan portfolio ($'000s)
30 000 ┤    ─·─ Volume of deposits ($'000s)
25 000 ┤    ······ No. of outstanding loans
20 000 ┤
15 000 ┤
10 000 ┤
 5 000 ┤
       └────┬──────┬──────┬──────┬──────┬──────┬──────┬──────┬
         June '99 Dec '99 June '00 Dec '00 June '01 Dec '01 Dec '02 June '03
```

the world: ten in Eastern Europe, including Georgia; five in Latin America, and three in Africa.

Since June 2003, the capital of ProCredit Bank has been fully owned by international financial organizations and banks. Two of the Georgian shareholder banks went into default and two banks (TBC Bank and Intellect Bank) sold their shares.

ProCredit Bank is the recognized microfinance leader in Georgia, with more than 32 000 customers. ProCredit Bank has now become the fourth largest bank in Georgia in terms of assets. Table 17.4 (opposite) provides major indicators on ProCredit Bank. Since its creation in 1999, ProCredit Bank has grown strongly, with its current loan portfolio standing in December 2003 at close to US$48m and with an average outstanding loan size of US$1940 (including all loans).

Figure 17.1 (above) demonstrates the strong growth of ProCredit Bank's loan portfolio. Interestingly, the graph shows that, from December 2002, the number of outstanding loans decreased while the gross loan portfolio kept increasing, which means that the average loan size increased. This trend is explained by the fact that ProCredit Bank ceased to offer Gold Pawn Loans (which are all under US$1000) in several outlets and branches in 2002, following a fraud (elaborated later).

ProCredit Bank's portfolio details are provided in Tables 17.5, 17.6 and 17.7 (below and overleaf). Table 17.5 reveals that 63 per cent of ProCredit Bank loans are 'gold pawn' loans. In terms of the number of

Table 17.5 ProCredit Bank portfolio (number of loans), as at December 2003

	Number	Percentage
Total loans	28 494	100
Total gold pawn loans	17 841	63
Total loans excl. gold pawn loans	10 653	37

Table 17.6 *ProCredit Bank portfolio (excluding Gold Pawn Loans), number of loans as at December 2003*

	Number of loans	**% of portfolio**
Up to US$ 1 000	4 588	43
US$1 001–US$10 000	5 039	47
US$10 001–US$50 000	838	8
> US$50 000	188	2
Total	10 653	100

Source: ProCredit Bank

loans (excluding 'gold pawn' loans), Table 17.6 shows that 90 per cent of the loans are under US$10 000. However, in terms of outstanding amounts (for all loans), Table 17.7 shows that a third of the loan portfolio is under US$10 000, while 36 per cent of the loan portfolio is more than US$50 000.

ProCredit Bank offers a full range of banking services to its clients (such as loans, deposits, account operation, transfer payments, etc.). In particular, ProCredit offers the loan products outlined in Table 17.8.

The newest loan product is the 'Express Micro Loan' (with simpler requirements than the regular micro-loans). ProCredit Bank is flexible regarding the collateral required. For 'Express Micro Loans' (up to US$750) no collateral is required, only third-party guarantees. For 'Regular Loans' up to US$3,000, ProCredit Bank does not require its clients to officially pledge fixed assets (such as real estate) or to go through the complicated legal procedures; movable assets (such as TV or fridge), which are not legally attached, are sufficient. For other loans, ProCredit Bank accepts pledges, personal belongings, fixed assets, personal guarantees, mortgages or gold as collateral.

As illustrated in Table 17.8, ProCredit provides a range of loans to its clients. ProCredit Bank's business loan performance is summarized in Table 17.9 (overleaf).

Table 17.7 *ProCredit Bank portfolio (outstanding amount), as at December 2003*

Loan amount	**Outstanding amount (US$m)**	**% of portfolio**
< US$10 000	15.80	33
US$10 001–US$50 000	14.53	31
> US$50 000	17.18	36

Source: ProCredit Bank

Table 17.8 ProCredit Bank loan products

Loan type	Loan amount (US$)	Currency	Maturity (months)	Interest rate (per annum)
Business loan				
Express Micro	Up to 750	only in GEL	up to 9 (12 in case of repeat loan)	48%
Micro (regular)	100–1 000	only in GEL	up to 12	48%
Micro (regular)	1 001–10 000	GEL, US$, euro	up to 12 (GEL) up to 18 for working capital up to 24 for fixed assets	30–36% GEL 24% US$, euro
Small (regular)	10 001–50 000	GEL, US$, euro	up to 12 (GEL) up to 24 for working capital up to 36 for fixed assets	22%–30% GEL 18% US$, euro
Medium (regular)	over 50 000	GEL, US$	up to 12 (GEL) up to 24 for working capital up to 60 for fixed assets	16% US$, euro 22%–30% GEL
Credit lines	over 1 000	GEL, US$, euro	up to 12	16%–36%
Consumer loans	up to 2 000	GEL	up to 12	36%–48%
Housing loans	up to 20 000	GEL, US$, euro	up to 12 (GEL) up to 36 (US$, euro)	22%–48% GEL 18%–24% US$, euro
Agricultural loans	up to 10 000	GEL, US$	up to 12 24% US$	30%–48% GEL
Gold pawn loans	Up to 1 000	only in GEL	up to 12	42%

Source: ProCredit Bank

Table 17.9 shows that business loans account for 31 per cent of total loans. The average outstanding loan size is US$4809. In term of outstanding amount, Table 17.9 shows that business loans account for 88 per cent of ProCredit Bank's outstanding portfolio. Business loans under US$10 000 account for 30 per cent of the total business loan portfolio.

Despite its success, ProCredit Bank's management recognizes a few challenges. First, ProCredit Bank strives to maintain a high portfolio quality. At the end of 2002, the share of loans in arrears increased from 1.61 per cent (in 2001) to 3.74 per cent of the loan portfolio. However, ProCredit Bank appears to have successfully improved its portfolio

Table 17.9 *Key indicators for business loans in US$ (as at 31 December 2003)*

Number of outstanding loans	8 714
Outstanding loan portfolio	US$41.90m
Loans under US$10 000	$12.73m
Loans above US$10 000	$29.17m
Average outstanding loan size	US$4 809
Portfolio at risk over 30 days (number of loans)	0.95%
Portfolio at risk over 30 days (volume of loans)	1.79%
Number of loan officers	100
	Source: ProCredit Bank

quality since the share of loans in arrears (over 30 days, for all loans) stood at 1.64 per cent in December 2003.

In 2002, ProCredit faced a serious crisis when it discovered that a number of employees had committed a fraud within the bank's Gold Pawn Loan department in Tbilisi (as illustrated by the amount of loan write-offs indicated in the Table 17.10, below). Following the discovery of the fraud, the bank's procedures and structure were changed to strengthen internal control and transparency.[14]

ProCredit Bank's management believes that the major challenges facing the bank are, on one side, to manage the strong growth of the bank and, on the other side, to secure the on-lending funds required to maintain this growth (either from commercial sources or from international financial institutions). An alternative for ProCredit Bank is to increase the amount of deposits raised. At the end of December 2003, ProCredit Bank had a deposit balance of US$17.6m, versus an outstanding loan balance of US$47.5m.

ProCredit launched a major campaign to attract deposits between September and December 2003. Every twenty-first depositor would receive gifts and every two-hundredth depositor would receive a free generator (a very useful piece of equipment considering the severe electricity shortage Georgia is facing). ProCredit Bank entitled this campaign, 'ProCredit Bank Delivers Light'.[15]

Table 17.10 *Loan write-offs (in volume and as a percentage of portfolio)*

	Dec. 2001	Dec. 2002	Dec. 2003
Total loans write-offs (US$)	151 000	1 554 000	564 834
% of portfolio	0.7	4.5	1.2

Two downscaling banks: Tbiluniversalbank and United Georgian Bank

In the early 1990s, Inter-American Development Bank (IADB) initiated the commercial bank downscaling approach in Latin America. IADB designed programmes that provided credit lines to selected commercial banks for the purpose of on-lending to microenterprises. The programme also included technical assistance for each partner bank. The partial success of downscaling in Latin America prompted the European Bank for Reconstruction and Development (EBRD) to invest in similar operations in Central and Eastern Europe and the New Independent States, starting in Russia in 1994.[16]

In Georgia, after the success of ProCredit Bank and with incentives from the EBRD, several Georgian commercial banks became interested in microfinance activities, in particular the Bank of Georgia, Tbiluniversalbank (TUB) and United Georgian Bank (UGB). In this section, we shall discuss the various experiences of TUB and UGB in microfinance.

The EBRD provided a US$1m credit line to TUB and a US$2.5m credit line to UGB. Both of these credit lines are targeted at micro-lending and are accompanied by technical assistance to develop the micro-lending departments within each bank. TUB started its micro-lending activities in March 2001, while UGB started in April 2002.

The first phase of the Small Enterprise Lending Programme (SELP) took place from January 2001 to December 2002 and the second phase started in January 2003.[17] The focus of the first phase was to build and strengthen the micro-lending departments of TUB and UGB, while the second phase focused on expanding the micro-lending programmes of TUB and UGB in the regions, as well as increasing the loan officers' productivity.

Table 17.11 (overleaf) summarises the main indicators of the micro-lending programmes of the two banks. A key difference between TUB and UGB is their size. TUB is a small bank with a very limited branch network (only one branch outside Tbilisi).

Tbiluniversalbank

Tbiluniversalbank (TUB) was formed as a limited liability partnership in 1995, and was granted a general banking licence from the National Bank of Georgia. In 2001, in accordance with the requirements of the National Bank of Georgia, TUB changed its legal status to a joint stock company. TUB is a full-fledged commercial bank.

TUB started its microfinance activities in March 2001. To do so, it first opened a new branch in a central location of Tbilisi. It then hired a new batch of loan officers who, following training in micro-lending techniques delivered by international experts, took charge of the new micro-lending department of the bank.

TUB microfinance activities are concentrated in Tbilisi. In 2002, TUB opened an additional outlet in the main market area of Tbilisi but

Table 17.11 Key indicators for TUB and UGB micro-lending programmes, as at 31 March 2004

	TUB	UGB
Number of outstanding loans	541	1 385
Outstanding loan portfolio (US$)	1 589 345	2 454 780
Average size of loan disbursed	5 773	1 644
Average outstanding loan size	2 938	1 772
Portfolio at risk over 30 days (number of loans)	0.92%	0.65%
Portfolio at risk over 30 days (volume of loans)	1.01%	0.85%
Number of loan officers	7	33
Number of branches participating in the microlending programme	One branch and one outlet in Tbilisi	One branch and one service centre in Tbilisi, two branches (Kutaisi and Akhaltsikhe) and four service centres (Gori, Rustavi, Marneuli and Poti) outside Tbilisi.

Source: Small Enterprise Lending Programme

could only disburse loans effectively from this location in 2003. Table 17.13 (opposite) summarizes the main characteristics of the microloans[19] provided by TUB.[20]

Table 17.12 TUB key indicators (US$m), as at 31 December 2003 [18]

Total assets	13.28
Outstanding loans	8.36
Deposits	8.52
Share capital	2.33
Branches	2
Number of outlets	1
Number of staff	86
Profit / loss	+ 0.35

Source: National Bank of Georgia

Table 17.13 Tbiluniversalbank micro-loans characteristics

Conditions	At least six months' working experience in any business Permanent location (office, trade or service unit) Major share of a business should be privately-owned by Georgian citizens
Activities that cannot be financed	Production and trade of light weaponry, tobacco production, production of drinks containing more than 15 per cent alcohol, gambling, business with high environmental risk
Standard loan	
Amount	US$200–20 000
Term	Working capital: 3–12 months Fixed assets and construction loans: 3–24 months
Interest rate	US$200–20,000 interest rate = 24% per annum
Fee	Approval commission of 2% non-refundable
Repayment schedule	Weekly, bi-weekly or monthly repayment
Collateral	Real estate, inventory, equipment, movable assets Market value of the collateral should correspond to the volume of the loan. Third-party guarantees are accepted For loans less than US$2 000, movable assets (not legally attached) are sufficient
Express Loan	
Amount	US$200–2 000
Term	Up to 12 months
Interest rate	36% per annum
Fee	Approval commission of 2% non-refundable
Repayment schedule	Weekly, bi-weekly or monthly repayment
Collateral	No fixed collateral (real estate) required
Disbursement time	1–3 days

During 2002 and 2003, TUB's micro-lending activities developed steadily. In 2003, a series of changes (introduction of the Express Loan product and simplification of lending procedures) was introduced to boost TUB's portfolio growth. However, TUB's growth is constrained by its limited branch network.

Figure 17.2 (overleaf) reveals that, as at December 2003, after 34 months of micro-lending, TUB had 521 loans outstanding, with a healthy portfolio value of US$1 396 218.

Figure 17.2 TUB loan portfolio evolution (US$)

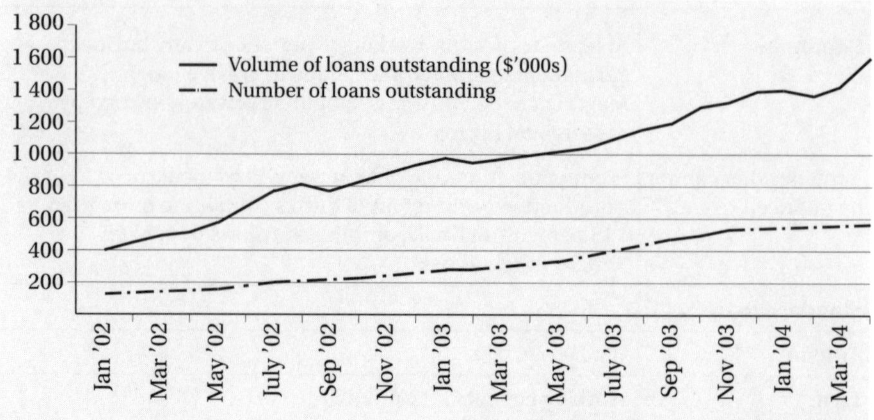

Source: Small Enterprise Lending Programme

United Georgian Bank

United Georgian Bank (UGB) is a joint stock company (with both Georgian and international shareholders) founded in 1995 after the merger of the three Georgian state banks: Exim Bank, Industrial Bank and New Georgian Bank (former Savings Bank). The National Bank of Georgia granted UGB a general licence authorizing banking operations. UGB currently has 18 branches and 18 service centres, half of the branches and service centres are located outside of the capital. UGB is the largest of the three main Georgian banks in term of assets.

In April 2002, UGB opened a new branch on the main avenue of Tbilisi and started its micro-lending operation. Following the same process as TUB, UGB hired a new batch of loan officers that were trained by international experts before starting their lending operations. UGB first focused on micro-lending operations in Tbilisi. In September 2002, taking advantage of its branch network, UGB launched its micro-

Table 17.14 UGB key indicators (US$m) as at 31 December 2003[21]

Total assets	78.93
Outstanding loans	42.37
Deposits	45.15
Share capital	9.77
Branches	18
Outlets	18
Number of staff	1080
Profit / loss	+ 1.11
	Source: National Bank of Georgia

Table 17.15 *Characteristics of UGB's Georgian Lari (GEL) Loan*

Conditions	At least six months' work experience in any business Permanent location (office, trade or service unit) Major share of a business should be privately owned by Georgian citizens
Activities that cannot be financed	Production and trade of light weaponry, tobacco production, production of drinks containing more than 15 per cent alcohol, gambling, business with high environmental risk
Georgian Lari Loan	
Amount	GEL200–5 000 (might be reduced to GEL2 000)
Term	Up to 12 months
Interest rate	42% per annum
Fee	Commission fee of 2% non-refundable
Repayment schedule	Weekly, bi-weekly or monthly repayment
Collateral	No fixed collateral (real estate) required, movable assets not legally attached are sufficient

lending activities at a service centre in Gori, a small city 70 km out of Tbilisi. In 2003, UGB continued the expansion of its micro-lending activities and established microfinance units within one service centre in Tbilisi and two branches in two other cities (Akhaltsikhe and Kutaisi).

TUB and UGB loans are extremely similar. UGB offers the same standard loans and express loans as TUB. UGB has recently launched a new loan product: the Georgian Lari Loan, shown in Table 17.15 (above).

The UGB loan portfolio grew steadily in 2002. In 2003, following the introduction of several changes (the new loan product: the express loan and simplification of lending procedures), UGB accelerated the growth of its portfolio. UGB (conversely to TUB) was able to build on its vast branch network and it expanded its micro-lending activities to another area of Tbilisi and to three additional cities.

Figure 17.3 (overleaf) shows that as of December 2003, after nearly two years of lending, UGB microfinance programme had 1048 outstanding loans with an outstanding portfolio value of US$2 180 896.

Challenges

TUB and UGB are extremely different banks. TUB is a smaller bank, recently created, that focuses mainly on Tbilisi. Conversely, UGB is an older bank (since it is the merger of three banks that operated in the former Soviet Union), of a much bigger size, and covers the whole Georgian territory. As a consequence, the management style of these two banks is also very different. Despite these important distinctions, the TUB and UGB micro-lending programmes face similar difficulties.

Figure 17.3 *UGB's loan portfolio evolution (US$)*

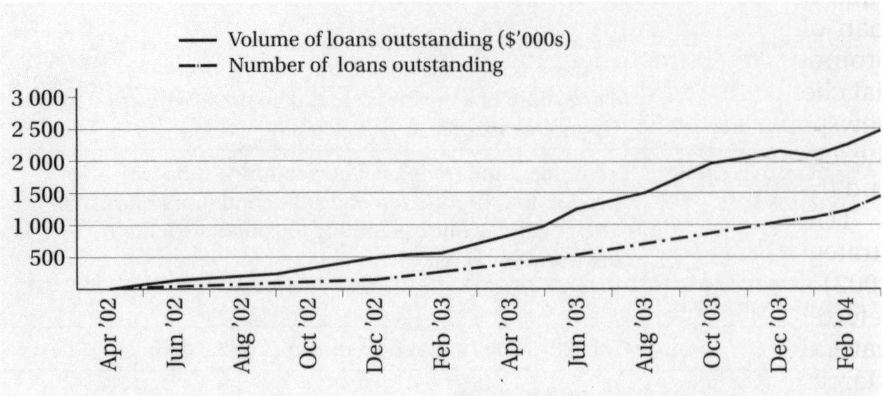

[Line graph showing Volume of loans outstanding ($'000s) and Number of loans outstanding from Apr '02 to Feb '04, with y-axis scale from 0 to 3,000 in increments of 500. Both lines show upward trends, with volume of loans outstanding reaching approximately 2,500 by Feb '04 and number of loans outstanding reaching approximately 1,500.]

Source: Small Enterprise Lending Programme

Competition

The main difficulty TUB and UGB have initially faced is the intense competition in the microfinance sector in Tbilisi. The main competitor to TUB and UGB is ProCredit Bank, which entered the microfinance market first and has thus enjoyed the benefits of early entrance.

In addition to this first-mover advantage, ProCredit Bank has an extensive branch network in Tbilisi (with eight branches and outlets) and outside Tbilisi (with ten branches and outlets). In comparison, TUB has one branch and one service centre in Tbilisi and one branch outside Tbilisi. However, the second partner bank of SELP, UGB, has seven branches and 10 service centres in Tbilisi and 11 branches and five service centres outside Tbilisi. UGB therefore has a well-developed branch network, which provides a solid base for further expansion of micro-lending operations.[22]

The up-to-date branches of ProCredit Bank and the bank's modern management contrast strongly with the branches and management style inherited from the Soviet era that characterizes several Georgian banks. However, it is noteworthy that the differences between Georgian banks in this regard are, in general, relatively large; some of them have shown substantial progress over the past few years in improving their infrastructure and establishing sustainable corporate governance.

Other competitors include Constanta, FINCA and World Vision, which compete with the lower end of TUB and UGB micro-lending market, as well as Bank of Georgia that has also developed a micro-lending programme with the initial technical support of the EBRD, which resumed in February 2004.

The supply of microfinance in Georgia is abundant, especially in Tbilisi, which is a relatively small city of around 1.5 million inhabitants. Many microfinance lenders are chasing few micro- and small entrepreneurs. Some microfinance actors are even wondering whether the supply of microfinance in Tbilisi is not exceeding demand.

Strong competition has led to several interesting developments. First, all microfinance lenders rely heavily on personal selling, with loan officers constantly visiting market areas and micro-businesses, promoting their micro-lending programme and identifying new potential clients. In addition, banks use traditional marketing tools, such as newspaper advertisements in the capital and television advertising in the regions on local channels (television advertising in Tbilisi is expensive and therefore not cost-effective).

TUB and UGB have also developed several marketing activities and strategies to attract additional customers. UGB for example offered (in 2002) a mobile phone recharge card to every client that successfully referred a new client to the bank.[23] With support of SELP, TUB and UGB have also implemented new loan products, such as express loans, in March 2003 (UGB, TUB) and loans in Georgian Lari in Gori (UGB), which UGB plans to introduce in other branches as well. Finally, most microfinance lenders (and TUB and UGB, in particular) have developed intricate incentive systems to increase the productivity of their loan officers while maintaining a healthy portfolio.

Competition has also an impact on interest rates, which have decreased since the beginning of micro-lending activities in Georgia. For example, until 2002, a standard US$2 000 loan was priced at 36 per cent per annum, now such loans are priced at 24 per cent.[24] After the successful introduction of express loans in SELP partner banks, some of the competing banks followed and introduced a similar product.

The challenge TUB and UGB are facing is to increase their client base in a very competitive environment while maintaining their portfolio quality. These two banks need not only to make more loans, but good loans.

Limited resources
Another challenge for TUB and UGB is limited resources. The EBRD provided credit lines (between US$1.5m and US$3m) with a 9.25 per cent annual interest rate and with technical assistance on a grant basis.

As a result, the two banks have been partly financing the development of their microfinance programmes themselves. For example, TUB relied on its own funding to open its first branch targeted at micro-lending, as well as its second the outlet. Similarly, UGB uses its own funding to renovate and equip the branches and service centres in which the bank intends to launch microfinance activities.

The EBRD covers the salaries and bonuses of the loan officers for the first six months of their lending activities but, after this period, the partner banks are responsible for paying their salaries and bonuses. The EBRD also provides technical and financial support for the selection and training of the loan officers, as well as full consultancy to newly established micro-lending departments in the initial phases of lending and partial support to experienced units.[25]

The senior management of both TUB and UGB has shown a strong commitment to the microfinance programmes and has therefore accepted to bear the cost of the development of the microfinance programmes. However, the senior management of these two banks has sometimes felt that they were facing unfair competition from ProCredit Bank, because of the heavy funding support it initially received from its donors and investors. It should be noted that ProCredit Bank no longer receives technical assistance since January 2003. ProCredit Bank now pays in full for its expatriate staff.

Internal challenges
Both banks have faced a range of internal challenges. Some of these challenges are linked to the important changes required when downscaling and include:

- the shift from traditional asset- and collateral-based lending to cash-flow lending;
- delegating lending decision making to the branch level;
- setting up strong monitoring systems;
- increasing their level of customer orientation.

For many commercial banks, such shifts are revolutionary and ensuring the buy-in of the senior management is crucial. Such changes can also create some tensions within the banks. Other challenges relate to the management capacity and internal organization of each bank.

For example, TUB and UGB have understood that loan officers in charge of micro-lending should be given competitive salaries to eliminate the temptation of staff taking bribes from potential clients. Incentive systems are also in place to increase their productivity. In return, the workload and the responsibility level of micro-loan officers are much higher than for other loan officers. However, this difference of treatment between traditional loan officers and micro-loan officers may become a source of tension and create institutional problems for the banks: micro-loan officers often do not fit within the traditional salary scales of the banks.

However it should be noted that the benefits of downscaling might, in some cases, outweigh the difficulties of downscaling. Downscaling can also be a vector of change for banks and it can help them strengthen their credit department as a whole. Through its micro-lending activities, TUB strengthened its credit methodology as well as its management information system.

Lessons from Georgia

The microfinance experience of Georgia can provide useful insights to actors already involved in microfinance (such as policy makers and donors) or to actors considering getting involved in microfinance (such as commercial banks). Georgia allows a direct comparison of two microfinance approaches: the microfinance bank versus the commercial downscaling bank.

The microfinance bank approach: strengths and potential weaknesses

Building on its microfinance experience (both with NGOs and with commercial banks), IPC became convinced that the ownership and governance structures of an institution are the essential factors that determine whether this institution will succeed in microfinance.[26] Following this finding, IMI created the microfinance bank approach, with a unique ownership and governance structure. IMI acquires equity stakes in the microfinance banks, while IPC manages the banks. This model is indeed one of the factors of ProCredit's success in Georgia. It gives a clear competitive edge to microfinance banks over commercial downscaling banks. In the latter situation, the technical assistance is only offered in an advisory role which therefore limits its impact.

As also demonstrated by ProCredit Bank in Georgia, microfinance banks can become profitable in a few years. At December 2003, ProCredit return on average equity stands at 7.2 per cent. However as the CGAP review[27] on microfinance demonstrates, microfinance banks are costly to set up. This study estimates initial investment and technical assicstance costs at about US$2m per bank. As a result, these banks are so far dependent on donor subsidy to start up.

In addition, microfinance banks may become dependent on the continued commitment of their foreign investors to sustain this growth. As explained above, one of the current challenges for ProCredit is to identify sufficient funding to fuel this growth, which is why ProCredit has started to mobilize deposits energetically.

The commercial downscaling bank approach: strengths and weaknesses

The downscaling approach became popular when it was realized that commercial banks might have several advantages in microfinance.

Some bankers doubt that microfinance can ever be profitable. However profitability analyses undertaken by SELP have proved that TUB and UGB's microfinance operation are profitable. At UGB, newly established micro-lending departments need one year maximum to break-even. For example, the microfinance programme in Gori became profitable after nine months of lending.

In Georgia, micro-lending loan officers are given higher salaries to end the temptation to take bribes from potential clients. The challenges of downscaling for commercial banks should therefore not be underestimated. The benefits of downscaling can outweigh the difficulties. It can be a vector for change for banks and it can help them strengthen their credit department as a whole. Because of its micro-lending activities TUB has strengthened its credit methodology as well as its management information system.

The case of Georgia shows that it can be advantageous to have both microfinance banks and downscaled commercial banks. ProCredit

Bank demonstrated that it is possible to lend to micro and small businesses in a profitable manner. As a result, commercial banks became interested in micro-lending. As a whole, this clearly benefited micro-entrepreneurs who now have several banks competing to serve them.

Discussion questions

1. Microfinance first evolved in response to the problems of poverty in underdeveloped and primarily rural economies. In Georgia, the same approach has been applied in very different circumstances. How applicable is it, and what changes may be necessary to allow banks both to assist and to profit from the continuing development of the country?

2. All three banks described are moving towards larger loans. Are they following the development trajectory of the market, or may they possibly be deserting the poorer sections of the population for whose benefit they were established?

3. Procredit Bank is lending out about three times its outstanding savings deposits, and is attempting to mobilize new funds from bulk sources as well as depositors. Most commercial banks mobilize more savings deposits than they lend out. Why is Procredit Bank not in this position, and is the bank likely to achieve a closer balance between savings and loans in the future?

4. There are large numbers of micro-lenders in Georgia, and there is strong competition, particularly in the capital city. Donors continue to support existing and new entrants. Is this appropriate, or might it even be potentially destructive?

Chapter Eighteen
Agricultural Bank of Mongolia (Khan Bank)

J. PETER MORROW, JAY DYER and ROBIN YOUNG

Introduction

In July 2000, the Agricultural Bank of Mongolia (AgBank) began a transformation that included a significant focus on microfinance and rural lending as a primary source of revenue to finance its turnaround. At that time, AgBank was technically insolvent and the majority of Mongolians were at risk of losing what access to financial services they had. Almost the entire loan portfolio had been written-off.

Building on an existing network of branches, the AgBank created innovative products to meet the needs of rural citizens and is now an extremely stable institution and the largest provider of financial services in the rural areas across Mongolia. The success of the turnaround was sealed by the privatization of the bank through international tender to a major Japanese company in March 2003.

Today, AgBank provides loan, deposit and transfer services at 379 locations across the country (up from 269 locations in year 2000), of which 93 per cent are in rural areas. The bank has disbursed 878 000 loans between late 2000 and February 2004, while maintaining an arrears rate consistently below 2 per cent and becoming the most profitable bank in Mongolia – with a return on equity of 44.19 percent in 2003. As at February 2004, 128 227 loans were outstanding for a portfolio value of almost US$50m with US$75.5m in 377 424 deposit accounts. The 15 433 domestic transfers totalled US$260 000 for the month. The average outstanding loan balance is US$382, deposit accounts average US$200, transfers US$17, and half of Mongolia's households conduct business with AgBank. The number of employees at the bank increased from 803 people in 2000 to a present level of 1833 personnel.

Mongolia rests just below Russia and above China with a very large land mass of 1.6 million km^2 and a population of only about 2.7 million people. There has been a traditional reliance on agriculture and the breeding of livestock, but there is a rapidly growing reliance on services and industry. Mongolia has extensive mineral deposits such as gold and copper.

Mongolia has a unique history. Under Genghis Khan and his descendants, the Mongolian Empire of the thirteenth-century included most of the known world, from Korea to Hungary and Vietnam to the Baltic Sea. Mongolia was subjugated by China during the Qing Dynasty (1644–1911) and declared independent in 1921. From 1921 to 1990 it was an independent country, but essentially a military colony of the Soviet Union. Upon dissolution of the Soviet Union, Mongolia declared itself a democracy and a free-market economy, which it remains today. Estimates show the GDP at US$1800 per capita with a growth rate of 5 per cent in 2003. Administratively, Mongolia is divided into 21 *aimags* (provinces) and one municipality, Ulaanbaatar (Ulan Bator), the capital of Mongolia.

AgBank history

After many years of operating deficits, loan losses, and a failed attempt at privatization, AgBank was placed in receivership in 1999, and many in the international community felt that it could never operate sustainably and should be closed. However, the importance of AgBank to Mongolia's rural sector could not be overstated. Although one of the smaller financial institutions in the country, it was the only bank with branches throughout Mongolia's vast territory to transfer money, make government pension and salary payments, and accept deposits.

As *The Economist* put it:

> ... *the Agricultural Bank, merits closure by any dispassionate measure. Yet its social importance is immense: in Mongolia's vast rural areas, it is the only bank that most people have ever walked into. Even though distant branches often have no money to dispense, the bank's removal would destroy any stirrings of a money economy. So the government will soon advertise for a foreign boss to turn the bank around.*
> (May 6, 2000)

Accepting the imperative to keep the bank open, donors entered into a unique agreement with the Government of Mongolia. The World Bank made reforming the bank a condition of its Financial Sector Adjustment Credit (FSAC) programme for Mongolia, and the US Agency for International Development (USAID) agreed to provide funds for an outside-management contract. The Government of Mongolia agreed to provide this outside manager with the full authority to manage the institution free from political or other interference.

A contract was signed with Development Alternatives, Inc. (DAI) of Bethesda, Maryland, USA, to manage the bank and, in July 2000, a team led by CEO J. Peter Morrow arrived in Mongolia. Debra Boyer filled the role of full-time Chief Operating Officer. DAI provided various short-term consultants from its home offices. At the start of the management contract, the team knew it would be crucial to:

1. cultivate internal staff capacities
2. develop proven products for the market
3. find a successful resolution to the political influence that had dominated the bank for years.

By agreement among all parties, the team's mission was to:

1. restore financial soundness to the bank;
2. bring financial services to the country's rural population
3. prepare the bank to operate independently and to be privatized

The management team developed a new lending programme; converted payment services into deposits; created an extensive marketing programme to improve AgBank's image and attract clients; implemented strong controls through new policies and procedures; created a more effective management structure; and significantly increased training activities.

In January 2003, the Government of Mongolia received three viable bids for the bank, all from strong and fully qualified private sector buyers. H.S. Securities of Japan was the highest bidder at US$6.85m and became the successful purchaser of the bank. The sale closed on 25 March 2003. The new owners have hired DAI to continue to provide management to the bank, a contract that is fully paid for out of bank income. H.S. Securities has stated that it wants to continue to expand based on the bank's target markets. It will be investing millions of dollars more into the bank to continue the outreach and market penetration. Since privatization, AgBank has continued to grow rapidly, practically doubling the loan portfolio from US$24.7m to US$49m during the first year.

The rural areas of Mongolia have been the bank's main focus, and its successes there have laid the foundation for substantial growth and new services for all Mongolians, urban and rural. AgBank's current mission statement is:

> To be the principal nationwide financial services company in Mongolia by delivering first-class products with the highest level of customer service.

Key to the turnaround of the institution was developing and implementing profitable products throughout the country. AgBank has shown that financial products can be created and delivered profitably even in scarcely populated and poor areas if they truly meet the needs of customers.

The institution has proven that it can sustain itself and contribute significantly to Mongolia's overall economic development. Aside from the large impact of its loan and deposit activity, the opening of 110 new branches and creation of more than 1000 well-paying jobs boosted the economies of many communities. In addition, AgBank is now one of the largest taxpayers in Mongolia, where before it was a cash drain on the government.

More generally, AgBank's leadership in bringing huge numbers of first-time depositors and borrowers into the banking system was key to intermediating Mongolia's money supply. Since 2000, the banking system has grown almost five-fold, and three-quarters of the country's money supply is in banks, up from less than half in 2000. AgBank's impact on the banking sector extends to several other institutions, who moved into the rural financial markets after seeing AgBank's successful rural lending activities.

Box 18.1 *Timeline of events in AgBank's history*

1991	The bank was founded as the Agricultural Cooperative Bank. The government arranged for agricultural co-operatives, herders and farmers to capitalize this new bank to take over the activities of the former monopoly State Bank. These comprised 326 rural branches and settlement centres, 2600 employees, and a portfolio of approximately US$2m in mostly non-performing loans and deposits whose interest rates were set by the Central Bank.
1992	The deterioration of AgBank's business and movement toward a market economy in Mongolia forced a reorganization of the institution. The bank expanded lending to offer larger loans after interference from the Government of Monoglia.
1996	The Bank's liquidity and financial position deteriorated to a level where the Central Bank appointed a receiver.
1999	Existing shareholders' interests were eliminated, and the Central Bank put together a restructuring plan. The government became the new sole owner through a capital infusion via Government Restructuring Bonds, converting debt to equity, and through injections of cash.
1999	The World Bank made reforming the bank a condition of its FSAC programme for Mongolia and USAID agreed to provide funds for an outside-management contract. The Government of Mongolia agreed to provide this outside manager with the full authority to manage the institution free from political or other interference.
2000	DAI won an international competition to manage the bank. In July 2000, the DAI team arrived in Mongolia to manage the bank.
2003	H.S. Securities of Japan was selected in an international bid as the buyer of the bank and retained DAI on a management contract. Growth and profitability continue to increase.

Product strategy

The management team developed a new lending programme, converted payment services into deposits, created an extensive marketing programme to increase deposits, implemented strong controls through new policies and procedures, created a more effective management structure, and significantly increased training activities. Products include loans, deposits, domestic and international transfer products, and government payment services. Clients are micro and small businesses, herders and farmers, consumers and government organizations.

The strategy has been to develop products that meet the needs of a large segment of the market, ensuring diversification by product and geographic area. The idea, from the beginning, was quickly to pilot products and then rapidly to expand the delivery countrywide, while a focus on quality lending always has been maintained. This differs from the strategy of a slower national rollout and a focus on quick saturation at each branch. All products were designed to be integrated into the branches by existing staff who are responsible for delivering an array of products. Combined with the quarterly goal-setting mentioned above, this strategy ensures the right products weigh properly in each market.

AgBank has introduced a large number of new products of all kinds. They are briefly described below.

Loans
- **Micro and Small Business Loans** This product is the mainstay of the lending programme in all markets. Although initially only for short-term working capital, qualified and experienced borrowers can now access term loans.
- **Small and Medium-Sized Enterprise (SME) Loans** This product was developed for medium-sized production companies. They are being made on a limited basis now as the lending team for SME loans is trained and the products are tested in the market.
- **Herder Loans** These loans were specifically designed to meet some of the unique needs of nomadic Mongolian herders based on cultural and business differences. Available on terms of up to one year, they help cover the gap between living and operating expenses in the months when herders are not generating income or wish to purchase herd-related goods.
- **Agricultural Production Loans** Introduced in May 2002, these loans have garnered interest primarily from vegetable growers, small private wheat farmers and hay producers.
- **Payroll Loans** Borrowers can borrow up to seven times their monthly salary for a variety of purposes for a term up to one year. Loan payments are made directly through a deduction from their regular salary. These loans provide significant cross-marketing opportunities for the bank.
- **Pensioner Loans** As part of the pension disbursement reform effort in 2001, a loan product was developed for this market. These small loans, which can be up to six times the value of a monthly pension, are repayable by assignment and automatic deduction from future pension payments. These loans empower pensioners to control their cash flow, enable them to borrow to help their family members venture into micro-businesses, and are an alternative to the traditional practice of borrowing from pawnshops and the informal sector.

Deposits
- **Personal or Business Current Accounts** These accounts are designed for those who are making regular financial transactions and who need regular statements.
- **Savings Accounts** Depositors may add and withdraw money at any time without fees. The account pays interest.
- **Time Deposits** This product pays a higher interest rate than a savings account. Deposits are encouraged to be for at least three

months, and incentives are given to savers to add to their deposits over the term.
- **Pension Direct Deposit** This programme was contractually agreed to with the Social Insurance Fund in early 2001. This meant opening accounts for each pensioner, which provided them with an additional service and raised the deposit base of the bank by opening hundreds of thousands of new accounts.
- **Payroll Direct Deposit** Similar to the Pension Direct Deposit, this product is marketed to large employers that want to eliminate the administrative expense of paying employees in cash. In addition to increased fee income for the bank, the bank also benefits from the many new individual deposit accounts and cross-selling opportunities.

Money-transfer products
- **Quick Pay** Key to the success of the bank has been this franchise that has been developed throughout the country. This product guarantees fast delivery (in three hours or less) of cash transfers between offices in the capital, Ulan Bator, and any one of the 77 on-line locations throughout the country.
- **Money Transfer** This is for the transfer of money from any AgBank location to any other AgBank location in the country. A transfer is delivered the next day if to a regional center and within three days if to a rural center.
- **Western Union** Money can be received at any AgBank location in Mongolia and funds can be sent to more than 180 countries worldwide.

Table 18.1 summarizes the results of the microenterprise and SME loans, the crop and herder credits, and pension and the salaried-based loans. Individuals who would not qualify for the bank's small business loans often use a consumer loan to get started in a new venture. AgBank has created a new class of bank borrowers. By recognizing the informal lending sector as a real competitor, AgBank has been able to provide a service that encourages many borrowers to successfully move into the formal financial system. AgBank's branches are quickly replacing pawnshops, store owners, and relatives for business and consumer borrowers. As a result, families and businesses are able to borrow more money at better terms and lower costs. As at February 2004, 878 976 loans had been disbursed and 128 227 were outstanding.

Another measure of the bank's impact is the growth in the small businesses that dominate rural Mongolia. Average small-business loan sizes have increased steadily over the past three years as increased inventory levels have translated into increased sales. Today, with loans to micro, small, and medium enterprises, AgBank's average outstanding business loan is US$1 807.

Pensioners were coming into the bank branches on a monthly basis to withdraw their payments, indicating this market was underserved

Table 18.1 AgBank loans as at February 2004

Product	Launch date	Total no. loans disbursed	Total value loans disbursed (US$'000)*	Total no. of loans outstanding	Total value of loan (US$'000)*	Av. loan outstanding (US$)
Micro & Small	Nov. 2000	80 835	98 780	13 485	19 135	1 419
Small & Medium	May 2001	3 300	15 555	1 633	8 184	5 011
Pensioners	May 2001	628 431	36 912	72 277	5 003	69
Herders	Aug. 2001	31 373	20 753	9 449	6 819	722
Payroll	Oct. 2001	132 784	34 177	30 539	6 654	218
Crop	May 2002	1 483	746	148	89	604
Mortgage	Apr. 2003	770	3 752	696	3 144	4 518
Total		878 976	210 674	128 227	49 028	382

*Note: Most loans and deposits are in the local currency, tugrug, and converted here to US dollars at the exchange rate of US$1 = 1174 tugrug.

for loans. As well, there were enormous transaction costs with paying so many small pensions per month. Another example of an important change has been the conversion of 200 000 government social security and salary payments into deposit accounts. Experience at AgBank shows that one-third of all government payments made through a deposit account stay in the account for an extended period. This conversion brought more deposits to the bank and helped build relationships with new customers who could then take advantage of other bank services and loans.

Money also has moved out from under mattresses, as individual deposits have grown from just over US$2m to US$54m in the period from December 2000 to February 2004. Most new depositors are people who were not previously depositors in banks, and the average deposit account at AgBank is US$168. (Please refer to Tables 18.2 and 18.3 for a breakdown in the distribution and evolution of deposits.)

AgBank's aggressive increase in deposits and loans and a subsequent expansion of other banks' operations throughout Mongolia have had an impact on the intermediation of Mongolia's money supply. In 2000, more than half the country's money supply was in the form of currency outside banks; today, less than one-third is held as currency. The long-term benefit of this intermediation for Mongolia's development is considerable as it provides internal resources for increased investment.

By creating products that meet the needs of the market, dropping withdrawal fees, and providing good customer service, AgBank has

Table 18.2 AgBank deposits (as at February 2004)

Deposit category	Outstanding balance (US$'000)	% of total outstanding balance	Number of depositor accounts	% of total depositor accounts	Av. account balance (US$)
Organizations	**15 849**	**20.99**	**14 354**	**3.8**	**1 104**
Current	12 024	15.92	14 318	3.79	840
Time	2 823	3.74	22	0.01	128 347
Demand	1 001	1.33	14	0.00	71 471
Individuals	**59 667**	**79.01**	**363 070**	**96.20**	**164**
Current	2 044	2.71	266 875	70.71	8
Time	47 265	62.59	39 971	10.59	1 182
Demand	10 358	13.72	56 224	14.90	184
Total	**75 515**	**100.00**	**377 424**	**100.00**	**200**

been able to increase its deposit base by 740 per cent since July 2000. This growth has in turn propelled the bank's expansion. The dependence on Government deposits dropped from 52 per cent of all deposits at the end of December 2000 to 6.7 per cent at the end of January 2004. Tables 18.2 and 18.3 summarise Agbank's deposit portfolio.

Lessons learned

Commitment and political economy for change

Management independence
A critical part of the turnaround was getting enforceable assurances from the Government that the new management team could operate free from political influence. The new management team was given the authority over personnel issues, credit policies and expenditures through a memorandum of understanding. Government agencies were prohibited from directing or interfering in any way with the bank. It also was given capital forbearance (that is, normal minimum capital and capital adequacy standards were suspended) for the period of the restructuring agreements. Observance of all these agreements was made a condition of the World Bank FSAC programme and the USAID funding arrangements. Shortly after the project started in July 2000, there was a complete change in government from the Democratic Party back to the former Communist Party. Although initially suspicious of the agreements made for AgBank's remediation, the new government eventually supported it fully.

Table 18.2 AgBank deposit evolution (converted to US$'000s)

Deposit category*	31 Dec. 2003		31 Dec. 2002		31 Dec. 2001		31 Dec. 2000	
Businesses	9 730	13.2%	9 798	22%	8 117	33%	3 663	28%
Government	4 293	6.7%	8 207	18%	8 570	35%	6 712	52%
Individuals	50 225	80.1%	27 028	60%	7 752	32%	2 520	20%
Total	64 248	100%	45 034	100%	24 439	100%	12 896	100%

*Note: Most loans and deposits are in the local currency, tugrug, and converted here to US dollars at the exchange rate of US$1 = 1174 tugrug.

Board of directors

Normal corporate governance was suspended for the remediation period. An independent board of directors – with two members from the Government of Mongolia, two nominated by USAID and an unaffiliated professional chairman – was appointed to monitor the remediation process and ensure the Government did not interfere. In effect, oversight by this board, a semiannual meeting between the management team and donors, an annual independent audit and Central Bank supervision formed an *ad hoc* corporate governance structure for the restructuring period. This arrangement was essential to break the pattern of interference that had previously contributed significantly to the bank's demise.

Central Bank guidelines

Early on, the turnaround team reached agreement with the Central Bank as to when AgBank's financial ratios would comply with prudential standards, and a conservative timetable was put in place. Management met all Central Bank guidelines a full year before the end of the period of remediation and has continued to exceed all requirements.

Privatization

Although the outside management had the authority and responsibility to run AgBank during the remediation, there was an obvious concern that when they left, when the 'firewall' came down, the bank and the Government would go back to the same practices that had caused the bank's problems in the first place. Thus, it was critical that, as part of the remediation agreement, the Government of Mongolia gave a commitment to the privatization of the bank. Thus, all parties understood that the remediation period would run until privatization. In 2002 the Government of Mongolia carried out its privatization agreements by organizing an international competitive tender with the successful privatization of AgBank to H.S. Securities of Japan for US$6.85m in early 2003.

Branch operations

Taking control of the decision process at AgBank was not merely a matter between the central government and senior bank management. Previously, the local branches functioned as part of their province or county administration. The branch managers were appointed in most cases by the local governor of the ruling party and considered part of his 'team'. A branch manager was a source of jobs and loans for people who desperately needed them. Based on this culture, they were more likely first to accommodate the need than to understand the implications from a business perspective. Managers had to be reoriented to understand the importance that the institution be strong, thus creating more outreach to even more viable clients and, hence, stimulating the overall economy. It also had to be made clear that the management team would hold them accountable for their actions. If managers took direction from local governors they would be disciplined, and if they performed well and independently they would be rewarded.

The foreign managers also recognized that these rural staff needed 'protection' from local pressures. Providing them a basis for operating independently required:

1. clear policies mandating transparency and independence that could be handed out to local officials
2. a mandate for local managers to speak up when they are asked to break policy
3. foreign managers' willingness to step in and refuse inappropriate requests
4. clear penalties for managers that followed the directives of local officials in violation of bank policies

The first encounter with a local official who wanted his way and did not get it often was difficult, but when people got the message that new management would not tolerate non-transparency, they usually stopped asking for favours or bribes.

Institutional innovation

Managerial leadership

The skill sets and competency of the senior management were critical. The team brought together experiences, knowledge and management skills from working in countries with similar economic situations, as well as strong knowledge and experiences from US banking. In addition, an executive team of some of the best Mongolian bankers was recruited and has clearly provided important technical and cultural input to the transformation of the bank. The management team set the tone and led the organization to develop a culture based on operating discipline and service innovation.

Management featuring clear lines of authority was a joint effort by expatriate and local professionals. The start of AgBank's turnaround was precarious. Decisions had to be reached and implemented quickly, and it was critical to deploy individuals with relevant outside experience who were not beholden to domestic political interests. Local departmental managers hired or promoted to the executive level were highly valued for their institutional memories as well as their keen understanding of the domestic market and culture. The project could not have been successful without this synergy between outside and inside management.

Credit culture
No bank in Mongolia had previously tried to develop and implement a fully transparent lending programme available to all who qualified. Some donors suggested that Mongolia's loan history was so bad that the bank should be remediated without lending. However, the team felt that it was critical to make loans; otherwise the bank would not recover financially or restore services to the public. Through the appropriate design of financial products and the right staff motivation, a new credit culture was developed.

Previously, most people in Mongolia had to rely on pawnbrokers and family members for loans. The bank's new lending products were truly welcome as they allowed people access to larger sums of money at a lower cost. Likewise, in the past, those loans that were secured from banks were associated with the government. Hence, institutional pressure to repay on time was often lax and, thus, as in many other countries, the culture of timely repayment to banks among potential borrowers was weak or non-existent.

For successful growth and profitability, the culture had to change, at the level of branch managers and loan officers and among customers. This challenge was met by holding the branch managers completely accountable for the decisions they made. Absolutely zero-tolerance was given to non-transparency, disobeying policies or acceding to pressure from politicians who tried to influence the lending. Because an outside management team was running the bank, it was easier to build this firewall. Local borrowers knew branch staff were subject to these constraints. Hence, clients realized their own failure to perform on their loans would cause problems for their friends and neighbours from whom they wanted to continue borrowing,

Brand and image of the bank
A major obstacle was changing the public's perception of the bank. Although the institution had many advantages, AgBank still suffered from a reputation for being politically driven, untrustworthy and insolvent. The first approach to change this image was to provide valuable products and services to customers as soon as possible. The 1 per cent withdrawal fee for deposits was immediately dropped – it had been a major impediment to mobilizing bank deposits – and rates on time deposits were raised to the top of the market, quickly giving the bank the liquidity it needed.

The management team brought in external marketing expertise and launched a major public relations campaign early on, telling Mongolia the bank was serious about business and was open to all. Likewise, the bank re-branded itself by adopting its acronym 'XAAH' as its public name. This translates to *khan* or 'king', a name with strong local appeal because of Genghis Khan. Television and radio campaigns reinforced this re-branding.

Demand for products and services
Before launching a bank restructuring and introducing new financial services, access to an under-served market with untapped demand sufficient to support the restructured bank must be ensured. If the prospective market is being adequately served by others, the cost and effort of a turnaround are probably not justified and could crowd out existing financial institutions. In Mongolia, studies were conducted to understand the general market potential before the turnaround contract began. The fact that a strong, informal market was offering loan rates of 12 to 15 per cent a month showed a demand that banks were not serving. Every project needs a golden goose, a competitive advantage. In the case of AgBank, a real need for sustainable financial services existed in the rural areas of the country. The bank was able to leverage existing branches and staff to deliver services quickly and efficiently.

Diversification
In addition to developing the new products, one important shift in the product and client mix was a diversification away from reliance on government. At the beginning of the remediation period, more than 50 per cent of the deposits were from the government. This reliance put AgBank's liquidity position at potential risk if the government were to withdraw significant funds. The bank sought and attracted deposits from private businesses and individuals. The result has been a shift from 52 per cent government deposits to the current 6.7 per cent. The private sector deposits are made up of hundreds of thousands of individual depositors, thus creating greater diversification.

Operational efficiency
If faced with challenging financial targets, the first reaction of many new managers is to start by cutting costs. A common problem at state-owned banks, however, is that not enough is being spent to generate required revenues. There are costs associated with delivering products and offering an acceptable level of customer service that are critical in a competitive market. It was found that small additional expenditures, primarily staff training and subsequently minor improvements to roofs, and purchases of furniture and computers, combined with prudent lending at the initial 269 AgBank points of service could lead to exponential growth in revenues.

However, to generate profitability, the increase in revenues needed to be met by cutting unnecessary expenses. For example, although new staff were brought in as part of improving the services or technical aspects of the bank, other staff had to be cut based on competency levels and redundancies. In the case of AgBank, most of these cuts took place while the bank was under Central Bank receivership. One of the first steps new management took on was cutting the right costs.

Learning and experimentation

Staff training

One of the advantages at AgBank was a well-trained and disciplined staff. Some felt the bank had too much of a 'state sector' mentality and that the staff would not be able to accept the changes necessary to turn the bank around to a position of growth, efficiency and profitability. However, the employees were well educated and good at performing many day-to-day banking tasks. It was clear a new organizational culture could not be developed overnight and that it would be an ongoing process. It was found that the staff quickly grasped the new products and marketing approaches and implemented them. In the countryside, staff and their families are embedded in the local communities, and they know who, where and how to find people to borrow money who will pay it back.

State-owned banks often have negative public images. It is important to capitalize on the existing positive aspects of the brand, but the institution also needs to be seen as 'new and improved' from both a customer and an employee perspective. AgBank had a particularly unfavorable reputation in the eyes of the public, but it was trusted because of its implicit government backing. Through efforts to develop brand identities, better customer service and overall public confidence, AgBank now commands much more favourable opinions. Staff buy-in is critical to the success of the institution. Within the bank, motivating the staff through training, fair and performance-based compensation, and recognition for good work has created better and more efficient working environments.

In the two-and-a-half years of the USAID-funded remediation, training was an integral part of reform for staff at all levels. The training programme focused on practical skills and information employees needed to deliver the bank's products and perform their jobs. Because of the importance training played in making the turnaround of AgBank possible, the German development agency, GTZ, provided assistance to establish a professional training department at the bank and significantly improve the skills of trainers.

Product development

In addition to staff training to promote learning, the product development and rollout process was based on a rapid but integral learning and experimentation process. Products were identified by managers at various levels. Once standard policies were drafted and approved, the products were pilot tested, refined and then rolled out nationally. Training for product rollout went from the national to the regional and branch levels, and decisions on how much to focus on a particular product were decided jointly at the local and national levels. In this way, staff were able to experiment and learn which products were most appropriate in each market.

Management information systems
One common reason why a business fails is uncontrolled growth. In a state-owned bank turnaround, it is imperative that revenue growth be balanced by a quality portfolio and by systems and procedures to detect and correct problems. Systems to monitor portfolio performance and to detect fraud are both crucially important. These systems do not have to be complex – at remote branches, they need not always be computerized – but they must be timely and complete. At AgBank, the lack of computers and networked informtion communication systems was not a hindrance to timely and accurate reporting. Managers developed simple paper reporting systems through which local, regional and national data are tracked and used for ongoing analysis and decision making. The data are critical to the learning and experimentation process, as they provide the evidence of which innovations work and which require refinement.

External catalysts

Donor agencies
Although a turnaround is conceptually feasible without international support, the turnaround in Mongolia would not have occurred without the participation of international donors. They helped ensure the decision-making authority of the turnaround teams by reaching consensus with the Mongolian government and provided critically needed funds for capital improvements and technical assistance.

Consultants and managers
As an expatriate on a management team, operating under a clear sense of corporate governance and of protecting AgBank's assets, the CEO and his team had clear power and the authority to say 'no'. Foreign managers working on the bank's turnaround did not have the societal imperatives that would create expectations and temptations contrary to the turnaround efforts. Therefore, it was critical that top managers came from outside of Mongolia for the rapid turnaround. Likewise, the external consultants were vital for managing a transparent valuation, bid and selection process.

Private investors
The private investors that purchased the bank were the final link in ensuring the turnaround efforts created economic value and that Agbank would continue to offer services to rural Mongolians in a sustainable

manner. Their international links have brought new ideas and resources to the institution.

Conclusion

From a cost-recovery perspective of the original work that began in July 2000, the value of the bank has increased so much over the period that it could have easily paid for the cost of the turnaround by the value that was created, as is witnessed by the sale price and the ongoing management contract between H.S. Securities and DAI. The earnings in 2003 were close to the entire cost of the three-year, donor-financed turnaround. Today, AgBank is the second most profitable bank in Mongolia with average monthly net income of US$300 000, including the cost of the DAI management contract that is paid out of earnings. In 2003, AgBank was the leading bank in the country in terms of return on assets (2.96 per cent) and return on equity (44.19 per cent).

The Government of Mongolia's commitment to change AgBank, as part of its overall privatization and economic modernization programme, was key to success. Its strategy to hire international consultants and privatize the bank was the right recipe. The experienced management team, coupled with the commitment of the local staff and strong business strategy, provided the skills to achieve the projected outcomes. Finally, the support and pressure from external forces encouraged political fortitude and kept the project on track.

It is challenging to turn around a large state-owned bank. Success rests on a confluence of political and financial circumstances, both internal and external. The driving factors summarized above should be considered as requirements for any successful turnaround effort. The most critical lessons learned are summarized below.

Management must be politically independent and qualified
Management was able to pursue successful turnaround strategies at AgBank because of the unique design of the recovery programme and the support of the bank's stakeholders. As the traditional state-owned bank in the countryside, AgBank was under very strong pressure to serve the government's political needs. Because the project team was given full authority for the bank, a new credit and operating culture could develop that has resulted in a very profitable and high quality credit portfolio. The carefully structured independence, buttressed with donor conditionalities, was essential.

The starting balance sheet must be clear
Before starting an assignment, the turnaround team must understand the true position of the bank's balance sheet and negotiate accordingly with the government. All earnings and fixed assets must be properly evaluated, and any capital needed must be put into the institution to raise the capital base to no less than zero. Capital can be injected as cash or as development bonds, depending on the institution's liquidity

position. If bonds, interest should be paid in cash to provide adequate cash flow. There should be adequate funds to cover initial operating costs and to purchase fixed assets that are required immediately. A long-term cash flow stream needs to be identified in order to support the ongoing operations.

Staff require training, incentives and protection from political pressures

Staff require on-going training in skills, policies, products and systems, especially during a time of significant organizational change. Transparent and performance-based incentive systems help ensure priorities and behaviour are aligned with the institution's best interests. When staff are threatened or pressurized by political forces, senior management should provide protection in the form of being used as an 'excuse' for not giving in.

Marketing is essential

A key lesson learned by AgBank is the importance of marketing: focused research, strong brand promotion, and products responsive to customer demand provide an income stream to sustain the organization. AgBank's managers used a combination of local knowledge from their branch managers, formal market surveys and experience from working in other developing countries to develop successful products and marketing campaigns.

Financial intermediaries can profitably service low-income markets

Some people doubt whether low-income populations are willing and able to pay for the financial products and services they need, but the experience in Mongolia proved different. Where per capita incomes are low, the experience has proven that there is a large market for the right kind of deposit and credit products, even if the interest rates and fees are relatively high. Low-income market segments will pay for the right products and good service.

Meeting clients' financial services needs has a positive economic impact

Often, small businesses will borrow lower amounts of money than they need, which can be valuable in building a borrowing history. However, if the lending products do not adequately meet the needs of the business and match their ability to service certain levels of debt, a large dropout rate will occur. Thus, the products (including the delivery and services attached to them) must grow and develop to reflect accurately the needs of the market. The most expensive part of a borrower relationship is acquisition – bringing the borrower into the institution for the first time. Profitability and sustainability will come from loan renewals and cross-selling other products.

Penny wise may be pound foolish when it comes to operating efficiency
Although competitive and profitable banks must operate efficiently, the focus should not be exclusively on cutting costs. Rather than closing branches, the focus should be on revenue-generating services that take advantage of the network. Incremental revenue can add up to significant net income. Nonetheless, operating costs should remain under control. State-owned banks can usually meet the needs of their market segment with relatively low-cost operations. The intent is not to compete with international banks going after high-end customers, but appropriately to serve rural and low-income market segments. Money should be spent to make the branches adequate and comfortable, but they do not have to be the best in town. Occasionally, only two people are needed in a location, and hand ledgers and a calculator may be adequate technology.

State-owned banks can be turned around
With a low operating cost basis and good returns from lending, AgBank was able to generate the profits to reinvest in physical and human infrastructure and make the bank sustainable while providing the needed services to the underserved market. The process evolved into a 'virtuous cycle' driven by the strong demand, as well as unmet need, for the new services. The AgBank experience contrasts with the commonly held view that state-owned 'dinosaur' banks cannot be turned around and successfully privatized. There may be other cases where, despite a poor history and state sector culture, latent but strong franchise value in a branch network or customer flow can be capitalized into profits and sustainability.

Discussion questions

1. Donor assistance and the whole restructuring programme for Mongolia were made conditional on AgBank's reform process being free of any political interference. How critical was this conditionality to the successful reform of the bank, and how likely is it that similar conditions could be applied in other countries?

2. Computerized special-purpose management information systems (MIS) are often seen as fundamental to the introduction of microfinance to commercial banks, but in this case many branches are said to have had only 'hand ledgers and a calculator'. How necessary is 'modern' information technology to successful microfinance?

3. There has been no attempt to separate micro-business loans from the other business of the bank; microfinance is totally integrated with other operations. Is this generally preferable to separation of the two types of business, at the branch and/or head-office level, as is preferred in many other banks?

Conclusions

A large proportion of the 2495 million people in low-income countries, and even many of the 2738 million in middle-income countries, still lack effective continuous access to banking services. It can be argued that financial services will follow increased prosperity, so that people without such services need to be richer and more accessible before banks and other financial institutions can consider serving them. We would argue, however, that improved access to banking services is a cause as well as an effect of economic development. Research has confirmed how access to financial services helps reduce vulnerability and enables people to seize economic opportunities. But we have met many economically active individuals, poor and non-poor, who live very close to bank branches but have no dealings with them. In the past 30 years, there have been enough initiatives in different locations to confirm that the bigger issue is how this market of small customers is perceived and served by banks. There is no longer any doubt that low-income consumers represent a large and growing market, and that very many of these customers who are currently un-served by banks have both the ability and willingness to pay for the banking services they need.

This book contains 18 case studies describing how existing banks have re-oriented themselves, or new banks have been set up to serve low-income customers and their enterprises. While development agencies and subsidies have played some part in this and have helped with the initial experiments, most banks are pursuing this market because it makes commercial sense. Many of these initiatives are recent but Bank Rakyat Indonesia (BRI), the subject of the first case study in the book, started offering such services 20 years ago. While many of the other case studies are nowhere near the scale of BRI, their results are as dramatic. It is clear that more bankers, investors and policy makers in many more countries are recognizing the market potential to serve large number of un-banked and under-banked people and are re-engineering financial institutions to serve this huge market. Once the promoters' conviction and capital are combined with the right skills and systems, it does not take very long to make profits out of this market. The case studies have shown how each institution evolved its approach to microfinance. The remainder of this chapter draws some key conclusions from the case studies and shows what they mean for bankers, policy makers and others.

Table c.1 overleaf summarizes some critical development indicators for the 15 countries where the banks are located, and it also includes some summary data from the 18 case studies themselves.

The sample of nine public sector and nine privately owned banks is neither representative nor random, and there are many other banks in the same and other countries, which are working in microfinance. The case studies cover a wide range of low and middle income countries, including some of the poorest nations in Africa, the poorest nation in Central and South America, as well as Bangladesh, Pakistan and India,

Table c.1 Development indicators and summary data from the case studies

Development indicators	Indonesia	Philippines	Pakistan	Bangladesh	India				Egypt
GNI/capita US$	710	1 030	420	380	470				1 470
% Urban population 2002	43	60	34	26	28				43
Domestic credit to private sector 2002 (% of GDP)	22	36	28	29	33				61
Case study indicators for microfinance activities	BRI	Producers Bank	Bank of Khyber	Sonali Bank	State Bank of India	Canara Bank	Oriental Bank of Commerce	ICICI Bank	Banque du Caire
Number of outlets	4 185	3	18	16	2 250	1	31		96
Number of depositors ('000)	29 869	51	*	*	5 100	7	12	*	*
Number of current borrowers ('000)	3 100	44	5		2 600	3	12	282	65
Deposits outstanding (US$ million)	3 527	1			73	1	1		
Loans disbursed (US$ million)	1 678	3	14	11	137		2		50
Loans outstanding (US$ million)			4	7		1	1	63	17
Deposit per account (US$)	118	20			14	189	53		
Average loan amount (US$)	541	77	825	n.a.	53	457	83	223	500
Average deposit as a % of GDP per capita	17	2	0	n.a.	3	40	11	n.a.	
Average loan as a % of GDP per capita	76	7	196	n.a.	11	97	18	48	34
Portfolio at risk (PAR)	0.0	0.0	0.0	2.5		1.0			1.5

CONCLUSIONS

Development indicators	Zimbabwe	Kenya	Benin	Ecuador	Guatemala	Haiti	Kosovo	Georgia	Mongolia
GNI/capita US$	n.a.	360	380	1 490	1 760	440	...	650	430
% Urban population 2002	37	35	44	64	40	37	...	57	57
Domestic credit to private sector 2002 (% of GDP)	37	23	12	28	19	16	...	8	19
Case study indicators for microfinance activities	Commercial Bank of Zimbabwe	Equity Building Society	Finadev	Banco Solidario	Bancafé	Sogesol	American Bank of Kosovo	ProCredit Bank	AgBank
Number of outlets		39		23	70	7	17	18	379
Number of depositors ('000)	3	296	14	91		*	77	32	377
Number of current borrowers ('000)	1	75	14	90	12	7	2	28	128
Deposits outstanding (US$ million)		49	1	127			65	18	76
Loans disbursed (US$ million)			43				74		211
Loans outstanding (US$ million)	0.3	27	10	92	17	5	32	48	49
Deposit per account (US$)		166	91	1 308			844	549	200
Average loan amount (US$)	97	360	656	1 484	1 500	685	30 833	1 667	382
Average deposit as a % of GDP per capita	n.a.	46	24	88		156	...	84	47
Average loan as a % of GDP per capita	n.a.	100	173	100	85	156	...	256	89
Portfolio at risk (PAR)	1.5	8.0	1.0	4.3	0.5	7.4	2.6	1.6	

* denotes no specific micro saving product

Source: *World Development Indicators 2004* and specific case studies

which are together home to by far the largest concentration of poor people on Earth. Poverty and a predominantly rural population is no bar to commercial banks' entry to microfinance.

The figure for domestic credit provided to the private sector is a useful indicator of the level of formal financial intermediation. This relates the amount of credit to the private sector, in the form of loans, trade credit and other obligations, to the total GDP. It is significant that this ratio is well below even the 27 per cent average for all low-income countries in six of the countries represented in our case studies. The banks in question have been able to reach out to large numbers of unbanked people in spite of the abysmally low level of formal financial activity in general. This shows that banks can intervene in the microfinance market even when formal financial transactions are at a very low level nationally

Small customers are a large and profitable market

The Microbanking Division of Bank Rakyat Indonesia today serves almost 30 million savers and three million borrowers through 4185 outlets. The US$3bn savings mobilized from savers are more than adequate to finance the substantial loan portfolio of US$1.7bn. During the 20 years from 1984 to 2003, the long-term loan loss ratio, calculated as total overdue by one day or more, including amounts written off, divided by the total which had fallen due during the period, was only 1.9 per cent. The micro-banking unit has made consistent profits and during the past five years (1998 to 2002), the average annual profit was US$139m, translating into an average annual return on assets of 5.8 per cent. This performance was achieved despite the fact that during the 20 year period, the Indonesia Rupiah exchange rate against the US dollar fluctuated between 1074 and 10 446. As the case study says: 'BRI has demonstrated that in a deregulated policy environment, a public bank is capable of serving vast numbers of micro-savers and micro-borrowers at competitive interest rates: mobilizing resources internally, covering its costs, and financing its expansion from its profits. BRI has proven that institutional viability, sustainability and outreach to low-income people are compatible.'

The success of BRI is not a recent phenomenon. By 1989, BRI had demonstrated that it was possible to transform an ailing public sector development bank into a viable, competitive and growing financial intermediary.

If the lessons from BRI were evident by 1989, why was the example not followed more widely elsewhere? Was the BRI success dependent on its particular context, or were other policy makers and private investors unable or unwilling to implement its lessons elsewhere?

Fortunately, BRI is no longer an isolated case. In Kenya, five private entrepreneurs set up Equity Building Society in 1984. The case study shows how Equity's focus on efficiently serving small customers helped an almost insolvent institution to revive and grow. Today, Equity serves

252 000 depositors and 66 000 borrowers from 15 branches and 24 other outlets. The numbers reached have grown dramatically in the past few years. Equity has also made growing profits since 1994 and, in 2003, it delivered a return on equity of 30 per cent and a return on assets of 3.6 per cent.

In Mongolia, a country over 10 times the physical size of Bangladesh with a population of only 2 million, a creative arrangement of private management working within the framework of public ownership was used to revive AgBank. As the case study says: 'The bank has disbursed 878 000 loans between late 2000 and February 2004 while maintaining an arrears rate consistently below 2 per cent and becoming the most profitable bank in Mongolia, with return on equity of 44 per cent in 2003. AgBank has shown that financial products can be created and delivered gainfully in even scarcely populated areas, if they truly meet the needs of the customers.'

As some of the above numbers indicate, the microfinance market is not just profitable, it is also enormous. Other case studies also report substantial growth and market potential:

- ICICI Bank in India only entered the market in 2001, by offering wholesale finance to other institutions, as well as direct service delivery. In two years, its microfinance portfolio grew from US$16m to US$63m, and the bank envisages a potential portfolio of US$4bn from this market.
- State Bank of India now allows informal self help groups (SHGs) of 10–20 women to open bank accounts and borrow from the bank. SBI was lending to 174 666 such SHGs in March 2004, against only 12 200 SHGs four years earlier, and the bank aims to be doing business with one million SHGs, with approximately 15 million mainly women members, by 2008.
- In Guatemala, Bancafé's portfolio grew from US$0.02m in 1999 to US$0.9m in 2001, and by 2003, it had reached US$16.9m.
- Banco Solidario is the microfinance market leader in Ecuador and has grown from less than US$30m portfolio in 1997 to more than US$130m in 2003.
- Banque du Caire estimates that only 7 per cent of the 2.4 million small entrepreneurs in Egypt have access to microfinance.
- Only 3 to 4 per cent of Georgians have a bank account.
- Bank of Khyber quotes a Pakistan microfinance network study that potential demand for microfinance services in Pakistan is around US$2bn per annum.
- Equity estimates that 6.7 million under-banked and un-banked Kenyans require comprehensive financial services.

Microfinance involves diversified risks, high loan repayments and customers who are concerned more with service quality than interest rates. Many commercial banks are discovering that the returns from this market are high in spite of the higher transaction costs.

Not all the case studies include complete data for the profitability of the banks' microfinance business, because microfinance is sometimes a small and relatively new part of the overall portfolio, and the banks' product and activity costing procedures may not be very rigorous. But where microfinance is housed in a subsidiary such as Sogesol and FINADEV, or makes up a significant part of the institution's business, as in BRI, Equity, or Banco Solidario, or where ownership has recently been transferred to private investors such as AgBank or American Bank of Kosovo, the numbers are more rigorous and profitability is substantial and sustained. What is more, most of the institutions in the case studies have substantial expansion plans for microfinance. They do not regret their entry to this market.

Profitability can be quickly achieved

Some bankers are initially exasperated as to why development practitioners make so much fuss about microfinance. After all, they say, they have been disbursing micro-loans and accepting micro-deposits even before the word 'microfinance' was coined. Most eventually appreciate that the excitement is about doing it profitably, with large numbers of customers who cannot offer collateral, with high loan repayment and manageable operating costs.

The BRI units achieved breakeven point 18 months after the inception of reforms in 1985. Sogesol in Haiti, despite being a new company and working in difficult circumstances, broke even in its twentieth month and achieved full profitability within two years of starting. Even though most commentators had written off the AgBank as recently as 1999, the bank was successfully turned around and sold to a private investor in less than three years. American Bank of Kosovo was set up from scratch, and in two-and-a-half years it had attained breakeven.

In many cases, the investors provided the initial commitment, and they may have entered into partnerships with international and/or social investors. Each case study shows how this commitment emerged and was institutionalized. Even though Sogebank in Haiti was an experienced retail bank, its managers realized that they did not internally have the expertise to build an effective microfinance operation. The bank decided to set up a service company in partnership with socially responsible investors.

International Micro Investments, a private investment company, are so confident of their business model that they have already invested in 18 microfinance banks around the world.

In India, with support from the National Bank for Agriculture and Rural Development, NGOs and donors have encouraged the public and private sector banks to experiment with informal self-help groups. The encouragement of the Central Bank, political support, positive experiences from the pilot programmes, and growing staff skills and confidence have helped to scale up the programme in the last few years. However, the scale is still small when compared to the potential customer demand or the banks' overall portfolio. Over 12 years, for example, the SBI has disbursed US$137m loans to the SHGs, but this is only 0.4 per cent of the bank's current loans outstanding of US$31bn.

In the case of AgBank, the commitment to reform a public sector bank emerged through an agreement between the government and international donors. The initial trigger for the chairman of Banque du Caire, another public sector bank, was the doubtful quality of the existing loan portfolio and the large and partly under-employed workforce. Carefully selected managers, along with external technical assistance for systems and staff development, helped convert these aspirations into a functioning programme.

Commercial banks not only have to have good systems but also constantly keep them under review. This is especially important with rapid growth of customers, staff and portfolio. Producers Bank portfolio quality deteriorated when its value tripled in 1996–97. During 2002, ProCredit Bank discovered that some employees committed a fraud in the Gold Pawn loan department and had to write off US$1.55m during the year, compared against US$0.15m loan write-off the previous year. ProCredit Bank had to strengthen its internal controls and procedures.

Some technical assistance providers are themselves investing in microfinance banks, such as ACCION, IMI and CARE. This is a healthy trend and should be welcomed. Donors have made significant contributions to the initiatives in many of the banks described in the case studies. A few banks such as United Georgian Bank, Tbiluniversalbank, Sonali Bank and Bank of Khyber have received credit lines from concessional sources such as the European Bank for Reconstruction and Development (EBRD), International Fund for Agricultural Development (IFAD) or elsewhere. Most of the development grants have been used for capacity building such as staff training, systems design or product development. In the case of Equity, the total subsidy is estimated to have been US$1.73m, excluding loans and equity. This amounts to less than US$7 per customer served. Operating cost support was provided by donors for the AgBank turnaround, but this was more than justified by increasing annual profits and the enhanced value of the bank.

It is clear that the benefit-to-cost ratio for assistance to banks in microfinance is much more favourable than for similar support to microfinance institutions for which both the loan capital and operating cost support has been much higher in relation to the numbers of customers served. Moreover, if the Co-operative Bank of Kenya, the Kenya Commercial Bank and even Barclays Bank are beginning to learn lessons from Equity's success just in Kenya itself, the larger benefits of such catalytic donor grants can go far beyond the original recipients.

Small customers strengthen banks' capacity to cope with big crises

This book is not about political and economic stability. We present the case studies from the perspective of the institutions, but the wider political, economic and social environment in which the institutions operate is, of course, critical to their success.

There are some indications that microfinance can materially assist a bank to weather severe economic and even political crises. Several of the countries from which the case studies are drawn have recently had crises or indeed still are in turmoil:

- In Zimbabwe, GDP has been declining since 1997, registering a 7.3 per cent drop in 2003. Inflation has fluctuated between 100 and 600 per cent over the period 2001–03 and the Zimbabwe/US dollar exchange rate has fallen from 40:1 in 2001 to 800:1 in 2003, and is still falling. Unemployment is estimated to be 60 per cent.
- Kosovo suffered from a decade of discrimination and neglect and was ravaged in 1999 by the Serb occupation and ethnic cleaning.
- Haiti's underdeveloped economy is the result of decades of political instability. The country has suffered severe political unrest during most of the past 15 years and the situation continues to be unstable.
- Civil war and massive economic disruption caused by the break-up of the Soviet Union followed Georgia's independence in 1991.

Political stability has a vital impact on economic opportunities and performance. Economic disruption can also emerge from other factors. The Ecuadorean economy performed poorly for some 10 years and faced the worst financial and economic crisis in its history in 1999. The crisis in the financial sector led to devaluation of the Sucre, rapid inflation and capital flight, and 20 banks closed, representing 45 per cent of the financial system.

The financial institutions in the countries described in the case studies are coping with these difficult circumstances very effectively, and it is clear that their microfinance portfolios have played an important part in enabling them to do this. Banco Solidario, the only private bank in Ecuador focused on microfinance, was able not only to remain open during the most difficult period but even to post modest profits. The liquidity of the microenterprise portfolio, and the risk diversification facilitated by many small loans and different financial products, helped the bank to weather the crisis. Microenterprises mainly use local inputs and supply to local markets and are thus better placed to deal with external shocks. At the peak of the financial crisis, microentrepreneurs lined up to repay their loans rather than to withdraw their money.

A year earlier, the microfinance division of BRI also showed that the impact of crisis could be positive. During June to August 1998, after Indonesia had been hit by both drought and an economic crisis, 1.29 million new saving deposit accounts were opened in BRI units. During the crisis year (August 1997 to August 1998), savings deposits increased by 90 per cent and loans outstanding by 5 per cent, when the inflation rate was 56 per cent. Because of the uncertain future, people were reluctant to take new loans, but they continued their loan repayments.

The loan loss ratio during this period was 2.16 per cent, virtually the same as the long term 2.17 per cent loss ratio experienced since 1984. Due to expanding deposits and an almost stable loan portfolio, the division's excess liquidity increased by 195 per cent during this period. This was extremely valuable, since confidence in the banking system was falling and might have triggered a run on the bank. Financial institutions with significant exposure to small customers seem to have better capacity to deal with such crises.

Small customers demand appropriate products and service delivery

Commercial banks have learned that small customers are no different from other customers in one respect – the onus is on the supplier to understand the location, the needs and the preferences of the customers and then to design and deliver products that best meet these needs. It is not more of the same – most small customers do not want complex product features, procedures or paperwork, and cannot afford frequent visits to the bank. They do not have balance sheets or securities and they have to work within very short time horizons. Microfinance can be a low-margin, high-volume mass market for the bank.

No matter where and how the idea to serve this market originates, the bank often has to redesign or refocus the financial products, the type of staff employed and their training, the management information systems and the incentives for both customers and staff.

When loan officers' and tellers' responses at the point of customer contact are effectively integrated with efficient back-office systems, such as credit manuals and management information systems, the results can be spectacular both in efficiency and customer response.

Equity conducted detailed process mapping to optimize the speed and efficiency of its customer service and introduced a new computerized system to improve its turnaround time from 30 to 40 minutes to about five minutes at the counter. Banque du Caire provides automatic approval in 10 minutes for repeat loans. The AgBank study reminds us that 'the intent is not to compete with international banks going after high-end customers, but appropriately to serve rural and low-income market segments. Money should be spent to make local branches adequate and comfortable, but they do not have to be the best in town. Occasionally, only two people are needed in a location, and hand ledgers and a calculator may be adequate technology.'

Several case studies mention efforts at branding and promotion, such as CBZ, Sogesol, ProCredit and Equity, including lottery prizes to mobilize deposits. The Equity case study shows that customers can be influenced by observing other's experiences. Product take-up grows rapidly once customers discover the quality of services on offer. Ninety per cent of FINADEV's clients heard of the bank through relatives or friends.

In 2000, AgBank discovered that large numbers of pensioners would crowd into the banking hall on a fixed day to collect their pensions, which was a problem for them and for the bank. In response, AgBank offered saving products to the pensioners, and their pension payments were automatically deposited in their accounts. The pensioners were able to withdraw these deposits when they wanted; this reduced pressure on the branches and led to a larger proportion of deposits remaining with the bank. The bank was also able to develop a loan product for these pensioners. Other customers, such as nomadic herders, had different needs but they also appreciated the new products.

Producers Bank in the Philippines was able to draw on Grameen Bank Bangladesh methodology to offer a standardized set of financial products, which were relatively easy for the management to understand, for the field staff to sell, and for low-income clients to access. As members of solidarity groups, poor women and men could access a loan of US$100 without any need for collateral. These loans are repayable in six months and customers can then access larger amounts. The bank started with less than 3000 such clients in 1999, and had reached 44 000 clients by 2003.

Even after offering the full range of banking services, including micro-loans of US$1000 to US$10 000, ProCredit introduced an express micro-loan ranging between US$100 and US$1000 and with simpler requirements and shorter repayment period (12 months), than the regular micro-loan. Banque du Caire is negotiating a micro-insurance product for its individual borrowers and sees the potential for bulk purchase of other products needed by its large customer base.

Bancafé and Bank of Khyber mention changes in banking hours. While many banks offer financial services to individuals, others work only through groups, and yet others serve both groups and individuals. Some banks offer a large range of microfinance, products, but BRI successfully serves its large customer base with two basic products, SIMPEDES savings and KUPEDES loans. The needs of microfinance customers also evolve and change and their bankers have to respond to this. Bancafé introduced community loans first in 1999, and individual loans only in 2001. By 2003, 88 per cent of its loans were to individuals.

Small customers pay back their loans and make substantial deposits

When formulating their initial plans for their entry into microfinance, Banque du Caire sought the reassurance of a 90 per cent guarantee for their micro-loans. When this was not forthcoming, the bank started cautiously with a more modest portfolio than they had originally planned. Three years later, and with the portfolio at risk at only 0.49 per cent, the bank planned to set up 150 new micro-lending branches, to employ 1000 new staff and to introduce new products.

Table c.1 shows that majority of banks have portfolio at risk (PAR) of only 2–4 per cent of their loan portfolio. The loans are not secured with physical collateral, and are thus considered as unsecured loans by the regulators. The reasons for this good performance include the following:

- Small customers value ongoing access to responsive financial institutions and go to great lengths to maintain or improve their credit record.
- In addition to the incentives of continued access and bigger loans, some banks offer interest discounts on prompt payment.
- With extremely large numbers of small customers, one customer getting into difficulty represents only a very small fraction of the overall portfolio.
- Regular contact with customers, and effective internal monitoring and information systems promptly spotlight problem cases for follow-up action.
- Prompt follow-up and recovery efforts ensure that other borrowers learn that wilful default is unacceptable.
- In some group-based methodologies, existing group members use their local knowledge to assess potential members while forming groups and when sanctioning loans.
- Bank staff are aware that their performance is being regularly tracked and compared against other staff. Some banks link staff compensation and incentives directly to the size and quality of portfolio managed. Often the loan officers disbursing the loan are also responsible for collection and thus build, and if necessary can use, their close relationships with clients to apply moral pressure on defaulters.

Institutions offering appropriate and diversified savings and loan products have found that saving depositors outnumber the borrowers and the deposits mobilized are more than adequate to fund loan demand. Table c.1 (pages 276–77) also shows that in six of the ten institutions which have specialized micro-savings products the total savings balances exceed the loans outstanding by a wide margin, and in every case the numbers of depositors exceed the numbers of borrowers. Equity found that even with 96 per cent of its depositors depositing less than US$50 each, it could still mobilize deposits of US$50m.

Similarly 71 per cent of the AgBank depositors operate current accounts with an average balance of only US$8. Because the bank also offers a range of useful savings products, the savings mobilized increased from US$13m in 2000 to US$64 m in 2003.

All poor people cannot immediately become bank customers

In Table c.1 (pages 276–77), Producers Bank of the Philippines has one of the lowest average size of loans and deposit balances. The average loan outstanding is US$74, which is 7 per cent of per capita gross national income and the average savings balance is US$20, or 2 per cent of per capita income. The bank acknowledges that in spite of these very small amounts, it is difficult to target the poorest segment of the population and very remote areas. BRI is in the same situation, in that distant villages, particularly on the outer islands of Indonesia, are sometimes totally un-served.

In countries with large numbers of very poor people, who tend to live in dispersed locations with inadequate roads, it is very hard for banks to cover the costs of reaching all the poor.

Strategic choices to serve small customers

In our Introduction, we indicated the different strategies pursued by the different institutions. The most common strategy for a commercial bank is to go down market, or downscaling, that is to reach out to poorer customers and neighbourhoods and to design and deliver appropriate products suitable for these customers. Existing banking licenses, staff, infrastructure and resources mean this can be done quickly. Seven of the nine public sector institutions in our case studies decided to take this route. These institutions face many challenges.

- Being public institutions they already have mixed experiences of this market, from earlier and often badly designed welfare programmes. It difficult to ensure that staff realize that this market segment is large and can be profitable, and that these customers need appropriate products and good quality services. The whole approach is totally different from the low-price, poor-quality services which they may have been used to providing in order to meet social obligations or satisfy government requirements.
- They have to develop the necessary culture and systems and to improve the motivation and skills of their existing staff. Many Banque du Caire staff were unwilling to spend time outside their offices developing business; they were used to waiting for customers to come to them.
- Staff have to accept that they are accountable and that transactions must be transparent. AgBank management had to protect staff from external pressures.
- Management have to sustain the focus over time and draw the right lessons. Bank of Khyber had various phases of centralization and decentralization in their efforts to deal effectively with microfinance customers.

Financial Bank, Benin, and Sogebank, Haiti, two private commercial banks, decided to pursue microfinance through a subsidiary. This enabled the banks to partner other investors who contributed both technical skills and financial resources. Sogesol was set up as a non-financial subsidiary, which did not require a separate banking licence or central bank supervision. The loans remain on the books of the parent bank, Sogebank, and the subsidiary earns fees based on the size and quality of the portfolio it has developed. Both subsidiaries leverage the reputation and systems of the parent. The subsidiaries are dedicated to microfinance and can thus remain totally focused on it.

This service company approach also presents a number of challenges. The interests of minority investors have to be protected; the tasks, costs, risks and remuneration have to be allocated carefully between the parent and the subsidiary; the back-office operations have to be integrated properly; and the senior staff of the parent bank have to ensure that the subsidiary has the access it needs to legal and other shared resources. State Bank of India, Producers Bank, and others are doing business with informal groups rather than individual customers. In India, this has received significant policy support and is currently the dominant microfinance model. In some cases, these groups are promoted by the bank, but in most cases other promoters are involved. Oriental Bank of Commerce now uses facilitators who are paid from a 1 per cent levy on loans. The advantage of this model is that groups help to identify customers and the groups also reduce the transaction costs per customer served. It is not easy, however, to reach out to the poorest people since they are often excluded from groups, and the costs of group promotion, support and supervision have to be covered.

ICICI Bank and Sonali Bank work through existing NGOs and MFIs to reach large numbers of customers. ICICI Bank has also bought out MFIs' existing portfolios. This enables MFIs with limited capital to extend their outreach. ICICI Bank does not have to develop its own retail delivery channels, and also benefits from first-loss guarantees. The bank hopes to develop a secondary market for microfinance receivables. The success of this policy will depend on sufficiently strong and substantial microfinance institutions that can offer the necessary retail delivery capacity and can also provide satisfactory guarantees.

The financial sector policy environment

Commercial banks are controlled by central banks. It is more expensive to handle large numbers of very small transactions than to work with more familiar corporate and middle-class personal accounts, and it may be necessary to charge microfinance customers higher interest rates. This can be politically difficult, even though the new customers' only alternative may be moneylenders who charge far higher rates.

The whole village unit microfinance system of BRI was only possible after interest rate deregulation in Indonesia in 1983. The Philippines deregulated interest rates in 1999, and most central banks now allow banks to fix their own interest rates, service charges and product features. As the Ecuador case study mentions, however, the threat of central bank intervention remains.

Similarly, the regulations usually only allow banks to have a certain limited proportion of their loan portfolio unsecured. The turnarounds of Equity and AgBank, both of which were insolvent, would have been impossible without sensitive handing by their respective central banks. The authorities in most countries are putting greater pressure on banks to improve the rigour and disclosure standards of asset classification, but there is still insufficient appreciation that short-term micro-loans are in fact more secure than many so-called secured loans, and that micro-loans can and should be judged by tougher norms than larger longer-term loans. Central Banks are also allowing increased competition, which will drive banks to improve the efficiency and quality of their services and also to keep charges down. This will lead some banks to concentrate on their core business, which is probably not microfinance, but the case studies show that liberalization is leading many others to reach out and to serve the enormous untapped demand.

Overall, the commercial banks have fewer regulatory problems than specialized non-bank microfinance institutions. Most MFIs still have to deal with many issues relating to the choice of act under which they should incorporate and how to access to equity finance in order to have sufficient capitalization to be allowed to mobilize deposits from savers. Banks are in a much stronger position, and the successes described in the cases demonstrate that they can profitably take advantage of this.

The way ahead

The case studies contain many messages for stakeholders, and every reader will draw conclusions from the material. We attempt below to draw together some of the most vital implications for bankers, policy makers, donors, microfinance practitioners and their customers.

Bankers

The main message of this book is for bankers. There are of course many different types of banks; in the public and the private sectors, large and small, local, national and multinational. There are also many postal banks, and co-operative banks, and some MFIs which have become banks. This book focuses mainly on existing commercial banks, but many of the lessons from the case studies are equally applicable to these other types of financial institutions.

All the case studies show how banks and their clients benefited from entry into the microfinance. Every bank has different reasons for joining the microfinance market, and the cases show that there are many different ways in which banks can become involved. The following arguments played an important role in most of the cases in this book.

- The financial services market is becoming globalized, and many national banks which earlier had a major share of local corporate business are losing out to international banks. One advantage that the national banks have is their extensive branch networks. Some treat this as a burden, and are trying to reduce their branch numbers, but previously unprofitable branches can be made viable with new microfinance business.
- Banks, like most kinds of business, aim to maximize their market shares, to grow, and to spread their risks. Microfinance can provide an ideal way of achieving all three of these broad goals.

- Microfinance can be profitable in its own right, but some micro-customers will also grow into big ones who can be profitable and loyal customers in the future. They will be unlikely to change their banking relationships if they have received good service when they were saving and borrowing only very small sums.
- Large private and corporate clients will shop around and are becoming more price sensitive and more willing to shift for small differences in interest rates. Poorer people need products which suit their needs, good service and convenient access; they will not move their accounts for a few percentage points in interest charges or returns on savings.
- It costs money to develop new customers, of whatever scale, but in many places NGOs and MFIs have promoted groups or other forms of intermediation to enable poorer people to be economical customers for financial services. The NGOs have in effect done the banks' customer development work for them, and banks can pick up ready-made customers at little or no cost to themselves.
- In some of the countries covered in the case studies, such as Bangladesh, Georgia, and Kenya, some MFIs have grown very rapidly and are obtaining full banking status. Existing banks are being threatened by these new competitors, and they may have to compete with them in the microfinance market in order to pre-empt competition for their own traditional customers.
- Microfinance should be seen primarily as a profitable long-term business opportunity, and not as an act of social responsibility for public relations' purposes. Nevertheless, banks are more dependent than most businesses on public opinion and government approval; they can enhance their image and their balance sheets at the same time by effective microfinance initiatives.

There are, of course, also many good reasons why commercial banks should not become involved in microfinance.

- Loans are unsecured, the clients and delivery channels are unfamiliar in social, gender and economic terms, both to bank staff and to their existing customers who may have to mingle with them at branch bank counters. Earlier misguided poverty alleviation programmes may have destroyed any credit culture among the poor, at least in the opinion of bank employees.
- Large numbers of small accounts require highly efficient accounting and management information systems, and aggressive follow-up of defaulters may create bad publicity for the bank as a whole. Similarly, the transaction costs of microfinance business may require a bank to charge higher than normal interest rates. These are unlikely to create problems for the clients, but journalists, the general public and particularly politicians may misinterpret these rates as usurious exploitation of the poor.

The case studies include examples of all these problems, and they show how banks have successfully overcome them. Direct entry into the microfinance market may also not always be appropriate for every institution. The case studies show how collaboration can, in some situations, be more appropriate than competition.

Donors and policy makers

Foreign donors can claim much of the credit for recognizing and supporting the various new institutions which came up in the 1970s and 1980s and which have pioneered most innovations in microfinance. Governments have responded more slowly, but in many countries they are now successfully encouraging rather than frustrating microfinance.

The principles of 'new paradigm' microfinance are now fairly well established, but the major task now is to extend the availability of micro-financial services to a larger proportion of the potential market, that is, the people who can benefit from them.

The examples in this book demonstrate that, in many if not most circumstances, existing commercial banks offer the most effective and efficient way of doing this. The main arguments for this proposition can be summarized as follows:

- It is less expensive, and quicker, to reach more poor people through the existing banks, rather than trying to do it by creating and developing entirely new institutions.
- Sound inclusive banking systems are a necessary component of economic development. Microfinance can strengthen and legitimize existing banks, and thus benefit both the 'un-banked' and the economy as a whole.
- New microfinance institutions usually owe their origin and survival to donor or other assistance, but commercial banks have their own independent existence. If microfinance is firmly embedded into a bank's profitable operations, it is likely to continue after external assistance is withdrawn.
- Most countries, quite rightly, insist that all banking institutions, and particularly those which mobilize small demand deposits, should conform to quite stringent regulations. Existing banks already do conform, and are usually already taking savings from potential micro-borrowers. There may be a need for some changes to regulations relating to unsecured loans, or to the location of banking transactions, before a bank can offer financial services, but there are far less regulatory hurdles to overcome than when setting up a new institution.
- Commercial banks do not need new equity to enable them to offer micro-financial services, and because they are usually flush with funds they do not need more finance. Encouragement, persuasion, training and some temporary operational support is all

- New institutions need new infrastructure and, most critically, they need new managers. It has been suggested that competent managers are the scarcest resource in most poor countries. It makes sense to use institutions which are already being managed, even if imperfectly, than to identify and build the capacity of completely new management teams.

We believe that our case studies demonstrate that these arguments are valid. There are of course some situations where there are no commercial banks, or they are so weak or hidebound by tradition as to be unwilling even to consider this new market, or when bank managers take a perfectly reasonable strategic decision not to become involved. It may also still be necessary, in an ever-reducing number of countries, to test and demonstrate the viability of microfinance to the banking community as part of the process of introducing the new market to them. In such instances, it may be necessary to start or expand specialist MFIs but this should not be the automatic response. If micro-financial services are needed, the existing banks should be the institutions to provide them unless there are compelling reasons why they cannot.

There are also some common but less legitimate reasons why both donors and governments may sometimes be reluctant to take this route. They may prefer to work with institutions which are more pliant and more grateful, and to look for 'projects' where they can claim credit for a complete new institution, rather than for a relatively minor component, in financial terms, of a large business portfolio. It is also difficult to nail a commemorative plaque to a new group of outstanding loans, or to ask an ambassador or minister to inaugurate a quite modest new department. It is important that these issues should be recognized, so that they can be avoided.

Microfinance practitioners

Some MFI staff may read this book in order to appraise the competition, or perhaps to help them in thinking about their own future. Some MFI staff in India and elsewhere have already moved to commercial banks, and this trend is likely to increase, as banks increase their market share.

Such moves are obviously excellent for the banks, in that they acquire ready-made expertise in what may for them be an unfamiliar market segment, which needs new types of financial products. There are also many reasons why MFI staff should think seriously of making such a move. There are likely to be more promotion opportunities, and a wider variety of work; and employment may be more secure, if sometimes less well remunerated, than in a donor-dependent 'project' or NGO. Work in the harsh commercial world may be less comfortable and more constrained by hierarchy and bureaucracy than in a socially-oriented NGO or MFI, but banking staff working in microfinance should be able to take satisfaction from the fact that they will probably be able to reach far more needy people, in a more sustainable way, than they ever could from most MFIs.

Some banks such as Sonali and ICICI Bank are also forging effective and mutually profitable partnerships with MFIs, rather than competing directly with them. Bank staff with experience of working for MFIs are already playing a vital role in initiating and managing these relationships.

Customers

Finally, we must briefly consider the customers' interests. These must of course be paramount, both from a social point of view but also to ensure that micro-financial services are properly marketed. If they are not, they will be unprofitable for the banks and useless to their clients.

For the poor, secure and accessible savings are at least as important as loans. Commercial bank deposits must usually be insured, by law, at least up to the likely level of most microfinance client's balances. Many MFIs do not offer savings facilities at all, or, if they do, they are uninsured. By mobilizing savings the MFIs may be putting savers' funds at risk, and they may be operating against or at least outside the law.

Many MFIs are critically dependent on donor or government subsidy of various kinds, and are likely to remain so. When this support is withdrawn, the institutions may go out of business. This is disastrous if they cannot repay savings deposits, and it can also be a serious blow to a poor household if they lose their main source of credit. Banks, on the other hand, are long-term institutions. Central banks ensure that banks do not get into trouble or at least that customers are 'rescued', in the interests of the credibility of the nation's financial system as a whole.

It is surely to be hoped that microfinance itself will become redundant, sooner rather than later, because most people will no longer need it. They will be able, like most of the readers of this book, to choose their own financial service providers and to do business with them individually, or in groups, as and when they wish. In individual cases this is already happening, and some microfinance clients have 'graduated' to regular client status. It is clearly much easier for a client to do this within the same institution than to have to establish her reputation from scratch with a new and unfamiliar bank.

The United Nations has designated 2005 as the International Year of Micro-Credit, and has invited governments, the private sector and other institutions to join in raising the profile and building the capacity of microfinance. This book addresses the experience and potential of one type of institution that can provide microfinance services – the commercial banks – but which has to some extent been neglected by comparison with specialized institutions. We believe that commercial banks alone have the potential to deliver micro-financial services in the volume and variety that are needed. We hope that this book will lead more banks to extend their outreach to greater numbers of poorer people who presently lack access to formal financial services.

Endnotes

GENERAL INTRODUCTION

1. This chapter is based on research variously supported by GTZ (1987-91), FAO (1998) and IFAD (1999–2001) and on recent information provided by the BRI Microbanking Division.

CHAPTER TWO

1. *Sources*: The World Bank (2002), Economist Intelligence Unit (2001), Philippines National Statistical Coordination Board (2002).
2. NCC Policy Paper, July 2002. For the purpose of this chapter, we have adopted an exchange rate of Filipino Pesos (P) 53.22 for US$1. It corresponds to the average IMF exchange rate for the months of June and July 2001, which represents the 'central' year in most of data.
3. IFAD (2002).
4. Philippines National Statistical Coordination Board (2002).
5. The case of CARD has been studied by, among others, Seibel and Torres (2001) and Drake and Rhyne (2002).

CHAPTER THREE

1. NWFP Statistics by Bureau of Statistics, Planning & Development Department, Government of NWFP.
2. *Economic Survey of Pakistan 2002–2003*.
3. *Pakistan Human Condition Report*, 2003 by UNDP Pakistan.
4. *Pakistan Human Condition Report*, 2003 by UNDP Pakistan.
5. Pakistan Development Forum, Islamabad: May 2003
6. RRP: Pak 29586, Asian Development Bank, November 2000
7. The Rural Support Programmes (RSPs) offer integrated rural development services to the poor communities by enhancing their capacities to help themselves. The RSP network is spread across Pakistan.
8. *Performance Indicators Report No. 6*, Pakistan Microfinance Network (PMN), Islamabad.
9. Based upon minimum caloric requirement of 2350 calories per day and price level of the year 2000-2001, the official poverty line is US$13.13 per capita per month.
10. A rate of US$1 = Pak Rupee 57 has been used throughout this study.
11. 'Maliha Hussain and Shazreh Hussain', Pakistan Microfinance Network, December 2003, Islamabad.
12. Gary M. Woller and Christopher Dunford (2002), *Where To Microfinance*, Romney Institute of Public Management, Marriott School, Brigham Young University.
13. Shariah compliant means in accordance with the principles of Islamic law.

CHAPTER FIVE

1. *www.sbi.co.in*

CHAPTER SIX

1. More information at *www.canbankindia.com*
2. More information at *www.dhan.org*

CHAPTER EIGHT

1. Micro Finance in India and Sa-Dhan, *www.sa-dhan.org/overview_micro.asp*
2. Vijay Mahajan and Bharti Gupta Ramola (Aug 2003), *Microfinance in India – Banyan Tree and Bonsai, A Review Paper for the World Bank.*
3. *www.icicibank.com*
4. ICICI Bank, Microfinance Products, December 2003.
5. *Scaling up Micro Financial Services: An Overview of Challenges and Opportunities*, Bindu Ananth, Soju Annie George, ICICI Bank, 2003.
6. Currently RBI norms require banks to extend 40% of their total advances to priority sectors like agriculture, small-scale industries, artisan, village and cottage industries, education, housing, self-help groups, food and agro-processing industry, etc, of which 13.5% has to go directly to farmers. Several of these loans can be classified as agriculture. All MFI loans can be classified as 'weaker section' loans, which has a sub-target of 10% of net bank credit. Potentially this is a large market if it works.
7. Microfinance: Productive Linkages, Editorial, *Economic and Political Weekly, March 6, 2004.*
8. Dr Nachiket Mor, Executive Director, ICICI Bank, as quoted in 'ICICI Bank bets on micro-finance – Ties up with Micro-credit Foundation', *The Hindu Business Line,* Wednesday, March 10, 2004.

CHAPTER NINE

1. *www.bdc.com.eg*

CHAPTER TEN

1. Some NGOs retain 10 per cent interest free deposit.

CHAPTER ELEVEN

1. Much of this chapter draws on Coetzee et al.'s 'Understanding the Re-birth of Equity Building Society in Kenya'.

2 This section is based on a DFID Project Memorandum for the Financial Sector Deepening Project, 2001.
3 Central Bank of Kenya, Ministry of Cooperatives, Association of Microfinance Institutions, Kenya Union of Savings and Credit Cooperatives.
4 For more on AfriCap, see *www.africapfund.com*
5 For more on the market-led approach to microfinance, see *www.microsave.org*
6 See Wright et al. (2003) for more on this.

CHAPTER THIRTEEN

1 United Nations Development Programme, '*Democracia, Pobreza y Exclusión Social en el Ecuador*', May 2001.
2 Maria Elena Perez, Soledad Burbano, Mónica Hernández, 'Banco Solidario: Strategy During Ecuador's Financial Crisis', November 2003, p.7.
3 Banco Central de Ecuador, *www.bce.fin.ec*, 19 March 2004.
4 Banco Solidario, Presentation to Consultants, 13 January 2004.
5 Santiago Ribadeneira Troya, 'Manejo de Costos en una Institución de Microfinanzas', *Microfinanzas en Ecuador*, Proyecto SALTO, January 2003, p.123.
6 Marín Bautista, 'Sistemas de Integración Financiera para Cooperativas de Ahorro y Crédito en Ecuador', FINANCOOP, October 2003, p.6.
7 Arie Sanders, Oscar Banegas, María Soledad Jarrín, et al; CDR-ULA and Fundación Alternativa Study; 'HIVOS, Alcance e Impacto de Crédito: Estudio de los casos Banco Solidario y Caja los Andes', December 2002, San José, Costa Rica, p. 3, annex 1.
8 Ribadeneira Troya, p.124.
9 Perez, p.4.
10 Sanders; p.*v*.
11 'Total portfolio' includes current, overdue and contaminated portfolio.
12 'Portfolio at risk' is measured taking into account the quotas that have become overdue and the principal that corresponds to this quota.
13 Total deposits includes demand deposits and time deposits.
14 The 'microenterprise portfolio at risk' is measured according to the traditional definition of portfolio at risk that incorporates the principal one day overdue while the total bank portfolio at risk is measured taking into account the quotas that have become overdue and the principal that corresponds to this quota.
15 Sanders, p.14.

CHAPTER FOURTEEN

1 Bancafé can be reached through its website, *www.bancafe.com.gt*

CHAPTER FIFTEEN

1. This case study is adapted from ACCION, *InSight* No. 6, 'The Service Company Model', 2003.
2. ACCION's experience with the service company model was first developed at Banco de Pichincha, the largest bank in Ecuador, with its microfinance service company, Credife. For more information on ACCION, see *www.accion.org*
3. World Bank, *World Development Indicators*, 2003.
4. The ACCION CAMEL™ is a diagnostic and management tool that measures the capital adequacy, asset quality, management, earnings and liquidity of microfinance institutions (MFIs). It is designed to help managers assess an organization's financial health and overall performance.
5. These findings are from ACCION, *InSight* No. 8, 'ACCION Poverty Outreach Findings: Sogesol, Haiti,' 2003.
6. DAI/FINNET, 2003.

CHAPTER SIXTEEN

1. Reliable data is weak as a result of a significant 'grey' economy and dislocations resulting from the 1999 conflict.
2. 'Support for the provision and institutionalization of business finance services in Kosovo,' Report to USAID/Kosovo, August 15, 2000.
3. Estimated total annual demand for credit among SMEs. Based on USAID's estimate of annual demand for fixed assets and working capital investments among small and medium-sized firms, multiplied by an estimated 3750 small firms and 1250 medium firms, multiplied by 75 per cent advance factor (i.e. a bank would not loan 100 per cent of investment needs).
4. The currency used in Kosovo was the DM until the euro was introduced. There were only remnants of Yugoslavian dinars in the provinces on a very small scale.
5. With the sale of the majority of ABK shares to RIB, the name of the bank was changed to Raiffeisen Bank Kosovo (RBKO). A re-branding campaign and formal ceremony was planned, and the name was changed in May 2003.

CHAPTER SEVENTEEN

1. The authors would like to thank Michael Kortenbusch from the Georgia Small Enterprise Lending Programme for his help.
2. As at May 2003. *Source*: Georgia, Country Profile, The Economist Intelligence Unit, 2003.
3. Georgia Enterprise Growth Initiative, USAID Caucasus, Office of Economic Restructuring, September 2002.
4. Georgia Microfinance, Stabilisation and Enhancement Activity, USAID Caucasus, Office of Economic Growth, November 2002.

5 Georgia Microfinance, Stabilisation and Enhancement Activity, USAID Caucasus, Office of Economic Growth, November 2002.
6 World Bank, *World Business Environment Survey*, 1999.
7 Georgia Enterprise Growth Initiative, USAID Caucasus, Office of Economic Restructuring, September 2002.
8 Strategy for Georgia, European Bank for Reconstruction and Development, 2002.
9 The following exchange rate is used: US$1 = GEL2.15.
10 *The State of Microfinance in Central and Eastern Europe and the New Independent States*, Sarah Forster, Seth Greene and Justyna Pytkowska, CGAP 2003.
11 Microfinance Bank of Georgia has become ProCredit Bank Georgia since 15 September 2003. The aim of this operation is to unify IMI-sponsored 'microfinance banks in Eastern Europe under a common name and logo' (*www.procredit.ge*).
12 CGAP, 2003.
13 GEL refers to the currency Georgian Lari.
14 Letter from management, *www.procredit.ge*
15 *www.procredit.ge/eng/10news/1001news.html*
16 CGAP, 2003.
17 The initial technical assistance was provided by Bannock Consulting, a British consultancy company. The current technical assistance is provided by Bankakademie and Business and Finance Consulting (BFC) GmbH as a subcontractor.
18 The following exchange rate was used: US$1 = GEL2.15.
19 TUB also offers pawn loans to its clients, but the pawn loan department is different from the micro-loan department and therefore is not discussed here.
20 The loans offered by TUB have evolved over time. Table 17.13 presents the current micro-loans offered by TUB.
21 Exchange rate used: US$1 = GEL2.15.
22 Not all these branches and service centres currently participate in micro-lending operations.
23 'Successfully' means that the bank disburses a loan to the new client referred by the old client.
24 Using the declining balance calculation.
25 As of December 2003, three international long-term experts and two local consultants provide support to TUB and UGB.
26 Sustainable microfinance banks – problems and perspectives, Philip Sigwart, General Manager of ProCredit Bank, Georgia.
27 CGAP, 2003.

References

ACPC (1995) *An Evaluation of the Grameen Bank Replication Project in the Philippines*, Manila.

APRACA-GTZ (1997) *The Linkage Banking in Asia*, Bangkok, APRACA, Eschborn, GTZ.

Asian Development Bank (2003) 'Draft Report Rural Microfinance Indonesia' (TA No.3810-INO).

Bango, B., Carlton, A., Manndorff, H., and Reiter, W. (1999) 'Microfinance in Zimbabwe, Evaluation of the Austrian support to Microfinance Institutions in Zimbabwe' [ILO-SDF, ZWFT and ZAMBUKO TRUST].

Bank Rakyat Indonesia (BRI) (1995) *One Hundred Years Bank Rakyat Indonesia 1895–1995*, Jakarta, BRI.

Bannock Consultants (2000) 'Output to Purpose Review, Credit for Informal Sector [CRISP], Zimbabwe Programme', Harare, Bannock Consulting.

Bannock Consulting (2000) 'Plan d'affaires et Rapport Final', Port-au-Prince, Bannock Consulting.

Bautista, Marín (2003) 'Sistemas de Integración Financiera para Cooperativas de Ahorro y Crédito en Ecuador', FINANCOOP, October, p.6.

Boyer, Debra and Jay Dyer (2003) 'The Agricultural Bank of Mongolia: From Insolvent State Bank to Thriving Private Bank', prepared for the USAID-sponsored 'Paving the Way Forward for Rural Finance An International Conference on Best Practices,' June 2003.

BRI (2004) Laporan Statistik BRI Unit, Jakarta, BRI.

CBZ (1995) 'CBZ Strategic Planning Document', Harare, Commercial Bank of Zimbabwe.

CGAP (2003) *The State of Microfinance in Central and Eastern Europe and the New Independent States*, Sarah Forster, Seth Greene and Justyna Pytkowska, CGAP.

Charitonenko, Stephanie, Richard H. Patten and Jacob Yaron (1998) 'Indonesia: Bank Rakyat Indonesia – Unit Desa 1970-1996. Sustainable Banking with the Poor – Case Studies in Microfinance'. Washington, D.C., The World Bank.

Coetzee, Gerhard, Kamau Kabbucho and Andrew Mnjama (2002) 'Understanding the Rebirth of Equity Building Society in Kenya'. Nairobi, MicroSave.

DAI/FINNET (2003) 'Base de Donnees sur les Institutions de Microfinance', Port-au-Prince, DAI/FINNET.

DFID (2001) 'Project Memorandum, Financial Sector Deepening, Kenya 2001–2006', Nairobi, DFID.

Drake, Deborah and Elisabeth Rhyne (2002) *The Commercialization of Microfinance: Balancing Business and Development*, Bloomfield, CT, Kumarian Press.

Dressen, Robert, Dyer, Jay and Northrip, Zan, 'Turning Around State-Owned Banks in Underserved Markets', *Small Enterprise Development*, Vol. 13, No. 4, December 2002.

Dyer, Jay, Morrow, J. Peter, and Robin Young (2004) 'Shanghai Poverty Conference – Scaling Up Poverty Reduction, Case Study – The Agricultural Bank of Monogolia', May, Shanghai.

European Bank for Reconstruction and Development (2002) 'Strategy for Georgia', EBRD.

Feekes, Fons (1993) 'Extending small credits profitably in Indonesia', *Small Enterprise Development* 4(2): 33–38.

Georgia Enterprise Growth Initiative, USAID Caucasus, Office of Economic Restructuring, September 2002.

Georgia Microfinance, Stabilisation and Enhancement Activity, USAID Caucasus, Office of Economic Growth, November 2002.

Georgia, Country Profile, The Economist Intelligence Unit, 2003

Government of Kenya (2000) Interim Poverty Reduction Strategy Paper, Nairobi, Government Printer.

Guy Stuart (2002) 'A Commercial Bank Does Microfinance: Sogesol in Haiti', Case Number CR16-02-1657, Cambridge, Massachusetts, Kennedy School of Government.

Hiemann, Wolfram (2003) 'Case Study: Bank Rakyat Indonesia', in Steinwand and Wiedmaier-Pfister.

Holloh, D. (1998) *Microfinance in Indonesia*, Hamburg, LIT Verlag.

Holloh, D. (2001) *Microfinance Institutions Study*, Jakarta, MoF, BI, GTZ-ProFi.

IFAD (2002) 'Interim Evaluation of the Rural Micro-enterprise Finance Project in the Philippines', Rome, International Fund for Agricultural Development.

Jewel Bank (2000) 'The Economic Vision', Jewel Bank, Zimbabwe.

Jewel Bank (2003) 'Zimbabwe Economy: Facts and Figures', Jewel Bank, Zimbabwe.

Lopez, Cesar, and Rhyne, Elisabeth (2003) 'The Service Company Model: A New Strategy for Commercial Banks in Microfinance'. *Insight,* Number 6, Boston, ACCION International.

Morrow, J. Peter (2002) 'Marketing for Profit in the Land of the Khans'. *DAI Developments*, Spring.

Perez, Maria Elena, Burbano, Soledad, Hernández, Mónica (2003) 'Banco Solidario: Strategy During Ecuador's Financial Crisis', November, p.7.

Quiñones, Benjamin R., and Seibel, Hans Dieter (2000, 2001) 'Social Capital in Microfinance: Case Studies in the Philippines' *Policy Sciences,* 33/3-4 (2000): 421-433, reprinted in John D. Montgomery and Alex Inkeles (2001) *Social Capital as a Policy Resource*, Boston, Kluwer, 195–207.

Reserve Bank of Australia (1999) 'International Comparison of Bank Branches, an update', Canberra, Reserve Bank of Australia.

Reserve Bank of Zimbabwe (2002) 'Monetary Policy Statement, Section 32.1', Harare, Reserve Bank of Zimbabwe.

Sanders, Arie, Banegas, Oscar, Jarrín, María Soledad, et al. (2002) CDR-ULA and Fundación Alternativa Study; 'HIVOS, Alcance e Impacto de Crédito: Estudio de los casos Banco Solidario y Caja los Andes', San José, Costa Rica, p. 3 Annex 1.

Seibel, Hans D. (1989) 'Finance with the Poor, by the Poor, for the Poor. Financial Technologies for the Informal Sector, with Case Studies from Indonesia', *Social Strategies* 3(2), Basel University.

Seibel, Hans D. (2000) 'Agricultural Development Banks: Close Them or Reform Them?', *Finance & Development*, June 2000: 45–48, Washington, D.C., International Monetary Fund.

Seibel, Hans D. and Dolores Torres (2001) 'Are Grameen Replications Sustainable and Do They Reach the Poor?' *The Journal of Microfinance* 1(1): 118–130.

Seibel, Hans D. (2003a) 'History Matters in Microfinance', *Small Enterprise Development* 14(2): 10–12.

Seibel, Hans D. (2003b) *Rural Finance in Indonesia*, Rome, IFAD.

Seibel, Hans D., and Parhusip, Uben (2003): 'Financial Innovations for Microenterprises: Linking Formal and Informal Financial Institutions', in Harper, Malcolm ed. (2003) *Microfinance: Evolution, Achievements and Challenges*, London: ITDG Publishing (reprinted).

Steinwand, Dirk (1997) 'PHBK Indonesia', Pp. 29-65 in vol. 1; pp. 1-11 in vol. 2, APRACA-GTZ.

Steinwand, Dirk (2001) *The Alchemy of Microfinance*, Berlin, VWF.

Steinwand, Dirk and Martina Wiedmaier-Pfister, eds (2003) *The Challenge of Sustainable Outreach: How can Public Banks Contribute to Outreach in Rural Areas? Five Case Studies from Asia*, Eschborn, GTZ.

UNCDF (1997) Zimbabwe Microfinance Assessment Report, UNDP.

UNDP (2001) 'Democracia, Pobreza y Exclusión Social en el Ecuador,' May 2001.

Welch, Karen Horn, Devaney, Patricia Lee, and Dewez, David (2003) 'ACCION Poverty Outreach Findings: SOGESOL, Haiti', *InSight*, No. 8, Boston, ACCION International.

World Bank (1999) Indonesia Country Assistance Note, March 29.

World Bank (2003) *World Development Indicators 2003*, Washington, D.C., World Bank.

World Bank (2003) *World Development Report 2003*, Oxford, Oxford University Press.

World Bank (2004) *World Development Indicators 2004*, Washington, D.C., World Bank.

Wright, Graham A.N. (2003) The Competitive Environment in Uganda: Implications for Microfinance Institutions and their Clients. Nairobi: MicroSave.

Wright, Graham, Cracknell, A.N. David, Mutesasira, Leonard, and Hudson, Rob (2003) *Strategic Marketing for MFIs*, Nairobi, MicroSave.

Index

ACCION 181, 185, 209, 212, 213, 219, 281
Africap 148, 149
Agricultural Bank of Mongolia 4, 257–273, 279, 280, 281, 283, 284, 285, 287
  branch operations 266
  clients 267, 268, 269, 272
  credit culture 267
  demand 268
  diversification 268
  efficiency 268–269, 272
  external catalysts 270
  impact 259, 262
  management 264–265, 266–267
  marketing 267–268, 272
  microfinance indicators 277
  MIS 270, 273
  history 258, 260
  privatization 265, 271
  products 260–264
    deposits 261–262, 264, 265
    loans 261, 263
    money transfer 262
  staff 268, 269, 272, 286
Agricultural Credit Policy Council (ACPC) 23
ALAFIA 168, 173
Alanganallur 77, 80, 88
Alexandria Business Association 117, 118
American Bank of Kosovo (ABK) 3, 4, 223–237, 280
  branches 228–229
  clients 231–232
  deposits 229
  impact 235
  microfinance indicators 277
  origins 227
  performance 234–235
  products 229–230
  staff 232–234, 236
    training 233
  techniques 230–231
arisan 7, 8
Asian financial crisis 9, 16, 18, 19, 30
Asian Development Bank (ADB) 23, 42
Association of Development Agencies in Bangldesh (ADAB) 63, 64
Asunción Mita 202–203

Bancafé 4, 195–208, 279, 284
  Asunción Mita 202–203
  BCC 198–199, 202, 203
  challenges 207
  clients 203–204, 206
  history 195–197
  indicators 196
  microfinance 195–197
  microfinance indicators 277
  MSME 197–200, 202, 205, 206
    products 198–200
      community-based 198–200, 202–203
      individual loans 199–200
    performance 205–206
    staff 201, 204, 206
    structure 200–201
    technology 204–205, 206
Banco Solidario 4, 179–193, 213, 279, 280, 282
  balance sheet 187
  challenges 191–92
  clients 182–183, 189, 190, 192
  impact 185–191, 189
  international investors 182–183
  microfinance indicators 277
  origins 180, 181–182
  performance 186
  products 180, 183–185
    Chauchera Card 180, 184, 192
    emigrants 184, 185
    'Pot of Gold' 180, 184
    social housing 184, 185
    solidarity group loans 183–184
  profitability 179, 188
  response to 1999 crisis 187–189
  vision and mission 179
Bangko Sentral ng Pilipinas (BSP) 21
Bangladesh 55–67
  bank coverage 2
  development indicators 276
  formal financial sector 59–60
  microfinance 55–61
  economy 55
Bangladesh Rural Development Board (BRDB) 56, 57, 62
Bank of Credit and Commerce International (BCCI) 132
Bank of India 69–76
Bank of Khyber 4, 37–54, 279, 284
  balance sheet 50
  collaboration 42–43
  commercial individual loans 42
  financial impact 47–49
  loan portfolio 45
  microfinance indicators 276
  microfinance loans 41, 47
  Microfinance Unit 40, 41, 45, 46, 47
  profit and loss 51
  revised lending methodology 49–52
  origins 40
  performance 48, 49
  staff 53–54, 286
Bank Rakyat Indonesia (BRI) 4, 7–20, 93, 275, 282, 280, 285, 287
  balance sheet 16
  capital and earnings 17
  cross-subsidization 16
  financial viability 45
  loans outstanding 11
  Microbanking Division 11, 16

INDEX

outreach 13–14
post-Asian financial crisis 14, 282
profitability 13, 16–17
rural MFIs 10–12
savings 12–13, 17–18
source of funds 12
transaction costs 13–14
transferring profits 16
Banque du Caire (BdC) 4, 115–130, 279, 283, 284
   branch structure 122–123
   client experience 126–127
   expansion 128–129
   history 116
   impact 125–127
   microfinance indicators 276
   loan officers 117, 120, 122, 126
   loan terms & conditions 124
   management 121
   micro-loan 115
   staff 119, 120–122, 126, 281, 286
BANRURAL 195, 197
Barclays Bank 131, 152, 281
BASIC Bank 59, 61
Basix 106, 107, 108, 109
Belthangady branch of SBI 75
Benin 165–178
   development indicators 277
   economy 165–166
   financial sector 166–169
Boisson, Pierre-Marie 212, 220
borrower-to-server ratio 13, 17
BRAC 57, 59, 60, 65, 67

Canara Bank 3, 4, 77–92
   Alanganallur branch peformance 80
   credit products 85–86
      term loans 85
      revolving online credit 85–86
   microfinance indicators 276
   origins 77
   performance 77
   repayment initiatives 86–88
      contact centres 87
      management information systems 87
      rescheduling 87
   SHG linkage 77–92
capacity building 66
capital deficiency 106–107, 110
CARE 111, 118, 133, 145, 172, 173, 181, 281
CASHPOR 107, 108, 109, 110
CDF 57, 58, 64, 65
central bank 21, 40, 70, 77, 85, 88, 98, 104, 105, 145, 148, 152, 168, 174, 182, 228, 235, 236, 247, 265, 280, 287, 288 292
Central Bank of Benin 168, 174
Central Bank of Kenya 148, 152
CGC 117, 119
CIDA (or ACDI) 117, 167
collateral 25, 144, 174, 200, 229, 230, 244, 251, 254, 284

Commercial Bank of Zimbabwe (CBZ) 4, 131–146, 283
   client experiences 143–144
   community banking 133–149
   delivery channels 135–136
   deposits 134–135, 140
   future directions 144–145
   history 132
   loans 141
   management & staff 132, 136–137
   marketing 135
   microfinance indicators 277
   performance 141–142
   pricing 136
   profitability 139–140
   service delivery 137–138
community banking 133–149, 198–199, 202–203
credit assessment 227, 230
credit enhancement 107, 108
credit-only institution 124
credit rating 63, 109
credit risk 124, 212
credit union 167, 241
customers 281–287
   see also individual institutions

DAI 258, 259, 260, 271
decentralization 204, 206
Dehradun 93, 95, 96
delinquency 27, 214, 229
delivery 98–100, 106–111, 135–138, 214
Deloitte 226, 229, 230
deposits 134–135, 158, 283, 285
deregulation 10, 13, 18, 116, 278
devaluation 125, 165, 180, 189, 282
development indicators 275, 276–277
development manager 95–96
DFID 132, 138, 145, 146, 149
Dhan Foundation 79–84, 87, 107, 110
   BLFs 81–84, 87, 89, 91, 92
   Kurinji Vattara Kalanjaim 83, 84
   CLAs 81–84, 87, 89, 91, 92
discipline 11, 33, 95, 98, 153
diversification 192, 260, 268, 285
donor projects 167–168, 290
downscaling 5, 220, 241, 247, 254, 255, 286

EBRD 240, 247, 252, 253, 281
Ecuador 179–193, 287
   crisis of 1999 187–189, 282
   development indicators 277
   'dollarization' 180, 184
   economy & finance 180–181, 282
Egypt 115–130
   bank coverage 2
   banking sector 115–116
   development indicators 276
   microenterprise 116–117
El Bardai, Ahmed Munir 115, 118, 120

EQI 117, 118, 119, 120, 122, 123
equity 106, 107, 177, 186, 255, 257, 257 290
Equity Building Society 3, 4, 147–163, 278, 283, 285, 287
   customers 151–152, 155
   deposits 158, 159
   external assistance 149
   financial impact 156–157
   loans 154, 160
   microfinance indicators 277
   origins 147–151
   performance 157, 161–163
   savings 151–153, 156, 158
   staff 150–151
excess liquidity 15, 17, 18, 19, 66, 283

facilitator 43, 44, 51, 94, 96, 97, 99, 286
FINADEV SA 4, 165–178, 280, 283
   balance sheet 177
   clients 172
   commercial banks and 173
   microfinance indicators 277
   origins 169–172
   performance 174
   products 174, 175
   profitability 176
   relationship with FBB 171
   staff 172, 178
Financial Bank (FBB) 171, 172, 173, 286
   statistics 169
first-loss default guarantee 108, 109
FMFBL 38, 53
Fundación Alternativa 181, 185, 190

Georgia 3, 239–256, 282
   bank coverage 2
   development indicators 277
   economy & society 239–240
   financial sector 240–241
   lessons from microfinance in 254–256
Gori 251, 253, 255
Grameen Bank, Bangladesh 21, 55, 57, 58, 59, 63, 93, 94, 102, 284
Grameen banking 21–35
   definition 25, 93
Grameen Foundation 108, 109
Grameen replication 23, 25, 33
group loan 43–44, 183–184, 185
Guatemala
   bank coverage 2
   banking system 196
   development indicators 277
   economy 195
Haiti 209–221, 282
   development indicators 277
   economy & society 209–210
H.S. Securities 259, 265, 271
IADB 181, 205, 211
ICICI Bank 4, 103–113, 279, 287, 292
   history 105

microfinance delivery 106–111
microfinance indicators 276
   on-tap securitization 107, 111
   partnership 107, 110–111
   portfolio buy-out 107, 109
   performance 112
   RMBG 106
IMI 242, 255, 280, 281
incentive 107, 122, 201, 204, 212, 214, 231, 253, 254, 285
India 69–113, 286
   bank coverage 2
   commercial banks & microfinance 104
   development indicators 276
   financial sector 69
   microfinance sector 103
   regulatory framework 106–107
   trend of advances 103
individual loans 24, 183, 213
Indonesia 7–20, 282
   development indicators 276
   financial infrastructure 7–8
   policy framework 8
inflation 8, 131, 141, 146, 195, 240, 282
information communication technology 118, 125, 157, 162, 192, 204, 215, 283
insurance 97, 128
interest rate 8, 20, 30, 35, 45, 90, 123, 136, 199, 208, 213, 245, 253, 287, 289
International Fund for Agricultural Development (IFAD) 23, 42, 63, 64, 65
International Project Consult (IPC) 211, 217, 241, 255

Kenya 147–163
   bank coverage 2
   development indicators 277
   economy 147
   financial sector 148
Khushali Bank 39, 53
Khyber, Bank of see Bank of Khyber
Kosovo 223–237, 282
   economy & war 223–224
Kosovo Business Finance (KBF) 223–237
   purpose 225–226
   timeline 227
Kosovo Business Finance Fund (KBFF) 227, 228
KUPEDES 10, 18

LDKP 8, 13
liability 57, 133, 138
liberalization 8–9, 147
liquidity 12, 189, 267, 268, 271, 282
loan guarantee 133
loan loss 119, 123, 126, 140, 144, 278, 283
loans outstanding 13, 15, 18, 29, 160, 161, 235, 245, 249, 251
loan tracking system 124, 125
loss ratio 13, 15–16, 108

management information systems
  27, 87, 138, 162, 205, 255, 270
marketing 135, 156, 157, 158, 214-215,
  227, 230, 253, 259, 283, 292
market-led approach 147-163, 157
market research 149, 152, 177, 211
mattress money 224, 235, 263
MFI 47-48
Micro Credit National 211, 217
Micro Enterprise Bank 225, 227
microfinance
  benefits of 281-285, 288, 289
  definition 3, 22
  drawbacks of 289
  origins 256
MicroSave 149, 157
Mongolia 257-273
  development indicators 277
  economy & society
monitoring 27, 57, 227, 231, 254
Multibanco 196, 197

NABARD 69-70, 77, 82, 88, 89, 93, 94,
  104, 105
Nairobi 148, 151
National Bank of Georgia 247
National Credit Council 22, 23
nationalization 93, 104
NCBA 117, 118, 123
'new paradigm' microfinance
  1, 5, 56, 64, 67, 290
NGO promotion of SHGs 79, 88
non-targeted loan 18
North-West Frontier Province 37
Nueva Ecija 24

'old paradigm' microfinance 61, 64, 66
operating costs 23, 214, 219, 234
Oriental Bank of Commerce (OBC)
    4, 93-102, 287
  client profile 96-97
  delivery mechanism 98-100
  development manager 95-96
  facilitator 96
  formation of groups 96
  expansion 100-102
  microfinance indicators 276
  origins 93
  performance 100
  profitability 99
  Rudrapur 98, 99
  savings products 97
outreach 13-14, 18, 19, 23, 30, 51, 109,
  129, 148, 150, 227, 230, 266, 278, 292
overdraft 85, 92, 108, 230

PADME 167, 168, 169, 173
Pakistan 37-54
  bank coverage 2
  development indicators 276
  economy 37-38

financial sector reach 39
microfinance 38-39
panchayat 81, 84
PAPME 167, 168, 173
PARMEC 168, 171
partnership 107, 110-111, 131-146, 177
People's Credit and Finance Corporation
  (PCFC) 23-24, 26
performing assets 88, 89
Philippines 7-20, 287
  bank coverage 2
  development indicators 276
  economy and finance 21-22
PKSF 58, 59, 60, 63, 64
policy environment 287-288
portfolio at risk (PAR) 122, 126, 156, 176,
  186, 198, 206, 276, 277, 284
portfolio buy-out 107, 109
Post Office Savings Bank (KPSB) 147, 148
primary lending rate 98, 136
priority sector 72, 74, 76, 77, 95, 104, 105,
  106, 108
Pristina 228, 230, 231
privatization 5, 116, 257, 258, 265, 271
Procredit Bank 240, 241, 252, 254, 255,
    283, 284
  establishment 241-242
  key indicators 242
  loan portfolio 243-246
  microfinance indicators 277
  ownership 242
Producers Bank 4, 21-35, 281, 284, 285,
    287
  balance sheet 31
  clients 30
  commercializing Grameen 25-27
  establishment 24
  expansion 24-25, 28-30
  human resources 27
  management information systems 27
  microfinance indicators 276
  outreach 27-28
  performance 28-29, 34
  profitability and productivity 29-30
  repayment 27-28
  social capital 33
productivity 28, 93, 214, 253, 254
products 283-284
  see also individual institutions
ProFund 181, 212
PROSHIKA 57, 64, 65, 67
public relations 156, 158, 268

receivables 110, 111
regulation 9, 19, 21, 22, 23, 39, 107, 147,
  171-172, 182, 211
repayment 9, 28, 77, 98, 279, 282
  initiatives 86-88
Reserve Bank of India 70, 77, 85, 88, 98,
  104, 105
Reserve Bank of Zimbabwe 145

return on assets 13, 29, 129, 186
revolving online credit 85–86
risk management 133, 210
ROSCA 145, 168
Rudrapur 98, 99, 100, 101
rural support programmes 38

savings and credit associations 7, 22
Savings and Credit Cooperatives 147, 148
savings mobiliziation 17, 24, 79, 171
savings scheme 10, 97
SDC 63, 66, 93
securitization 107, 111
self-help groups 59, 69–76, 77–92, 93, 94, 102, 104
   definition 69
   financing advantages 88–89
SELP 247, 252, 255
service 283–284
   see also individual institutions
service company model 209–221, 286–287
   definition 210–211
   lessons from Sogesol 218–219
Shakti Foundation 57, 63, 64, 65
SHARE 107, 108, 109
SKDRDP 75, 76
SIMPEDES 10, 12
social collateral 44
social loan 169
Sogebank 209, 286
   interface with Sogesol 214–215, 286
Sogesol 209–221, 280, 283, 286
   balance sheet 217
   customers 213–214, 215
   delivery 214
   ICT 215
   interface with Sogebank 214–215
   marketing 214–215
   microfinance indicators 277
   origins 210, 211
   performance 216, 218
   products 213
   prospects 217–218
   staff 214, 215
solidarity group loans 25, 284
Sonali Bank 4, 55–67, 287, 292
   Micro-Credit Division 66
   microfinance indicators 276
   NGO linkage 63–67
   origins 60
   staff 66–67
staff 285, 286
   see also individual institutions
State Bank of India (SBI) 3, 4, 69–76, 279, 287
   branch network 72
   financial position 71
   microfinance indicators 276
   microfinance strategy 73–75
   SHG linkage 72–76
   history 70

State Bank of Pakistan 40
state ownership 269, 270, 273
subsidy 48, 52, 113, 145, 205, 219, 292
subsidized credit 9, 56

Tamil Nadu 78, 105
Tbilisi 239, 247, 250, 251, 252, 253
Tbiluniversalbank 247, 255, 281
   competition 252–253
   internal challenges 254
   key indicators 248
   loans 249–250
   resources 253–254
third-party guarantee 108, 230
transaction cost 13–14, 19, 74, 91, 94, 212, 279, 289

Uganda 129
UNDP 149, 205, 239
United Georgian Bank 240, 247, 255, 281
   competition 252–253
   internal challenges 254
   key indicators 248, 250
   loans 251
   resources 253–254
UNMIK 223, 225, 228
USAID 10, 116–117, 119, 120, 123, 129, 130, 181, 218, 226, 227, 229, 235, 236, 258, 260, 264, 265, 269

VITAL FINANCE 173, 174

WAEMU 166, 168, 171
wholesale 5, 55–67, 75, 178, 279
women 5, 30, 81, 104, 126, 128, 142, 172, 173
World Bank 12, 167, 240, 258, 264

Yunus, Muhammad, Professor 1, 25, 63

Zambuko Trust 141
Zimbabwe 131–146
   development indicators 277
   economy 131, 282